S0-BYD-439

Java 1.1

No experience required.

Java™ 1.1

No experience required.™

Steven Holzner

SYBEX®

San Francisco • Paris • Düsseldorf • Soest

Associate Publisher: Gary Masters
Acquisitions Manager: Kristine Plachy
Acquisitions & Developmental Editor: Suzanne Rotondo
Editor: Brenda Frink
Technical Editor: Kevin Russo
Book Designer: Patrick Dintino, Catalin Dulfu
Desktop Publisher: Maureen Forys
Production Coordinator: Nathan Johanson
Indexer: Ted Laux
Cover Designer: Ingalls & Associates

Screen reproductions produced with Collage Complete.

Collage Complete is a trademark of Inner Media Inc.

SYBEX is a registered trademark of SYBEX Inc.

No experience required is a trademark of SYBEX Inc.

TRADEMARKS: SYBEX has attempted throughout this book to distinguish proprietary trademarks from descriptive terms by following the capitalization style used by the manufacturer.

The author and publisher have made their best efforts to prepare this book, and the content is based upon final release software whenever possible. Portions of the manuscript may be based upon pre-release versions supplied by software manufacturer(s). The author and the publisher make no representation or warranties of any kind with regard to the completeness or accuracy of the contents herein and accept no liability of any kind including but not limited to performance, merchantability, fitness for any particular purpose, or any losses or damages of any kind caused or alleged to be caused directly or indirectly from this book.

Photographs and illustrations used in this book have been downloaded from publicly accessible file archives and are used in this book for news reportage purposes only to demonstrate the variety of graphics resources available via electronic access. Text and images available over the Internet may be subject to copyright and other rights owned by third parties. Online availability of text and images does not imply that they may be reused without the permission of rights holders, although the Copyright Act does permit certain unauthorized reuse as fair use under 17 U.S.C. Section 107.

Copyright ©1997 SYBEX Inc., 1151 Marina Village Parkway, Alameda, CA 94501. World rights reserved. No part of this publication may be stored in a retrieval system, transmitted, or reproduced in any way, including but not limited to photocopy, photograph, magnetic or other record, without the prior agreement and written permission of the publisher.

Library of Congress Card Number: 97-65363
ISBN: 0-7821-2083-0

Manufactured in the United States of America

10 9 8 7 6 5 4 3

Software License Agreement: Terms and Conditions

The media and/or any online materials accompanying this book that are available now or in the future contain programs and/or text files (the "Software") to be used in connection with the book. SYBEX hereby grants to you a license to use the Software, subject to the terms that follow. Your purchase, acceptance, or use of the Software will constitute your acceptance of such terms.

The Software compilation is the property of SYBEX unless otherwise indicated and is protected by copyright to SYBEX or other copyright owner(s) as indicated in the media files (the "Owner(s)"). You are hereby granted a single-user license to use the Software for your personal, noncommercial use only. You may not reproduce, sell, distribute, publish, circulate, or commercially exploit the Software, or any portion thereof, without the written consent of SYBEX and the specific copyright owner(s) of any component software included on this media.

In the event that the Software or components include specific license requirements or end-user agreements, statements of condition, disclaimers, limitations or warranties ("End-User License"), those End-User Licenses supersede the terms and conditions herein as to that particular Software component. Your purchase, acceptance, or use of the Software will constitute your acceptance of such End-User Licenses.

By purchase, use or acceptance of the Software you further agree to comply with all export laws and regulations of the United States as such laws and regulations may exist from time to time.

Software Support

Components of the supplemental Software and any offers associated with them may be supported by the specific Owner(s) of that material but they are not supported by SYBEX. Information regarding any available support may be obtained from the Owner(s) using the information provided in the appropriate read.me files or listed elsewhere on the media.

Should the manufacturer(s) or other Owner(s) cease to offer support or decline to honor any offer, SYBEX bears no responsibility. This notice concerning support for the Software is provided for your information only. SYBEX is not the agent or principal of the Owner(s), and SYBEX is in no way responsible for providing any support for the Software, nor is it liable or responsible for any support provided, or not provided, by the Owner(s).

Warranty

SYBEX warrants the enclosed media to be free of physical defects for a period of ninety (90) days after purchase. The Software is not available from SYBEX in any other form or media than that enclosed herein or posted to www.sybex.com. If you discover a defect in the media during this warranty period, you may obtain a replacement of identical format at no charge by sending the defective media, postage prepaid, with proof of purchase to:

SYBEX Inc.
Customer Service Department
1151 Marina Village Parkway
Alameda, CA 94501
(510) 523-8233
Fax: (510) 523-2373
e-mail: info@sybex.com
WEB: HTTP://WWW.SYBEX.COM

After the 90-day period, you can obtain replacement media of identical format by sending us the defective disk, proof of purchase, and a check or money order for $10, payable to SYBEX.

Disclaimer

SYBEX makes no warranty or representation, either expressed or implied, with respect to the Software or its contents, quality, performance, merchantability, or fitness for a particular purpose. In no event will SYBEX, its distributors, or dealers be liable to you or any other party for direct, indirect, special, incidental, consequential, or other damages arising out of the use of or inability to use the Software or its contents even if advised of the possibility of such damage. In the event that the Software includes an online update feature, SYBEX further disclaims any obligation to provide this feature for any specific duration other than the initial posting.

The exclusion of implied warranties is not permitted by some states. Therefore, the above exclusion may not apply to you. This warranty provides you with specific legal rights; there may be other rights that you may have that vary from state to state. The pricing of the book with the Software by SYBEX reflects the allocation of risk and limitations on liability contained in this agreement of Terms and Conditions.

Shareware Distribution

This Software may contain various programs that are distributed as shareware. Copyright laws apply to both shareware and ordinary commercial software, and the copyright Owner(s) retains all rights. If you try a shareware program and continue using it, you are expected to register it. Individual programs differ on details of trial periods, registration, and payment. Please observe the requirements stated in appropriate files.

Copy Protection

The Software in whole or in part may or may not be copy-protected or encrypted. However, in all cases, reselling or redistributing these files without authorization is expressly forbidden except as specifically provided for by the Owner(s) therein.

To Tamsen Conner, future computer genius.
(You can just tell.)

Acknowledgments

Any book is a collaborative effort. Many people helped me along the way. Of course, there is not space to thank all the people who made contributions to this book. Certain people stand out as having made a difference.

In particular, I would like to thank Brenda Frink, Kevin Russo, Suzanne Rotondo, Nathan Johanson, Maureen Forys, Linda Good, and Ted Laux. These people made specific contributions to my book, from the concept to working through the physical pages. Many thanks for all the hours you've contributed—thanks to you all!

Contents at a Glance

Table of Contents

Introduction

Java is very, very popular right now, and no wonder: Java has transformed the Web and Web programming in many ways. Java makes your Web pages come alive, displaying buttons, menus, images, and animation. Because you can program for many different types of computers using Java, Java applications have also become very popular. And now that Java has arrived in its new 1.1 version, it's even more popular than before. As more and more Web browsers become Java-enabled, as more and more computers support Java, its popularity continues to spread.

Why Use Java?

Although it's possible to create Web pages without Java, they just can't compare to Java pages. Rather than have static images, why not have something that *moves*? Rather than have text that doesn't change, why not allow the user to enter their own text? There's nothing like an interactive Web page to get the attention of casual Web surfers.

Java is coming into its own as a programming language for non-Web applications as well. This is because it's a very powerful cross-platform language, allowing you to develop programs on one computer type and run them on many others. In today's world, that's a strong reason to use Java. Java 1.1 allows you many powerful options, from popup menus to using the clipboard to JAR files. We're going to explore them all in this book.

How This Book Is Organized

Our emphasis in this book will be seeing Java 1.1 at work and giving you the skills needed to use it effectively. If you want to get something from a programming book, there's nothing like seeing working code. Many programming books start off with abstractions, programming constructs, and theory; but here you will look at Java not as an end in itself but as a tool for creating programs you are interested in.

In this book, you'll see things from a different point of view—the getting things done point of view. Instead of Chapters named "If Statements," "Java Modifiers," or "Abstract Java Classes," each unit in this book teaches a specific Skill, such as "Check boxes," "Radio Buttons," "Menus," and "Graphics Animation." You'll put Java to work creating the programs you want.

You'll work through plenty of bite-sized examples because trying to learn Java without running it is like trying to learn to fly by reading an airplane parts manual. These examples will be short and to the point, covering topics such as:

Text fields and text areas	JAR files
Popup calculators	Radio buttons and check boxes
The Java ScrollPane class	Printing
Popup menus	The system clipboard
Scroll bars and scrolling lists	The Java 1.1 Delegated event model
Employee databases	Image maps
Menus	Popup windows
Popup dialog boxes	Layouts
Panels	Buttons
Navigating to other URLs	Multi-threading
Mouse-driven paint programming	Mouse-driven image resizing
Accessing the keyboard directly	Fonts
Graphics animation	The Sun Animator class

The plan, then, is to put Java to work for you, using all its power and classes in the process of creating working Java programs. Java has a great deal to offer, and you'll see just about all of it in this book, from creating Java applets to creating Java applications; from creating new dialog boxes to printing directly from a program. Java provides a great many tools, and you'll use them fully as you create the programs in this book.

Look What's on the CD!

The CD-ROM provides you with cutting-edge third-party tools including Java Developers Kit 1.1, Jamba, Mojo, ED for Windows, Widgets, and Jet Effects. To install and use these tools, see the readme.txt file in the CD-ROM's root directory.

The code you'll use in this book will also appear on the CD-ROM, which means that you don't have to type anything in as you work through the examples. It's all there on the CD-ROM. You'll find the .java files, which hold the source code for the programs, and the .class files, which are ready to run. To install the files on your hard disk, see the readme.txt file in the CD-ROM's root directory.

Conventions Used in This Book

The examples in this book will be built incrementally; when you add a new line or lines of code, the new lines will be indicated with arrows, like this:

```
      drawbutton = new Button("Draw freehand");
      linebutton = new Button("Draw a line");
  ➡   ovalbutton = new Button("Draw an oval");
  ➡   rectbutton = new Button("Draw a rectangle");
  ➡   roundedbutton = new Button("Draw a rounded rectangle");
```

Throughout the book, Notes, Tips, and Warnings appear to give you extra insight.

 Notes indicate points of special concern such as why working with the mouse one way instead of another is important at a particular time, or what you can do with one Web browser in Java that you can't with another.

 Tips are written to save you time or to point out additional helpful information, such as a programming shortcut.

 **A Warning tells you about common programming errors or other potential mix-ups you should watch out for.**

What You'll Need

Although Java is an object-oriented language, you don't need to have object-oriented programming experience to use this book. If you do have experience with an object-oriented programming language, there's still a lot to learn from this book.

You'll need an editor or word processor, such as Microsoft WordPad, to enter your Java programs into files you can compile and run. Your editor or word processor must be able to save files in simple text format.

And, of course, to use your completed Java programs on the Web, you should have a place to host your Web pages. Although Java can produce stand-alone applications, the majority of Java programmers target the Web in their Java development. In Skill 1, you'll learn how to embed Java applets in a Web page.

Your Internet Service Provider should be able to instruct you on how to upload your applets so you can use them in your Web pages. Usually you need to find out where to install your Web pages and applets (what directory in the ISP computer), and then you can use a File Transfer Protocol (FTP) program to upload your files to that directory.

You can find more information about Java on the Internet. Some resources include Sun's Java site, `http://www.javasoft.com` and `http://www.javasoft.com/doc`. You can also check out the Usenet group `comp.lang.java.programmer`. For updates to this book, visit the Sybex site, `http://www.sybex.com`.

R. Jones 356-555-3398.

PROGRAMMERS
C, C, VB, Cobol, exp. Call 534-555-6543 or fax 534-555-6544.

PROGRAMMING
MRFS Inc. is looking for a Sr. Windows NT developer. Reqs. 3-5 yrs. Exp. in C under Windows, Win95 & NT, using Visual C. Excl. OO design & implementation skills a must. OLE2 & ODBC are a plus. Excl. Salary & bnfts. Resume & salary history to HR, 8779 HighTech Way, Computer City, AR

PROGRAMMERS
Contractors Wanted for short & long term assignments; Visual C, MFC Unix C/C, SQL Oracle Dev clop ers PC Help Desk Support Windows NT & NetWareTelecommunications Visual Basic, Access, HTMT, CGI, Perl MMI & Co.. 885-555-9933

PROGRAMMER World Wide Web Links wants your HTML & Photoshop skills. Develop great WWW sites. Local & global customers. Send samples & resume to WWWL, 2000 Apple Road, Santa Rosa, CA.

TECHNICAL WRITER Software firm seeks writer/editor for manuals, research notes, project mgmt. Min 2 years tech. writing, DTP & programming experience. Send resume & writing samples to: Software Systems, Dallas, TX.

TECHNICAL Software development firm looking for Tech Trainers. Ideal candidates have programming experience in Visual C, HTML & JAVA. Need quick start starter. Call (443) 555-6868 for interview.

TECHNICAL WRITE R/ Premier Computer Corp is seeking a combination of technical skills, knowledge and experience in the following areas: UNIX, Windows 95/NT, Visual Basic, on-line help & documentation, and the Internet. Candidates must possess excellent writing skills, and be comfortable working in a quality vs. deadline driven environment. Competitive salary. Fax resume & samples to Karen Fields, Premier Computer Corp. 444 Industrial Blvd. Concord, CA. Or send to our website at www.premier.com.

WEB DESIGNER
BA/BS or equivalent programming/multimedia production. 3 years of experience in use and design of WWW services streaming audio and video HTML, PERL, CGI, GIF, JPEG. Demonstrated interpersonal, organization, communication, multi-tasking skills. Send resume to The Learning People at www.learning.com.

WEBMASTER-TECHNICAL
BSCS or equivalent. 2 years of experience in CGI, Windows 95/NT, UNIX, C, Java, Perl. Demonstrated ability to design, code, debug and test on-line services. Send resume to The Learning People at www.learning.com.

PROGRAMMER World Wide Web Links wants your HTML & Photoshop skills. Develop great WWW sites.

---

ing tools. Experienced in documentation preparation & programming languages (Access, C, FoxPro) are a plus. Financial or banking customer service support is required along with excellent verbal & written communication skills with multi levels of end-users. Send resume to KKUP Enterprises, 45 Orange Blvd. Orange, CA.

COMPUTERS Small Web Design firm seeks indiv. w/NT, Webserver & Database management exp. fax resume to 556-555-4221.

COMPUTER/ Visual C/C, Visual Basic Exp'd Systems Analysts/ Programmers for growing software dev. team in Roseburg. Computer Science or related degree preferred. Develop adv. Engineering applications for engineering firm. Fax resume to 707-555-8744.

COMPUTER Web Master for dynamic SF Internet co. Site. Dev. test. coord. train 2 yrs prog. Exp. C C. Web C. FTP. Fax resume to Best Staffing 845-555-7722.

COMPUTER PROGRAMMER
Ad agency seeks programmer w/exp. in UNIX/NT Platforms, Web Server, CGI/Perl. Programmer Position avail. on a project basis with the possibility to move into F/T. Fax resume & salary req. to R. Jones 334-555-8332.

COMPUTERS Programmer/Analyst Design and maintain C based SQL database applications. Required skills: Visual Basic, C, SQL, ODBC. Document existing and new applications. Novell or NT exp. a plus. Fax resume & salary history to 235-555-9935.

GRAPHIC DESIGNER
Webmaster's Weekly is seeking a creative Graphic Designer to design high impact marketing collater al, including direct mail promos. CD-ROM packages, ads and WWW pages. Must be able to juggle multiple projects and learn new skills on the job very rapidly. Web design experience a big plus. technical troubleshooting also a plus. Call 435-555-1235.

GRAPHICS - ART DIRECTOR - WEB-MULTIMEDIA
Leading internet development company has an outstanding opportunity for a talented, high-end Web Experienced Art Director In addition to a great portfolio and fresh ideas, the ideal candidate has excellent communication and presentation skills. Working as a team with innovative producers and programmers, you will create dynamic, interactive web sites and application interfaces. Some programming experience required. Send samples and resume to: SuperSites, 333 Main. Seattle, WA.

MARKETING
Fast paced software and services provider looking for MARKETING COMMUNICATIONS SPECIALIST to be responsible for its webpage.

PROGRAMMERS Multiple short term assignments available: Visual C, 3 positions SQL ServerNT Server, 2 positions JAVA & HTML, long term NetWare Various locations. Call for more info 356-555-3398.

PROGRAMMERS
C, C, VB, Cobol, exp.
Call 534-555-6543
or fax 534-555-6544.

PROGRAMMING
MRFS Inc. is looking for a Sr. Windows NT developer. Reqs. 3-5 yrs. Exp. In C under Windows, Win95 & NT, using Visual C. Excl. OO design & implementation skills a must. OLE2 & ODBC are a plus. Excl. Salary & bnfts. Resume & salary history to HR, 8779 HighTech Way, Computer City, AR

PROGRAMMERS/ Contractors Wanted for short & long term assignments; Visual C MFC Unix C/C, SQL Oracle Developers PC Help Desk Support Windows NT & NetWareTelecommunications Visual Basic, Access, HTMT, CGI, Perl MMI & Co.. 885-555-9933

PROGRAMMER World Wide Web Links wants your HTML & Photoshop skills. Develop great WWW sites. Local & global customers. Send samples & resume to WWWL, 2000 Apple Road, Santa Rosa, CA.

TECHNICAL WRITER Software firm seeks writer/editor for manuals, research notes, project mgmt. Min 2 years tech. writing, DTP & programming experience. Send resume & writing samples to: Software Systems, Dallas, TX.

COMPUTER PROGRAMMER
Ad agency seeks programmer w/exp. in UNIX/NT Platforms, Web Server, CGI/Perl. Programmer Position avail on a project basis with the possibility to move into F/T. Fax resume & salary req. to R. Jones 334-555-8332.

TECHNICAL WRITER Premier Computer Corp is seeking a combination of technical skills, knowledge and experience in the following areas: UNIX, Windows 95/NT, Visual Basic, on-line help & documentation and the internet. Candidates must possess excellent writing skills, and be comfortable working in a quality vs. deadline driven environment. Competitive salary. Fax resume & samples to Karen Fields. Premier Computer Corp. 444 Industrial Blvd. Concord, CA. Or send to our website at www.premier.com.

WEB DESIGNER
BA/BS or equivalent programming/multimedia production. 3 years of experience in use and design of WWW services streaming audio and video HTML, PERL, CGI, GIF, JPEG. Demonstrated interpersonal, organization, communication, multi-tasking skills. Send resume to The Learning People at www.learning.com.

WEBMASTER-TECHNICAL
BSCS or equivalent, 2 years of experience in CGI, Windows 95/NT,

---

COMPUTERS Small Web Design Firm seeks indiv. w/NT. Webserver & Database management exp. fax resume to 556-555-4221.

COMPUTER Visual C/C. Visual Basic Exp'd Systems Analysts/ Programmers for growing software dev. team in Roseburg. Computer Science or related degree preferred. Develop adv. Engineering applications for engineering firm. Fax resume to 707-555-8744.

COMPUTER Web Master for dynamic SF Internet co. Site. Dev. test. coord. train. 2 yrs prog. Exp. C C Web C. FTP. Fax resume to Best Staffing 845-555-7722.

COMPUTERS/ QA SOFTWARE TESTERS Qualified candidates should have 2 yrs exp. performing integration & system testing using automated testing tools. Experienced in documentation preparation & programming languages (Access, C, FoxPro) are a plus. Financial or banking customer service support is required along with excellent verbal & written communication skills with multi levels of end-users. Send resume to KKUP Enterprises, 45 Orange Blvd. Orange, CA.

COMPUTERS Programmer/Analyst Design and maintain C based SQL database applications. Required skills: Visual Basic, C, SQL, ODBC. Document existing and new applications. Novell or NT exp. a plus. Fax resume & salary history to 235-555-9935.

GRAPHIC DESIGNER
Webmaster's Weekly is seeking a creative Graphic Designer to design high impact marketing collater al, including direct mail promo's. CD-ROM packages, ads and WWW pages. Must be able to juggle multiple projects and learn new skills on the job very rapidly. Web design experience a big plus. technical troubleshooting also a plus. Call 435-555-1235.

GRAPHICS - ART DIRECTOR - WEB-MULTIMEDIA
Leading internet development company has an outstanding opportunity for a talented, high-end Web Experienced Art Director. In addition to a great portfolio and fresh ideas, the ideal candidate has excellent communication and presentation skills. Working as a team with innovative producers and programmers, you will create dynamic, interactive web sites and application interfaces. Some programming experience required. Send samples and resume to: SuperSites, 333 Main. Seattle, WA.

COMPUTER PROGRAMMER
Ad agency seeks programmer w/exp. in UNIX/NT Platforms, Web Server, CGI/Perl. Programmer Position avail. on a project basis with the possibility to move into F/T. Fax resume & salary req. to R. Jones 334-555-8332.

PROGRAMMERS / Established software company seeks program-

---

ment. Must be a self-starter, energetic, organized. Must have 2 yrs web experience. Programming plus. Call 985-555-9854.

PROGRAMMERS Multiple short term assignments available: Visual C, 3 positions SQL ServerNT Server, 2 positions JAVA & HTML, long term NetWare Various locations. Call more info. 356-555-3398.

PROGRAMMERS
C, C, VB, Cobol, exp. Call 534-555-6543 or fax 534-555-6544.

PROGRAMMING
MRFS Inc. Is looking for a Sr. Windows NT developer. Reqs. 3-5 yrs. Exp. In C under Windows, Win95 & NT, using Visual C & OO design & implementation skills a must. OLE2 & ODBC are a plus. Excl. Salary & bnfts. Resume & salary history to HR. 8779 HighTech Way, Computer City, AR

PROGRAMMERS/ Contractors Wanted for short & long term assignments: Visual C, MFCUnix C/C, Oracle Developers PC Help Desk Support Windows NT & NetWare Telecommunications Visual Basic, Access, HTMT, CGI, Perl MMI & Co.. 885-555-9933

PROGRAMMER World Wide Web Links wants your HTML & Photoshop skills. Develop great WWW sites. Local & global customers. Send samples & resume to WWWL, 2000 Apple Road, Santa Rosa, CA.

TECHNICAL WRITER Software firm seeks writer/editor for manuals, research notes, project mgmt. Min 2 years tech. writing, DTP & programming experience. Send resume & writing samples to: Software Systems, Dallas, TX.

TECHNICAL Software development firm looking for Tech Trainers. Ideal candidates have programming experience in Visual C, HTML & JAVA. Need quick self starter. Call (443) 555-6868 for interview.

TECHNICAL WRITER Premier Computer Corp is seeking a combination of technical skills, knowledge and experience in the following areas: UNIX, Windows 95/NT, Visual Basic, on-line help & documentation and the internet. Candidates must possess excellent writing skills, be comfortable working in a quality vs. deadline driven environment. Competitive salary. Fax resume & samples to Karen Fields. Premier Computer Corp. 444 Industrial Blvd. Concord, CA. Or send to our website at www.premier.com.

WEB DESIGNER
BA/BS or equivalent programming/multimedia production years of experience in use. design of WWW services streaming audio and video HTML, PERL, GIF, JPEG. Demonstrated interpersonal, organization, communication, multi-tasking skills. Send resume The Learning People at www.learning.com.

WEBMASTER-TECHNIC

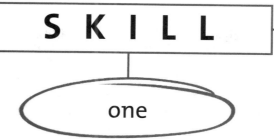

S K I L L

one

1

Building the First
Java Examples

- ❑ Installing the JDK 1.1
- ❑ The Java applet viewer
- ❑ Creating Java applets
- ❑ Customizing applets
- ❑ Object-oriented programming
- ❑ Connecting Java and HTML

Welcome to Java 1.1! We have an ambitious agenda before us: We're going to get a firm grip on Java programming, creating both powerful Java programs and Web pages. We're going to take a guided tour through Java 1.1—including seeing the differences between Java 1.0 and Java 1.1. There is no more exciting programming package available. As you are probably aware, the popularity of Java has skyrocketed as more and more people have seen how versatile and powerful it is. Web programmers have found it an excellent tool because it allows them to write programs that will run on many different types of computers. They have started using it to make their Web pages actually *do* something.

With Java, you will be able to display animation and images, accept mouse clicks and text, use controls like scrollbars and check boxes, print graphics, support popup menus, and even support additional windows and menu bars.

Each of the Skills in this book is specially set up to cover a Java skill, and you'll see plenty of bite-sized examples as you learn how to handle Java in depth. Other books might have only a few examples, partial examples, or examples that are too long to deal with comfortably; but in this book, the examples will be plentiful and will be small enough to target a single skill.

We'll start working on our Java skills right away. Other books may start with chapters of abstractions before getting to work, but not this one. We will concentrate on examples in this book—that is, on seeing things from the programmer's point of view. On seeing Java at *work*.

Java programs come two ways: as stand-alone applications and as small programs you can embed in Web pages, called *applets*. Of the two, applets are the most popular, and we'll concentrate primarily on them.

Building the Hello Example

Our first example will be a simple one because right now we just want to get started in Java without too many extra details to weigh us down. We will create a small Java applet, the type of Java program you can embed in a Web page, that will display the words, "Hello from Java!"

What's an Applet?

Just what do we mean by an applet? An applet is a special program that you can embed in a Web page such that the applet gains control over a certain part of the Web page. On that part of the page, the applet can display buttons, list boxes, images, and more. It's applets that make Web pages "come alive."

Each applet is given the amount of space (usually measured in pixels) that it requests in a Web page, such as the amount of space shown in Figure 1.1. (Soon we'll see how an applet "requests" space.) This is the space that the applet will use for its display. We'll place the words "Hello from Java!" in our applet, as shown in Figure 1.2.

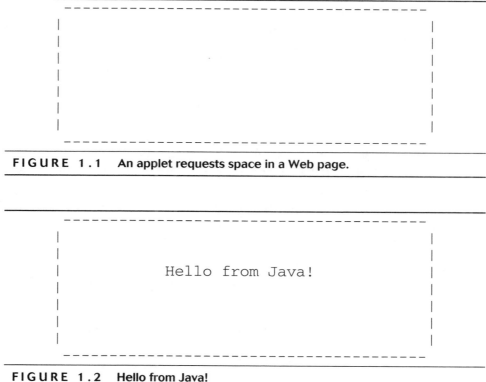

FIGURE 1.1   An applet requests space in a Web page.

FIGURE 1.2   Hello from Java!

That's how our applet will work; after it is created, we will be able to embed it in a Web page. Let's create and run our applet now.

Creating the Hello Example

Let's call this first applet hello. We will store the actual Java code (that is, the lines of text that make up our program) for this applet in the file hello.java. You'll need an editor of some kind to create this file (such as Windows Wordpad). We'll be creating .java files throughout the book, so use an editor you are comfortable with. Another point to notice is that if you are going to use a word processor, like Microsoft Word, you'll have to save your .java files as straight text—something you can type out at the DOS prompt and not see any funny characters. Check your word processor's Save As menu item or your word processor's documentation to see how to do this. The Sun Java system won't be able to handle anything but straight text files. Now type the following text into the file hello.java (this is the traditional first program in most java books):

```
import java.awt.Graphics;
public class hello extends java.applet.Applet
{
    public void paint(Graphics g)
    {
        g.drawString("Hello from Java!", 60, 30 );
    }
}
```

This is the text of our first Java program, and soon you'll see what each line means. Having typed the text in, save it to disk as hello.java.

NOTE   **Note that capitalization counts here—make sure you type** hello.java, **not** Hello.java **or** hello.Java.

In general, the name of the file will match exactly (including case) the name given in the "class" statement in the file; in our case, that is hello:

```
import java.awt.Graphics;
```
→
```
public class hello extends java.applet.Applet
{
    public void paint( Graphics g )
    {
        g.drawString("Hello from Java!", 60, 30 );
    }
}
```

In this book, we will place our programs into subdirectories of a new directory we will call java1-1 (this is optional—you can choose any name). That means we'll save the hello.java file as c:\java1-1\hello\hello.java.

Now we have created hello.java. This is the source code for our applet, and it contains the Java code that we have written. The next step is to compile this Java code into a working applet and see our applet at work. Applets have the extension .class, making the name of our actual applet hello.class. We'll see just exactly *why* applets have the extension .class shortly.

For example, if we had set up a class named, say, screenclass, we can create an object of that class named screen this way:

```
screenclass screen;
```

You'll see how to actually create a class soon (creating a class like screenclass is not hard—when we create a class in code, we will just group all its functions and data inside the class definition), and then you'll see how to create objects of that class. What's important to remember is this: the object itself is what holds the data we want to work with; the class itself holds no data but just describes how the object should be set up.

Object-oriented programming at root is nothing more than a way of grouping functions and the data they work on together to make your program less cluttered. We'll see more about object-oriented programming throughout this book, including how to create a class, how to create an object of that class, and how to reach the functions and data in that object when we want to.

That completes our mini-overview of classes and objects. As you can see, a class is just a programming construct that groups together, or *encapsulates*, functions and data, and an object may be thought of as a variable of that class's type, as our object screen is to the class screenclass.

As it turns out, Java comes complete with several libraries of pre-defined classes, which save us a great deal of work. To a considerable extent, this book is an examination of these pre-defined and very useful Java classes. Using those predefined classes, we'll create objects needed to handle buttons, text fields, scroll bars, and much more.

Learning about Java Packages

These class libraries are called *packages* in Java, and one such library is called java.awt (where awt stands for Abstract Window Toolkit). This library holds the Graphics class, which will handle the graphics work we undertake. So this line in our first applet:

```
import java.awt.Graphics;
```

actually means that we want to include the Java Graphics class and make use of it in our program. In a minute, we'll see that we will use an object of the Graphics class for our graphics output.

We've added support for graphics handling by including the java.awt.Graphics class (and in Java, displaying the text string "Hello from Java!" is considered graphics handling). Next, it's time to set up our applet itself, which we have named hello. To do so, we will define a new class named hello. This is the standard way of setting up an applet in Java, and in fact, the applet itself has the file extension .class. That's because each class we define in a .java file ends up being exported to a .class file, where we can make use of it. You'll learn more details about this soon.

It would be quite difficult to write all the code an applet class needs from scratch. For example, we'd need to interact with the Web browser, reserve a section of screen, initialize the appropriate Java packages, and much more. It turns out that all that functionality is already built into the Java Applet class, which is part of the java.applet package. But how do we make use of the Applet class? That is, we want to customize our applet to display our text string, and the java.applet.Applet class itself knows nothing about that.

Understanding Java Inheritance

We can customize the java.applet.Applet class by *deriving* our hello class from the java.applet.Applet class. This makes java.applet.Applet the *base* class of the hello class, and it makes hello a class derived from java.applet .Applet. This gives us all the power of the java.applet.Applet class without the worries of writing it ourselves, and we can add what we want to this class by adding code to our derived class hello.

This is an important part of object-oriented programming, and it's called *inheritance*. In this way, a derived class inherits the functionality of its base class and adds more on top of it. For example, we may have a base class called chassis. We can derive various classes from this base class called, say, car and truck. In this way, two derived classes can share the same base class, saving time and effort programmatically. Although our car and truck classes share the same base class, chassis, they added different items to the base class, ending up as two quite different classes, car and truck.

Using inheritance, then, we will *extend* the base class java.applet.Applet by creating our own class hello and adding onto the base class. We indicate that the hello class is derived from the java.applet.Applet class like this—note that we use the keyword *class* to indicate that we are defining a new class:

```
    import java.awt.Graphics;

➜   public class hello extends java.applet.Applet
➜   {
        .
        .
        .
```

Now we're starting to set up our new class, hello, and we've given it all the power of the java.applet.Applet class (like the ability to request space from the Web browser and to respond to many browser-created commands). But how do we make additions and even alterations to the java.applet.Applet class to customize our own hello class? How do we display our text string? One way is by *overriding* the base class's built-in functions (overriding is an important part of object-oriented programming). When we re-define a base class's function in a derived class, the new version of the function is the one that takes over. In this way, we can customize the functions from the base class as we like them in the derived class.

For example, one function in the java.applet.Applet class is called paint(). This is a very important function that is called when the Web browser tells the applet to create its display on the screen. This happens when the applet first begins and every time that it has to be re-displayed later (for example, if the Web browser was minimized and then maximized, or if some window was moved and the applet's display area was uncovered after having been covered).

Our goal in the hello class is to display the string "Hello from Java!" on the screen, and in fact, we will override the java.applet.Applet class's paint() function to do so. We override a base class's function simply by redefining it in our new class. We'll do that now for the paint() function, noting first that the built-in functions of a class are called that class's *methods*. In this case, then, we override (that is, re-define) the paint() method like this:

```
import java.awt.Graphics;

public class hello extends java.applet.Applet
{
    public void paint( Graphics g )[
    {
        .
        .
        .
```

NOTE   The built-in functions of a class are called *methods*. Classes can also have built-in variables—called *data members*—and even constants. Collectively, all these parts are called a class's *members*.

What Are Java Access Modifiers?

The keyword *public* is called an *access modifier*. A class's methods can be declared `public`, `private`, or `protected`. If they are declared `public`, than you can call them from anywhere in the program, not just in the class in which they are defined. If they are `private`, they may be called from only the class in which they are defined. If they are `protected`, they may be called in only the class in which they are defined and the classes derived from that class.

Next, we indicate the *return* type of the `paint()` method. When we call a method, we can pass parameters to it, and it can return data to us. In this case, `paint()` has no return value, which we indicate as the return type *void*. Other return types are `int` for an integer return value (this variable is usually 32 bits long), `long` for a long integer (this variable is usually 64 bits long), `float` for a floating point return, or `double` for a double-precision floating point value. You can also return arrays and objects in Java.

Finally, note that we indicate that the `paint()` method is automatically passed one parameter—an object of the `Graphics` class that we will call g:

```
import java.awt.Graphics;

public class hello extends java.applet.Applet
{
     public void paint(Graphics g)
     {   .
             .
             .
```

This `Graphics` object represents the physical display of the applet. That is, we can use the built-in methods of this object—such as `drawImage()`, `drawLine()`, `drawOval()`, and others—to drawn on the screen. In this case, we want to place the string "Hello from Java!" on the screen, and we can do that with the `drawString()` method.

How do we reach the methods of an object like the `Graphics` object we have named g? We do that with a dot operator (.) like this: `g.drawString()`, where here we are invoking g's `drawString()` method to "draw" a string of text on the screen (text is handled like any other type of graphics in a windows environment—that is, it is drawn on the screen rather than "printed," just as you would draw a rectangle or circle). We supply three parameters to the `drawString()` method—the string of text we want to display, and the (x, y) location of that string's lower left corner (called the starting point of the string's *baseline*) in pixels on the screen, passed in two integer values. As shown in Figure 1.3, we can draw our string at the pixel location (60, 30), where (0, 0) is the upper left corner of the applet's display.

```
                (0, 0)    x increases -->
  y increases    ------------------------------------
       |        |                                     |
       V        |                                     |
                |                                     |
  (60, 30) _____Hello from Java!            |
                |                                     |
                |                                     |
                |                                     |
                 ------------------------------------
```

F I G U R E 1 . 3   Drawing a string at (60,30)

TIP   The coordinate system in a Java program is set up with the origin (0, 0) at the upper left, with x increasing horizontally to the right, and y increasing vertically downwards; this fact will be important throughout the book. If it seems backwards to you, you might try thinking of it in terms of reading a page of text, like this one, where you start at the upper left and work your way to the right and down. The units of measurement in Java coordinate systems are almost always screen pixels.

This means that we add a call to the drawString() method this way:

```java
import java.awt.Graphics;

public class hello extends java.applet.Applet
{
    public void paint( Graphics g )
    {
        g.drawString( "Hello from Java!", 60, 30 );
    }
}
```

Note that Java uses the same convention as C or C++ to indicate that a code statement is finished: it ends the statement with a semicolon (;).

TIP   In general, Java adheres very strongly to C++ coding conventions. If you know C++, you already know a great deal of Java.

We have completed the code necessary for our applet, which is to say the code for our new class, hello. When the Java compiler creates hello.class, the entire specification of our new class will be in that file. This is the actual binary file that you upload to your Internet Service Provider so it may be included in your Web page. A Java-enabled Web browser takes this class specification and creates an object of that class and then gives it control to display itself and, if applicable, handle user input.

But how? We have not yet completed the dissection of our first example; all we have done so far is to trace the development of `hello.java` into `hello.class`. How did we get our applet to be displayed in the Applet Viewer?

Understanding the Applet's Web Page

We saw that the Applet Viewer took our `hello.class` applet and displayed it in a Web page as shown in Figure 1.4.

FIGURE 1.4   Displaying an applet in a Web page

How did it get there? What happened is that we created a Web page for our applet and then opened that Web page in the Applet Viewer, which then displayed our applet. That Web page looks like this:

```
<html>

<!- Web page written for the Sun Applet Viewer>
```

```
<head>
<title>hello</title>
</head>

<body>
<hr>

<applet
code=hello.class
width=200
height=200>

</applet>

<hr>
</body>
</html>
```

Web pages are written in HTML (HyperText Markup Language). Because applets appear in Web pages, we will take the time to briefly work through the above page to make sure you know what's going on. If you're familiar with HTML, you can skip much of this review, but you should take a look at how to use the <applet> tag to embed applets in Web pages.

Connecting Java and HTML

Let's take apart the Web page we created for our applet now. We start with the <html> tag:

```
<html>
   .
   .
   .
```

Instructions in .html pages are placed into tags surrounded by angle brackets: < and >. The tags hold directions to the Web browser and are not displayed on the screen. Here, the <html> tag indicates to the Web browser that this .html file is written in HTML.

Next comes a comment. Comments in .html pages are written using the ! symbol like this: <! This is a comment.>. As follows, we indicate that this is a Web page written so we can use the Sun Applet Viewer:

```
<html>
```

```
<!- Web page written for the Sun Applet Viewer>
                    .
                    .
                    .
```

Next comes the header portion of our Web page, which we declare with the
<head> tag, ending the header section with the corresponding end header tag,
</head> (many HTML tags are used in pairs like this, such as <head> and </head>
or <center> and </center> to center text and images). In this case, the .html file
gets the title (set up with the <title> tag) of "hello", to match our applet:

```
<html>

<!- Web page written for the Sun Applet Viewer>

→       <head>
→       <title>hello</title>
→       </head>
            .
            .
            .
```

The title is the name given to a Web page, and it's usually displayed in the Web
browser's title bar. Next comes the body of the Web page. Here is where all the
actual items for display will go. We start the page off with a ruler line (visible in
Figure 1.4), using the <hr> tag:

```
<html>

<!- Web page written for the Sun Applet Viewer>

<head>
<title>hello</title>
</head>

→       <body>
→       <hr>
            .
            .
            .
```

Now we come to our applet. Applets are embedded with the <applet> tag,
and here we use the *code* keyword to indicate our applet is supported by the
hello.class file. We also indicate the size of the applet as 200 x 200 pixels (you
can choose any size you like here) this way:

```
<html>

<!- Web page written for the Sun Applet Viewer>
```

```
         <head>
         <title>hello</title>
         </head>

         <body>
         <hr>
    →    <applet
    →    code=hello.class
    →    width=200
    →    height=200>

    →    </applet>
            .
            .
            .
```

TIP   You can also use the java.applet.Applet.resize() method to request that the Web browser resize applets.

The <applet> tag is one that has a good deal of importance for us, so let's take a closer look at it now. Here's how the <applet> tag works in general:

```
<APPLET
     [ALIGN = LEFT or RIGHT or TOP or TEXTTOP or MIDDLE or
         ABSMIDDLE  or BASELINE or BOTTOM or ABSBOTTOM]
         [ALT = AlternateText]
         CODE = AppletName.class
         [CODEBASE = URL of .class file]
         HEIGHT = AppletPixelsHeight
         [HSPACE = PixelSpaceToLeftOfApplet]
         [NAME = AppletInstanceName]
         [VSPACE = PixelSpaceAboveApplet]
         WIDTH = AppletPixelsWidth
     >
     [<PARAM NAME = Parameter1 VALUE = VALUE1]
     [<PARAM NAME = Parameter2 VALUE = VALUE2]
            .
            .
            .
     </APPLET>
```

TIP   You can specify the URL of the applet's .class file with the CODEBASE keyword. This is often useful if you want to store your applets together in a directory in your ISP, away from the .html files.

Note that we indicate to the Web browser here how much space we'll need for our applet, using the HEIGHT and WIDTH keywords. We can also pass parameters to our applets with the PARAM keyword like this: <applet> PARAM today = "friday" </applet>. Passing parameters in this way allows us to customize our applets to fit different Web pages because we can read the parameters from inside an applet and make use of them. We'll see how this works in an example later in the book.

TIP   We'll see that there are enhancements to the <applet> tag in Java 1.1, such as the ability to pass the name of .jar files as parameters.

Not all Web browsers support Java. In practice, this means that those browsers just ignore the <applet> tag. This, in turn, means that you can place text between the <applet> and </applet> tags that will be displayed in non-Java browsers (and not in Java-enabled browsers), like this:

```
<applet code=hello>
Your Web browser does not support Java, so you can't see my applets, sorry!
</applet>
```

That's it for the <applet> tag. Using this tag, we can embed our applets in our Web pages, as Java has done for us in this temporary page. We finish off our Web page with the </body> and </html> tags as follows:

```
<html>

<!- Web page written for the Sun Applet Viewer>

<head>
<title>hello</title>
</head>

<body>
<hr>

<applet
code=hello.class
width=200
height=200>

</applet>

<hr>
</body>
</html>
```

Skill 1

And that completes our first example—we've gotten a glimpse into the process of creating and running an applet. It was as quick as that—we created and ran our first applet.

In this Skill, our example applet demonstrated only the easiest way to get an applet to work. Let's continue on to get a better idea of how we'll be working with Java throughout the book as we give our applet more power in Skill 2.

Are You Experienced?

Now you can...

- ☑ **create your own Java source code files**
- ☑ **understand the inner workings of a simple applet**
- ☑ **create a small working Java applet**
- ☑ **use the Applet Viewer to embed an applet in a Web page**
- ☑ **understand the basic object-oriented programming topics that will be useful throughout the book**

2. Jones 356-555-3398.

PROGRAMMERS
C. C. VB, exp. Call 534-555-6543 or fax 534-555-6544.

PROGRAMMING
MRFS Inc. is looking for a Sr Windows NT developer. Reqs. 3-5 yrs. Exp. In C under Windows, Win95 & NT, using Visual C. Excl. OO design & implementation skills a must. OLE2 & ODBC are a plus. Excl. Salary & bnfts. Resume & salary history to HR. 8779 HighTech Way, Computer City, AR

PROGRAMMERS
Contractors Wanted for short & long term assignments; Visual C. MFC Unix C/C, SQL Oracle Dev elop ers PC Help Desk Support Windows NT & NetWareTelecommunications Visual Basic, Access, HTMT, CGI, Perl MMI & Co. 885-555-9933

PROGRAMMER World Wide Web Links wants your HTML & Photoshop skills. Develop great WWW sites. Local & global customers. Send samples & resume to WWWL 2000 Apple Road, Santa Rosa, CA.

TECHNICAL WRITER Software firm seeks writer/editor for manuals, research notes, project mgmt. Min 2 years tech. writing, DTP & programming experience. Send resume & writing samples to: Software Systems, Dallas, TX.

TECHNICAL Software development firm looking for Tech Trainers. Ideal candidates have programming experience in Visual C HTML & JAVA. Need quick self starter. Call (443) 555-6868 for interview.

TECHNICAL WRITER/ Premier Computer Corp is seeking a combination of technical skills, knowledge and experience in the following areas: UNIX, Windows 95/NT, Visual Basic, on-line help & documentation and the Internet. Candidates must possess excellent writing skills, and be comfortable working in a quality vs. deadline driven environment. Competitive salary. Fax resume & samples to Karen Fields, Premier Computer Corp. 444 Industrial Blvd. Concord, CA. Or send to our website at www.premier.com.

WEB DESIGNER
BA/BS or equivalent programming/multimedia production. 3 years of experience in use and design of WWW services streaming audio and video HTML, PERL, CGI, GIF, JPEG. Demonstrated interpersonal, organization, communication, multi-tasking skills. Send resume to The Learning People at www.learning.com.

WEBMASTER-TECHNICAL
BSCS or equivalent. 2 years of experience in CGI, Windows 95/NT, UNIX, C, Java, Perl. Demonstrated ability to design, code, debug and test on-line services. Send resume to The Learning People at www.learning.com.

PROGRAMMER World Wide Web Links wants your HTML & Photoshop skills. Develop great WWW sites.

ing tools. Experienced in documentation preparation & programming languages (Access, C FoxPro) are a plus. Financial or banking customer service support is required along with excellent verbal & written communication skills with multi levels of end-users. Send resume to KKUP Enterprises, 45 Orange Blvd. Orange, CA.

COMPUTERS Small Web Design firm seeks indiv w/NT. Webserver & Database management exp. Fax resume to 556-555-4221.

COMPUTER/ Visual C/C. Visual Basic Exp'd Systems Analysts/Programmers for growing software dev. team in Roseburg. Computer Science or related degree preferred. Develop adv. Engineering applications for engineering firm. Fax resume to 707-555-8744.

COMPUTER Web Master for dynamic SF internet co. Site. Dev. test. coord. train. 2 yrs prog. Exp. C C Web C. FTP. fax resume to Best Staffing 845-555-7722.

COMPUTER PROGRAMMER
Ad agency seeks programmer w/exp. in UNIX/NT Platforms, Web Server, CGI/Perl. Programmer Position avail. on a project basis with the possibility to move into F/T. Fax resume & salary req. to R. Jones 334-555-8332.

COMPUTERS Programmer/Analyst Design and maintain C based SQL database applications. Required skills: Visual Basic, C, SQL, ODBC. Document existing and new applications, Novell or NT exp. a plus. Fax resume & salary history to 235-555-9935.

GRAPHIC DESIGNER
Webmaster's Weekly is seeking a creative Graphic Designer to design high impact marketing collateral, including direct mail promos. CD-ROM packages, ads and WWW pages. Must be able to juggle multiple projects and learn new skills on the job very rapidly. Web design experience a big plus. technical troubleshooting also a plus. Call 435-555-1235.

GRAPHICS - ART DIRECTOR - WEB-MULTIMEDIA
Leading internet development company has an outstanding opportunity for a talented, high-end Web Experienced Art Director. In addition to a great portfolio and fresh ideas, the ideal candidate has excellent communication and presentation skills. Working as a team with innovative producers and programmers you will create dynamic, interactive web sites and application interfaces. Some programming experience required. Send samples and resume to: SuperSites, 333 Main, Seattle, WA.

MARKETING
Fast paced software and services provider looking for MARKETING COMMUNICATIONS SPECIALIST to be responsible for its webpage.

PROGRAMMERS Multiple short term assignments available: Visual C. 3 positions SQL ServerNT Server. 2 positions JAVA & HTML. long term NetWare Various locations. Call for more info. 356-555-3398.

PROGRAMMERS
C. C. VB, Cobol, exp.
Call 534-555-6543
or fax 534-555-6544

PROGRAMMING
MRFS Inc. is looking for a Sr Windows NT developer. Reqs. 3-5 yrs. Exp. In C under Windows. Win95 & NT. using Visual C. Excl. OO design & implementation skills a must. OLE2 & ODBC are a plus. Resume & salary history to HR. 8779 HighTech Way. Computer City, AR

PROGRAMMERS/ Contractors Wanted for short & long term assignments: Visual C. MFC Unix C/C. SQL Oracle Developers PC Help Desk Support Windows NT & NetWareTelecommunications Visual Basic, Access, HTMT, CGI, Perl MMI & Co. 885-555-9933

PROGRAMMER World Wide Web Links wants your HTML & Photoshop skills. Develop great WWW sites. Local & global customers. Send samples & resume to WWWL 2000 Apple Road, Santa Rosa, CA.

TECHNICAL WRITER Software firm seeks writer/editor for manuals, research notes, project mgmt. Min 2 years tech. writing, DTP & programming experience. Send resume & writing samples to: Software Systems, Dallas, TX.

COMPUTER PROGRAMMER
Ad agency seeks programmer w/exp. in UNIX/NT Platforms, Web Server, CGI/Perl. Programmer Position avail. on a project basis with the possibility to move into F/T. Fax resume & salary req. to R. Jones 334-555-8332.

TECHNICAL WRITER Premier Computer Corp is seeking a combination of technical skills, knowledge and experience in the following areas: UNIX, Windows 95/NT, Visual Basic, on-line help & documentation and the internet. Candidates must possess excellent writing skills, and be comfortable working in a quality vs. deadline driven environment. Competitive salary. Fax resume & samples to Karen Fields, Premier Computer Corp. 444 Industrial Blvd. Concord, CA. Or send to our website at www.premier.com.

WEB DESIGNER
BA/BS or equivalent programming/multimedia production. 3 years of experience in use and design of WWW services streaming audio and video HTML. PERL. CGI. GIF, JPEG. Demonstrated interpersonal, organization, communication, multi-tasking skills. Send resume to The Learning People at www.learning.com.

WEBMASTER-TECHNICAL
BSCS or equivalent. 2 years of experience in CGI, Windows 95/NT,

COMPUTERS Small Web Design firm seeks indiv w/NT. Webserver & Database management exp. fax resume to 556-555-4221.

COMPUTER Visual C/C. Visual Basic Exp'd Systems Analysts/Programmers for growing software dev. team in Roseburg. Computer Science or related degree preferred. Develop adv. Engineering applications for engineering firm. Fax resume to 707-555-8744.

COMPUTER Web Master for dynamic SF internet co. Site. Dev. test. coord. train. 2 yrs prog. Exp. C C Web C. FTP. fax resume to Best Staffing 845-555-7722.

COMPUTERS/ QA SOFTWARE TESTERS Qualified candidates should have 2 yrs exp. performing integration & system testing using automated testing tools. Experienced in documentation preparation & programming languages (Access, C, FoxPro) are a plus. Financial or banking customer service support is required along with excellent verbal & written communication skills with multi levels of end-users. Send resume to KKUP Enterprises, 45 Orange Blvd. Orange, CA.

COMPUTERS Programmer/Analyst Design and maintain C based SQL database applications. Required skills: Visual Basic, C, SQL, ODBC. Document existing and new applications, Novell or NT a plus. Fax resume & salary history to 235-555-9935.

GRAPHIC DESIGNER
Webmaster's Weekly is seeking a creative Graphic Designer to design high impact marketing collateral including direct mail promo's. CD-ROM packages, ads and WWW pages. Must be able to juggle multiple projects and learn new skills on the job very rapidly. Web design experience a big plus. technical troubleshooting also a plus. Call 435-555-1235.

GRAPHICS - ART DIRECTOR - WEB-MULTIMEDIA
Leading internet development company has an outstanding opportunity for a talented, high-end Web Experienced Art Director. In addition to a great portfolio and fresh ideas, the ideal candidate has excellent communication and presentation skills. Working as a team with innovative producers and programmers you will create dynamic, interactive web sites and application interfaces. Some programming experience required. Send samples and resume to: SuperSites, 333 Main, Seattle, WA.

COMPUTER PROGRAMMER
Ad agency seeks programmer w/exp. in UNIX/NT Platforms, Web Server. CGI/Perl. Programmer Position avail. on a project basis with the possibility to move into F/T. Fax resume & salary req. to R. Jones 334-555-8332.

PROGRAMMERS / Established software company seeks program

ment. Must be a self-starter, energetic, organized. Must have 2 yrs web experience. Programming plus. Call 985-555-9854.

PROGRAMMERS Multiple short term assignments available: Visual C. 3 positions SQL ServerNT Server. 2 positions JAVA & HTML. long term NetWare Various locations. Call more info. 356-555-3398.

PROGRAMMERS
C. C. VB, Cobol. exp. Call 534-555-6543 or fax 534-555-6544.

PROGRAMMING
MRFS Inc. is looking for a Windows NT developer. Reqs. yrs. Exp. In C under Windows. Win95 & NT. using Visual C. OO design & implementation skills a must. OLE2 & ODBC are a plus. Excl. Salary & bnfts. Resume salary history to HR. 8779 HighTech Way. Computer City, AR

PROGRAMMERS/ Contractors Wanted for short & long term assignments: Visual C. MFCUnix C/C. Oracle Developers PC Help Desk Support Windows NT & NetWare Telecommunications Visual Basic. Access, HTMT, CGI, Perl MMI & Co. 885-555-9933

PROGRAMMER World Wide Web Links wants your HTML & Photoshop skills. Develop great WWW sites. Local & global customers. Send samples & resume to WWWL 2000 Apple Road, Santa Rosa, CA.

TECHNICAL WRITER Software firm seeks writer/editor for manuals, research notes, project mgmt. Min 2 years tech. writing, DTP & programming experience. Send resume & writing samples to: Software Systems, Dallas, TX.

TECHNICAL Software development firm looking for Tech Trainers. Ideal candidates have programming experience in Visual C HTML & JAVA. Need quick self starter. Call (443) 555-6868 for interview.

TECHNICAL WRITER Premier Computer Corp is seeking a combination of technical skills, knowledge and experience in the following areas: UNIX, Windows 95/NT, Visual Basic, on-line help & documentation and the internet. Candidates possess excellent writing skills, be comfortable working in a quality vs. deadline driven environment. Competitive salary. Fax resume & samples to Karen Fields, Premier Computer Corp. 444 Industrial Blvd. Concord, CA. Or send to our website at www.premier.com.

WEB DESIGNER
BA/BS or equivalent programming/multimedia production. years of experience in use and design of WWW services streaming audio and video HTML. PERL. GIF, JPEG. Demonstrated interpersonal, organization, communication, multi-tasking skills. Send resume to The Learning People at www.learning.com.

WEBMASTER-TECHNICAL

S K I L L

two

Handling Java Text Fields

- ❏ Adding buttons and other Java controls
- ❏ Adding and using text fields
- ❏ Using Java class constructors
- ❏ Using the new operator
- ❏ Using the init() function
- ❏ Initializing Java controls

PC Help Desk Support Windows NT & NetWare Visual Basic Access HTML SQL Perl MMI & Co., 885-555-9933

PROGRAM Links wants your HTML & Photoshop skills. Develop great WWW sites. Local & glo ples & resume to WWWL 2000 Apple Road. Santa Rosa, CA.

TECHNICAL seeks writer/editor for manuals, research notes, project mgmt. Min 2 years tech. ming experience. Send resume & writing Samples to: Software Systems D

MARKE ed softwa looking for NICATION onsible fo ordinatio st be a se anized. P erience Call 98

MER s your H velop gre bal cust resume

Science or related degree preferred. Develop adv. Engineering applica- resume to 707-555-8744.

COMPUTER web master for dynam- Dev. test. coord. train. 2 yrs. prog. Exp. C.C. Web C. FTP, Fax resume to Best

COMPUTER PROGRAMMER Ad agency seeks programmer w/exp in UNIX/NT Platforms, Web Server ogrammer Posit- ion avail. on a project basis with the possibility to move into F/T. Fax req to R Jones 334-555-8332.

TECHNICAL Software development

Resume & salary history to HR. 8779 HighTech Way, Computer City, AR

PROGRAMMERS/ Contractors Wanted for short & long term assignments. Visual C MFC Unix C/C SQL Oracle Developers PC Help Desk Support Windows NT & NetWareTelecommunications Visual Basic, Access, HTML, CGI, Perl MMI & Co., 885-555-9933

PROGRAMMER World Wide Web Links wants your HTML & Photoshop skills. Develop great WWW sites. Local & global customers. Send sam- ples & resume to WWWL 2000 Apple Road. Santa Rosa, CA.

TECHNICAL WRITER Software firm seeks writer/editor for manuals, research notes, project mgmt. Min

In Skill 1, we saw the basics of a simple Java applet. In Skill 2, we're going to add *controls* to our programs. Controls are the interactive items you find in applets, like text boxes, buttons, and scrolling list boxes, and they're very powerful parts of Java programs. The next two skills are two of the most important and fundamental controls: text boxes—called *text fields* in Java—and buttons. After exploring text fields here, we'll see how to integrate them with buttons in Skill 3. For example, we'll see how to create an applet with a text field and a button marked Click Here, as shown in Figure 2.1.

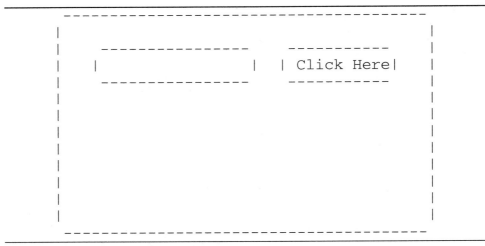

FIGURE 2.1 An applet with a text field and a button

When the user clicks the Click Here button, we can place a new message that reads, "Welcome to Java" in the text field, as shown in Figure 2.2.

Using controls is a very strong technique in Java—in fact, using the included controls is often the whole point of an applet.

Declaring a Text Field

The first control we add to an applet will be the text field. Familiar to all Windows users, a *text field* is just a box that can hold text. (Text fields are also called text boxes and edit controls.) Our goal might be to place a text field in our applet, as shown in Figure 2.3.We can even start the text field out with the message,

"Welcome to Java," as shown in Figure 2.4. After this text field appears, the users can edit the text as they like, using the mouse and keyboard.

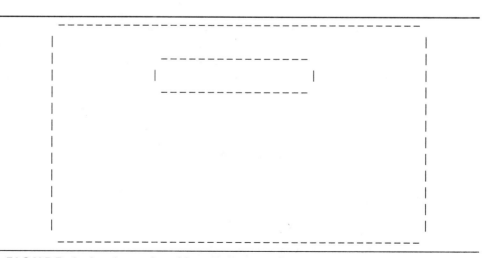

```
    ---------------------------------------------------
  |                                                     |
  |      -----------------      -------------           |
  |     |Welcome to Java |     | Click Here |           |
  |      -----------------      -------------           |
  |                                                     |
  |                                                     |
  |                                                     |
  |                                                     |
  |                                                     |
  |                                                     |
  |                                                     |
    ---------------------------------------------------
```

F I G U R E 2 . 2   **When the user clicks the Click Here button, a message appears in the text field.**

```
      -------------------------------------------------
    |                                                   |
    |            -----------------                      |
    |           |                 |                     |
    |            -----------------                      |
    |                                                   |
    |                                                   |
    |                                                   |
    |                                                   |
    |                                                   |
    |                                                   |
    |                                                   |
      -------------------------------------------------
```

F I G U R E 2 . 3   **An applet with an empty text field**

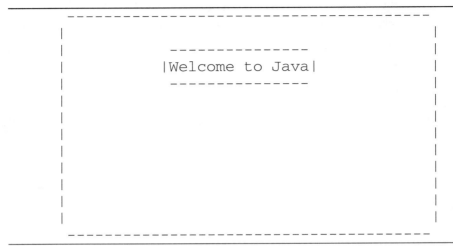

FIGURE 2.4 The message "Welcome to Java" can be displayed in a text field.

TIP Sometimes you may not want the user to edit the text you display in a Java program. In that case, you can use the `TextField setEditable()` method, which allows you to make text fields read-only. In addition, you can use *Label* controls, instead of text fields. Label controls display text that cannot be altered by the user. We'll learn about these controls in Skill 4.

Create a new subdirectory now to contain the code for our text field example, naming it `text`. Now create a new file, named `text.java`, with your editor. We can start our new text field program the same way we started the `hello.java` file:

```
import java.awt.*;

public class text extends java.applet.Applet
{
    .
    .
    .
}
```

Here, we are importing all the classes in the Java AWT package with the statement `import java.awt.*`. These are the classes that will let us add text fields and buttons to our applet—for example, two of the classes in this package that we will use are `Button` and `TextField`. In addition, we are declaring a new public class named `text` as our applet's main class, based on the `java.applet.Applet` class.

Next, we create our text field. We first have to declare it, setting up an object named, say, `text1` of the `TextField` class:

```
import java.awt.*;

public class text extends java.applet.Applet
{
        TextField text1;
             .
             .
             .
}
```

The above declares our new text field, which we have named `text1`. The methods of the Java class `TextField`, which is the class we will use for text fields, appear in Table 2.1.

NOTE   **Note the distinction between the terms** `TextField` **and** `text1`. `TextField` **is a Java class, and** `text1` **is the object of that class that we will actually work with.**

T A B L E   2 . 1 : Java `TextField` class methods

Method	Does This
addActionListener(ActionListener)	Adds action listener to textfield.
addNotify()	Creates `TextField`'s peer.
echoCharIsSet()	Returns true if `TextField` has echoing.
getColumns()	Returns the number of columns.
getEchoChar()	Returns the echoing character.
getMinimumSize()	Returns minimum size for `TextField`.
getMinimumSize(int)	Returns minimum size needed for `TextField` with specified columns.
getPreferredSize()	Returns preferred size for `TextField`.
getPreferredSize(int)	Returns preferred size for `TextField` with the specified columns.
minimumSize()	Deprecated. Replaced by getMinimumSize().
minimumSize(int)	Deprecated. Replaced by getMinimumSize(int).
paramString()	Returns the String of parameters for `TextField`.

TABLE 2.1 CONTINUED: Java `TextField` class methods

Method	Does This
`preferredSize()`	Deprecated. Replaced by `getPreferredSize()`.
`preferredSize(int)`	Deprecated. Replaced by `getPreferredSize(int)`.
`processActionEvent(ActionEvent)`	Processes action events by dispatching them to `ActionListener` objects.
`processEvent(AWTEvent)`	Processes events on textfield.
`removeActionListener(ActionListener)`	Removes the specified action listener.
`setColumns(int)`	Sets number of columns in `TextField`.
`setEchoChar(char)`	Sets echo character for `TextField`.
`setEchoCharacter(char)`	Deprecated. Replaced by setEchoChar(char).

 TIP   Note the `getText()` and `setText()` methods in the `TextField` class; these are the usual ways to get text from a text field or set the text in that text field.

Placing `text1` as we have done in our applet makes it a *global class variable*. What we mean by global is that it will be available to all the methods (i.e., built-in functions) of our text class, and all the code in those methods, because it is declared outside any such method.

As far as variables go, a variable is just a place set aside in memory for data; we will find that variable's numeric data types in Java are just the same as most standard Basic, C or C++ implementations. For example, to set aside space for integer data, we set up an integer variable of type `int`:

```
int the_integer;
```

To place values in variable, we just assign them to that variable as follows:

```
the_integer = 5;
```

The built-in Java numeric data types like `int` and `float` appear in Table 2.2.

 **WARNING**   It is usually good to restrict the number of global class variables you use to a minimum. Because these variables can be reached anywhere, there is always the possibility of conflict with another variable of the same name in one of your methods. Using too many global variables goes directly against the spirit of object-oriented programming, which was originally developed to handle larger programs by getting variables and methods out of the global space, placing them in objects to clear the global space of clutter.

TABLE 2.2: The Java numeric data types

Type	Bits	Means
byte	8	Holds a byte of data.
Short	16	Short integer.
Int	32	Integer value.
Long	64	Long integer.
Float	32	Floating point value.
Double	64	Double precision floating point value.
Char	16	Unicode character.
Boolean	—	Takes true or false values.

NOTE   We can declare a class's data as private, protected, or public, just as we can for a class's methods.

Initializing with the init() Method

Declaring a text field, however, just sets aside memory for it and does nothing to display it in our applet. We have to handle that ourselves, and we do that in the init() method.

When we want to initialize an applet, by, for example, adding text fields to it, we do that in the init() method. As you'll see throughout this book, all kinds of initialization can take place in the init() function. It runs automatically when the applet starts, so you should place code that you want run first in the init() function. To use init(), we just add it to our class as follows:

```
import java.awt.*;

public class text extends java.applet.Applet
{
    TextField text1;
```

```
→        public void init()
         {
             .
             .
             .
→        }

    }
```

Note that the `init()` function is like any other function, except that it doesn't return a value (which is why the return type is listed as `void` above) and it runs automatically when the applet starts. Our task in `init()` is to create the new text field and install it in our applet. Creating Java controls is a two-step process: we first declare the new object as we have done above, and then we have to actually create the new object in the `init()` function, using the Java **new** operator.

Handling Memory with the new **Operator**

The Java **new** operator is just like the C++ **new** operator; it is used to allocate memory for objects, variables, arrays—for anything we'd like. If you know C, the **new** operator largely replaces `malloc()`, `calloc()` and all the memory allocation functions; and it is much easier to work with.

 NOTE While the standard memory-allocating functions like `malloc()` and `calloc()` in C are functions, the **new** operator is indeed an operator (like +, − and so on) not a function. This operator is a built-in part of Java and does not come from any class library.

Let's put the **new** operator to work. We'll create our new object named `text1` in our applet's `init()` method, using the following syntax:

```
import java.awt.*;

public class text extends java.applet.Applet
{
    TextField text1;

    public void init()
```

```
    {
→       text1 = new TextField();
            .
            .
            .
    }

}
```

This syntax creates a new TextField object and places it in our text1 variable. This is a two-step process that we'll see many times in this book: you first *declare* a control's object and then use the new operator to *create* that object in the init() method.

The above new line of code creates a new text field, but it's only one character wide. To make the text field, say, 20 characters wide, we pass a value of 20 to the TextField class's *constructor*.

What Are Java Constructors?

Using constructors is a very popular technique in object-oriented programming; a constructor for a particular class is simply a method that is automatically run when you create an object of that class, and its purpose is to initialize that object as you want it. That is, constructors are used to initialize objects. A class's constructor is called when a new object is being created of that class, and we can set the object up as we like it. Because a constructor is a method, we can pass data to constructors (if they are written to accept such data), allowing us to set up an object as we want when that object is created. In this case, we'll pass a value of 20 to our new text field's constructor. We can do that using the following syntax:

```
import java.awt.*;

public class text extends java.applet.Applet
{
    TextField text1;

    public void init()
    {
→       text1 = new TextField(20);
            .
            .
            .
    }
```

This makes our new text field 20 characters wide. If we wanted to set up an initial string in the text field instead of using a set number of characters, we could just pass that string to `TextField`'s constructor as follows:

```
text1 = new TextField("Welcome to Java");
```

Overloading Java Methods

If you are not familiar with C++, this might seem odd—how can we call a function with a numeric value like 20 *or* a string like "Welcome to Java"? The reason is that in Java, as in C++, you can *overload* functions. This means that you can set up a function to be called with different types and numbers of parameters. The Java compiler determines which version of the function to call depending on what parameters—and how many of them—you pass. For that reason, both these lines are valid Java code:

```
text1 = new TextField(20);
text2 = new TextField("Welcome to Java");
```

 NOTE **Don't confuse overloading functions with overriding them. Overloading a function means that the function can be called with different parameter lists, while overriding a function redefines the version of the function that appears in the class's base class.**

Now that we've created our new text field, the next step is to *add* it to our applet's display. In Skill 3, we'll see that Java handles the display of our controls automatically. That is, Java handles what's called the *layout* of our controls automatically, although we will take more control of this process as time goes on. To add our text field to our applet's display, we use the `add()` method as follows, where we add the new control `text1` to our applet's default layout:

```
import java.awt.*;

public class text extends java.applet.Applet
{
    TextField text1;

    public void init()
    {
        text1 = new TextField(20);
```

→   add(text1);
                .
                .
                .
        }

    }

At this point, then, our new text field appears in the applet as shown in Figure 2.5. We add the text shown in Figure 2.6 to the text field as follows, using the TextField class's setText() method (see Table 2.1).

```
import java.awt.*;

public class text extends java.applet.Applet
{
    TextField text1;

    public void init()
    {
        text1 = new TextField(20);
        add(text1);
        text1.setText("Welcome to Java");
    }

}
```

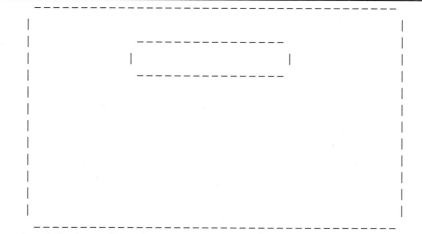

FIGURE 2.5   Our new text field

```
 ------------------------------------------
|                                          |
|           ------------------             |
|          |Welcome to Java  |             |
|           ------------------             |
|                                          |
|                                          |
|                                          |
|                                          |
|                                          |
|                                          |
|                                          |
 ------------------------------------------
```

FIGURE 2.6   We want to add the text, "Welcome to Java."

NOTE   We could also place this text into the text box by passing it to the text field's constructor this way: `text1 = new TextField("Welcome to Java");`

NOTE   Note again the syntax here: `text1.setText("Welcome to Java");`. **This is the standard way of executing an object's internal method (here, that's the** `setText()` **method of the** `text1` **object) with the dot operator. Again, this is standard C++ terminology, but if you're not used to it, it might take a while before it becomes second nature. In general, if you want to execute, say, a method named** `the_method()`, **which is a built-in function of an object named** `the_object`, **the correct syntax is:** `the_object.the_method();`.

And that's all there is to it—we've created a new text field and added it to our applet's display. Create the `text.class` file now with javac. We'll need a Web page to display our new class file in the Applet Viewer, so create a new .htm file called `text.htm` now, adding the following HTML code to it:

```
<html>

<!- Web page written for the Sun Applet Viewer>
```

```
<head>
<title>text</title>
</head>

<body>
<hr>

<applet
code=text.class
width=200
height=200>

</applet>

<hr>
</body>
</html>
```

We're ready to run the Applet Viewer with this new Web page. The result appears below—you can see our text field, with our message in it. Our first text field applet is a success—the listing for this applet appears in text.java.

text.java

```java
import java.awt.*;

public class text extends java.applet.Applet
{
    TextField text1;

    public void init()
    {
```

```
        text1 = new TextField(20);
        add(text1);
        text1.setText("Welcome to Java");
    }

}
```

TIP   Java text fields support the standard Windows editing shortcuts like Ctrl+V to paste from the clipboard, Ctrl+X to cut selected text, Ctrl+C to copy selected text, and so on.

Creating and using text fields is a good start. However, it's only a start. Let's turn now to Skill 3, where we'll work with a new Java control: buttons.

Are You Experienced?

Now you can...

☑ **add Java controls to a program and initialize them**

☑ **add and use text fields**

☑ **display multiple lines of text**

☑ **use text areas**

☑ **allocate memory**

☑ **use the Java new operator**

356-555-3398.

PROGRAMMERS
C. C. VB. Cobol, exp. Call 534-555-6543 or fax 534-555-6544.

PROGRAMMING

MRFS Inc. is looking for a Sr. Windows NT developer. Reqs. 3-5 yrs. Exp. In C under Windows, Win95 & NT, using Visual C. Excl. OO design & implementation skills a must. OLE2 & ODBC are a plus. Excl. Salary & bnfts. Resume & salary history to HR, 8779 HighTech Way, Computer City, AR

PROGRAMMERS

Contractors Wanted for short & long term assignments: Visual C, MFC Unix C/C, SQL Oracle Dev elop ers PC Help Desk Support Windows NT & NetWareTelecommunications Visual Basic, Access, HTMT, CGI, Perl MMI & Co., 885-555-9933

PROGRAMMER World Wide Web Links wants your HTML & Photoshop skills. Develop great WWW sites. Local & global customers. Send samples & resume to WWWL, 2000 Apple Road, Santa Rosa, CA.

TECHNICAL WRITER Software firm seeks writer/editor for manuals, research notes, project mgmt. Min 2 years tech. writing, DTP & programming experience. Send resume & writing samples to: Software Systems, Dallas, TX.

TECHNICAL Software development firm looking for Tech Trainers. Ideal candidates have programming experience in Visual C, HTML & JAVA. Need quick self starter. Call (443) 555-6868 for interview.

TECHNICAL WRITER/ Premier Computer Corp is seeking a combination of technical skills, knowledge and experience in the following areas: UNIX, Windows 95/NT, Visual Basic, on-line help & documentation, and the internet. Candidates must possess excellent writing skills, and be comfortable working in a quality vs. deadline driven environment. Competitive salary. Fax resume & samples to Karen Fields, Premier Computer Corp., 444 Industrial Blvd. Concord, CA. Or send to our website at www.premier.com.

WEB DESIGNER

BA/BS or equivalent programming/multimedia production. 3 years of experience in use and design of WWW services streaming audio and video HTML, PERL, CGI, GIF, JPEG. Demonstrated interpersonal, organization, communication, multi-tasking skills. Send resume to The Learning People at www.learning.com.

WEBMASTER-TECHNICAL

BSCS or equivalent, 2 years of experience in CGI, Windows 95/NT, UNIX, C, Java, Perl. Demonstrated ability to design, code, debug and test on-line services. Send resume to The Learning People at www.learning.com.

PROGRAMMER World Wide Web Links wants your HTML & Photoshop skills. Develop great WWW sites. Local & global customers. Send sam-

ing tools. Experienced in documentation preparation & programming languages (Access, C, FoxPro) are a plus. Financial or banking customer service support is required along with excellent verbal & written communication skills with multi levels of end-users. Send resume to KKUP Enterprises, 45 Orange Blvd., Orange, CA.

COMPUTERS Small Web Design Firm seeks indiv. w/NT, Webserver & Database management exp. Fax resume to 556-555-4221.

COMPUTER/ Visual C/C, Visual Basic Exp'd Systems Analysts/ Programmers for growing software dev. team in Roseburg. Computer Science or related degree preferred. Develop adv. Engineering applications for engineering firm. Fax resume to 707-555-8744.

COMPUTER Web Master for dynamic SF Internet co. Site. Dev., test, coord., train. 2 yrs prog. Exp. C C. Web C. FTP. Fax resume to Best Staffing 845-555-7722.

COMPUTER PROGRAMMER

Ad agency seeks programmer w/exp. in UNIX/NT Platforms, Web Server, CGI/Perl. Programmer Position avail. on a project basis with the possibility to move into F/T. Fax resume & salary req. to R. Jones 334-555-8332.

COMPUTERS Programmer/Analyst Design and maintain C based SQL database applications. Required skills: Visual Basic, C, SQL, ODBC. Document existing and new applications. Novell or NT exp. a plus. Fax resume & salary history to 235-555-9935.

GRAPHIC DESIGNER
Webmaster's Weekly is seeking a creative Graphic Designer to design high impact marketing collater al, including direct mail promois, CD-ROM packages, ads and WWW pages. Must be able to juggle multiple projects and learn new skills on the job very rapidly. Web design experience a big plus, technical troubleshooting also a plus. Call 435-555-1235.

GRAPHICS - ART DIRECTOR - WEB-MULTIMEDIA
Leading internet development company has an outstanding opportunity for a talented, high-end Web Experienced Art Director. In addition to a great portfolio and fresh ideas, the ideal candidate has excellent communication and presentation skills. Working as a team with innovative producers and programmers, you will create dynamic, interactive web sites and application interfaces. Some programming experience required. Send samples and resume to: SuperSites, 333 Main, Seattle, WA.

MARKETING

Fast paced software and services provider looking for MARKETING COMMUNICATIONS SPECIALIST to be responsible for its webpage, seminar coordination, and ad place-

PROGRAMMERS Multiple short term assignments available: Visual C, 3 positions SQL ServerNT Server, 2 positions JAVA & HTML, long term NetWare. Various locations. Call for more info. 356-555-3398.

PROGRAMMERS

C. C. VB, Cobol, exp. Call 534-555-6543 or fax 534-555-6544.

PROGRAMMING
MRFS Inc. is looking for a Sr. Windows NT developer. Reqs. 3-5 yrs. Exp. In C under Windows, Win95 & NT, using Visual C. Excl. OO design & implementation skills a must. OLE2 & ODBC are a plus. Excl. Salary & bnfts. Resume & salary history to HR, 8779 HighTech Way, Computer City, AR

PROGRAMMERS/ Contractors Wanted for short & long term assignments: Visual C MFC Unix C/C SQL Oracle Developers PC Help Desk Support Windows NT & NetWareTelecommunications Visual Basic, Access, HTMT, CGI, Perl MMI & Co., 885-555-9933

PROGRAMMER World Wide Web Links wants your HTML & Photoshop skills. Develop great WWW sites. Local & global customers. Send samples & resume to WWWL, 2000 Apple Road, Santa Rosa, CA.

TECHNICAL WRITER Software firm seeks writer/editor for manuals, research notes, project mgmt. Min 2 years tech. writing, DTP & programming experience. Send resume & writing samples to: Software Systems, Dallas, TX.

COMPUTER PROGRAMMER

Ad agency seeks programmer w/exp. in UNIX/NT Platforms, Web Server, CGI/Perl. Programmer Position avail. on a project basis with the possibility to move into F/T. Fax resume & salary req. to R. Jones 334-555-8332.

TECHNICAL WRITER Premier Computer Corp is seeking a combination of technical skills, knowledge and experience in the following areas: UNIX, Windows 95/NT, Visual Basic, on-line help & documentation, and the internet. Candidates must possess excellent writing skills, and be comfortable working in a quality vs. deadline driven environment. Competitive salary. Fax resume & samples to Karen Fields, Premier Computer Corp., 444 Industrial Blvd. Concord, CA. Or send to our website at www.premier.com.

WEB DESIGNER
BA/BS or equivalent programming/multimedia production. 3 years of experience in use and design of WWW services streaming audio and video HTML, PERL, CGI, GIF, JPEG. Demonstrated interpersonal, organization, communication, multi-tasking skills. Send resume to The Learning People at www.learning.com.

WEBMASTER-TECHNICAL
BSCS or equivalent, 2 years of experience in CGI, Windows 95/NT, UNIX, C, Java, Perl. Demonstrated

COMPUTERS Small Web Design Firm seeks indiv. w/NT, Webserver & Database management exp. Fax resume to 556-555-4221.

COMPUTER Visual C/C, Visual Basic Exp'd Systems Analysts/ Programmers for growing software dev. team in Roseburg. Computer Science or related degree preferred. Develop adv. Engineering applications for engineering firm. Fax resume to 707-555-8744.

COMPUTER Web Master for dynamic SF Internet co. Site. Dev., test, coord., train. 2 yrs prog. Exp. C C. Web C. FTP. Fax resume to Best Staffing 845-555-7722.

COMPUTERS/ QA SOFTWARE TESTERS Qualified candidates should have 2 yrs exp. performing integration & system testing using automated testing tools. Experienced in documentation preparation & programming languages (Access, C, FoxPro) are a plus. Financial or banking customer service support is required along with excellent verbal & written communication skills with multi levels of end-users. Send resume to KKUP Enterprises, 45 Orange Blvd., Orange, CA.

COMPUTERS Programmer/Analyst Design and maintain C based SQL database applications. Required skills: Visual Basic, C, SQL, ODBC. Document existing and new applications. Novell or NT exp. a plus. Fax resume & salary history to 235-555-9935.

GRAPHIC DESIGNER

Webmaster's Weekly is seeking a creative Graphic Designer to design high impact marketing collater al, including direct mail promo's, CD-ROM packages, ads and WWW pages. Must be able to juggle multiple projects and learn new skills on the job very rapidly. Web design experience a big plus, technical troubleshooting also a plus. Call 435-555-1235.

GRAPHICS - ART DIRECTOR - WEB-MULTIMEDIA
Leading internet development company has an outstanding opportunity for a talented, high-end Web Experienced Art Director. In addition to a great portfolio and fresh ideas, the ideal candidate has excellent communication and presentation skills. Working as a team with innovative producers and programmers, you will create dynamic, interactive web sites and application interfaces. Some programming experience required. Send samples and resume to: SuperSites, 333 Main, Seattle, WA.

COMPUTER PROGRAMMER
Ad agency seeks programmer w/exp. in UNIX/NT Platforms, Web Server, CGI/Perl. Programmer Position avail. on a project basis with the possibility to move into F/T. Fax resume & salary req. to R. Jones 334-555-8332.

PROGRAMMERS / Established software company seeks programmers with extensive Windows NT

ment. Must be a self-starter, energetic, organized. Must have 2 years web experience. Programming a plus. Call 985-555-9854.

PROGRAMMERS Multiple short term assignments available: Visual C, 3 positions SQL ServerNT Server, 2 positions JAVA & HTML, long term NetWare. Various locations. Call for more info. 356-555-3398.

PROGRAMMERS

C. C. VB, Cobol, exp. Call 534-555-6543 or fax 534-555-6544.

PROGRAMMING

MRFS Inc. is looking for a Sr. Windows NT developer. Reqs. 3-5 yrs. Exp. In C under Windows, Win95 & NT, using Visual C. Excl. OO design & implementation skills a must. OLE2 & ODBC are a plus. Excl. Salary & bnfts. Resume & salary history to HR, 8779 HighTech Way, Computer City, AR

PROGRAMMERS/ Contractors Wanted for short & long term assignments: Visual C, MFCUnix C/C, SQL Oracle Developers PC Help Desk Support Windows NT & NetWareTelecommunications Visual Basic, Access, HTMT, CGI, Perl MMI & Co., 885-555-9933

PROGRAMMER World Wide Web Links wants your HTML & Photoshop skills. Develop great WWW sites. Local & global customers. Send samples & resume to WWWL, 2000 Apple Road, Santa Rosa, CA.

TECHNICAL WRITER Software firm seeks writer/editor for manuals, research notes, project mgmt. Min 2 years tech. writing, DTP & programming experience. Send resume & writing samples to: Software Systems, Dallas, TX.

TECHNICAL Software development firm looking for Tech Trainers. Ideal candidates have programming experience in Visual C, HTML & JAVA. Need quick self starter. Call (443) 555-6868 for interview.

TECHNICAL WRITER Premier Computer Corp is seeking a combination of technical skills, knowledge and experience in the following areas: UNIX, Windows 95/NT, Visual Basic, on-line help & documentation, and the internet. Candidates must possess excellent writing skills, and be comfortable working in a quality vs. deadline driven environment. Competitive salary. Fax resume & samples to Karen Fields, Premier Computer Corp., 444 Industrial Blvd. Concord, CA. Or send to our website at www.premier.com.

WEB DESIGNER

BA/BS or equivalent programming/multimedia production. 3 years of experience in use and design of WWW services streaming audio and video HTML, PERL, CGI, GIF, JPEG. Demonstrated interpersonal, organization, communication, multi-tasking skills. Send resume to The Learning People at www.learning.com.

WEBMASTER-TECHNIC

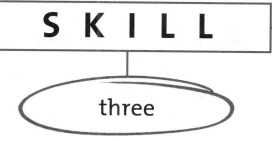

S K I L L

three

3

Using Java Buttons

❑ Using the new Java 1.1 delegation-based event model

❑ Adding and using Java buttons

❑ Using multiple buttons

❑ Using Java events

❑ The Java String class

❑ Adding and using text areas

In Skill 2, we got our start with Java controls by taking a look at text fields. Here, we're going to flesh out our programs by adding buttons. Every GUI user is familiar with buttons—you click them to make some action occur. Buttons connect naturally with text fields in Java—when we click a button, we can display something in a text field. These are fundamental GUI controls, so let's start working with buttons now.

Working with Buttons in Java

You have already learned a little about handling text fields. Next, let's see how we can control what happens even more, by using buttons. For example, we might set up a new applet with a text field and a button that has the caption "Click Here." (See Figure 3.1.) When the user clicks the button, we might display a message such as "Welcome to Java" in our text field, as shown in Figure 3.2.

Let's create this example now. We can call our new applet clicker. Create a new file named `clicker.java` and start with our usual beginning-of-applet code:

```java
import java.applet.Applet;
import java.awt.*;

public class clicker extends Applet {
    .
    .
    .
}
```

We start by adding the text field for our new applet, which, as before, we can name `text1`. We declare that new control at the beginning of our class's declaration. This is where we will place all our control's declarations, to make them global class variables because, as we'll see, we need to reach them from more than one method:

```java
import java.applet.Applet;
import java.awt.*;

public class clicker extends Applet {

→    TextField text1;
    .
    .
    .
```

```
 --------------------------------------------
|                                            |
|   -------------------    ------------      |
|  |                   |  | Click Here |     |
|   -------------------    ------------      |
|                                            |
|                                            |
|                                            |
|                                            |
|                                            |
|                                            |
|                                            |
 --------------------------------------------
```

FIGURE 3.1   Using a text field and a button together in an applet

```
 ---------------------------------------------
|                                             |
|   -------------------    ------------       |
|  |Welcome to Java    |  | Click Here |      |
|   -------------------    ------------       |
|                                             |
|                                             |
|                                             |
|                                             |
|                                             |
|                                             |
|                                             |
 ---------------------------------------------
```

FIGURE 3.2   "Welcome to Java" appears in the text field.

Next, we create the new text field with the new operator and add it to our applet's display with the add() method:

```
import java.applet.Applet;
import java.awt.*;
```

TABLE 3.2 CONTINUED: The Java String class methods

Method	Does This
trim()	Trims leading and trailing white space from this String.
valueOf(boolean)	Returns a String object that represents the state of the given boolean.
valueOf(char)	Returns a String object that contains a single character.
valueOf(char[])	Returns a String that is equivalent to the given character array.
valueOf(char[], int, int)	Returns a String that is equivalent to the given character array.
valueOf(double)	Returns a String that represents the value of the double.
valueOf(float)	Returns a String that represents the value of the float.
valueOf(int)	Returns a String that represents the value of the integer.
valueOf(long)	Returns a String that represents the value of the long.
valueOf(Object)	Returns String that represents the value of object.

TIP

The String class's methods now make use of the Java 1.1 Internationalization techniques, like using character-encoding converters and being locale-aware. Using the Java Locale class, you can set the formation of Strings with constants like Locale.FRENCH, Locale.GERMAN, and so on.

And now our new applet is complete. Build it now and run it. Click the button and watch the "Welcome to Java" message appear in the text field as shown below. The code for this applet appears in clicker.java.

C   clicker.java

```
import java.applet.Applet;
import java.awt.*;
import java.awt.event.*;

public class clicker extends Applet implements ActionListener {

    TextField text1;
    Button button1;

    public void init(){
        text1 = new TextField(20);
        add(text1);
        button1 = new Button("Click Me");
        add(button1);
        button1.addActionListener(this);
    }

    public void actionPerformed(ActionEvent event){
        String msg = new String ("Welcome to Java");
        if(event.getSource() == button1){
            text1.setText(msg);
        }
    }
}
```

So far, then, we've seen how to add both a text field and a button to our applet. Now let's turn to the next case—multiple buttons.

How to Handle Multiple Buttons

Let's say that we want to set up a new applet that has two buttons, labeled "Welcome to" and "Java", along with a text box, as shown in Figure 3.4. When the user clicks the Welcome To button, we can display "Welcome to" in the text box, as shown in Figure 3.5. When they click the Java button, we can display "Java" in the text box, as shown in Figure 3.6.

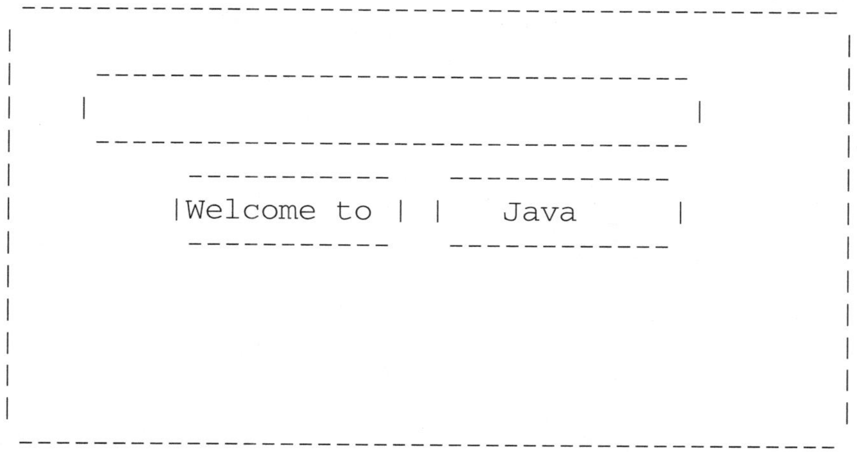

FIGURE 3.4 An applet with a text box and two buttons

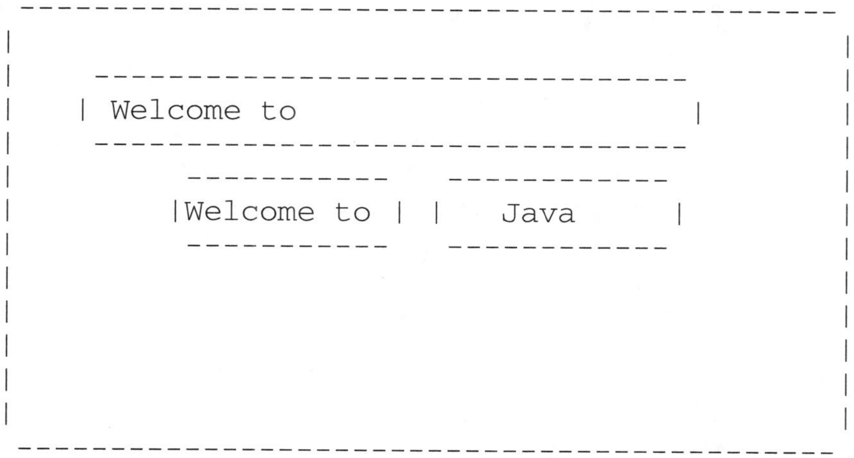

FIGURE 3.5 Click the Welcome To button and "Welcome to" appears in the text box.

```
 ------------------------------------------------------
|                                                      |
|      ----------------------------------             |
|     | Java                            |             |
|      ----------------------------------             |
|      -----------    -----------                     |
|     |Welcome to |  |   Java    |                    |
|      -----------    -----------                     |
|                                                      |
|                                                      |
|                                                      |
|                                                      |
|                                                      |
 ------------------------------------------------------
```

FIGURE 3.6   **Click the Java button and "Java" appears in the text box.**

Creating `clickers.java`

This exercise will give you the chance to see how to keep buttons separate and to learn a new and faster method of determining which button was clicked. Let's put this together now. Create a new file called `clickers.java` now. We'll need two buttons, `button1` and `button2`, and a text field, `text1`. We add those to the beginning of our class definition as follows:

```
import java.applet.Applet;
import java.awt.*;
import java.awt.event.*;

public class clickers extends Applet {

     TextField text1;
     Button button1, button2;
          .
          .
          .

}
```

Next, we create and add those controls to our applet in an `init()` method as we did in the last two examples:

```
import java.applet.Applet;
import java.awt.*;
import java.awt.event.*;

public class clickers extends Applet {

    TextField text1;
    Button button1, button2;

➜   public void init(){

            .
            .
            .

➜       }
    }
```

In this case, we want a text field and two buttons, one button with the caption "Welcome to" and the other with the caption "Java":

```
import java.applet.Applet;
import java.awt.*;
import java.awt.event.*;

public class clickers extends Applet {

    TextField text1;
    Button button1, button2;

    public void init(){
➜       text1 = new TextField(20);
➜       add(text1);
➜       button1 = new Button("Welcome to");
➜       add(button1);
➜       button2 = new Button("Java");
➜       add(button2);
    }
}
```

At this point, then, we've added all the controls we'll need to our applet, as shown in Figure 3.7.

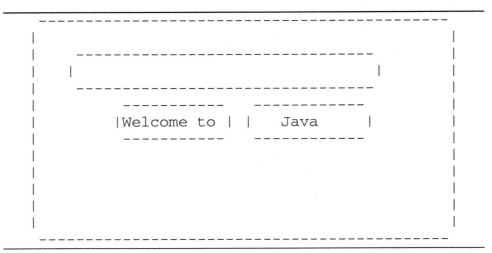

F I G U R E 3 . 7   Our applet contains three controls: two buttons and a text field.

Making `clickers.java` **Work**

Now it's time to get the new controls working. As before, we'll do that with the `actionPerformed()` method, so add that to our class now, as well as the keywords `implements ActionListener`:

```
import java.applet.Applet;
import java.awt.*;
import java.awt.event.*;
```

→   ```
public class clickers extends Applet implements ActionListener{

    TextField text1;
    Button button1, button2;

    public void init(){
        text1 = new TextField(20);
        add(text1);
        button1 = new Button("Welcome to");
        add(button1);
        button2 = new Button("Java");
        add(button2);
    }
```
```

→
```
        public void actionPerformed(ActionEvent e){
                .
                .
                .
→       }
    }
```

In addition to adding the actionPerformed() method and our keywords, we will connect our buttons to the ActionListener now—note that both buttons will be connected to the same ActionListener this way, as we use addActionListener():

```
    import java.applet.Applet;
    import java.awt.*;
    import java.awt.event.*;
```
→
```
    public class clickers extends Applet implements ActionListener{

        TextField text1;
        Button button1, button2;

        public void init(){
            text1 = new TextField(20);
            add(text1);
            button1 = new Button("Welcome to");
            add(button1);
→           button1.addActionListener(this);
            button2 = new Button("Java");
            add(button2);
→           button2.addActionListener(this);
        }

        public void actionPerformed(ActionEvent e){
                .
                .
                .
        }
    }
```

Now our buttons are connected to the actionPerformed() method. The next step is to determine which button caused the click event that caused actionPerformed() to be called, and we can do that with the ActionEvent class's getSource() method. Here, the two buttons are button1 and button2, and we check to see which one was clicked as follows:

```
    import java.applet.Applet;
    import java.awt.*;
    import java.awt.event.*;
```

```
public class clickers extends Applet implements ActionListener {

    TextField text1;
    Button button1, button2;

    public void init(){
        text1 = new TextField(20);
        add(text1);
        button1 = new Button("Welcome to");
        add(button1);
        button1.addActionListener(this);
        button2 = new Button("Java");
        add(button2);
        button2.addActionListener(this);
    }

    public void actionPerformed(ActionEvent e){
➜        if(e.getSource() == button1){
                .
                .
                .
➜        }
➜        if(e.getSource() == button2){
                .
                .
                .
➜        }
    }
}
```

In case button1 *was* clicked, we want to place the text "Welcome to" in the text field text1, and we do that like this:

```
import java.applet.Applet;
import java.awt.*;
import java.awt.event.*;

public class clickers extends Applet implements ActionListener {

    TextField text1;
    Button button1, button2;

    public void init(){
        text1 = new TextField(20);
        add(text1);
        button1 = new Button("Welcome to");
        add(button1);
        button1.addActionListener(this);
```

```
            button2 = new Button("Java");
            add(button2);
            button2.addActionListener(this);
        }

        public void actionPerformed(ActionEvent e){
            if(e.getSource() == button1){
→               text1.setText("Welcome to");
            }
            if(e.getSource() == button2){
                .
                .
                .
            }
        }
    }
}
```

We can do the same for button2, which places the text "Java" in text1, as follows:

```
import java.applet.Applet;
import java.awt.*;
import java.awt.event.*;

public class clickers extends Applet implements ActionListener {

    TextField text1;
    Button button1, button2;

    public void init(){
        text1 = new TextField(20);
        add(text1);
        button1 = new Button("Welcome to");
        add(button1);
        button1.addActionListener(this);
        button2 = new Button("Java");
        add(button2);
        button2.addActionListener(this);
    }

    public void actionPerformed(ActionEvent e){
        if(e.getSource() == button1){
            text1.setText("Welcome to");
        }
        if(e.getSource() == button2){
→           text1.setText("Java");
        }
    }
}
```

And that's all there is to it—our applet is complete. Build that applet now and execute it, as shown below. As we designed it, when the user clicks the Welcome To button, "Welcome to" appears in the text field; when they click the Java button, "Java" appears in the text field. Our applet is working. The listing for this applet appears in `clickers.java`.

clickers.java

```
import java.applet.Applet;
import java.awt.*;
import java.awt.event.*;

public class clickers extends Applet implements ActionListener {

    TextField text1;
    Button button1, button2;

    public void init(){
        text1 = new TextField(20);
        add(text1);
        button1 = new Button("Welcome to");
        add(button1);
        button1.addActionListener(this);
        button2 = new Button("Java");
        add(button2);
        button2.addActionListener(this);
    }

    public void actionPerformed(ActionEvent e){
        if(e.getSource() == button1){
```

```
            text1.setText("Welcome to");
        }
        if(e.getSource() == button2){
            text1.setText("Java");
        }
    }
}
```

While we're working on text fields and buttons, we'll take a look at the multi-line text field called a *text area*. Java uses a text area to support text that takes up more than one line.

Handling Java Text Areas

A text area really works in almost the same way that a text field does, but it can have several lines, as shown in Figure 3.8.

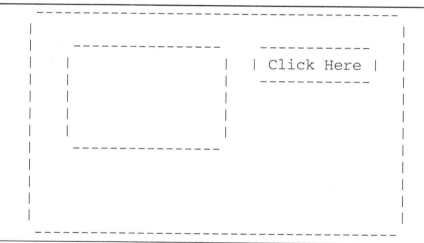

FIGURE 3.8   An empty text area

This is the control to use when you have multiple lines of text to display, such as a set of instructions, or when you let the user edit a large amount of text. Text fields can do the same job, but for large amounts of text—especially text that has carriage returns or paragraphs—text areas are the way to go.

Creating `txtarea.java`

Let's put together an example applet using a text area. When the user clicks a button labeled "Click Here", we can place a message saying: "Welcome to Java" in the text area, as shown in Figure 3.9.

```
 --------------------------------------------
|                                            |
|    ----------------------    ------------  |
|   |Welcome to Java       |   | Click Here | |
|   |                      |   | ---------- | |
|   |                      |   |            |  |
|   |                      |   |            |  |
|    ----------------------                  |
|                                            |
|                                            |
|                                            |
|                                            |
 --------------------------------------------
```

FIGURE 3.9   When the user clicks the button, "Welcome to Java" appears in the text area.

We handle a text area much as we would handle a text field; let's see one in action. Create a new file named `txtarea.java`. Open that file now and add our usual starting code:

```java
import java.applet.Applet;
import java.awt.*;
import java.awt.event.*;

public class txtarea extends Applet {
    .
    .
    .
}
```

As with our previous examples, we add a button, `button1`, to our applet. Next, we add a text area object of the Java class `TextArea`, calling that object, say, `textarea1`, giving it five rows, twenty columns, and starting it off with an empty string, `" "` to display. (That is, the text area will appear blank.)

```java
import java.applet.Applet;
```

```
import java.applet.Applet;
import java.awt.*;
import java.awt.event.*;

public class txtarea extends Applet {

→       TextArea textarea1;
→       Button button1;

        public void init(){
→           textarea1 = new TextArea("", 5, 20);
→           add(textarea1);
→           button1 = new Button("Click Me");
            add(button1);
               .
               .
               .
        }
```

The Java TextArea class methods appear in Table 3.3.

T A B L E 3 . 3 : TextArea **class methods**

Method	Does This
TextArea()	Constructs new TextArea.
TextArea(int, int)	Deprecated. Replaced by TextArea(String, int, int).
TextArea(String)	Constructs new TextArea with the specified text.
TextArea(String, int, int)	Constructs new TextArea with given text and number of rows and columns.
TextArea(String, int, int, int)	Constructs new TextArea with given text and number of rows, columns, and scrollbar "visibility".
addNotify()	Creates TextArea's peer.
append(String)	Appends given text to end of TextArea.
appendText(String)	Deprecated. Replaced by append(String).
getColumns()	Returns number of columns in TextArea.
getMinimumSize()	Returns minimum size Dimensions of TextArea.
getMinimumSize(int, int)	Returns given minimum size Dimensions of TextArea.
getPreferredSize()	Returns the preferred Dimensions of TextArea.
getPreferredSize(int, int)	Returns given row and column Dimensions of the TextArea.
getRows()	Returns the number of rows in the TextArea.

TABLE 3.3 CONTINUED: TextArea **class methods**

Method	Does This
getScrollbarVisibility()	Returns enumerated value describing which scrollbars the TextArea has.
insert(String, int)	Inserts the given text at the given position.
insertText(String, int)	Deprecated. Replaced by insert(String, int).
minimumSize()	Deprecated. Replaced by getMinimumSize().
minimumSize(int, int)	Deprecated. Replaced by getMinimumSize(int, int).
paramString()	Returns the String of parameters for this TextArea.
preferredSize()	Deprecated. Replaced by getPreferredSize().
preferredSize(int, int)	Deprecated. Replaced by getPreferredSize(int, int).
replaceRange(String, int, int)	Replaces text from the indicated start to end position with the new text given.
replaceText(String, int, int)	Deprecated. Replaced by replaceRange(String, int, int).
setColumns(int)	Sets the number of columns for TextArea.
setRows(int)	Sets number of rows for TextArea.

Making txtarea.java Work

Now we add the keywords implements ActionListener and make the applet's main class a listener for the Click Me button:

```
import java.applet.Applet;
import java.awt.*;
import java.awt.event.*;

public class txtarea extends Applet implements ActionListener{

    TextArea textarea1;
    Button button1;

    public void init(){
        textarea1 = new TextArea("", 5, 20);
        add(textarea1);
        button1 = new Button("Click Me");
        add(button1);
        button1.addActionListener(this);
    }
}
```

In addition, we'll need an `actionPerformed()` method to catch button clicks:

```java
import java.awt.*;
import java.awt.event.*;

public class txtarea extends Applet implements ActionListener {

    TextArea textarea1;
    Button button1;

    public void init(){
        textarea1 = new TextArea("", 5, 20);
        add(textarea1);
        button1 = new Button("Click Me");
        add(button1);
        button1.addActionListener(this);
    }

    public void actionPerformed (ActionEvent e){
             .
             .
             .
    }
}
```

If the button is indeed clicked, we can place our "Welcome to Java" text into the text area. Instead of using `setText()` to set the text of our text area as we did for text fields, we will use the `TextArea` class's `insert()` method.

TIP   The `insert()` method, which lets you insert text at a specific location, is unique to text areas—text fields do not have this method. With `insert()`, you treat all the text in the text area as one long string, each character counting as one place, and you indicate the position at which you want to insert your new text by passing that location as an integer to `insert()`.

We can insert our text at a specified position in the text area. In this case, we'll place the "Welcome to Java" message at the beginning of the text area so we pass a location of 0. We create a new String object named `msg` and then display that string using `insert()` to place it into the text area:

```java
import java.applet.Applet;
import java.awt.*;
import java.awt.event.*;

public class txtarea extends Applet implements ActionListener {
```

```
TextArea textarea1;
Button button1;

public void init(){
    textarea1 = new TextArea("", 5, 20);
    add(textarea1);
    button1 = new Button("Click Me");
    add(button1);
    button1.addActionListener(this);
}

public void actionPerformed (ActionEvent e){
    String msg = "Welcome to Java";
    if(e.getSource() == button1){
        textarea1.insert(msg, 0);
    }
}
}
```

Run the new applet, as shown below. As you can see, our new text area is working. Now we're able to support not only buttons and text fields, but text areas as well. If the user were to edit the text in the text area, they'd find out that it supports multiple lines and that they can use the Enter key as they type. The listing for this applet appears in `txtarea.java`.

txtarea.java

```
import java.applet.Applet;
import java.awt.*;
import java.awt.event.*;
```

```
public class txtarea extends Applet implements ActionListener {

    TextArea textarea1;
    Button button1;

    public void init(){
        textarea1 = new TextArea("", 5, 20);
        add(textarea1);
        button1 = new Button("Click Me");
        add(button1);
        button1.addActionListener(this);
    }

    public void actionPerformed (ActionEvent e){
        String msg = "Welcome to Java";
        if(e.getSource() == button1){
            textarea1.insert(msg, 0);
        }
    }
}
```

That's all for now in our guided tour of buttons and text fields. We've learned how to add controls to our programs, use text boxes, use buttons, and use text areas. Let's turn now to Skill 4, in which we start working with a new Java control: check boxes.

Are You Experienced?

Now you can...

- ☑ add and use a button in a program, allowing the user to initiate an action simply by clicking the button you've created
- ☑ store strings of text in a program, using the Java String class
- ☑ use Java events to interact with the user
- ☑ handle multiple buttons in the actionPerformed() method
- ☑ display multiple lines of text
- ☑ add and use text areas

Jones 356-555-3398.

PROGRAMMERS
C, C, VB, Cobol, exp. Call 534-555-6543 or fax 534-555-6544.

PROGRAMMING
MRFS Inc. is looking for a Sr. Windows NT developer. Reqs. 3-5 yrs. Exp. in C under Windows, Win95 & NT, using Visual C. Excl. OO design & implementation skills a must. OLE2 & ODBC are a plus. Exd. Salary & bnfts. Resume & salary history to HR. 8779 HighTech Way. Computer City, AR

PROGRAMMERS
Contractors Wanted for short & long term assignments; Visual C, MFC Unix C/C, SQL Oracle Dev elop ers PC Help Desk Support Windows NT & NetWare Telecommunications Visual Basic, Access, HTML, CGI, Perl MMI & Co., 885-555-9933

PROGRAMMER World Wide Web Links wants your HTML & Photoshop skills. Develop great WWW sites. Local & global customers. Send samples & resume to WWWI. 2000 Apple Road, Santa Rosa, CA.

TECHNICAL WRITER Software firm seeks writer/editor for manuals, research notes, project mgmt. Min 2 years tech. writing, DTP & programming experience. Send resume & writing samples to: Software Systems, Dallas, TX.

TECHNICAL Software development firm looking for Tech Trainers. Ideal candidates have programming experience in Visual C. HTML & JAVA. Need quick self starter. Call (443) 555-6868 for interview.

TECHNICAL WRITER / Premier Computer Corp is seeking a combination of technical skills, knowledge and experience in the following areas: UNIX, Windows 95/NT, Visual Basic, on-line help & documentation, and the Internet. Candidates must possess excellent writing skills, and be comfortable working in a quality vs. deadline driven environment. Competitive salary. Fax resume & samples to Karen Fields. Premier Computer Corp., 444 Industrial Blvd. Concord, CA. Or send to our website at www.premier.com.

WEB DESIGNER
BA/BS or equivalent programming/multimedia production. 3 years of experience in use and design of WWW services streaming audio and video HTML, PERL, CGI, GIF, JPEG. Demonstrated interpersonal, organization, communication, multi-tasking skills. Send resume to The Learning People at www.learning.com.

WEBMASTER-TECHNICAL
BSCS or equivalent. 2 years of experience in CGI. Windows 95/NT. UNIX, C, Java, Perl. Demonstrated ability to design, code, debug, and test on-line services. Send resume to The Learning People at www.learning.com.

PROGRAMMER World Wide Web Links wants your HTML & Photoshop skills. Develop great WWW sites. Local & global customers. Send sam-

ing tools. Experienced in documentation preparation & programming languages (Access, C, FoxPro) are a plus. Financial or banking customer service support is required along with excellent verbal & written communication skills with multi levels of end-users. Send resume to KKUP Enterprises, 45 Orange Blvd., Orange, CA.

COMPUTERS Small Web Design firm seeks indiv. w/NT, Webserver & Database management exp. Fax resume to 556-555-4221.

COMPUTER/ Visual C/C, Visual Basic Exp'd Systems Analysts/Programmers for growing software dev. team in Roseburg. Computer Science or related degree preferred. Develop adv. Engineering applications for engineering firm. Fax resume to 707-555-8744.

COMPUTER Web Master for dynamic SF Internet co. Site. Dev. test, coord. train. 2 yrs prog. Exp. C C Web C FTP fax resume to Best Staffing 845-555-7722.

COMPUTER PROGRAMMER
Ad agency seeks programmer w/exp. in UNIX/NT Platforms, Web Server, CGI/Perl. Programmer Position avail. on a project basis with the possibility to move into F/T. Fax resume & salary req. to R. Jones 334-555-8332.

COMPUTERS Programmer/Analyst Design and maintain C based SQL database applications. Required skills: Visual Basic, C, SQL, ODBC. Document existing and new applications. Novell or NT exp. a plus. Fax resume & salary history to 235-555-9935.

GRAPHIC DESIGNER
Webmaster's Weekly is seeking a creative Graphic Designer to design high impact marketing collateral, including direct mail promo's. CD-ROM packages, ads and WWW pages. Must be able to juggle multiple projects and learn new skills on the job very rapidly. Web design experience a big plus, technical troubleshooting also a plus. Call 435-555-1235.

GRAPHICS - ART DIRECTOR - WEB-MULTIMEDIA
Leading internet development company has an outstanding opportunity for a talented, high-end Web Experienced Art Director. In addition to a great portfolio and fresh ideas, the ideal candidate has excellent communication and presentation skills. Working as a team with innovative producers and programmers, you will create dynamic, interactive web sites and application interfaces. Some programming experience required. Send samples and resume to: SuperSites, 333 Main, Seattle, WA.

MARKETING
Fast paced software and services provider looking for MARKETING COMMUNICATIONS SPECIALIST to be responsible for its webpage, seminar coordination, and ad place-

PROGRAMMERS Multiple short term assignments available: Visual C 3 positions SQL ServerNT Server, 2 positions JAVA & HTML, long term NetWare Various locations. Call for more info. 356-555-3398.

PROGRAMMERS
C, C, VB, Cobol, exp.
Call 534-555-6543
or fax 534-555-6544.

PROGRAMMING
MRFS Inc. is looking for a Sr. Windows NT developer. Reqs. 3-5 yrs. Exp. in C under Windows, Win95 & NT, using Visual C. Excl. OO design & implementation skills a must. OLE2 & ODBC are a plus. Exd. Salary & bnfts. Resume & salary history to HR. 8779 HighTech Way, Computer City, AR

PROGRAMMERS/ Contractors Wanted for short & long term assignments; Visual C, MFC Unix C/C, SQL Oracle Developers PC Help Desk Support Windows NT & NetWare Telecommunications Visual Basic, Access, HTML, CGI, Perl MMI & Co. 885-555-9933

PROGRAMMER World Wide Web Links wants your HTML & Photoshop skills. Develop great WWW sites. Local & global customers. Send samples & resume to WWWI. 2000 Apple Road, Santa Rosa, CA.

TECHNICAL WRITER Software firm seeks writer/editor for manuals, research notes, project mgmt. Min 2 years tech. writing, DTP & programming experience. Send resume & writing samples to Software Systems, Dallas, TX.

COMPUTER PROGRAMMER
Ad agency seeks programmer w/exp. in UNIX/NT Platforms, Web Server, CGI/Perl. Programmer Position avail. on a project basis with the possibility to move into F/T. Fax resume & salary req. to R. Jones 334-555-8332.

TECHNICAL WRITER Premier Computer Corp is seeking a combination of technical skills, knowledge and experience in the following areas: UNIX, Windows 95/NT, Visual Basic, on-line help & documentation, and the Internet. Candidates must possess excellent writing skills, and be comfortable working in a quality vs. deadline driven environment. Competitive salary. Fax resume & samples to Karen Fields, Premier Computer Corp. 444 Industrial Blvd. Concord, CA. Or send to our website at www.premier.com.

WEB DESIGNER
BA/BS or equivalent programming/multimedia production. 3 years of experience in use and design of WWW services streaming audio and video HTML, PERL, CGI, GIF, JPEG. Demonstrated interpersonal, organization, communication, multi-tasking skills. Send resume to The Learning People at www.learning.com.

WEBMASTER-TECHNICAL
BSCS or equivalent, 2 years of experience in CGI, Windows 95/NT,

COMPUTERS Small Web Design firm seeks indiv. w/NT, Webserver & Database management exp. Fax resume to 556-555-4221.

COMPUTER Visual C/C Visual Basic Exp'd Systems Analysts/Programmers for growing software dev. team in Roseburg. Computer Science or related degree preferred. Develop adv. Engineering applications for engineering firm. Fax resume to 707-555-8744.

COMPUTER Web Master for dynamic SF Internet co. Site. Dev. test, coord. train 2 yrs prog. Exp. C C Web C. FTP fax resume to Best Staffing 845-555-7722.

COMPUTERS/ QA SOFTWARE TESTERS Qualified candidates should have 2 yrs exp. performing integration & system testing using automated testing tools. Experienced in documentation preparation & programming languages (Access, C, FoxPro) are a plus. Financial or banking customer service support is required along with excellent verbal & written communication skills with multi levels of end-users. Send resume to KKUP Enterprises, 45 Orange Blvd. Orange, CA.

COMPUTERS Programmer/Analyst Design and maintain C based SQL database applications. Required skills: Visual Basic, C, SQL, ODBC. Document existing and new applications. Novell or NT exp. a plus. Fax resume & salary history to 235-555-9935.

GRAPHIC DESIGNER
Webmaster's Weekly is seeking a creative Graphic Designer to design high impact marketing collateral, including direct mail promo's. CD-ROM packages, ads and WWW pages. Must be able to juggle multiple projects and learn new skills on the job very rapidly. Web design experience a big plus, technical troubleshooting also a plus. Call 435-555-1235.

GRAPHICS - ART DIRECTOR - WEB-MULTIMEDIA
Leading internet development company has an outstanding opportunity for a talented, high-end Web Experienced Art Director. In addition to a great portfolio and fresh ideas, the ideal candidate has excellent communication and presentation skills. Working as a team with innovative producers and programmers, you will create dynamic, interactive web sites and application interfaces. Some programming experience required. Send samples and resume to: SuperSites, 333 Main, Seattle, WA.

COMPUTER PROGRAMMER
Ad agency seeks programmer w/exp. in UNIX/NT Platforms, Web Server, CGI/Perl. Programmer Position avail. on a project basis with the possibility to move into F/T. Fax resume & salary req. to R. Jones 334-555-8332.

PROGRAMMERS / Established software company seeks program-

ment. Must be a self-starter, energetic, organized. Must have 2 ye web experience. Programming plus. Call 985-555-9854

PROGRAMMERS Multiple s term assignments available: Vi C. 3 positions SQL ServerNT Ser 2 positions JAVA & HTML, long t NetWare Various locations. Call more info. 356-555-3398.

PROGRAMMERS
C, C, VB, Cobol, exp. Call 534-5 6543 or fax 534-555-6544.

PROGRAMMING
MRFS Inc. is looking for a Windows NT developer. Reqs. yrs. Exp. in C under Windo Win95 & NT, using Visual C. E OO design & implementation s a must. OLE2 & ODBC are a p Excl. Salary & bnfts. Resume salary history to HR, 8779 HighT Way, Computer City, AR

PROGRAMMERS/ Contract Wanted for short & long term assi ments: Visual C, MFC Unix C/C, Oracle Developers PC Help D Support Windows NT & NetW Telecommunications Visual B Access, HTML, CGI, Perl MMI & 885-555-9933

PROGRAMMER World Wide Links wants your HTML & Photos skills. Develop great WWW s Local & global customers. Send s ples & resume to WWWI. 2 Apple Road, Santa Rosa, CA.

TECHNICAL WRITER Software seeks writer/editor for manu research notes, project mgmt. M years tech. writing, DTP & progr ming experience. Send resume writing samples to Softw Systems, Dallas, TX.

TECHNICAL Software develop firm looking for Tech Trainers. I candidates have programming e rience in Visual C. HTML & JA Need quick self starter. Call (4 555-6868 for interview.

TECHNICAL WRITER Pre Computer Corp is seeking a con nation of technical skills, knowle and experience in the follow areas: UNIX, Windows 95/NT, V Basic, on-line help & documenta and the Internet. Candidates possess excellent writing skills, be comfortable working in a qu vs. deadline driven environm Competitive salary. Fax resum samples to Karen Fields, Pre Computer Corp. 444 Industrial Concord, CA. Or send to our web at www.premier.com.

WEB DESIGNER
BA/BS or equivalent progr ming/multimedia production. years of experience in use design of WWW services stream audio and video HTML, PERL, GIF, JPEG. Demonstrated inter sonal, organization, communica multi-tasking skills. Send resume The Learning People at www.learning.com.

WEBMASTER-TECHNIC

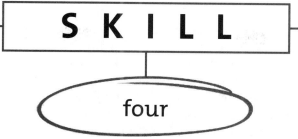

SKILL

four

Using Java Layouts and Check Boxes

In this book, you've already come far: you've worked with text fields, text areas, and buttons. However, there are many more powerful Java controls, and one of those is the check box. And in this Skill, we're going to take a look at check boxes. This new control is important by itself, but we'll also learn more about coordinating controls (handling and arranging a number of controls together) in a Java program. The reason we'll learn more about coordinating controls like this is that controls like check boxes and radio buttons are meant to be handled in *groups*. You often use check boxes to choose one or more selections among a group of selections, and radio buttons are even more group-oriented—they are used to allow the user to select one option among many.

What Is a Java Layout?

In Skills 1–3 we did not perform any special placement of our text fields and buttons in our applets—Java handled the placement of our controls for us. That is both good and bad—it's good if things work out the way you want them, but bad otherwise.

In fact, we have been using Java's default *layout manager*, the FlowLayout manager. Layout managers control the placement of controls in an applet for us. We can select which layout manager to use, and that's a good thing because oftentimes the default layout manager will not arrange our controls the way we want them.

Let's take a look at an example. In this case, we want to build a small adding calculator applet. All we'll do is take two integers from the user, add them together, and display the result.This applet will require us to handle both text and numeric input, as well as layout managers. Let's get started now.

Building the Adder Applet

Our goal is simply to create a Java applet that acts as an adding calculator. We can make this calculator up of text fields and buttons: one text field for the first number, one for the second, a button for the equals sign, and another text field for the answer. To add 2 + 2, the user will enter that data into the first two text fields, as shown in Figure 4.1. Then, when they click the button whose caption is "=", they will see the result in the bottom text field, as shown in Figure 4.2.

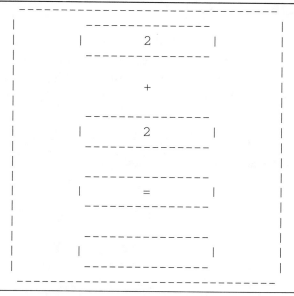

FIGURE 4.1 The user enters data into the first two text fields of our applet.

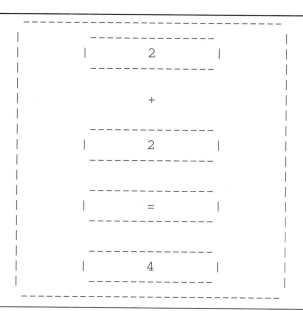

FIGURE 4.2 When the user clicks the = button, the sum of the first two text fields appears in the third text field.

The Label **Control**

You may wonder at first how we can place a plus sign between the top two text boxes and may assume that we'll use drawString() as we did in Skill 1, but in fact we'll place the plus sign in a new type of control: a Label control. This control is a control like any other—it displays text and nothing more. The methods of the Label control appear in Table 4.1.

T A B L E   4 . 1 : The Label **class methods**

Method	Does This
Label()	Constructs an empty label.
Label(String)	Constructs a label with given text.
Label(String, int)	Constructs a label with given text and alignment (Label.RIGHT, Label.CENTER, or Label.LEFT).
addNotify()	Creates a peer for Label.
getAlignment()	Gets alignment of Label.
getText()	Gets caption of Label.
paramString()	Returns parameter string of Label.
setAlignment(int)	Sets alignment for Label (label.RIGHT, Label.CENTER, or Label.LEFT).
setText(String)	Sets text in Label.

TIP

Note that you can set the text of a label control with the setText() method just as you can in a text field. You can also align the text in the label to the right, left, or center by passing one of the Label class's pre-defined constants to the constructor or the setAlignment() method: Label.RIGHT, Label.Left, or Label.CENTER.

Let's start this project. Create a new file named, say, adder.java now, and add our usual starting code, including a new class named adder:

```
import java.applet.Applet;
import java.awt.*;
import java.awt.event.*;

public class adder extends Applet {


}
```

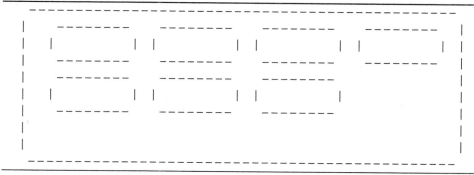

FIGURE 4.4   When the default layout manager comes to the end of a row, it wraps the next controls.

Working with the Java Grid Layout

We want the controls on our calculator to be placed as shown in Figure 4.5: vertically, not horizontally. We can do that by replacing the default FlowLayout manager in our applet with another layout manager—the GridLayout manager.

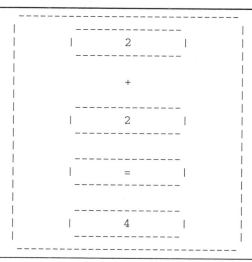

FIGURE 4.5   We want our controls to be arranged vertically.

Using the GridLayout Manager

The FlowLayout manager simply places controls in an applet one by one, wrapping them at the end of a row. The GridLayout manager, on the other hand, is often more useful, because it places controls in a grid, as shown in Figure 4.6. To arrange our adding calculator's controls vertically, we can add them to our applet in a grid of dimensions 9x3, as shown in Figure 4.7.

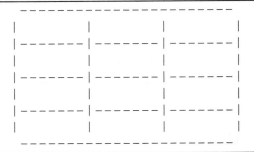

FIGURE 4.6   The GridLayout manager places controls on a grid.

To do so, we'll install the GridLayout manager in our applet and then add the controls to it. As we add controls to the layout manager, it will place them in the grid, one after the other, row by row. That means that we have to fill all of the entries in the grid, not just the entries that hold the controls we want to display. One way of solving this problem is to use a set of labels without any text that act as spacers. We can add those labels now, giving them the names shown in Figure 4.8.

We add these labels now to the adder class as shown below.

```
import java.applet.Applet;
import java.applet.Applet;
import java.awt.*;
import java.awt.event.*;

public class adder2 extends Applet implements ActionListener {

    TextField text1, text2, answertext;
    Label pluslabel, fill1, fill2, fill3, fill4, fill5,
    fill6, fill7, fill8, fill9, fill10;
    Label spacer1, spacer2, spacer3, spacer4, spacer5, spacer6;
```

```
    Button button1;
         .
         .
         .
}
```

Now we can install the GridLayout manager as our new layout manager.

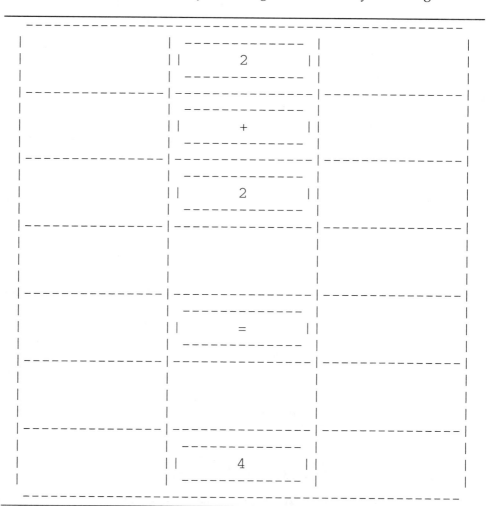

FIGURE 4.7   Our calculator with padded cells arranged in a grid

```
-------------------------------------------------------
|                |  ------------  |                    |
|     fill1      | |      2     | |      fill2         |
|                |  ------------  |                    |
|----------------|----------------|--------------------|
|                |  ------------  |                    |
|     fill3      | |      +     | |      fill4         |
|                |  ------------  |                    |
|----------------|----------------|--------------------|
|                |  ------------  |                    |
|     fill5      | |      2     | |      fill6         |
|                |  ------------  |                    |
|----------------|----------------|--------------------|
|                |                |                    |
|    spacer1     |    spacer2     |     spacer3         |
|                |                |                    |
|----------------|----------------|--------------------|
|                |  ------------  |                    |
|     fill7      | |      =     | |      fill8         |
|                |  ------------  |                    |
|----------------|----------------|--------------------|
|                |                |                    |
|    spacer4     |    spacer5     |     spacer6         |
|                |                |                    |
|----------------|----------------|--------------------|
|                |  ------------  |                    |
|     fill9      | |      4     | |     fill10         |
|                |  ------------  |                    |
-------------------------------------------------------
```

FIGURE 4.8   Adding labels to every entry in the grid

Adding a GridLayout Manager

We install the GridLayout manager (replacing the default FlowLayout manager) in the init() method before we have added any controls to the layout. In this case,

we want a grid of 9 rows and 3 columns, and we set that up with the setLayout()
method as follows:

```
import java.applet.Applet;
import java.awt.*;
import java.awt.event.*;

public class adder2 extends Applet implements ActionListener {

    TextField text1, text2, answertext;
    Label pluslabel, fill1, fill2, fill3, fill4, fill5,
    fill6, fill7, fill8, fill9, fill10;
    Label spacer1, spacer2, spacer3, spacer4, spacer5, spacer6;
    Button button1;

    public void init(){

        setLayout(new GridLayout(9, 3));
                    .
                    .
                    .
    }
}
```

That's all there is to it—now our applet uses a grid layout. We add the other
controls, including the spacer labels, the same way (note in particular that we
place the plus sign in the middle of its label by including the class constant
Label.CENTER in the call to the Label class's constructor):

```
import java.applet.Applet;
import java.awt.*;
import java.awt.event.*;

public class adder2 extends Applet implements ActionListener {

    TextField text1, text2, answertext;
    Label pluslabel, fill1, fill2, fill3, fill4, fill5,
    fill6, fill7, fill8, fill9, fill10;
    Label spacer1, spacer2, spacer3, spacer4, spacer5, spacer6;
    Button button1;

    public void init(){

        setLayout(new GridLayout(9, 3));

        fill1 = new Label();
        add(fill1);
        text1 = new TextField(10);
```

Skill 4

```
→          add(text1);
→          fill2 = new Label();
→          add(fill2);

           fill3 = new Label();
→          add(fill3);
→          pluslabel = new Label("+", Label.CENTER);
→          add(pluslabel);
→          fill4 = new Label();
→          add(fill4);

→          fill5 = new Label();
→          add(fill5);
→          text2 = new TextField(10);
→          add(text2);
→          fill6 = new Label();
→          add(fill6);

→          spacer1 = new Label();
→          add(spacer1);
→          spacer2 = new Label();
→          add(spacer2);
→          spacer3 = new Label();
→          add(spacer3);

→          fill7 = new Label();
→          add(fill7);
→          button1 = new Button("=");
→          add(button1);
→          button1.addActionListener(this);
→          fill8 = new Label();
→          add(fill8);

→          spacer4 = new Label();
→          add(spacer4);
→          spacer5 = new Label();
→          add(spacer5);
→          spacer6 = new Label();
→          add(spacer6);

→          fill9 = new Label();
→          add(fill9);
→          answertext = new TextField(10);
→          add(answertext);
→          fill10 = new Label();
→          add(fill10);
→      }
    }
```

Now our controls will be aligned vertically. Build and run the new version of the numbers applet now. As you can see in the graphic below, our controls are placed as we want them—our grid layout example is a success. The code for this applet appears in adder.java, version 2.

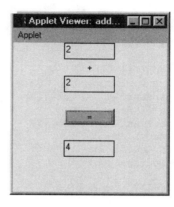

adder.java, version 2 (with layout)

```java
import java.applet.Applet;
import java.awt.*;
import java.awt.event.*;

public class adder2 extends Applet implements ActionListener {

    TextField text1, text2, answertext;
    Label pluslabel, fill1, fill2, fill3, fill4, fill5,
    fill6, fill7, fill8, fill9, fill10;
    Label spacer1, spacer2, spacer3, spacer4, spacer5, spacer6;
    Button button1;

    public void init(){

        setLayout(new GridLayout(9, 3));

        fill1 = new Label();
        add(fill1);
        text1 = new TextField(10);
        add(text1);
        fill2 = new Label();
        add(fill2);

        fill3 = new Label();
        add(fill3);
```

```
pluslabel = new Label("+", Label.CENTER);
add(pluslabel);
fill4 = new Label();
add(fill4);

fill5 = new Label();
add(fill5);
text2 = new TextField(10);
add(text2);
fill6 = new Label();
add(fill6);

spacer1 = new Label();
add(spacer1);
spacer2 = new Label();
add(spacer2);
spacer3 = new Label();
add(spacer3);

fill7 = new Label();
add(fill7);
button1 = new Button("=");
add(button1);
button1.addActionListener(this);
fill8 = new Label();
add(fill8);

spacer4 = new Label();
add(spacer4);
spacer5 = new Label();
add(spacer5);
spacer6 = new Label();
add(spacer6);

fill9 = new Label();
add(fill9);
answertext = new TextField(10);
add(answertext);
fill10 = new Label();
add(fill10);
}

public void actionPerformed(ActionEvent e){
    if(e.getSource() == button1){
        int sum = Integer.parseInt(text1.getText()) +
        ➥ Integer.parseInt(text2.getText());
        answertext.setText(String.valueOf(sum));
    }
}
}
```

Now that we have some familiarity with layouts, we will press on to work with check boxes and radio buttons, two controls which are often used in special layouts, as we'll soon see.

Building Programs with Check Boxes

We will begin our exploration of check boxes with a simple check box example. In this case, we'll just put five check boxes into our applet, as shown in Figure 4.9. When the user clicks one of these check boxes, we can indicate that action in a text field, as shown in Figure 4.10.

```
-----------------------------------------------------------
|   _         _           _           _          _        |
|  |_| 1     |_| 2       |_| 3       |_| 4      |_| 5      |
|                                                         |
|          -------------------------------------------    |
|         |                                           |   |
|          -------------------------------------------    |
|                                                         |
|                                                         |
-----------------------------------------------------------
```

FIGURE 4.9 An applet with five check boxes and a text field

```
-----------------------------------------------------------
|   _         _           _           _          _        |
|  |_| 1     |_| 2       |v| 3       |_| 4      |_| 5      |
|                                                         |
|          -------------------------------------------    |
|         |Check box 3 clicked!                       |   |
|          -------------------------------------------    |
|                                                         |
|                                                         |
-----------------------------------------------------------
```

FIGURE 4.10 When the user clicks check box 3, the message "Check box 3 clicked!" appears in the text field.

Let's create a new applet called checker. Create a new file named
checker.java and create a new class named checker as shown below:

```
import java.applet.Applet;
import java.awt.*;
import java.awt.event.*;

public class checker extends Applet {

}
```

Now we can declare the five check boxes we'll need—naming them, checkbox1
to checkbox5—and the text field, called text1, that we'll use to report when the
user clicks a check box. Check boxes are created with the Java Checkbox class, so
we declare our five check boxes as follows:

```
import java.applet.Applet;
import java.awt.*;
import java.awt.event.*;

public class checker extends Applet implements ItemListener {

        Checkbox checkbox1, checkbox2, checkbox3, checkbox4, checkbox5;
        TextField text1;
            .
            .
            .
}
```

The Java Checkbox class methods appear in Table 4.2.

As with other controls, we actually create and add the new check boxes to our
applet in the init() method, so create that method now:

```
import java.applet.Applet;
import java.awt.*;
import java.awt.event.*;

public class checker extends Applet {

        Checkbox checkbox1, checkbox2, checkbox3, checkbox4, checkbox5;
        TextField text1;

        public void init(){

        }

}
```

T A B L E 4 . 2 : The Checkbox **class methods**

Method	Does This
Checkbox()	Constructs a Checkbox with an empty label.
Checkbox(String)	Constructs a Checkbox with the given label.
Checkbox(String, boolean)	Constructs a Checkbox with the given label.
Checkbox(String, boolean, CheckboxGroup)	Constructs a Checkbox with the given label, set to the given state, and in the given check box group.
Checkbox(String, CheckboxGroup, boolean)	Deprecated. Replaced by Checkbox(String, boolean, CheckboxGroup).
addItemListener(ItemListener)	Adds the given item listener to receive item events from this Checkbox.
addNotify()	Creates the peer of the Checkbox.
getCheckboxGroup()	Returns the Checkbox group.
getLabel()	Gets the label of the Checkbox.
getSelectedIndexes()	Returns an array (length 1) containing the selected index or null if the Checkbox is not selected.
getSelectedItems()	Returns the array (length 1) containing the checkbox label or null if the Checkbox is not selected.
getState()	Returns the boolean state of the Checkbox.
paramString()	Returns the parameter String of this Checkbox.
processEvent(AWTEvent)	Processes events on this Checkbox.
processItemEvent(ItemEvent)	Processes item events occurring on this checkbox by dispatching them to any registered ItemListener objects.
removeItemListener(ItemListener)	Removes the given item listener so that it no longer receives item events from this Checkbox.
setCheckboxGroup(CheckboxGroup)	Sets the CheckboxGroup to the given group.
setLabel(String)	Sets this Checkbox's label to be the given string.
setState(boolean)	Sets the Checkbox to the specified boolean state.

All we have to do here is add the check boxes and the text field. We add the check box checkbox1 like this:

```
import java.applet.Applet;
import java.awt.*;
import java.awt.event.*;
```

```
public class checker extends Applet {

    Checkbox checkbox1, checkbox2, checkbox3, checkbox4, checkbox5;
    TextField text1;

    public void init(){

➜        checkbox1 = new Checkbox("1");
➜        add(checkbox1);
            .
            .
            .

    }
}
```

Note that we can give the check box a label (here that label is simply 1) by passing a string to the Checkbox class's constructor, as we have done above. All that remains now is to add the other check boxes and the text field:

```
import java.applet.Applet;
import java.awt.*;
import java.awt.event.*;

public class checker extends Applet {

    Checkbox checkbox1, checkbox2, checkbox3, checkbox4, checkbox5;
    TextField text1;

    public void init(){

        checkbox1 = new Checkbox("1");
        add(checkbox1);
➜        checkbox2 = new Checkbox("2");
➜        add(checkbox2);
➜        checkbox3 = new Checkbox("3");
➜        add(checkbox3);
➜        checkbox4 = new Checkbox("4");
➜        add(checkbox4);
➜        checkbox5 = new Checkbox("5");
➜        add(checkbox5);
➜        text1 = new TextField(20);
➜        add(text1);
    }
}
```

Now our new check boxes are installed. The next step is to connect them to our code. You might expect to use an ActionListener interface, but in fact, you use a different interface with check boxes because unlike buttons, check boxes can be either checked or unchecked (and the way to test their state is with the `getState()` method). The interface we use here is called `ItemListener`, and we implement that as follows:

```
import java.applet.Applet;
import java.awt.*;
import java.awt.event.*;
```

→
```
public class checker extends Applet implements ItemListener{

    Checkbox checkbox1, checkbox2, checkbox3, checkbox4, checkbox5;
    TextField text1;

    public void init(){

        checkbox1 = new Checkbox("1");
        add(checkbox1);
        checkbox2 = new Checkbox("2");
        add(checkbox2);
        checkbox3 = new Checkbox("3");
        add(checkbox3);
        checkbox4 = new Checkbox("4");
        add(checkbox4);
        checkbox5 = new Checkbox("5");
        add(checkbox5);
        text1 = new TextField(20);
        add(text1);
    }
}
```

We make our applet into the listener for our check boxes (that is, our applet will handle the events that occur when the check boxes are clicked or unclicked) with the check box `addItemListener()` method this way:

```
import java.applet.Applet;
import java.awt.*;
import java.awt.event.*;

public class checker extends Applet implements ItemListener {

    Checkbox checkbox1, checkbox2, checkbox3, checkbox4, checkbox5;
    TextField text1;

    public void init(){

        checkbox1 = new Checkbox("1");
```

```
            add(checkbox1);
→           checkbox1.addItemListener(this);
            checkbox2 = new Checkbox("2");
            add(checkbox2);
→           checkbox2.addItemListener(this);
            checkbox3 = new Checkbox("3");
            add(checkbox3);
→           checkbox3.addItemListener(this);
            checkbox4 = new Checkbox("4");
            add(checkbox4);
→           checkbox4.addItemListener(this);
            checkbox5 = new Checkbox("5");
            add(checkbox5);
→           checkbox5.addItemListener(this);
            text1 = new TextField(20);
            add(text1);
        }
    }
```

Now we've added our new check boxes to the applet and connected them up to our applet so that check box events will be sent to our applet. We're almost done; all we have to do now is to handle the check box events. The method to override when using the ItemListener interface (so we will be notified when check boxes are checked) is itemStateChanged(), and we add that now:

```
import java.applet.Applet;
import java.awt.*;
import java.awt.event.*;

public class checker extends Applet implements ItemListener {

    Checkbox checkbox1, checkbox2, checkbox3, checkbox4, checkbox5;
    TextField text1;

    public void init(){

        checkbox1 = new Checkbox("1");
        add(checkbox1);
        checkbox1.addItemListener(this);
        checkbox2 = new Checkbox("2");
        add(checkbox2);
        checkbox2.addItemListener(this);
        checkbox3 = new Checkbox("3");
        add(checkbox3);
        checkbox3.addItemListener(this);
        checkbox4 = new Checkbox("4");
        add(checkbox4);
```

```
            checkbox4.addItemListener(this);
            checkbox5 = new Checkbox("5");
            add(checkbox5);
            checkbox5.addItemListener(this);
            text1 = new TextField(20);
            add(text1);
        }

→       public void itemStateChanged(ItemEvent e) {
                    .
                    .
                    .
→       }
    }
```

itemStateChanged() is the method that will be called if the user clicks one of our check boxes and we are passed an object of class ItemEvent in that method. We can examine which check box was clicked with the ItemEvent class's getItemSelectable() method for checkbox1, as follows:

```
import java.applet.Applet;
import java.awt.*;
import java.awt.event.*;

public class checker extends Applet implements ItemListener {

    Checkbox checkbox1, checkbox2, checkbox3, checkbox4, checkbox5;
    TextField text1;

    public void init(){

        checkbox1 = new Checkbox("1");
        add(checkbox1);
        checkbox1.addItemListener(this);
        checkbox2 = new Checkbox("2");
        add(checkbox2);
        checkbox2.addItemListener(this);
        checkbox3 = new Checkbox("3");
        add(checkbox3);
        checkbox3.addItemListener(this);
        checkbox4 = new Checkbox("4");
        add(checkbox4);
        checkbox4.addItemListener(this);
        checkbox5 = new Checkbox("5");
        add(checkbox5);
        checkbox5.addItemListener(this);
        text1 = new TextField(20);
```

Skill 4

```
            add(text1);
        }

        public void itemStateChanged(ItemEvent e) {
→           if(e.getItemSelectable() == checkbox1){
                        .
                        .
                        .
            }
        }
    }
```

If checkbox1 is clicked, we can place a message in the text field saying: "Check box 1 clicked!" using the TextField setText() method, as follows:

```java
import java.applet.Applet;
import java.awt.*;
import java.awt.event.*;

public class checker extends Applet implements ItemListener {

    Checkbox checkbox1, checkbox2, checkbox3, checkbox4, checkbox5;
    TextField text1;

    public void init(){

        checkbox1 = new Checkbox("1");
        add(checkbox1);
        checkbox1.addItemListener(this);
        checkbox2 = new Checkbox("2");
        add(checkbox2);
        checkbox2.addItemListener(this);
        checkbox3 = new Checkbox("3");
        add(checkbox3);
        checkbox3.addItemListener(this);
        checkbox4 = new Checkbox("4");
        add(checkbox4);
        checkbox4.addItemListener(this);
        checkbox5 = new Checkbox("5");
        add(checkbox5);
        checkbox5.addItemListener(this);
        text1 = new TextField(20);
        add(text1);
    }

    public void itemStateChanged(ItemEvent e) {
        if(e.getItemSelectable() == checkbox1){
```

→
```
            text1.setText("Check box 1 clicked!");
        }               .
                        .
                        .
    }
}
```

We can respond to clicks on the other check boxes in the same way:

```
import java.applet.Applet;
import java.awt.*;
import java.awt.event.*;

public class checker extends Applet implements ItemListener {

    Checkbox checkbox1, checkbox2, checkbox3, checkbox4, checkbox5;
    TextField text1;

    public void init(){

        checkbox1 = new Checkbox("1");
        add(checkbox1);
        checkbox1.addItemListener(this);
        checkbox2 = new Checkbox("2");
        add(checkbox2);
        checkbox2.addItemListener(this);
        checkbox3 = new Checkbox("3");
        add(checkbox3);
        checkbox3.addItemListener(this);
        checkbox4 = new Checkbox("4");
        add(checkbox4);
        checkbox4.addItemListener(this);
        checkbox5 = new Checkbox("5");
        add(checkbox5);
        checkbox5.addItemListener(this);
        text1 = new TextField(20);
        add(text1);
    }

    public void itemStateChanged(ItemEvent e) {
        if(e.getItemSelectable() == checkbox1){
            text1.setText("Check box 1 clicked!");
        }
        if(e.getItemSelectable() == checkbox2){
            text1.setText("Check box 2 clicked!");
        }
        if(e.getItemSelectable() == checkbox3){
            text1.setText("Check box 3 clicked!");
        }
```

→
→
→
→
→
→

```
→          if(e.getItemSelectable() == checkbox4){
→              text1.setText("Check box 4 clicked!");
→          }
→          if(e.getItemSelectable() == checkbox5){
→              text1.setText("Check box 5 clicked!");
→          }
        }
    }
```

And our check box example is ready to go. Build the new applet now and run it, as shown below. As you can see, when the user clicks a check box, our applet responds and indicates what happened. Our check box example works exactly as we want it to. The code for this applet appears in checker.java.

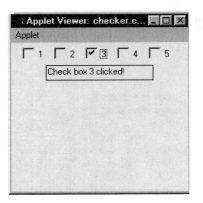

 TIP   To see at any time whether a check box is clicked or not, you can use the getState() method like this: checkbox1.getState(), which returns true if the check box is checked and false otherwise.

checker.java

```java
import java.applet.Applet;
import java.awt.*;
import java.awt.event.*;

public class checker extends Applet implements ItemListener {

    Checkbox checkbox1, checkbox2, checkbox3, checkbox4, checkbox5;
    TextField text1;
```

```java
public void init(){

    checkbox1 = new Checkbox("1");
    add(checkbox1);
    checkbox1.addItemListener(this);
    checkbox2 = new Checkbox("2");
    add(checkbox2);
    checkbox2.addItemListener(this);
    checkbox3 = new Checkbox("3");
    add(checkbox3);
    checkbox3.addItemListener(this);
    checkbox4 = new Checkbox("4");
    add(checkbox4);
    checkbox4.addItemListener(this);
    checkbox5 = new Checkbox("5");
    add(checkbox5);
    checkbox5.addItemListener(this);
    text1 = new TextField(20);
    add(text1);
}

public void itemStateChanged(ItemEvent e) {
    if(e.getItemSelectable() == checkbox1){
        text1.setText("Check box 1 clicked!");
    }
    if(e.getItemSelectable() == checkbox2){
        text1.setText("Check box 2 clicked!");
    }
    if(e.getItemSelectable() == checkbox3){
        text1.setText("Check box 3 clicked!");
    }
    if(e.getItemSelectable() == checkbox4){
        text1.setText("Check box 4 clicked!");
    }
    if(e.getItemSelectable() == checkbox5){
        text1.setText("Check box 5 clicked!");
    }
}
}
```

We've gotten a good introduction to check boxes in the checkers applet. Now we're able to use check boxes in our Java programs. In the next Skill we will turn to the other control that acts very much like check boxes: radio buttons. Check boxes and radio buttons are often used together.

Skill 4

Are You Experienced?

Now you can...

- ☑ allow the user to use check boxes in Java programs
- ☑ display text in a Java program
- ☑ add and use labels
- ☑ use Java layouts
- ☑ read input from text fields
- ☑ use Java methods to convert the text you read from text fields to a number
- ☑ install and use the GridLayout manager in Java programs

Jones 356-555-3398.

PROGRAMMING
C, C, VB, Cobol, exp. Call 534-555-6543 or fax 534-555-6544.

PROGRAMMING
MRFS Inc. is looking for a Sr. Windows NT developer. Reqs. 3-5 yrs. Exp. in C under Windows, Win95 & NT, using Visual C. Excl. OO design & implementation skills a must. OLE2 & ODBC are a plus. Excl. Salary & bnfts. Resume & salary history to HR. 8779 HighTech Way, Computer City, AR

PROGRAMMERS
Contractors Wanted for short & long term assignments; Visual C, MFC Unix, C/C, SQL Oracle Dev clpp ers, PC Help Desk Support Windows NT & NetWare Telecommunications Visual Basic, Access, HTMT, CGI, Perl MMI & Co., 885-555-9933

PROGRAMMER World Wide Web Links wants your HTML & Photoshop skills. Develop great WWW sites. Local & global customers. Send samples & resume to WWWL, 2000 Apple Road, Santa Rosa, CA.

TECHNICAL WRITER Software firm seeks writer/editor for manuals, research notes, project mgmt. Min 2 years tech. writing, DTP & programming experience. Send resume & writing samples to: Software Systems, Dallas, TX.

TECHNICAL Software development firm looking for Tech Trainers. Ideal candidates have programming experience in Visual C, HTML & JAVA. Need quick self starter. Call (443) 555-6868 for interview.

TECHNICAL WRITER / Premier Computer Corp is seeking a combination of technical skills, knowledge and experience in the following areas: UNIX, Windows 95/NT, Visual Basic, on-line help & documentation, and the Internet. Candidates must possess excellent writing skills, and be comfortable working in a quality vs. deadline driven environment. Competitive salary. Fax resume & samples to Karen Fields. Premier Computer Corp. 444 Industrial Blvd. Concord, CA. Or send to our website at www.premier.com

WEB DESIGNER
BA/BS or equivalent programming/multimedia production. 3 years of experience in use and design of WWW services streaming audio and video HTML, PERL, CGI, GIF, JPEG. Demonstrated interpersonal, organization, communication, multi-tasking skills. Send resume to The Learning People at www.learning.com

WEBMASTER-TECHNICAL
BSCS or equivalent, 2 years of experience in CGI, Windows 95/NT, UNIX, C, Java, Perl. Demonstrated ability to design, code, debug and test on-line services. Send resume to The Learning People at www.learning.com

PROGRAMMER World Wide Web Links wants your HTML & Photoshop skills. Develop great WWW sites. Local & global customers. Send sam-

---

...tation preparation & programming languages (Access, C, FoxPro) are a plus. Financial or banking customer service support is required along with excellent verbal & written communication skills with multi levels of end-users. Send resume to KKUP Enterprises, 45 Orange Blvd. Orange, CA.

COMPUTERS Small Web Design firm seeks indiv. w/NT, Webserver & Database management exp. Fax resume to 556-555-4221.

COMPUTER/ Visual C/C, Visual Basic Exp'd Systems Analysts/ Programmers for growing software dev. team in Roseburg. Computer Science or related degree preferred. Develop adv. Engineering applications for engineering firm. Fax resume to 707-555-8744.

COMPUTER Web Master for dynamic SF Internet co. Site. Dev. test, coord. train. 2 yrs prog. Exp. C,C Web C FTP. Fax resume to Best Staffing 845-555-7722.

COMPUTER PROGRAMMER
Ad agency seeks programmer w/exp. in UNIX/NT Platforms. Web Server, CGI/Perl. Programmer Position avail. on a project basis with the possibility to move into F/T. Fax resume & salary req. to R. Jones 334-555-8332.

COMPUTERS Programmer/Analyst Design and maintain C based SQL database applications. Required skills: Visual Basic, C, SQL, ODBC, Document existing and new applications. Novell or NT exp. a plus. Fax resume & salary history to 235-555-9935.

GRAPHIC DESIGNER
Webmaster's Weekly is seeking a creative Graphic Designer to design high impact marketing collater al, including direct mail promols. CD-ROM packages, ads and WWW pages. Must be able to juggle multiple projects and learn new skills on the job very rapidly. Web design experience a big plus, technical troubleshooting also a plus. Call 435-555-1235.

GRAPHICS - ART DIRECTOR - WEB-MULTIMEDIA
Leading internet development company has an outstanding opportunity for a talented, high-end Web Experienced Art Director. In addition to a great portfolio and fresh ideas, the ideal candidate has excellent communication and presentation skills. Working as a team with innovative producers and programmers, you will create dynamic, interactive web sites and application interfaces. Some programming experience required. Send samples and resume to: SuperSites, 333 Main. Seattle, WA.

MARKETING
Fast paced software and services provider looking for MARKETING COMMUNICATIONS SPECIALIST to be responsible for its webpage, seminar coordination, and ad place-

---

PROGRAMMERS Multiple short term assignments available: Visual C, 3 positions SQL Server NT Server, 2 positions JAVA & HTML, long term NetWare. Various locations. Call for more info. 356-555-3398.

PROGRAMMERS

C, C, VB, Cobol, exp.
Call 534-555-6543
or fax 534-555-6544.

PROGRAMMING
MRFS Inc. is looking for a Sr. Windows NT developer. Reqs. 3-5 yrs. Exp. in C under Windows, Win95 & NT, using Visual C. Excl. OO design & implementation skills a must. OLE2 & ODBC are a plus. Resume & salary history to HR. 8779 HighTech Way, Computer City, AR

PROGRAMMERS/ Contractors Wanted for short & long term assignments; Visual C, MFC Unix C/C, SQL Oracle Developers PC Help Desk Support Windows NT & NetWare Telecommunications Visual Basic, Access, HTMT, CGI, Perl MMI & Co., 885-555-9933

PROGRAMMER World Wide Web Links wants your HTML & Photoshop skills. Develop great WWW sites. Local & global customers. Send samples & resume to WWWL, 2000 Apple Road, Santa Rosa, CA.

TECHNICAL WRITER Software firm seeks writer/editor for manuals, research notes, project mgmt. Min 2 years tech. writing, DTP & programming experience. Send resume & writing samples to: Software Systems, Dallas, TX.

COMPUTER PROGRAMMER
Ad agency seeks programmer w/exp. in UNIX/NT Platforms, Web Server, CGI/Perl. Programmer Position avail. on a project basis with the possibility to move into F/T. Fax resume & salary req. to R. Jones 334-555-8332.

TECHNICAL WRITER Premier Computer Corp is seeking a combination of technical skills, knowledge and experience in the following areas: UNIX, Windows 95/NT, Visual Basic, on-line help & documentation, and the Internet. Candidates must possess excellent writing skills, and be comfortable working in a quality vs. deadline driven environment. Competitive salary. Fax resume & samples to Karen Fields, Premier Computer Corp. 444 Industrial Blvd, Concord, CA. Or send to our website at www.premier.com

WEB DESIGNER
BA/BS or equivalent programming/multimedia production. 3 years of experience in use and design of WWW services streaming audio and video HTML, PERL, CGI, GIF, JPEG. Demonstrated interpersonal, organization, communication, multi-tasking skills. Send resume to The Learning People at www.learning.com

WEBMASTER-TECHNICAL
BSCS or equivalent, 2 years of experience in CGI, Windows 95/NT, UNIX, C, Java, Perl. Demonstrated

---

COMPUTERS Small Web Design firm seeks indiv. w/NT, Webserver & Database management exp. Fax resume to 556-555-4221.

COMPUTER Visual C/C, Visual Basic Exp'd Systems Analysts/ Programmers for growing software dev. team in Roseburg. Computer Science or related degree preferred. Develop adv. Engineering applications for engineering firm. Fax resume to 707-555-8744.

COMPUTER Web Master for dynamic SF Internet co. Site. Dev. test, coord. train. 2 yrs prog. Exp. C,C Web C FTP. Fax resume to Best Staffing 845-555-7722.

COMPUTERS/ QA SOFTWARE TESTERS Qualified candidates should have 2 yrs exp. performing integration & system testing using automated testing tools. Experienced in documentation preparation & programming languages (Access, C, FoxPro) are a plus. Financial or banking customer service support is required along with excellent verbal & written communication skills with multi levels of end-users. Send resume to KKUP Enterprises, 45 Orange Blvd. Orange, CA.

COMPUTERS Programmer/Analyst Design and maintain C based SQL database applications. Required skills: Visual Basic, C, SQL, ODBC, Document existing and new applications. Novell or NT exp. a plus. Fax resume & salary history to 235-555-9935.

GRAPHIC DESIGNER
Webmaster's Weekly is seeking a creative Graphic Designer to design high impact marketing collater al including direct mail promo's. CD-ROM packages, ads and WWW pages. Must be able to juggle multiple projects and learn new skills on the job very rapidly. Web design experience a big plus, technical troubleshooting also a plus. Call 435-555-1235.

GRAPHICS - ART DIRECTOR - WEB-MULTIMEDIA
Leading internet development company has an outstanding opportunity for a talented, high-end Web Experienced Art Director. In addition to a great portfolio and fresh ideas, the ideal candidate has excellent communication and presentation skills. Working as a team with innovative producers and programmers you will create dynamic, interactive web sites and application interfaces. Some programming experience required. Send samples and resume to: SuperSites, 333 Main. Seattle, WA.

COMPUTER PROGRAMMER
Ad agency seeks programmer w/exp. in UNIX/NT Platforms, Web Server, CGI/Perl. Programmer Position avail. on a project basis with the possibility to move into F/T. Fax resume & salary req. to R. Jones 334-555-8332.

PROGRAMMERS / Established software company seeks programmers with extensive Windows NT

...ment. Must be a self-starter, energetic, organized. Must have 2 yrs web experience. Programming plus. Call 985-555-9854.

PROGRAMMERS Multiple s... term assignments available: Vi... C, 3 positions SQL ServerNT Ser... 2 positions JAVA & HTML, long... NetWare Various locations. Call... more info. 356-555-3398.

PROGRAMMERS
C, C, VB, Cobol exp. Call 534-5... 6543 or fax 534-555-6544.

PROGRAMMING
MRFS Inc. is looking for a... Windows NT developer. Reqs... yrs. Exp. in C under Wind... Win95 & NT, using Visual C... OO design & implementation... a must. OLE2 & ODBC are a... Excl. Salary & bnfts. Resum... salary history to HR, 8779 Hi... Way, Computer City, AR

PROGRAMMERS/ Contra... Wanted for short & long term as... ments. Visual C, MFCUnix C/C... Oracle Developers PC Help... Support Windows NT & NetW... Telecommunications Visual B... Access, HTMT, CGI, Perl MMI &... 885-555-9933

PROGRAMMER World Wide... Links wants your HTML & Photo... skills. Develop great WWW... Local & global customers. Send... ples & resume to WWWL,... Apple Road, Santa Rosa, CA.

TECHNICAL WRITER Software... seeks writer/editor for man... research notes, project mgmt.... years tech. writing, DTP & prog... ming experience. Send resum... writing samples to: Soft... Systems, Dallas, TX.

TECHNICAL Software develop... firm looking for Tech Trainers... candidates have programming e... rience in Visual C, HTML &... Need quick self starter. Call... 555-6868 for interview.

TECHNICAL WRITER Pre... Computer Corp is seeking a... nation of technical skills, know... and experience in the follo... areas: UNIX, Windows 95/NT,... Basic, on-line help & documents... and the Internet. Candidates... possess excellent writing skills... be comfortable working in a q... vs. deadline driven environ... Competitive salary. Fax resum... samples to Karen Fields, Pr... Computer Corp. 444 Industrial... Concord, CA. Or send to our we... at www.premier.com

WEB DESIGNER

BA/BS or equivalent prog... ming/multimedia production... years of experience in use... design of WWW services strea... audio and video HTML, PERL... GIF, JPEG. Demonstrated inte... sonal, organization, communic... multi-tasking skills. Send resum... The Learning People at www... ing.com.

WEBMASTER-TECHNIC...

S K I L L

five

5

Working with Radio Buttons

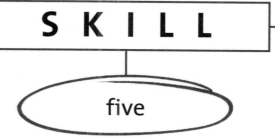

- ❑ Adding Java panels in a program
- ❑ Placing controls in a panel
- ❑ Reaching controls in other panels
- ❑ Grouping radio buttons together
- ❑ Using the CheckboxGroup class

In Skill 4, we took a look at Java check boxes. Here, we're going to take a look at radio buttons. In addition, you'll start to learn how to group controls together, both with the CheckboxGroup class and the Panel class. We'll bring radio buttons and check boxes together in a relatively large-scale example. Let's start at once with a guided tour of radio buttons.

Building Programs with Radio Buttons

Radio buttons (also called option buttons) are much like check boxes, but there is an important difference. You can check a number of check boxes at the same time, as shown in Figure 5.1. Option buttons, however, operate in a group, and only one can be clicked at one time, as shown in Figure 5.2.

```
[v] 1        [ ] 2        [v] 3        [ ] 4        [v] 5
```

FIGURE 5.1   You can check more than one check box at a time.

```
( ) 1        (*) 2        ( ) 3        ( ) 4        ( ) 5
```

FIGURE 5.2   Only one radio button can be active at a time.

To associate radio buttons together in this way, we use a CheckboxGroup object. When we add radio buttons to a group, the CheckboxGroup class's internal methods will make sure that only one of the radio buttons is checked at any time automatically—we won't have to worry about "unchecking" radio buttons when one of a group is checked.

The Radios Applet

To see radio buttons at work, let's write a new applet much like our check box applet that will present radio buttons, instead of check boxes, to the user. When the user clicks one of the radio buttons, we can report that fact as shown in Figure 5.3.

```
------------------------------------------------------------
|                                                          |
| ( ) 1        ( ) 2        (*) 3        ( ) 4        ( ) 5 |
|                                                          |
|         ------------------------------------             |
|         |Radio button 3 clicked!           |             |
|         ------------------------------------             |
|                                                          |
|                                                          |
------------------------------------------------------------
```

FIGURE 5.3   **When the user clicks a button, a message appears in the text field.**

Create a new project now named radios and create the new class named radios like this:

```
import java.applet.Applet;
import java.awt.*;
import java.awt.event.*;

public class radios extends Applet {
        .
        .
        .
}
```

You might be expecting a new Java class called RadioButton or something. However, in Java, radio buttons are actually just check boxes that have been added to a check box group. When you add check boxes to a check box group, they change their appearance automatically and become radio buttons. That means that we can create five new Checkbox objects for our radio controls:

```
import java.applet.Applet;
import java.awt.*;
import java.awt.event.*;


public class radios extends Applet {
```
→   Checkbox checkbox1, checkbox2, checkbox3, checkbox4, checkbox5;
```
}
```

Next, we will need an object of class CheckboxGroup to add our check boxes too (so they can act in a coordinated fashion). The CheckboxGroup class methods appear in Table 5.1. In our applet, we declare a new object of class CheckboxGroup which we can name checkboxgroup1, and we declare the text field:

```
import java.applet.Applet;
import java.awt.*;
import java.awt.event.*;

public class radios extends Applet {
```
→   CheckboxGroup checkboxgroup1;
```
        Checkbox checkbox1, checkbox2, checkbox3, checkbox4, checkbox5;
```
→   TextField text1;

```
}
```

T A B L E   5 . 1 : The CheckboxGroup **class methods**

Method	Does This
CheckboxGroup()	Creates a CheckboxGroup.
getCurrent()	Gets current selection. Deprecated.
getSelectedCheckbox()	Gets current selected check box.
setCurrent(Checkbox)	Sets current selection to indicated Checkbox. Deprecated.
setSelectedCheckbox()	Sets the current choice to the specified Checkbox.
toString()	Returns string of CheckboxGroup's options.

```
     public class checkpanels extends Applet {

→        checkboxpanel panel1, panel2, panel3;
                 .
                 .
                 .
     }

     class checkboxpanel extends Panel {
         Checkbox check1, check2, check3, check4;

         checkboxpanel(){
             check1 = new Checkbox("1");
             add(check1);
             check2 = new Checkbox("2");
             add(check2);
             check3 = new Checkbox("3");
             add(check3);
             check4 = new Checkbox("4");
             add(check4);
         }
     }
```

Next, we have to initialize these panels in the init() method. We will use the GridLayout manager to make these panels appear side by side, so we start off by installing that manager first:

```
     import java.applet.Applet;
     import java.awt.*;

     public class checkpanels extends Applet {

         checkboxpanel panel1, panel2, panel3;

         public void init(){
→            setLayout(new GridLayout(1, 3));
                 .
                 .
                 .
         }
     }

     class checkboxpanel extends Panel {
         Checkbox check1, check2, check3, check4;

         checkboxpanel(){
             check1 = new Checkbox("1");
```

Skill 5

```
        add(check1);
        check2 = new Checkbox("2");
        add(check2);
        check3 = new Checkbox("3");
        add(check3);
        check4 = new Checkbox("4");
        add(check4);
    }
}
```

Now we create and add our three checkbox panels, panel1, panel2, and panel3 of our new class checkpanels to our applet:

```
import java.applet.Applet;
import java.awt.*;

public class checkpanels extends Applet {

    checkboxpanel panel1, panel2, panel3;

    public void init(){
        setLayout(new GridLayout(1, 3));
→       panel1 = new checkboxpanel();
→       panel2 = new checkboxpanel();
→       panel3 = new checkboxpanel();
→       add(panel1);
→       add(panel2);
→       add(panel3);
    }

}

class checkboxpanel extends Panel {
    Checkbox check1, check2, check3, check4;

    checkboxpanel(){
        check1 = new Checkbox("1");
        add(check1);
        check2 = new Checkbox("2");
        add(check2);
        check3 = new Checkbox("3");
        add(check3);
        check4 = new Checkbox("4");
        add(check4);
    }
}
```

And that's all there is to it—now we've created a new panel type, added controls to the panel, and added panels of that type to our applet. As you can see in the graphic below, we have successfully installed three panels in our applet. Our check-panels applet is a success. The code for this applet appears in checkpanels.java.

checkpanels.java

```java
import java.applet.Applet;
import java.awt.*;

public class checkpanels extends Applet {

    checkboxpanel panel1, panel2, panel3;

    public void init(){
        setLayout(new GridLayout(1, 3));
        panel1 = new checkboxpanel();
        panel2 = new checkboxpanel();
        panel3 = new checkboxpanel();
        add(panel1);
        add(panel2);
        add(panel3);
    }

}

class checkboxpanel extends Panel {
    Checkbox check1, check2, check3, check4;

    checkboxpanel(){
```

```
        check1 = new Checkbox("1");
        add(check1);
        check2 = new Checkbox("2");
        add(check2);
        check3 = new Checkbox("3");
        add(check3);
        check4 = new Checkbox("4");
        add(check4);
    }
}
```

As you can see, panels make up a powerful technique for grouping controls together. We'll use panels in our next example, in which we bring Skill 5 together with Skill 4 by using radio buttons, check boxes, panels, and layouts all in the same applet.

Putting Check Boxes and Radio Buttons Together

Let's say that we decide to set up a sandwich shop on the Web. In particular, we want to embed an applet in a Web page giving customers the price of various sandwiches. That applet might look something like Figure 5.6, in which we let the customer select from various sandwich options, indicate the ingredients in each sandwich, and give the customer a price for what they have selected.

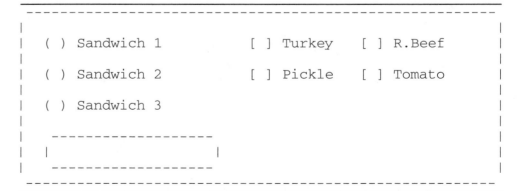

FIGURE 5.6   An online sandwich shop

For example, if the user clicks the Sandwich 1 radio button, we set the corresponding check boxes to indicate what's in this sandwich, and indicate the total price in a text field, as shown in Figure 5.7. If the user then clicks another radio button, all the other radio buttons are cleared, a new set of sandwich ingredients is indicated, and a new price appears, as shown in Figure 5.8. We can put the controls in our applet into two panels, as shown in Figure 5.9.

```
------------------------------------------------------------
|                                                          |
|   (*)  Sandwich 1         [v]  Turkey    [ ]  R.Beef     |
|                                                          |
|   ( )  Sandwich 2         [v]  Pickle    [ ]  Tomato     |
|                                                          |
|   ( )  Sandwich 3                                        |
|                                                          |
|   ------------------                                     |
|   |Price $2.95      |                                    |
|   ------------------                                     |
------------------------------------------------------------
```

FIGURE 5.7   When the user selects a sandwich, the applet indicates the ingredients and price of the sandwich.

```
------------------------------------------------------------
|                                                          |
|   ( )  Sandwich 1         [v]  Turkey    [v]  R.Beef     |
|                                                          |
|   ( )  Sandwich 2         [v]  Pickle    [v]  Tomato     |
|                                                          |
|   (*)  Sandwich 3                                        |
|                                                          |
|   ------------------                                     |
|   |Price $4.00      |                                    |
|   ------------------                                     |
------------------------------------------------------------
```

FIGURE 5.8   When the user selects a new sandwich, the applet displays information about the new sandwich.

```
----------Panel1----------------------Panel2------------
|                                                        |
|   ----------------------    ----------------------     |
|   | ( )  Sandwich 1    |    |[ ]  Turkey    [ ]  R.Beef |  |
|   |                    |    |                       |  |
|   | ( )  Sandwich 2    |    |[ ]  Pickle    [ ]  Tomato |  |
|   |                    |    |                       |  |
|   | ( )  Sandwich 3    |    |                       |  |
|   |                    |    |                       |  |
|   |  ----------------- |    |                       |  |
|   | |                 ||    |                       |  |
|   |  ----------------- |    |                       |  |
|   ----------------------    ----------------------     |
----------------------------------------------------------
```

FIGURE 5.9   We'll divide our controls into two panels.

To see this idea in action, create a new applet named sandwich.java. We will begin by designing the new panels we'll use, starting with the panel with the radio buttons and the text field:

```
----------------------
| ( )  Sandwich 1    |
|                    |
| ( )  Sandwich 2    |
|                    |
| ( )  Sandwich 3    |
|                    |
|  ----------------- |
| |                 ||
|  ----------------- |
----------------------
```

Creating the Menu Panel

We do so as we did in our previous panels applet, by deriving a new class named, say, Menu, from the Java Panel class (add this new class to the sandwich.java file):

```
class Menu extends Panel {
    .
    .
    .
}
```

Now we add the controls we'll need—note that since this panel holds radio buttons, we'll need a check box group object:

```
class Menu extends Panel {
    CheckboxGroup CGroup;
    Checkbox sandwich1, sandwich2, sandwich3;
    TextField Pricebox;
            .
            .
            .
}
```

And we add our controls to the new `Panel` class in that class's constructor:

```
class Menu extends Panel {
    CheckboxGroup CGroup;
    Checkbox Sandwich1, Sandwich2, Sandwich3;
    TextField Pricebox;

    Menu(){
➜       CGroup = new CheckboxGroup();
➜       add(Sandwich1 = new Checkbox("Sandwich 1", CGroup, false));
➜       add(Sandwich2 = new Checkbox("Sandwich 2", CGroup, false));
➜       add(Sandwich3 = new Checkbox("Sandwich 3", CGroup, false));
➜       Pricebox = new TextField(15);
➜       add(Pricebox);
    }
}
```

That's it—we've set up our first panel:

```
 ---------------------
| ( )  Sandwich 1     |
|                     |
| ( )  Sandwich 2     |
|                     |
| ( )  Sandwich 3     |
|                     |
|  ------------------ |
| |                | ||
|  ------------------ |
 ---------------------
```

Skill 5

Creating the Ingredients Panel

The other panel we need looks like this, with four labeled check boxes:

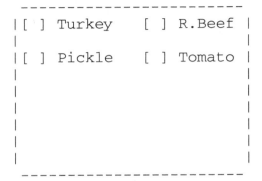

We can call this new panel class `Ingredients` and add the definition of this new class to the `sandwich.java` file. All we'll need in this new class are four check boxes, labeled with the ingredients in our sandwiches, so that class looks like this:

```
class Ingredients extends Panel {

Checkbox Ingredient1, Ingredient2, Ingredient3, Ingredient4;

    Ingredients(){
        add(Ingredient1 = new Checkbox("Turkey"));
        add(Ingredient2 = new Checkbox("R.Beef"));
        add(Ingredient3 = new Checkbox("Pickle"));
        add(Ingredient4 = new Checkbox("Tomato"));
    }
}
```

And that's it for this panel.

At this point, then, our new panels are ready to add to the `sandwich` class. Add that class now and declare a panel of each of our new panel classes as follows:

```
import java.applet.Applet;
import java.awt.*;
import java.awt.event.*;

public class sandwich extends Applet {

    Menu Panel1;
```

```
➡        Ingredients Panel2;
                .
                .
                .

    }

    class Menu extends Panel {
        CheckboxGroup CGroup;
        Checkbox Sandwich1, Sandwich2, Sandwich3;
        TextField Pricebox;

        Menu(){
            CGroup = new CheckboxGroup();
            add(Sandwich1 = new Checkbox("Sandwich 1", CGroup, false));
            add(Sandwich2 = new Checkbox("Sandwich 2", CGroup, false));
            add(Sandwich3 = new Checkbox("Sandwich 3", CGroup, false));
            Pricebox = new TextField(15);
            add(Pricebox);
        }
    }

    class Ingredients extends Panel {
        Checkbox Ingredient1, Ingredient2, Ingredient3, Ingredient4;

        Ingredients(){
            add(Ingredient1 = new Checkbox("Turkey"));
            add(Ingredient2 = new Checkbox("R.Beef"));
            add(Ingredient3 = new Checkbox("Pickle"));
            add(Ingredient4 = new Checkbox("Tomato"));
        }
    }
```

Now we can create and add those panels. To make sure they appear side by side, we'll use the GridLayout manager. We install that manager now in the applet's init() method:

```
import java.applet.Applet;
import java.awt.*;
import java.awt.event.*;

public class sandwich extends Applet {

    Menu Panel1;
    Ingredients Panel2;

    public void init(){
```

```
→            setLayout(new GridLayout(1, 2));
                      .
                      .
                      .
         }
   }
```

Then we simply add our two new panels like this:

```
import java.applet.Applet;
import java.awt.*;
import java.awt.event.*;

public class sandwich extends Applet {

    Menu Panel1;
    Ingredients Panel2;

    public void init(){
        setLayout(new GridLayout(1, 2));
→       Panel1 = new Menu();
→       Panel2 = new Ingredients();
→       add(Panel1);
→       add(Panel2);
                  .
                  .
                  .
    }

}
```

At this point, then, our applet will look like Figure 5.10.

```
 ---------------------------------------------------------
|                                                         |
|   ( ) Sandwich 1          [ ] Turkey    [ ] R.Beef      |
|                                                         |
|   ( ) Sandwich 2          [ ] Pickle    [ ] Tomato      |
|                                                         |
|   ( ) Sandwich 3                                        |
|                                                         |
|      ------------------                                 |
|     |                  |                                |
|      ------------------                                 |
|                                                         |
 ---------------------------------------------------------
```

FIGURE 5.10   Our applet so far

NOTE   **Panels do not have any predefined outlines that appear around them in an applet. They are really just constructs to arrange controls, not GUI objects.**

We haven't done anything yet to make this applet functional—we still need to connect up the buttons. We start that process by adding the ItemListener interface to our applet:

```
import java.applet.Applet;
import java.awt.*;
import java.awt.event.*;
```

→
```
public class sandwich extends Applet implements ItemListener{

    Menu Panel1;
    Ingredients Panel2;

    public void init(){
        setLayout(new GridLayout(1, 2));
        Panel1 = new Menu();
        Panel2 = new Ingredients();
        add(Panel1);
        add(Panel2);
    }

}
```

Now we have to connect the option button's ItemListener interfaces to our applet. The option buttons are named Sandwich1, Sandwich2, and Sandwich3, but we can't just execute a statement such as

```
Sandwich1.addItemListener(this)
```

because Sandwich1 is not an object in our applet, but in the Panel1 object. That means we will reach those option buttons another way, using the Java dot operator (.):

```
import java.applet.Applet;
import java.awt.*;
import java.awt.event.*;
```

→
```
public class sandwich extends Applet implements ItemListener{

    Menu Panel1;
    Ingredients Panel2;
```

```
        public void init(){
            setLayout(new GridLayout(1, 2));
            Panel1 = new Menu();
            Panel2 = new Ingredients();
            add(Panel1);
→           Panel1.Sandwich1.addItemListener(this);
→           Panel1.Sandwich2.addItemListener(this);
→           Panel1.Sandwich3.addItemListener(this);
            add(Panel2);
        }
    }
```

Next, we add the itemStateChanged() method to handle radio button clicks:

```
import java.applet.Applet;
import java.awt.*;
import java.awt.event.*;

public class sandwich extends Applet implements ItemListener {

    Menu Panel1;
    Ingredients Panel2;

    public void init(){
        setLayout(new GridLayout(1, 2));
        Panel1 = new Menu();
        Panel2 = new Ingredients();
        add(Panel1);
        Panel1.Sandwich1.addItemListener(this);
        Panel1.Sandwich2.addItemListener(this);
        Panel1.Sandwich3.addItemListener(this);
        add(Panel2);
    }


→   public void itemStateChanged(ItemEvent e) {
            .
            .
            .
→       }
    }
```

Now let's handle the case in which the user clicks the radio button marked "Sandwich 1." We can use the following syntax to check whether that button was clicked:

```
import java.applet.Applet;
import java.awt.*;
```

```
import java.awt.event.*;

public class sandwich extends Applet implements ItemListener {

    Menu Panel1;
    Ingredients Panel2;

    public void init(){
        setLayout(new GridLayout(1, 2));
        Panel1 = new Menu();
        Panel2 = new Ingredients();
        add(Panel1);
        Panel1.Sandwich1.addItemListener(this);
        Panel1.Sandwich2.addItemListener(this);
        Panel1.Sandwich3.addItemListener(this);
        add(Panel2);
    }


        public void itemStateChanged(ItemEvent e) {
➔       if(e.getItemSelectable() == Panel1.Sandwich1){

➔       }
        }
    }
```

If, in fact, the Sandwich1 button is clicked, we want the check boxes to indicate what is in the sandwich, as shown in Figure 5.11.

```
-----------------------------------------------------------
|                                                         |
|  (*)  Sandwich 1         [v]  Turkey    [ ] R.Beef      |
|                                                         |
|  ( )  Sandwich 2         [v]  Pickle    [ ] Tomato      |
|                                                         |
|  ( )  Sandwich 3                                        |
|                                                         |
|     -------------------                                 |
|    |Price $2.95        |                                |
|     -------------------                                 |
|                                                         |
-----------------------------------------------------------
```

FIGURE 5.11   When the user clicks the Sandwich1 button, the check boxes should indicate what's in the sandwich.

If the Sandwich1 was clicked, we will set the check boxes appropriately in
Panel2. The check boxes are actually objects internal to the Panel2 object
that we have named Ingredient1 to Ingredient4, so we address them as
Panel2.Ingredient1 to Panel2.Ingredient4. We can use the check box
method setState() to set the check boxes as we want them—passing a value
of true makes them appear checked, and a value of false makes them appear
unchecked:

```
import java.applet.Applet;
import java.awt.*;
import java.awt.event.*;

public class sandwich extends Applet implements ItemListener {

    Menu Panel1;
    Ingredients Panel2;

    public void init(){
        setLayout(new GridLayout(1, 2));
        Panel1 = new Menu();
        Panel2 = new Ingredients();
        add(Panel1);
        Panel1.Sandwich1.addItemListener(this);
        Panel1.Sandwich2.addItemListener(this);
        Panel1.Sandwich3.addItemListener(this);
        add(Panel2);
    }


    public void itemStateChanged(ItemEvent e) {
        if(e.getItemSelectable() == Panel1.Sandwich1){
            Panel2.Ingredient1.setState(true);
            Panel2.Ingredient2.setState(false);
            Panel2.Ingredient3.setState(true);
            Panel2.Ingredient4.setState(false);
            Panel1.Pricebox.setText("Price: $2.95");
        }
    }
}
```

In this way, we've handled the Sandwich 1 button. The other sandwich buttons
are the same with different options, so activating them looks like this:

```
import java.applet.Applet;
import java.awt.*;
```

```java
import java.awt.event.*;

public class sandwich extends Applet implements ItemListener {

    Menu Panel1;
    Ingredients Panel2;

    public void init(){
        setLayout(new GridLayout(1, 2));
        Panel1 = new Menu();
        Panel2 = new Ingredients();
        add(Panel1);
        Panel1.Sandwich1.addItemListener(this);
        Panel1.Sandwich2.addItemListener(this);
        Panel1.Sandwich3.addItemListener(this);
        add(Panel2);
    }


    public void itemStateChanged(ItemEvent e) {
        if(e.getItemSelectable() == Panel1.Sandwich1){
            Panel2.Ingredient1.setState(true);
            Panel2.Ingredient2.setState(false);
            Panel2.Ingredient3.setState(true);
            Panel2.Ingredient4.setState(false);
            Panel1.Pricebox.setText("Price: $2.95");
        }
        if(e.getItemSelectable() == Panel1.Sandwich2){
            Panel2.Ingredient1.setState(false);
            Panel2.Ingredient2.setState(true);
            Panel2.Ingredient3.setState(true);
            Panel2.Ingredient4.setState(true);
            Panel1.Pricebox.setText("Price: $2.95");
        }
        if(e.getItemSelectable() == Panel1.Sandwich3){
            Panel2.Ingredient1.setState(true);
            Panel2.Ingredient2.setState(true);
            Panel2.Ingredient3.setState(true);
            Panel2.Ingredient4.setState(true);
            Panel1.Pricebox.setText("Price: $4.00");
        }
    }
}
```

And that's it—we've completed our sandwich example applet, which uses panels, check boxes, radio buttons, and a grid layout. Run the completed applet now, as shown below. When the user clicks various system options, the corresponding price and component list are indicated. Our applet is a success. The code for this applet appears in sandwich.java.

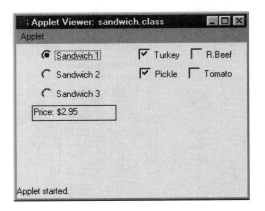

sandwich.java

```java
import java.applet.Applet;
import java.awt.*;
import java.awt.event.*;

public class sandwich extends Applet implements ItemListener {

    Menu Panel1;
    Ingredients Panel2;

    public void init(){
        setLayout(new GridLayout(1, 2));
        Panel1 = new Menu();
        Panel2 = new Ingredients();
        add(Panel1);
        Panel1.Sandwich1.addItemListener(this);
        Panel1.Sandwich2.addItemListener(this);
        Panel1.Sandwich3.addItemListener(this);
        add(Panel2);
    }


    public void itemStateChanged(ItemEvent e) {
        if(e.getItemSelectable() == Panel1.Sandwich1){
            Panel2.Ingredient1.setState(true);
            Panel2.Ingredient2.setState(false);
```

```
                Panel2.Ingredient3.setState(true);
                Panel2.Ingredient4.setState(false);
                Panel1.Pricebox.setText("Price: $2.95");
            }
            if(e.getItemSelectable() == Panel1.Sandwich2){
                Panel2.Ingredient1.setState(false);
                Panel2.Ingredient2.setState(true);
                Panel2.Ingredient3.setState(true);
                Panel2.Ingredient4.setState(true);
                Panel1.Pricebox.setText("Price: $2.95");
            }
            if(e.getItemSelectable() == Panel1.Sandwich3){
                Panel2.Ingredient1.setState(true);
                Panel2.Ingredient2.setState(true);
                Panel2.Ingredient3.setState(true);
                Panel2.Ingredient4.setState(true);
                Panel1.Pricebox.setText("Price: $4.00");
            }
        }
}

class Menu extends Panel {
    CheckboxGroup CGroup;
    Checkbox Sandwich1, Sandwich2, Sandwich3;
    TextField Pricebox;

    Menu(){
        CGroup = new CheckboxGroup();
        add(Sandwich1 = new Checkbox("Sandwich 1", CGroup, false));
        add(Sandwich2 = new Checkbox("Sandwich 2", CGroup, false));
        add(Sandwich3 = new Checkbox("Sandwich 3", CGroup, false));
        Pricebox = new TextField(15);
        add(Pricebox);
    }
}

class Ingredients extends Panel {
    Checkbox Ingredient1, Ingredient2, Ingredient3, Ingredient4;

    Ingredients(){
        add(Ingredient1 = new Checkbox("Turkey"));
        add(Ingredient2 = new Checkbox("R.Beef"));
        add(Ingredient3 = new Checkbox("Pickle"));
        add(Ingredient4 = new Checkbox("Tomato"));
    }
}
```

Skill 5

Now we're working with all three of the elements we've introduced in this Skill and the last one: check boxes, radio buttons, and panels. We've also gained some practical experience accessing members of another class by reaching the buttons in our panels from our applet class. Now we'll turn now to another powerful Java control—scroll bars—in Skill 6.

Are You Experienced?

Now you can...

- ☑ add and use radio buttons for more power in your Java programs
- ☑ use the `Panel` class as a base class to derive your own panel class to group Java controls together
- ☑ use the `CheckboxGroup` class to group radio buttons together so that only one of them will appear checked at any time
- ☑ reach objects embedded in other objects

Design server & xp. Fax

C, Visual nalysts/ software omputer referred. applica- m. fax

dynam- y. test, xp. C C to Best

Testers have 2 ration & ted test- ocumen- ramming o) are a ustomer d along en com- levels o o KKUP Blvd.

Analyst sed SQL equired ODBC applica- a plus tory to

eking o design ilateral. o's, CD- WWW le multi- skills on design ical trou- all 435-

OR -

nt com- portuni- nd Web addition h ideas, excellent entation h innov- ammers. teractive terfaces perience l resume Seattle.

software king for ATIONS le for its tion, and f-starter, have 2 ramming

---

PROGRAMMERS
C, C, VB, Cobol, exp. Call 534-555-6543 or fax 534-555-6544.

PROGRAMMING
MRFS Inc. Is looking for a Sr. Windows NT developer. Reqs. 3-5 yrs. Exp. In C under Windows, Win95 & NT, using Visual C. Excl. OO design & implementation skills a must. OLE2 & ODBC are a plus. Excl. Salary & bnfts. Resume & salary history to HR, 8779 HighTech Way, Computer City, AR

PROGRAMMERS
Contractors Wanted for short & long term assignments: Visual C, MFC Unix C/C, SQL Oracle Dev elopers PC Help Desk Support Windows NT & NetWare Telecommunications Visual Basic, Access, HTML, CGI, Perl MMI & Co., 885-555-9933

PROGRAMMER World Wide Web Links wants your HTML & Photoshop skills. Develop great WWW sites. Local & global customers. Send sam- ples & resume to WWWL, 2000 Apple Road, Santa Rosa, CA.

TECHNICAL WRITER Software firm seeks writer/editor for manuals, research notes, project mgmt. Min 2 years tech. writing, DTP & program- ming experience. Send resume & writing samples to: Software Systems, Dallas, TX.

TECHNICAL Software development firm looking for Tech Trainers, Ideal candidates have programming expe- rience in Visual C, HTML & JAVA. Need quick self starter. Call (443) 555-6868 for interview.

TECHNICAL WRITER/ Premier Computer Corp is seeking a combi- nation of technical skills, knowledge and experience in the following areas: UNIX, Windows 95/NT, Visual Basic, on-line help & documentation, and the internet. Candidates must possess excellent writing skills, and be comfortable working in a quality vs. deadline driven environment. Competitive salary. Fax resume & samples to Karen Fields, Premier Computer Corp., 444 Industrial Blvd. Concord, CA. Or send to our website at www.premier.com.

WEB DESIGNER
BA/BS or equivalent program- ming/multimedia production. 3 years of experience in use and design of WWW services streaming audio and video HTML, PERL, CGI, GIF, JPEG. Demonstrated interper- sonal, organization, communication, multi-tasking skills. Send resume to The Learning People at www.learn- ing.com.

WEBMASTER-TECHNICAL
BSCS or equivalent, 2 years of experience in CGI, Windows 95/NT, UNIX, C, Java, Perl. Demonstrated ability to design, code, debug and test on-line services. Send resume to The Learning People at www.learn- ing.com.

PROGRAMMER World Wide Web Links wants your HTML & Photoshop skills. Develop great WWW sites. Local & global customers. Send sam-

---

tation preparation & programming languages (Access, C, FoxPro) are a plus. Financial or banking customer service support is required along with excellent verbal & written com- munication skills with multi levels of end-users. Send resume to KKUP Enterprises. 45 Orange Blvd. Orange, CA.

COMPUTERS Small Web Design Firm seeks indiv. w/NT. Webserver & Database management exp. Fax resume to 556-555-4221.

COMPUTER/ Visual C/C, Visual Basic Exp'd Systems Analysts/ Programmers for growing software dev. team in Roseburg. Computer Science or related degree preferred. Develop adv. Engineering applica- tions for engineering firm. Fax resume to 707-555-8744.

COMPUTER Web Master for dynam- ic SF internet co. Site. Dev. test, coord. train. 2 yrs prog. Exp. C C Web C FTP. Fax resume to Best Staffing 845-555-7722.

COMPUTER PROGRAMMER
Ad agency seeks programmer w/exp. in UNIX/NT Platforms, Web Server, CGI/Perl. Programmer Posit- ion avail. on a project basis with the possibility to move into F/T. Fax resume & salary req. to R. Jones 334-555-8332.

COMPUTERS Programmer/Analyst Design and maintain C based SQL database applications. Required skills: Visual Basic, C, SQL, ODBC. Document existing and new applica- tions. Novell or NT exp a plus. Fax resume & salary history to 235-555-9935.

GRAPHIC DESIGNER
Webmaster's Weekly is seeking a creative Graphic Designer to design high impact marketing collateral, including direct mail promo's. CD-ROM packages, ads and WWW pages. Must be able to juggle mul- tiple projects and learn new skills on the job very rapidly. Web design experience a big plus. technical troubleshooting also a plus. Call 435-555-1235.

GRAPHICS - ART DIRECTOR - WEB-MULTIMEDIA
Leading internet development com- pany has an outstanding opportuni- ty for a talented, high-end Web Experienced Art Director. In addition to a great portfolio and fresh ideas, the ideal candidate has excellent communication and presentation skills. Working as a team with innov- ative producers and programmers, you will create dynamic, interactive web sites and application interfaces. Some programming experience required. Send samples and resume to: SuperSites, 333 Main, Seattle. WA.

MARKETING
Fast paced software and services provider looking for MARKETING COMMUNICATIONS SPECIALIST to be responsible for its webpage, seminar coordination, and ad place-

---

PROGRAMMERS Multiple short term assignments available: Visual C 3 positions SQL ServerNT Server. 2 positions JAVA & HTML, long term NetWare Various locations. Call for more info. 356-555-3398.

PROGRAMMERS

C, C, VB, Cobol, exp. Call 534-555-6543 or fax 534-555-6544.

PROGRAMMING
MRFS Inc. Is looking for a Sr Windows NT developer. Reqs. 3-5 yrs. Exp. In C under Windows. Win95 & NT, using Visual C. Excl. OO design & implementation skills a must. OLE2 & ODBC are a plus. Excl. Salary & bnfts. Resume & salary history to HR, 8779 HighTech Way, Computer City, AR

PROGRAMMERS/ Contractors Wanted for short & long term assignments: Visual C, MFC Unix C/C. SQL Oracle Developers PC Help Desk Support Windows NT & NetWare Telecommunications Visual Basic, Access, HTML, CGI, Perl MMI & Co., 885-555-9933

PROGRAMMER World Wide Web Links wants your HTML & Photoshop skills. Develop great WWW sites. Local & global customers. Send sam- ples & resume to WWWL, 2000 Apple Road, Santa Rosa, CA.

TECHNICAL WRITER Software firm seeks writer/editor for manuals, research notes, project mgmt. Min 2 years tech. writing, DTP & program- ming experience. Send resume & writing samples to: Software Systems, Dallas, TX.

COMPUTER PROGRAMMER
Ad agency seeks programmer w/exp. in UNIX/NT Platforms, Web Server, CGI/Perl. Programmer Position avail. on a project basis with the possibili- ty to move into F/T. Fax resume & salary req. to R. Jones 334-555-8332.

TECHNICAL WRITER Premier Computer Corp is seeking a combi- nation of technical skills, knowledge and experience in the following areas: UNIX, Windows 95/NT, Visual Basic, on-line help & documentation, and the internet. Candidates must possess excellent writing skills, and be comfortable working in a quality vs. deadline driven environment. Competitive salary. Fax resume & samples to Karen Fields, Premier Computer Corp., 444 Industrial Blvd. Concord, CA. Or send to our website at www.premier.com.

WEB DESIGNER
BA/BS or equivalent program- ming/multimedia production. 3 years of experience in use and design of WWW services streaming audio and video HTML, PERL, CGI, GIF, JPEG. Demonstrated interper- sonal, organization, communication, multi-tasking skills. Send resume to The Learning People at www.learn- ing.com.

WEBMASTER-TECHNICAL
BSCS or equivalent, 2 years of experience in CGI, Windows 95/NT, UNIX, C, Java, Perl. Demonstrated

---

COMPUTERS Small Web Design Firm seeks indiv. w/NT, Webserver & Database management exp. Fax resume to 556-555-4221.

COMPUTER Visual C/C, Visual Basic Exp'd Systems Analysts/ Programmers for growing software dev. team in Roseburg. Computer Science or related degree preferred. Develop adv. Engineering applica- tions for engine ering firm. Fax resume to 707-555-8744.

COMPUTER Web Master for dynam- ic SF internet co. Site. Dev. test, coord. train. 2 yrs prog. Exp. C C Web C FTP. fax resume to Best Staffing 845-555-7722.

COMPUTERS/ QA SOFTWARE TESTERS Qualified candidates should have 2 yrs. performing integra- tion & system testing using automat- ed testing tools. Experienced in docu- mentation preparation & program- ming languages (Access, C, FoxPro) are a plus. Financial or banking cus- tomer service support is required along with excellent verbal & written communication skills with multi levels of end-users. Send resume to KKUP Enterprises, 45 Orange Blvd. Orange, CA.

COMPUTERS Programmer/Analyst Design and maintain C based SQL database applications. Required skills: Visual Basic, C, SQL, ODBC. Document existing and new appli- cations. Novell or NT exp. a plus. Fax resume & salary history to 235-555-9935.

GRAPHIC DESIGNER
Webmaster's Weekly is seeking a creative Graphic Designer to design high impact marketing collater al, including direct mail promo's. CD-ROM packages, ads and WWW pages. Must be able to juggle mul- tiple projects and learn new skills on the job very rapidly. Web design experience a big plus. technical troubleshooting also a plus. Call 435-555-1235.

GRAPHICS - ART DIRECTOR - WEB-MULTIMEDIA
Leading internet development com- pany has an outstanding opportuni- ty for a talented, high-end Web Experienced Art Director. In addition to a great portfolio and fresh ideas, the ideal candidate has excellent communication and presentation skills. Working as a team with innov- ative producers and programmers, you will create dynamic, interactive web sites and application interfaces. Some programming experience required. Send samples and resume to: SuperSites, 333 Main, Seattle. WA.

COMPUTER PROGRAMMER
Ad agency seeks programmer w/exp. in UNIX/NT Platforms, Web Server, CGI/Perl. Programmer Position avail. on a project basis with the possibili- ty to move into F/T. Fax resume & salary req. to R. Jones 334-555-8332.

PROGRAMMERS / Established software company seeks program- mers with extensive Windows NT

---

ment. Must be a self-starter, e getic, organized. Must have 2 y web experience. Programmin plus. Call 985-555-9854.

PROGRAMMERS Multiple term assignments available: V C, 3 positions SQL ServerNT Se 2 positions JAVA & HTML, long NetWare Various locations. Cal more info. 356-555-3398.

PROGRAMMERS
C, C, VB, Cobol, exp. Call 534- 6543 or fax 534-555-6544.

PROGRAMMING
MRFS Inc. Is looking for a Windows NT developer. Reqs yrs. Exp. In C under Wind Win95 & NT using Visual C OO design & implementation a must. OLE2 & ODBC are a Excl. Salary & bnfts. Resum salary history to HR, 8779 Hig Way, Computer City, AR

PROGRAMMERS/ Contra Wanted for short & long term as ments: Visual C, MFCUnix C/C, Oracle Developers PC Help Support Windows NT & Neti Telecommunications Visual B Access, HTML, CGI, Perl MMI a 885-555-9933

PROGRAMMER World Wide Links wants your HTML & Photo skills. Develop great WWW Local & global customers. Send ples & resume to WWWL, Apple Road, Santa Rosa, CA.

TECHNICAL WRITER Software seeks writer/editor for mar research notes, project mgmt. f years tech. writing, DTP & pros ming experience. Send resum writing samples to: Soft Systems, Dallas, TX.

TECHNICAL Software develop firm looking for Tech Trainers. candidates have programming e rience in Visual C, HTML & J Need quick self starter. Call 555-6868 for interview.

TECHNICAL WRITER Pre Computer Corp is seeking a co nation of technical skills, know and experience in the follo areas: UNIX, Windows 95/NT, Basic, on-line help & document and the internet. Candidates possess excellent writing skills be comfortable working in a q vs. deadline driven environm Competitive salary. Fax resur samples to Karen Fields. Pr Computer Corp., 444 Industrial Concord, CA. Or send to our w at www.premier.com.

WEB DESIGNER

BA/BS or equivalent prog ming/multimedia production years of experience in use design of WWW services strea audio and video HTML, PERL GIF, JPEG. Demonstrated inte sonal, organization, communic multi-tasking skills. Send resu The Learning People at www ing.com.

WEBMASTER-TECHNIC

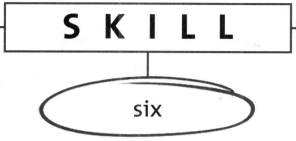

S K I L L

six

6

Adding
Scroll Bars

- ❑ Adding and using scroll bars in Java programs
- ❑ Updating scroll settings to match scrolling actions
- ❑ Coordinating multiple scroll bars
- ❑ Using the Border layout manager
- ❑ Using AdjustmentListeners

In Skill 5, we got a good introduction to the use of radio buttons, and we put radio buttons and check boxes together in our sandwich applet. In this Skill, we're going to continue our guided tour of Java by examining a new control: scroll bars. As any user of a windowed environment can tell you, scroll bars are very important controls. We'll also examine some additional Java layout techniques—layouts are an important part of Java programming, and we'll become more familiar with what Java has to offer us here. We'll also take a look at the new Java 1.1 ScrollPane class.

Adding Scroll Bars to Programs

We'll start off with a scroll bar example. There are two types of scroll bar controls—horizontal and vertical scroll bars, and we'll see both here. For example, let's create a new applet named scroller that contains both types of scroll bars, as shown in Figure 6.1. When the user moves a scroll bar, we'll report on the new horizontal or vertical position of the bars in a text field, as shown in Figure 6.2.

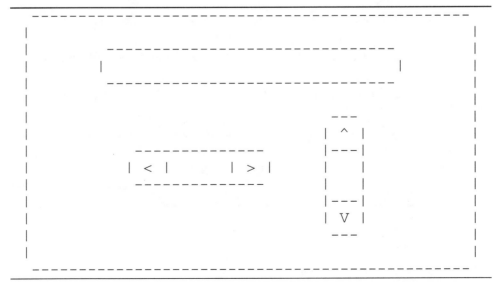

FIGURE 6.1   Our applet will contain a vertical scroll bar and a horizontal scroll bar.

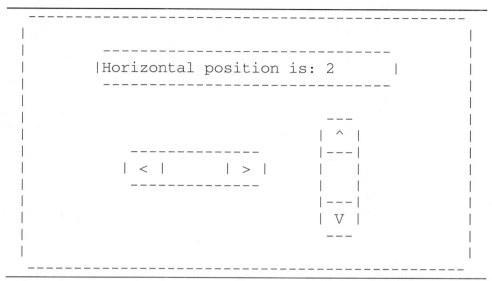

FIGURE 6.2   The text field will report the new position of the scroll bar.

Skill 6

This will be an easy example. Create a new file named scroller.java. Begin by adding the text field we'll need, text1, and the two scroll bars, scroll1 and scroll2, which are objects of the Java Scrollbar class:

```
import java.applet.Applet;
import java.awt.event.*;
import java.awt.*;

public class scroller extends Applet {

        TextField text1;
        Scrollbar scroll1, scroll2;
            .
            .
            .

    }
```

The Java Scrollbar class's methods appear in Table 6.1.

TABLE 6.1 : The Scrollbar **class's methods**

Method	Does This
Scrollbar()	Constructs a Scrollbar (vertical).
Scrollbar(int)	Constructs a Scrollbar with specified orientation: Scrollbar.HORIZONTAL or Scrollbar.VERTICAL.
Scrollbar(int, int, int, int, int)	Constructs a Scrollbar with given orientation, initial value, scroll thumb size, minimum and maximum values.
AddAdjustmentListener (AdjustmentListener)	Adds new adjustment listener to get adjustment events from this Scrollbar.
addNotify()	Adds the Scrollbar's peer.
GetBlockIncrement()	Gets block increment for Scrollbar.
GetLineIncrement()	Deprecated. Gets line-by-line increment for Scrollbar.
getMaximum()	Gets maximum setting of Scrollbar.
getMinimum()	Gets minimum setting of Scrollbar.
getOrientation()	Gets orientation of Scrollbar.
getPageIncrement()	Deprecated. Gets page-by-page increment for Scrollbar.
getUnitIncrement()	Gets unit increment for Scrollbar.
getValue()	Gets current value of Scrollbar.
getVisible()	Deprecated. Gets the visible portion of Scrollbar.
getVisibleAmount()	Gets visible amount of Scrollbar.
paramString()	Gets string parameters for Scrollbar.
processAdjustmentEvent (AdjustmentEvent)	Processes adjustment events of scroll bar, dispatching them to AdjustmentListener objects.
processEvent(AWTEvent)	Processes events of Scrollbar.
removeAdjustmentListener (AdjustmentListener)	Removes the specified adjustment listener so that it no longer gets adjustment events.
setBlockIncrement(int)	Sets block increment for Scrollbar.
setLineIncrement(int)	Deprecated. Sets line-by-line increment for Scrollbar.
setMaximum(int)	Sets maximum value for Scrollbar.

TABLE 6.1 CONTINUED: The Scrollbar class's methods

Method	Does This
setMinimum(int)	Sets minimum value for Scrollbar.
setOrientation(int)	Sets orientation for Scrollbar.
setPageIncrement(int)	Deprecated. Sets page-by-page increment for Scrollbar.
setUnitIncrement(int)	Sets unit increment for Scrollbar.
setValue(int)	Sets value of Scrollbar to given value.
setValues(int, int, int, int)	Sets values for Scrollbar.
setVisibleAmount(int)	Sets visible amount of Scrollbar.

Installing Scroll Bars

In the init() method, we will add our scroll bars and text fields to the applet. We start with the text field we'll need to report the scroll bars' positions, text1:

```
import java.applet.Applet;
import java.awt.event.*;
import java.awt.*;

public class scroller extends Applet {

→      TextField text1;
       Scrollbar scroll1, scroll2;

       public void init(){
→          text1 = new TextField(20);
→          add(text1);
                .
                .
                .

       }
}
```

Now we continue constructing our horizontal scroll bar, scroll1, by passing these parameters to its constructor (see Table 6.1): its orientation (we use the pre-defined Scrollbar class constants Scrollbar.HORIZONTAL or Scrollbar.VERTICAL—these constants are built into the Scrollbar class), the scroll bar's initial value (i.e., the location of the scroll box in the scroll bar—called the *thumb*), the size of the scroll thumb in pixels, and the scroll bar's minimum possible value (we'll use 1) and its maximum possible value (we'll use 100):

```java
import java.applet.Applet;
import java.awt.event.*;
import java.awt.*;


public class scroller extends Applet {

    TextField text1;
    Scrollbar scroll1, scroll2;

    public void init(){
        text1 = new TextField(20);
        add(text1);

        scroll1 = new Scrollbar(Scrollbar.HORIZONTAL, 1, 10, 1, 100);
        add(scroll1);
            .
            .
            .
    }
}
```

TIP Using the `setValues()` method, you can change a scroll bar's maximum and minimum possible values while your applet is running. You can also scroll the scroll bar from code with the `setValue()` method. (It's a common error to confuse `setValue()` with `setValues()`, but note that these are two different methods.)

In this way, we've created a new horizontal scroll bar whose values can range from 1 to 100, and whose initial value is 1.

In the same way, we create a similar scroll bar, `scroll2`, which has the same value range but is vertical:

```java
import java.applet.Applet;
import java.awt.event.*;
import java.awt.*;


public class scroller extends Applet {

    TextField text1;
    Scrollbar scroll1, scroll2;
```

```
      public void init(){
          text1 = new TextField(20);
          add(text1);
          scroll1 = new Scrollbar(Scrollbar.HORIZONTAL, 1, 10, 1, 100);
          add(scroll1);

➡         scroll2 = new Scrollbar(Scrollbar.VERTICAL, 1, 10, 1, 100);
➡         add(scroll2);
      }
}
```

That's it—our scroll bars appear in our applet now.

Connecting Scroll Bars to Code

The next step is to connect them to code, and you might think we do that with an
ActionListener or ItemListener interface—but in fact, we use the *AdjustmentListener*
interface this time, because scroll bars are considered *adjustable* controls. We use the
addAdjustmentListener() method of the Scrollbar class like we used the
addItemListener() and addActionListener().

```
import java.applet.Applet;
import java.awt.event.*;
import java.awt.*;

➡ public class scroller extends Applet implements AdjustmentListener {

      TextField text1;
      Scrollbar scroll1, scroll2;

      public void init(){
          text1 = new TextField(20);
          add(text1);
          scroll1 = new Scrollbar(Scrollbar.HORIZONTAL, 1, 10, 1, 100);
          add(scroll1);
➡         scroll1.addAdjustmentListener(this);
          scroll2 = new Scrollbar(Scrollbar.VERTICAL, 1, 10, 1, 100);
          add(scroll2);
➡         scroll2.addAdjustmentListener(this);
      }


}
```

We can determine which scroll bar caused the event by overriding the `adjustmentValueChanged()` method. That method takes a parameter of class `AdjustmentEvent`:

```java
import java.applet.Applet;
import java.awt.event.*;
import java.awt.*;


public class scroller extends Applet implements AdjustmentListener {

    TextField text1;
    Scrollbar scroll1, scroll2;

    public void init(){
        text1 = new TextField(20);
        add(text1);
        scroll1 = new Scrollbar(Scrollbar.HORIZONTAL, 1, 10, 1, 100);
        add(scroll1);
        scroll1.addAdjustmentListener(this);
        scroll2 = new Scrollbar(Scrollbar.VERTICAL, 1, 10, 1, 100);
        add(scroll2);
        scroll2.addAdjustmentListener(this);
    }

    public void adjustmentValueChanged(AdjustmentEvent e){
            .
            .
            .

    }
}
```

We can determine which scroll bar caused the event with the `AdjustableEvent` class's `getAdjustable()` method the following way, where we check to see if `scroll1` caused the scroll event:

```java
import java.applet.Applet;
import java.awt.event.*;
import java.awt.*;


public class scroller extends Applet implements AdjustmentListener {

    TextField text1;
    Scrollbar scroll1, scroll2;

    public void init(){
        text1 = new TextField(20);
```

```
        add(text1);
        scroll1 = new Scrollbar(Scrollbar.HORIZONTAL, 1, 10, 1, 100);
        add(scroll1);
        scroll1.addAdjustmentListener(this);
        scroll2 = new Scrollbar(Scrollbar.VERTICAL, 1, 10, 1, 100);
        add(scroll2);
        scroll2.addAdjustmentListener(this);
    }

    public void adjustmentValueChanged(AdjustmentEvent e){
➜        if(e.getAdjustable() == scroll1) {
                 .
                 .
                 .
➜        }
    }
}
```

Our first step is to set the scroll bar's thumb position to the place the user scrolled it to. That might seem funny, but it turns out that unless we update the scroll bar's thumb ourselves, it will spring back when the user releases it to the position it occupied before it was scrolled. The reason that we have to move it ourselves is because the user may have moved the thumb to some location we consider "forbidden," and Java allows us the option of not accepting the user's scroll actions in that case. To set the thumb's new location, we use the Scrollbar class's setValue() method, and to get its current value, we use the getValue() method. To place the thumb at the location the user moved it to, then, we execute this code:

```
import java.applet.Applet;
import java.awt.event.*;
import java.awt.*;


public class scroller extends Applet implements AdjustmentListener {

    TextField text1;
    Scrollbar scroll1, scroll2;

    public void init(){
        text1 = new TextField(20);
        add(text1);
        scroll1 = new Scrollbar(Scrollbar.HORIZONTAL, 1, 10, 1, 100);
        add(scroll1);
        scroll1.addAdjustmentListener(this);
        scroll2 = new Scrollbar(Scrollbar.VERTICAL, 1, 10, 1, 100);
        add(scroll2);
```

```
                    scroll2.addAdjustmentListener(this);
            }

            public void adjustmentValueChanged(AdjustmentEvent e){
                    if(e.getAdjustable() == scroll1) {
                    scroll1.setValue(scroll1.getValue());
                                  .
                                  .
                                  .

            }
        }
    }
```

Don't forget to set the scroll bar thumb to its new value when it has been scrolled, or it will appear to "jump" back on its own when the user releases it.

Because `scroll1`, the horizontal scroll bar, was scrolled, we display the new setting of that scroll bar in the text field `text1`. To do so, we convert the value of `scroll1` to an integer and display it in `text1` this way:

```
import java.applet.Applet;
import java.awt.event.*;
import java.awt.*;


public class scroller extends Applet implements AdjustmentListener {

        TextField text1;
        Scrollbar scroll1, scroll2;

        public void init(){
                text1 = new TextField(20);
                add(text1);
                scroll1 = new Scrollbar(Scrollbar.HORIZONTAL, 1, 10, 1, 100);
                add(scroll1);
                scroll1.addAdjustmentListener(this);
                scroll2 = new Scrollbar(Scrollbar.VERTICAL, 1, 10, 1, 100);
                add(scroll2);
                scroll2.addAdjustmentListener(this);
        }

        public void adjustmentValueChanged(AdjustmentEvent e){
                if(e.getAdjustable() == scroll1) {
```

```
              scroll1.setValue(scroll1.getValue());
→             text1.setText("Horizontal position: " + scroll1.getValue());
          }
        }
     }
```

TIP   **We can concatenate—that is, join—strings in Java with the + operator as in the line**
`text1.setText("horizontal position:" + String.valueOf(scroll1.getValue()));`.

And we do the same for `scroll2` as follows:

```java
import java.applet.Applet;
import java.awt.event.*;
import java.awt.*;


public class scroller extends Applet implements AdjustmentListener {

    TextField text1;
    Scrollbar scroll1, scroll2;

    public void init(){
        text1 = new TextField(20);
        add(text1);
        scroll1 = new Scrollbar(Scrollbar.HORIZONTAL, 1, 10, 1, 100);
        add(scroll1);
        scroll1.addAdjustmentListener(this);
        scroll2 = new Scrollbar(Scrollbar.VERTICAL, 1, 10, 1, 100);
        add(scroll2);
        scroll2.addAdjustmentListener(this);
    }

    public void adjustmentValueChanged(AdjustmentEvent e){
        if(e.getAdjustable() == scroll1) {

            scroll1.setValue(scroll1.getValue());
            text1.setText("Horizontal position: " + scroll1.getValue()); }
→       if(e.getAdjustable() == scroll2) {
→           scroll2.setValue(scroll2.getValue());
→           text1.setText("Vertical position: " + scroll2.getValue());
→       }
        }
    }
```

Our scroll bar applet is ready to go. As shown below, the user can move the scroll bar thumbs, and their new position will be reported in the text fields. Our scrolling applet is a success! The code for this applet appears in `scroller.java`.

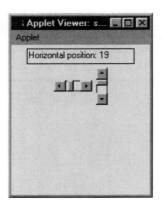

scroller.java

```java
import java.applet.Applet;
import java.awt.event.*;
import java.awt.*;


public class scroller extends Applet implements AdjustmentListener {

    TextField text1;
    Scrollbar scroll1, scroll2;

    public void init(){
        text1 = new TextField(20);
        add(text1);
        scroll1 = new Scrollbar(Scrollbar.HORIZONTAL, 1, 10, 1, 100);
        add(scroll1);
        scroll1.addAdjustmentListener(this);
        scroll2 = new Scrollbar(Scrollbar.VERTICAL, 1, 10, 1, 100);
        add(scroll2);
        scroll2.addAdjustmentListener(this);
    }

    public void adjustmentValueChanged(AdjustmentEvent e){
        if(e.getAdjustable() == scroll1) {
            scroll1.setValue(scroll1.getValue());
            text1.setText("Horizontal position: " + scroll1.getValue());
        }
```

```
if(e.getAdjustable() == scroll2) {
    scroll2.setValue(scroll2.getValue());
    text1.setText("Vertical position: " + scroll2.getValue());
}
}
}
```

There is a special Java layout manager—the BorderLayout manager—that is perfect for use with scroll bars although even many Java experts do not know about it. Let's use this layout to add power to the following applet.

Using Scroll Bars and Border Layouts

The BorderLayout manager will allow us to surround our applet with scroll bars, as shown in Figure 6.3. When the user scrolls the horizontal or vertical scroll bars, we can report the new settings of the changed scroll bar in the text field, as shown in Figure 6.4.

FIGURE 6.3   **Using the BorderLayout manger to place the scroll bars**

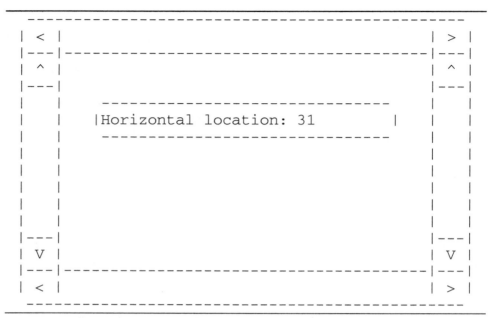

FIGURE 6.4   Reporting the new position of the scroll bar

Let's see this feature in action. Create a new file named, say, scrollborder.java now. We declare the controls we need—two horizontal scroll bars hScroll1 and hScroll2, and two vertical scroll bars, vScroll1 and vScroll2—as follows:

```java
import java.applet.Applet;
import java.awt.*;
import java.awt.event.*;

public class scrollborder extends Applet implements AdjustmentListener {

        Scrollbar hScroll1, hScroll2, vScroll1, vScroll2;
            .
            .
            .

}
```

We want to display a text field in the center of the applet. To accommodate this, we will place our two text fields in a panel (named Panel1) of a new class named textpanel:

```java
import java.applet.Applet;
```

```
import java.awt.*;
import java.awt.event.*;

public class scrollborder extends Applet implements AdjustmentListener {

        Scrollbar hScroll1, hScroll2, vScroll1, vScroll2;
→       textPanel Panel1;
                .
                .
                .
}
```

Let's create our `textpanel` class now. To do so, add this code to the end of the `scrollborder.java` file:

```
class textpanel extends Panel {

}
```

You learned how to work with panels in Skill 5. All we need here is a text field, which we might call `Text1`:

```
class textPanel extends Panel {
→       TextField Text1;

        textPanel(){
→           Text1 = new TextField(20);
→           add(Text1);
        }
}
```

Now that our new panel class is ready, we can set up our new layout. This layout will consist of four scroll bars surrounding our central panel, and as we'll see, that's easy to set up with the BorderLayout manager. First, we install that as our new layout manager in the applet's `init()` method:

```
import java.applet.Applet;
import java.awt.*;
import java.awt.event.*;

public class scrollborder extends Applet implements AdjustmentListener {

        Scrollbar hScroll1, hScroll2, vScroll1, vScroll2;
        textPanel Panel1;

        public void init(){
```

```
→            setLayout(new BorderLayout());
                 .
                 .
                 .
        }

    }
```

We can now add our controls to this new layout. When you add controls to the BorderLayout manager, you specify where the new control goes—around the edges of the applet, which are designated north, south, east, and west, or in the center, as shown in Figure 6.5.

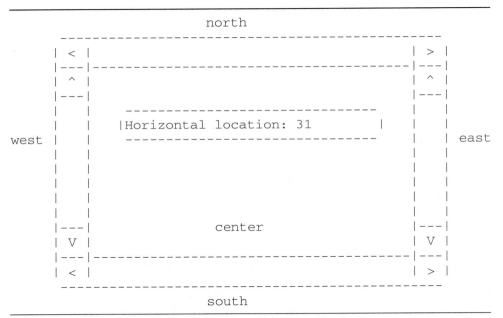

FIGURE 6.5 Locations in the layout are designated as north, south, east, west, **and** center.

For example, we create and add a scroll bar on the top of the applet—the "North" position—like this, where we also connect our applet as its AdjustmentListener:

```
import java.applet.Applet;
import java.awt.*;
import java.awt.event.*;

public class scrollborder extends Applet implements AdjustmentListener {
```

```
        Scrollbar hScroll1, hScroll2, vScroll1, vScroll2;
        textPanel Panel1;

        public void init(){
            setLayout(new BorderLayout());

→           hScroll1 = new Scrollbar(Scrollbar.HORIZONTAL, 1, 1, 1, 200);
→           add("North", hScroll1);
→           hScroll1.addAdjustmentListener(this);
                    .
                    .
                    .

        }
    }
```

We continue on, adding the other scroll bars, and the Panel1 object in the center of our applet:

```
    import java.applet.Applet;
    import java.awt.*;
    import java.awt.event.*;

    public class scrollborder extends Applet implements AdjustmentListener {

        Scrollbar hScroll1, hScroll2, vScroll1, vScroll2;
        textPanel Panel1;

        public void init(){
            setLayout(new BorderLayout());

            hScroll1 = new Scrollbar(Scrollbar.HORIZONTAL, 1, 1, 1, 200);
            add("North", hScroll1);
            hScroll1.addAdjustmentListener(this);

→           vScroll1 = new Scrollbar(Scrollbar.VERTICAL, 1, 1, 1, 200)
→           add("West", vScroll1);
→           vScroll1.addAdjustmentListener(this);

→           hScroll2 = new Scrollbar(Scrollbar.HORIZONTAL, 1, 1, 1, 200);
→           add("South", hScroll2);
→           hScroll2.addAdjustmentListener(this);

→           vScroll2 = new Scrollbar(Scrollbar.VERTICAL, 1, 1, 1, 200);

→           add("East", vScroll2);
→           vScroll2.addAdjustmentListener(this);

→           Panel1 = new textPanel();
```

Skill 6

```
→            add("Center", Panel1);
→            Panel1.Text1.SetLocation(0, 0);
        }
    }
```

Now our scroll bars are laid out correctly in our applet. All that remains is to connect them to our code in the adjustmentValueChanged() method, so add the following code to scrollborder.java now:

```java
import java.applet.Applet;
import java.awt.*;
import java.awt.event.*;

public class scrollborder extends Applet implements AdjustmentListener {

    Scrollbar hScroll1, hScroll2, vScroll1, vScroll2;
    textPanel Panel1;

    public void init(){
        setLayout(new BorderLayout());

        hScroll1 = new Scrollbar(Scrollbar.HORIZONTAL, 1, 1, 1, 200);
        add("North", hScroll1);
        hScroll1.addAdjustmentListener(this);

        vScroll1 = new Scrollbar(Scrollbar.VERTICAL, 1, 1, 1, 200);
        add("West", vScroll1);
        vScroll1.addAdjustmentListener(this);

        hScroll2 = new Scrollbar(Scrollbar.HORIZONTAL, 1, 1, 1, 200);
        add("South", hScroll2);
        hScroll2.addAdjustmentListener(this);

        vScroll2 = new Scrollbar(Scrollbar.VERTICAL, 1, 1, 1, 200);
        add("East", vScroll2);
        vScroll2.addAdjustmentListener(this);

        Panel1 = new textPanel();
        add("Center", Panel1);
        Panel1.Text1.SetLocation(0, 0);
    }

    public void adjustmentValueChanged(AdjustmentEvent e){
            .
            .
            .

    }
}
```

Note that we should keep the scroll bars coordinated (i.e., if the user scrolls one, we should update the other as well). That looks like this in code:

```java
import java.applet.Applet;
import java.awt.*;
import java.awt.event.*;

public class scrollborder extends Applet implements AdjustmentListener {

        Scrollbar hScroll1, hScroll2, vScroll1, vScroll2;
        textPanel Panel1;

        public void init(){
            setLayout(new BorderLayout());

            hScroll1 = new Scrollbar(Scrollbar.HORIZONTAL, 1, 1, 1, 200);
            add("North", hScroll1);
            hScroll1.addAdjustmentListener(this);

            vScroll1 = new Scrollbar(Scrollbar.VERTICAL, 1, 1, 1, 200);
            add("West", vScroll1);
            vScroll1.addAdjustmentListener(this);

            hScroll2 = new Scrollbar(Scrollbar.HORIZONTAL, 1, 1, 1, 200);
            add("South", hScroll2);
            hScroll2.addAdjustmentListener(this);

            vScroll2 = new Scrollbar(Scrollbar.VERTICAL, 1, 1, 1, 200);
            add("East", vScroll2);
            vScroll2.addAdjustmentListener(this);

            Panel1 = new textPanel();
            add("Center", Panel1);
            Panel1.Text1.SetLocation(0, 0);
        }

        public void adjustmentValueChanged(AdjustmentEvent e){
            if(e.getAdjustable() == hScroll1){

                hScroll1.setValue(hScroll1.getValue());
                hScroll2.setValue(hScroll1.getValue());
            }
            if(e.getAdjustable() == vScroll1){

                vScroll1.setValue(vScroll1.getValue());
                vScroll2.setValue(vScroll1.getValue());
        }

            if(e.getAdjustable() == hScroll2){
```

```
→          hScroll2.setValue(hScroll2.getValue());
→          hScroll1.setValue(hScroll2.getValue());
        }
        if(e.getAdjustable() == vScroll2){

→          vScroll2.setValue(vScroll2.getValue());
→          vScroll1.setValue(vScroll2.getValue());
        }
    }

}
```

Finally, we can report the new scroll bar positions in the appropriate text field as follows:

```
import java.applet.Applet;
import java.awt.*;
import java.awt.event.*;

public class scrollborder extends Applet implements AdjustmentListener {

    Scrollbar hScroll1, hScroll2, vScroll1, vScroll2;
    textPanel Panel1;

    public void init(){
        setLayout(new BorderLayout());
                .
                .
                .
    }

    public void adjustmentValueChanged(AdjustmentEvent e){
        if(e.getAdjustable() == hScroll1){
            hScroll1.setValue(hScroll1.getValue());
            hScroll2.setValue(hScroll1.getValue());
→           Panel1.Text1.setText("Horizontal location: " + hScroll1.getValue());
        }
        if(e.getAdjustable() == vScroll1){

            vScroll1.setValue(vScroll1.getValue());
            vScroll2.setValue(vScroll1.getValue());
→           Panel1.Text1.setText("Vertical location: " + vScroll1.getValue());
        }
        if(e.getAdjustable() == hScroll2){
            hScroll2.setValue(hScroll2.getValue());
            hScroll1.setValue(hScroll2.getValue());
→           Panel1.Text1.setText("Horizontal location: " + hScroll2.getValue());
        }
```

```
        if(e.getAdjustable() == vScroll2){
            vScroll2.setValue(vScroll2.getValue());
            vScroll1.setValue(vScroll2.getValue());
            Panel1.Text1.setText("Vertical location: " + vScroll2.getValue());
        }
    }
}
```

And that's it—our scrollborder applet is finished. Run the scrollborder applet now. As you can see, our scroll bars appear surrounding the central panel. When the user scrolls the scroll bars, the new horizontal and vertical positions appear in the text fields below. The code for this applet appears in `scrollborder.java`.

TIP   If you want to move controls around in the central panel in response to the action of the surrounding scroll bars, just use the control's `SetLocation()` method (which most Java controls have). This can give the user the impression they are scrolling the controls around inside the applet.

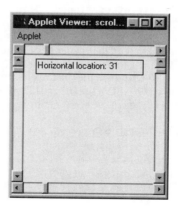

scrollborder.java

```
import java.applet.Applet;
import java.awt.*;
import java.awt.event.*;

public class scrollborder extends Applet implements AdjustmentListener {

    Scrollbar hScroll1, hScroll2, vScroll1, vScroll2;
    textPanel Panel1;
```

```java
public void init(){
    setLayout(new BorderLayout());

    hScroll1 = new Scrollbar(Scrollbar.HORIZONTAL, 1, 1, 1, 200);
    add("North", hScroll1);
    hScroll1.addAdjustmentListener(this);

    vScroll1 = new Scrollbar(Scrollbar.VERTICAL, 1, 1, 1, 200);
    add("West", vScroll1);
    vScroll1.addAdjustmentListener(this);

    hScroll2 = new Scrollbar(Scrollbar.HORIZONTAL, 1, 1, 1, 200);
    add("South", hScroll2);
    hScroll2.addAdjustmentListener(this);

    vScroll2 = new Scrollbar(Scrollbar.VERTICAL, 1, 1, 1, 200);
    add("East", vScroll2);
    vScroll2.addAdjustmentListener(this);

    Panel1 = new textPanel();
    add("Center", Panel1);
    Panel1.Text1.SetLocation(0, 0);
}

public void adjustmentValueChanged(AdjustmentEvent e){
    if(e.getAdjustable() == hScroll1){
        hScroll1.setValue(hScroll1.getValue());
        hScroll2.setValue(hScroll1.getValue());
        Panel1.Text1.setText("Horizontal location: " + hScroll1.getValue());
    }
    if(e.getAdjustable() == vScroll1){

        vScroll1.setValue(vScroll1.getValue());
        vScroll2.setValue(vScroll1.getValue());
        Panel1.Text1.setText("Vertical location: " + vScroll1.getValue());
    }
    if(e.getAdjustable() == hScroll2){
        hScroll2.setValue(hScroll2.getValue());
        hScroll1.setValue(hScroll2.getValue());
        Panel1.Text1.setText("Horizontal location: " + hScroll2.getValue());
    }
    if(e.getAdjustable() == vScroll2){
        vScroll2.setValue(vScroll2.getValue());
        vScroll1.setValue(vScroll2.getValue());
        Panel1.Text1.setText("Vertical location: " + vScroll2.getValue());
    }
}
```

```
    }

class textPanel extends Panel {
    TextField Text1;

    textPanel(){
        Text1 = new TextField(20);
        add(Text1);
    }
}
```

That's it—now we can use scroll bars with the border layout, giving our Java programs a professional air.

Working with the
ScrollPane **Class**

Java 1.1 includes a class called ScrollPane, which lets us place a control in the middle of a container object and display it. Scroll bars will appear around the edges of this container as needed. This is something like the example we just developed, except the ScrollPane class scrolls the controls we place in its pane automatically, instead of letting us handle the scrolling events ourselves. It's easy to implement, so let's see it at work now—create a new file named scrpane.java and start it off as usual:

```
import java.applet.Applet;
import java.awt.*;

public class scrpane extends Applet {

}
```

Now we add our ScrollPane object, which we might call scrollpane1:

```
import java.applet.Applet;
import java.awt.*;

public class scrpane extends Applet {

→       ScrollPane scrollpane1;

        public void init(){
```

```
→              scrollpane1 = new ScrollPane();
                    .
                    .
                    .
        }

    }
```

All we have to do is to create a new control and add it to our ScrollPane object.
We will add a new text field to the ScrollPane object as follows:

```
import java.applet.Applet;
import java.awt.*;

public class scrpane extends Applet {

    ScrollPane scrollpane1;
→   TextField text1;

    public void init(){
        scrollpane1 = new ScrollPane();
→       text1 = new TextField("Welcome to Java");
→       scrollpane1.add(text1);
                    .
                    .
                    .

    }
}
```

The Java ScrollPane class's methods appear in Table 6.2

T A B L E 6 . 2 : The ScrollPane **class's methods**

Method	Does This
ScrollPane()	Creates a new scroll pane container with a display policy of "as needed".
ScrollPane(int)	Create a new scroll pane container.
add(Component, int)	Adds given component to this scrollpane container.
addNotify()	Creates scroll pane's peer.
doLayout()	Lays out container by resizing its child to its preferred size.
getHAdjustable()	Returns the Adjustable object which represents the horizontal scrollbar.
getHScrollbarHeight()	Returns the height that would be occupied by a horizontal scroll bar.

TABLE 6.2 CONTINUED: The ScrollPane **class's methods**

Method	Does This
getScrollbarDisplayPolicy()	Returns the display policy for the scroll bars.
getScrollPosition()	Returns the current x,y position within the child which is displayed at the 0,0 location of the scrolled panel's view.
getVAdjustable()	Returns the Adjustable object which represents the vertical scroll bar.
getViewportSize()	Returns the current size of the scroll pane's view port.
getVScrollbarWidth()	Returns the width that would be occupied by a vertical scroll bar.
paramString()	Returns the parameter String of this Container.
printComponents(Graphics)	Prints the component in this scroll pane.
setLayout(LayoutManager)	Sets the layout manager for this container.
setScrollPosition(int, int)	Scrolls to the given position in the child component.
setScrollPosition(Point)	Scrolls to the given position in the child component.

All that's left is to add our ScrollPane object to our applet, and we do that like this:

```
import java.applet.Applet;
import java.awt.*;

public class scrpane extends Applet {

    ScrollPane scrollpane1;
    TextField text1;
        .
    public void init(){
        scrollpane1 = new ScrollPane();
        text1 = new TextField("Welcome to Java");
        scrollpane1.add(text1);
        add(scrollpane1);
    }

}
```

You can run the applet now, as shown below. As you can see, the ScrollPane is active, and by using the scroll bar, the user can scroll our control in the

ScrollPane. In this way, you can put controls into a ScrollPane and let the user scroll as needed. This new applet appears in scrpane.java.

scrpane.java

```
import java.applet.Applet;
import java.awt.*;

public class scrpane extends Applet {

    ScrollPane scrollpane1;
    TextField text1;

    public void init(){
        scrollpane1 = new ScrollPane();
        text1 = new TextField("Welcome to Java");
        scrollpane1.add(text1);
        add(scrollpane1);
    }

}
```

That's all there is to it—now we're using the ScrollPane class. We've come far in Skill 6, adding scrolling to our arsenal of Java techniques. That's it for scroll bars for the moment. Let's move on now to another set of powerful Java controls—choice controls and scrolling lists.

Are You Experienced?

Now you can...

- ☑ let the user display more information by using scroll bars in Java programs, allowing the user to manipulate scroll bar thumbs for program input

- ☑ use the BorderLayout manager to handle scroll bars

- ☑ use the `ScrollPane` class to scroll controls easily

- ☑ create multiple scroll bars in one Java program and keep them coordinated as the user manipulates them

- ☑ match the user's scrolling actions by updating scroll bar settings

- ☑ ignore the user's scrolling actions if the user scrolls to a region you consider "forbidden"

Skill 6

R. Jones 356-555-3398.

PROGRAMMERS
C. C. VB, Cobol, exp. Call 534-555-6543 or fax 534-555-6544.

PROGRAMMING
MRFS Inc. is looking for a Sr. Windows NT developer. Reqs. 3-5 yrs. Exp. In C under Windows, Win95 & NT, using Visual C. Excl. OO design & implementation skills a must. OLE2 & ODBC are a plus. Excl. Salary & bnfts. Resume & salary history to HR. 8779 HighTech Way. Computer City, AR

PROGRAMMERS
Contractors Wanted for short & long term assignments; Visual C, MFC Unix C/C, SQL Oracle Dev elop ers PC Help Desk Support Windows NT & NetWareTelecommunications Visual Basic, Access, HTML, CGI, Perl MMI & Co., 885-555-9933

PROGRAMMER World Wide Web Links wants your HTML & Photoshop skills. Develop great WWW sites. Local & global customers. Send samples & resume to WWWL, 2000 Apple Road, Santa Rosa, CA.

TECHNICAL WRITER. Software firm seeks writer/editor for manuals, research notes, project mgmt. Min 2 years tech. writing, DTP & programming experience. Send resume & writing samples to: Software Systems, Dallas, TX.

TECHNICAL. Software development firm looking for Tech Trainers. Ideal candidates have programming experience in Visual C, HTML & JAVA. Need quick self starter. Call (443) 555-6868 for interview.

TECHNICAL WRITER / Premier Computer Corp is seeking a combination of technical skills, knowledge and experience in the following areas: UNIX, Windows 95/NT, Visual Basic, on-line help & documentation, and the internet. Candidates must possess excellent writing skills, and be comfortable working in a quality vs. deadline driven environment. Competitive salary. Fax resume & samples to Karen Fields, Premier Computer Corp. 444 Industrial Blvd. Concord, CA. Or send to our website at www.premier.com.

WEB DESIGNER
BA/BS or equivalent programming/multimedia production. 3 years of experience in use and design of WWW services streaming audio and video HTML, PERL, CGI, GIF, JPEG. Demonstrated interpersonal, organization, communication, multi-tasking skills. Send resume to The Learning People at www.learning.com.

WEBMASTER-TECHNICAL
BSCS or equivalent. 2 years of experience in CGI, Windows 95/NT, UNIX, C, Java, Perl. Demonstrated ability to design, code, debug and test on-line services. Send resume to The Learning People at www.learning.com.

PROGRAMMER World Wide Web Links wants your HTML & Photoshop skills. Develop great WWW sites. Local & global customers. Send sam-

---

ing tools. Experienced in documentation preparation & programming languages (Access, C, FoxPro) are a plus. Financial or banking customer service support is required along with excellent verbal & written communication skills with multi levels of end-users. Send resume to KKUP Enterprises, 45 Orange Blvd. Orange, CA.

COMPUTERS Small Web Design firm seeks indiv. w/NT Webserver & Database management exp. Fax resume to 556-555-4221.

COMPUTER/ Visual C/C, Visual Basic Exp'd Systems Analysts/ Programmers for growing software dev. team in Roseburg. Computer Science or related degree preferred. Develop adv. Engineering applications for engineering firm. Fax resume to 707-555-8744.

COMPUTER Web Master for dynamic SF Internet co. Site. Dev. test, coord. train. 2 yrs prog. Exp. C C Web C. FTP. Fax resume to Best Staffing 845-555-7722.

COMPUTER PROGRAMMER
Ad agency seeks programmer w/exp. in UNIX/NT Platforms. Web Server, CGI/Perl. Programmer Position avail on a project basis with the possibility to move into F/T. Fax resume & salary req to R. Jones 334-555-8332.

COMPUTERS Programmer/Analyst Design and maintain C based SQL database applications. Required skills: Visual Basic, C SQL, ODBC. Document existing and new applications. Novell or NT exp. a plus. Fax resume & salary history to 235-555-9935.

GRAPHIC DESIGNER
Webmaster's Weekly is seeking a creative Graphic Designer to design high impact marketing collateral, including direct mail promos, CD-ROM packages, ads and WWW pages. Must be able to juggle multiple projects and learn new skills on the job very rapidly. Web design experience a big plus, technical troubleshooting also a plus. Call 435-555-1235

GRAPHICS - ART DIRECTOR - WEB-MULTIMEDIA
Leading internet development company has an outstanding opportunity for a talented, high-end Web Experienced Art Director. In addition to a great portfolio and fresh ideas, the ideal candidate has excellent communication and presentation skills. Working as a team with innovative producers and programmers, you will create dynamic, interactive web sites and application interfaces. Some programming experience required. Send samples and resume to: SuperSites, 333 Main, Seattle, WA.

MARKETING
Fast paced software and services provider looking for MARKETING COMMUNICATIONS SPECIALIST to be responsible for its webpage, seminar coordination and ad place-

---

PROGRAMMERS Multiple short term assignments available: Visual C, 3 positions SQL ServerNT Server. 2 positions JAVA & HTML, long term NetWare Various locations, Call for more info. 356-555-3398.

PROGRAMMERS

C. C, VB, Cobol, exp
Call 534-555-6543
or fax 534-555-6544.

PROGRAMMING
MRFS Inc. is looking for a Sr. Windows NT developer. Reqs. 3-5 yrs. Exp. In C under Windows, Win95 & NT, using Visual C. Excl. OO design & implementation skills a must. OLE2 & ODBC are a plus. Excl. Salary & bnfts. Resume & salary history to HR, 8779 HighTech Way, Computer City, AR.

PROGRAMMERS/ Contractors Wanted for short & long term assignments: Visual C, MFC Unix C/C, SQL Oracle Developers PC Help Desk Support Windows NT & NetWareTelecommunications Visual Basic, Access, HTML, CGI, Perl MMI & Co., 885-555-9933

PROGRAMMER World Wide Web Links wants your HTML & Photoshop skills. Develop great WWW sites. Local & global customers. Send samples & resume to WWWL, 2000 Apple Road, Santa Rosa, CA.

TECHNICAL WRITER Software firm seeks writer/editor for manuals, research notes, project mgmt. Min 2 years tech. writing, DTP & programming experience. Send resume & writing samples to Software Systems, Dallas, TX.

COMPUTER PROGRAMMER
Ad agency seeks programmer w/exp. in UNIX/NT Platforms, Web Server CGI/Perl. Programmer Position avail. on a project basis with the possibility to move into F/T. Fax resume & salary req. to R. Jones 334-555-8332.

TECHNICAL WRITER Premier Computer Corp is seeking a combination of technical skills, knowledge and experience in the following areas: UNIX, Windows 95/NT, Visual Basic, on-line help & documentation and the internet. Candidates must possess excellent writing skills, and be comfortable working in a quality vs. deadline driven environment. Competitive salary. Fax resume & samples to Karen Fields, Premier Computer Corp. 444 Industrial Blvd Concord, CA. Or send to our website at www.premier.com.

WEB DESIGNER
BA/BS or equivalent programming/multimedia production. 3 years of experience in use and design of WWW services streaming audio and video HTML, PERL, CGI, GIF, JPEG. Demonstrated interpersonal, organization, communication, multi-tasking skills. Send resume to The Learning People at www.learning.com.

WEBMASTER-TECHNICAL
BSCS or equivalent, 2 years of experience in CGI, Windows 95/NT, Unix C, Java, Perl. Demonstrated

---

COMPUTERS Small Web Design firm seeks indiv. w/NT Webserver & Database management exp. fax resume to 556-555-4221.

COMPUTER Visual C/C, Visual Basic Exp'd Systems Analysts/ Programmers for growing software dev. team in Roseburg. Computer Science or related degree preferred. Develop adv. Engineering applications for engineering firm. Fax resume to 707-555-8744.

COMPUTER Web Master for dynamic SF Internet co. Site. Dev. test, coord. train. 2 yrs prog. Exp. C C. Web C. FTP. Fax resume to Best Staffing 845-555-7722.

COMPUTERS/ QA SOFTWARE TESTERS Qualified candidates should have 2 yrs. exp. performing integration & system testing using automated testing tools. Experienced in documentation preparation & programming languages (Access, C, FoxPro) are a plus. Financial or banking customer service support is required along with excellent verbal & written communication skills with multi levels of end-users. Send resume to KKUP Enterprises, 45 Orange Blvd. Orange, CA.

COMPUTERS Programmer/Analyst Design and maintain C based SQL database applications. Required skills: Visual Basic, C SQL, ODBC. Document existing and new applications. Novell or NT exp. a plus. Fax resume & salary history to 235-555-9935.

GRAPHIC DESIGNER
Webmaster's Weekly is seeking a creative Graphic Designer to design high impact marketing collateral and including direct mail promo's, CD-ROM packages, ads and WWW pages. Must be able to juggle multiple projects and learn new skills on the job very rapidly. Web design experience a big plus, technical troubleshooting also a plus. Call 435-555-1235

GRAPHICS - ART DIRECTOR - WEB-MULTIMEDIA
Leading internet development company has an outstanding opportunity for a talented, high-end Web Experienced Art Director. In addition to a great portfolio and fresh ideas, the ideal candidate has excellent communication and presentation skills. Working as a team with innovative producers and programmers, you will create dynamic, interactive web sites and application interfaces. Some programming experience required. Send samples and resume to: SuperSites, 333 Main, Seattle, WA.

COMPUTER PROGRAMMER
Ad agency seeks programmer w/exp. in UNIX/NT Platforms, Web Server, CGI/Perl. Programmer Position avail. on a project basis with the possibility to move into F/T. Fax resume & salary req. to R. Jones 334-555-8332.

PROGRAMMERS / Established software company seeks programmers with extensive Windows NT

---

ment. Must be a self-starter, energetic, organized. Must have 2 years web experience. Programming plus. Call 985-555-9854.

PROGRAMMERS Multiple term assignments available: Visual C, 3 positions SQL ServerNT Server 2 positions JAVA & HTML, long term NetWare Various locations. Call for more info. 356-555-3398.

PROGRAMMERS

C. C, VB, Cobol, exp. Call 534-555-6543 or fax 534-555-6544.

PROGRAMMING
MRFS Inc. is looking for a Windows NT developer. Reqs. yrs. Exp. In C under Windows, Win95 & NT using Visual C. OO design & implementation a must. OLE2 & ODBC are a Excl. Salary & bnfts. Resume salary history to HR, 8779 HighTech Way, Computer City, AR

PROGRAMMERS/ Contractors Wanted for short & long term assignments. Visual C, MFCUnix C/C, Oracle Developers PC Help Support Windows NT & Net Telecommunications Visual Access, HTML, CGI, Perl MMI & 885-555-9933

PROGRAMMER World Wide Links wants your HTML & Photoshop skills. Develop great WWW Local & global customers. Send ples & resume to WWWL, Apple Road, Santa Rosa, CA.

TECHNICAL WRITER Software seeks writer/editor for manuals, research notes, project mgmt. years tech. writing, DTP & programming experience. Send resume writing samples to: Software Systems, Dallas, TX.

TECHNICAL Software development firm looking for Tech Trainers, candidates have programming experience in Visual C, HTML & JAVA. Need quick self starter. Call 555-6868 for interview.

TECHNICAL WRITER Premier Computer Corp is seeking a combination of technical skills, knowledge and experience in the following areas: UNIX, Windows 95/NT, Basic, on-line help & documentation and the internet. Candidates possess excellent writing skills be comfortable working in a quality vs. deadline driven environment. Competitive salary. Fax resume samples to Karen Fields, Premier Computer Corp. 444 Industrial Concord, CA. Or send to our website at www.premier.com.

WEB DESIGNER

BA/BS or equivalent programming/multimedia production. years of experience in use and design of WWW services streaming audio and video HTML, PERL, GIF, JPEG. Demonstrated interpersonal, organization, communication, multi-tasking skills. Send resume The Learning People at www.learning.com.

WEBMASTER-TECHNICAL

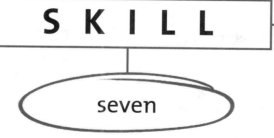

SKILL

seven

Using Choice Controls and Scrolling Lists

7

❏ Adding and using choice controls in Java programs

❏ Adding and using scrolling lists in Java programs

❏ Passing parameters to an applet

❏ Determining which selection was made in a scrolling list

In Skill 6, we took a look at handling scroll bars. In this chapter we're going to examine two other popular Java controls, Choice controls and Scrolling Lists. Both of these controls present a number of options to the user and let them select which one—or ones—they like. We'll also see how to use the built-in Java support for applet *parameters*—values we can pass our applet from the data placed in the <applet> tag in the .html page. Java adds a great deal of support for parameters for us, and using parameters we can customize our applet to work in many different Web pages without being recompiled. We'll also explore the most powerful—and most complex—of the Java layouts: the GridBagLayout. Let's start now with Java Choice controls.

Using Choice Controls

The choice control is really just the drop-down list box that Windows users are familiar with. For example, if we had a choice control, the user would see the first choice in the choice control and an arrow button next to it, as shown in Figure 7.1. When the user clicks the arrow button, the list of choices opens, as shown in Figure 7.2. When the user selects a choice (by clicking it), we can display the result in a text field, as shown in Figure 7.3.

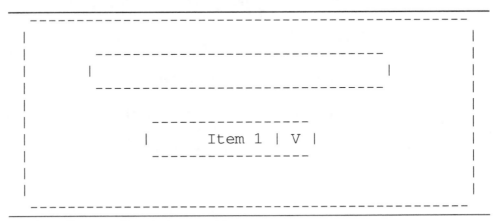

FIGURE 7.1   The choice control

```
 ------------------------------------------------
|                                                |
|      ------------------------------            |
|     |                              |           |
|      ------------------------------            |
|                                                |
|           ----------------                     |
|          |   Item 1     | V |                  |
|          |   Item 2     |----                  |
|          |   Item 3     |                       |
|          |   Item 4     |                       |
|           ----------                            |
|                                                |
 ------------------------------------------------
```

FIGURE 7.2   Clicking the arrow button displays a list of choices.

```
 ------------------------------------------------
|                                                |
|       ----------------------------------       |
|      |Item 2                           |       |
|       ----------------------------------       |
|                                                |
|              -----------------                 |
|             |   Item 2   | V |                 |
|              -----------------                 |
|                                                |
 ------------------------------------------------
```

FIGURE 7.3   We can report which choice was selected.

We will put choice controls to work in minute. As it turns out, choice controls will give us the chance to first explore another facet of Java—handling parameters. Parameters are values you can pass to an applet and use to customize the applet's behavior. For example, we might pass the items that the choice control is to display. In this way, you can use the same applet with the same choice control in many different Web pages.

Let's see how this all works. Create a new file named choices.java. Here, we'll pass the choices that the choice control is to display as parameters embedded in the applet's Web page. Create the Web page choices.htm now. This file will look just like our standard Web page—but with one addition: we'll include param tags giving the values we want to display in the choice control (i.e., the strings "Item 1" to "Item 4"), giving those strings the names selection1 to selection4:

```
<html>
<head>
<title>choices</title>
</head>
<body>
<hr>
<applet
    code=choices.class
    width=200
    height=200 >
    <param name=selection1 value="Item 1">
    <param name=selection2 value="Item 2">
    <param name=selection3 value="Item 3">
    <param name=selection4 value="Item 4">
</applet>
<hr>
</body>
</html>
```

We'll be able to read and make use of those parameters from our applet. If you want to, you can have many different sets of parameters in many different Web pages but still use the same applet. In this way, we can customize the applet's behavior easily.

Now let's write choices.java. Here we'll see how to retrieve the parameters we've set up and place them in our Choice control. We begin by adding the controls we'll need—a choice control and a text field—this way:

```
import java.applet.Applet;
import java.awt.*;
import java.awt.event.*;

public class choices extends Applet {

        Choice choice1;
        TextField text1;
            .
            .
            .

}
```

→
```
            list1 = new List(2, true);
                        .
                        .
                        .

        }
    }
```

Next, we add the list, the text field, and the selections in the List control. We'll add the items to the List control with the List class's add() method this way:

```
import java.applet.Applet;
import java.awt.*;
import java.awt.event.*;

public class scrolllist extends Applet {

    List list1;
    TextField text1;

    public void init(){
        text1 = new TextField(20);
        add(text1);
        list1 = new List(2, true);
        list1.add("Item 1");
        list1.add("Item 2");
        list1.add("Item 3");
        add(list1);
                .
                .
                .

        }
    }
```

In addition, we add an ActionListener to our applet's class and the List control:

```
import java.applet.Applet;
import java.awt.*;
import java.awt.event.*;

public class scrolllist extends Applet implements ActionListener{

    List list1;
    TextField text1;

    public void init(){
        text1 = new TextField(20);
        add(text1);
        list1 = new List(2, true);
        list1.add("Item 1");
```

Skill 7

```
            list1.add("Item 2");
            list1.add("Item 3");
            add(list1);
  ➜         list1.addActionListener(this);
        }
    }
```

Now the applet displays the scrolling list control and the text field—our next step is to make the scrolling list active with an `actionPerformed()` method:

```
import java.applet.Applet;
import java.awt.*;
import java.awt.event.*;

public class scrolllist extends Applet implements ActionListener {

    List list1;
    TextField text1;

    public void init(){
        text1 = new TextField(20);
        add(text1);
        list1 = new List(2, true);
        list1.add("Item 1");
        list1.add("Item 2");
        list1.add("Item 3");
        add(list1);
        list1.addActionListener(this);
    }

  ➜     public void actionPerformed(ActionEvent e) {
                    .
                    .
                    .
  ➜         }
    }
```

If the user has indeed made a selection, we can get the currently selected item in the scrolling list this way:

```
((List) e.getSource()).getSelectedItem()
```

and we display that selection in the text field `text1` as follows:

```
import java.applet.Applet;
import java.awt.*;
import java.awt.event.*;
```

```
public class scrolllist extends Applet implements ActionListener {

    List list1;
    TextField text1;

    public void init(){
        text1 = new TextField(20);
        add(text1);
        list1 = new List(2, true);
        list1.add("Item 1");
        list1.add("Item 2");
        list1.add("Item 3");
        add(list1);
        list1.addActionListener(this);
    }

    public void actionPerformed(ActionEvent e) {
        if(e.getSource() == list1){
            text1.setText(((List) e.getSource()).getSelectedItem());
        }
    }
}
```

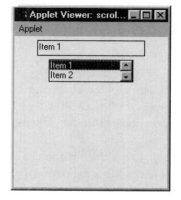

NOTE   To handle multiple selections (our list control is set up to accept multiple selections), we would use `getSelectedItems()` here instead. In this simple example, we're using just a single selection.

We're finished! Our scrolling list applet is ready to run. The user can scroll up and down our list, and when they make a selection, we report what that selection is, as shown below. The code for this applet appears in `scrolllist.java`.

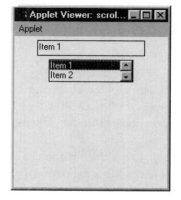

scrolllist.java

```java
import java.applet.Applet;
import java.awt.*;
import java.awt.event.*;

public class scrolllist extends Applet implements ActionListener {

    List list1;
    TextField text1;

    public void init(){
        text1 = new TextField(20);
        add(text1);
        list1 = new List(2, true);
        list1.add("Item 1");
        list1.add("Item 2");
        list1.add("Item 3");
        add(list1);
        list1.addActionListener(this);
    }

    public void actionPerformed(ActionEvent e) {
        if(e.getSource() == list1){
        text1.setText(((List) e.getSource()).getSelectedItem());
        }
    }
}
```

We will turn now to the final topic for this chapter—another powerful Java layout manager—the GridBagLayout manager.

Using the GridBagLayout Manager

In this last example of the chapter, we'll explore what is probably the most powerful native Java layout of all—the GridBagLayout. This layout manager lets us specify the position of our controls more exactly than any other layout manager we've seen.

For example, using the GridBagLayout manager, we can create an applet that provides the user with a list of employees. We can display the names of employees in buttons at the top of the applet. When the user clicks a button, we can display the corresponding employee ID number in a text area, as shown in Figure 7.6.

```
+-----------------------------------------------------------+
|  --------------------------------------------------------  |
| |        |        |        |        |        |         |  |
| | Britta |  Mark  |  Nancy |  Ted   |                     |
| |        |        |        |        |                     |
| |--------------------------------------------------------| |
| |ID: 838939                                               | |
| |                                                         | |
| |                                                         | |
| |                                                         | |
| |                                                         | |
| |                                                         | |
| |                                                         | |
| |                                                         | |
|  --------------------------------------------------------  |
+-----------------------------------------------------------+
```

FIGURE 7.6   Displaying a number in a text field at the click of a button

We'll give this new layout a try. Create a new file now named `employee.java`. We add the controls we'll need—buttons `button1` to `button4`, and a text area named `text1`:

```
import java.applet.Applet;
import java.awt.*;
import java.awt.event.*;

public class employee extends Applet {

→       Button button1, button2, button3, button4;
→       TextArea text1;
            .
            .
            .
    }
```

Now let's set up our new GridBagLayout manager to see how it works. We do that by creating a new object of the `GridBagLayout` class named `gridbag`, as follows in the `init()` method:

```
import java.applet.Applet;
import java.awt.*;
```

```
import java.awt.event.*;

public class employee extends Applet {

    Button button1, button2, button3, button4;
    TextArea text1;

    public void init(){

        GridBagLayout gridbag = new GridBagLayout();
            .
            .
            .

    }
}
```

We specify how we want our controls to be arranged under the GridBagLayout manager using an object of the Java class `GridBagConstraints`, as we'll see in the example. We use this object to arrange the controls in a GridBagLayout. In the following code, we create an object of that class and we name it `constraints`:

```
import java.applet.Applet;
import java.awt.*;
import java.awt.event.*;

public class employee extends Applet {

    Button button1, button2, button3, button4;
    TextArea text1;

    public void init(){

        GridBagLayout gridbag = new GridBagLayout();
        GridBagConstraints constraints = new GridBagConstraints();
            .
            .
            .

    }
}
```

Now we can install our new GridBagLayout in our applet:

```
import java.applet.Applet;
import java.awt.*;
import java.awt.event.*;

public class employee extends Applet {
```

```
Button button1, button2, button3, button4;
TextArea text1;

public void init(){

    GridBagLayout gridbag = new GridBagLayout();
    GridBagConstraints constraints = new GridBagConstraints();
    setLayout(gridbag);
        .
        .
        .
    }
}
```

The next step is to start specifying how we want our controls to be "constrained" in our new layout, and we'll turn to that now.

Using GridBagConstraints

GridBagLayouts work with the relative "weights" of controls in the x and y directions—for example, since all of these buttons have the same width, they each have the same x weight, as shown in Figure 7.7. If one control is twice as wide as the others, it will have double the x weight, as shown in Figure 7.8.

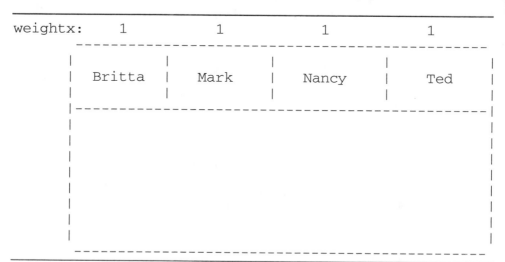

```
weightx:      1           1           1           1
          ---------------------------------------------------
         |           |           |           |           |
         |  Britta   |   Mark    |   Nancy   |   Ted     |
         |           |           |           |           |
         | ----------------------------------------------|
         |                                               |
         |                                               |
         |                                               |
         |                                               |
         |                                               |
         |                                               |
         |                                               |
          - - - - - - - - - - - - - - - - - - - - - - - - -
```

FIGURE 7.7 If each button is the same width, then each button has the same x weight.

Skill 7

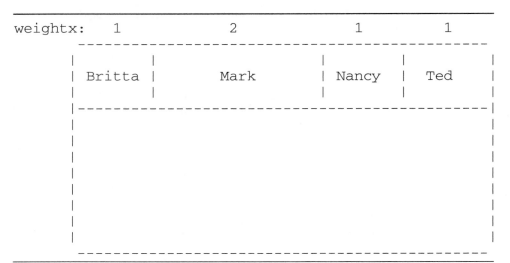

FIGURE 7.8   If one button is twice as wide as the others, it's x weight is double.

We specify x and y weights with the `weightx` and `weighty` members of the `GridBagConstraints` object we have named `constraints`. Since all our buttons have the same height, they have the same value for `weighty`, which we can just set to 1:

```
import java.applet.Applet;
import java.awt.*;
import java.awt.event.*;

public class employee extends Applet {

    Button button1, button2, button3, button4;
    TextArea text1;

    public void init(){

        GridBagLayout gridbag = new GridBagLayout();
        GridBagConstraints constraints = new GridBagConstraints();
        setLayout(gridbag);
        constraints.weighty = 1;
            .
            .
            .
    }
}
```

We can specify that the controls in our applet be stretched to fill their allotted space in the layout, and we do that by setting the fill member of our `constraints` object. We could set this data member to the constant `GridBagConstraints.HORIZONTAL` to stretch our controls horizontally, to `GridBagConstraints.VERTICAL` to stretch them vertically, or to `GridBagConstraints.BOTH` to stretch them in both dimensions to fill the space allotted for them. In our case, we'll stretch our controls in both dimensions:

```java
import java.applet.Applet;
import java.awt.*;
import java.awt.event.*;

public class employee extends Applet {

    Button button1, button2, button3, button4;
    TextArea text1;

    public void init(){

        GridBagLayout gridbag = new GridBagLayout();
        GridBagConstraints constraints = new GridBagConstraints();
        setLayout(gridbag);
        constraints.weighty = 1;
        constraints.fill = GridBagConstraints.BOTH;
             .
             .
             .
    }
}
```

TIP

In the Java naming convention, the built-in data members of a class are referred to with small letters, while constants use capital letters. Therefore, we know the fill member of a `GridBagConstraints` object is a variable, while `GridBagConstraints.VERTICAL` is a built-in constant of the class.

At this point, we're ready to add our first button to the grid bag. We do that by giving this first button an x weight of 1, and create the new button, `button1`, giving it the caption of the first name in our employee directory, "Britta," and adding an ActionListener to it:

```java
import java.applet.Applet;
import java.awt.*;
import java.awt.event.*;
```

```
→   public class employee extends Applet implements ActionListener {

        Button button1, button2, button3, button4;
        TextArea text1;

        public void init(){

            GridBagLayout gridbag = new GridBagLayout();
            GridBagConstraints constraints = new GridBagConstraints();
            setLayout(gridbag);
            constraints.weighty = 1;
            constraints.fill = GridBagConstraints.BOTH;

→           constraints.weightx = 1;
→           button1 = new Button("Britta");
→           button1.addActionListener(this);
                            .
                            .
                            .

        }
    }
```

Adding this button to the GridBagLayout is a two-step process. First, we set up the grid bag's constraints, using our `constraints` object, and then we add the control itself. That looks like this:

```
import java.applet.Applet;
import java.awt.*;
import java.awt.event.*;

public class employee extends Applet implements ActionListener {

        Button button1, button2, button3, button4;
        TextArea text1;

        public void init(){


            GridBagLayout gridbag = new GridBagLayout();
            GridBagConstraints constraints = new GridBagConstraints();
            setLayout(gridbag);
            constraints.weighty = 1;
            constraints.fill = GridBagConstraints.BOTH;

            constraints.weightx = 1;
            button1 = new Button("Britta");
→           gridbag.setConstraints(button1, constraints);
→           add(button1);
```

```
            button1.addActionListener(this);
                .
                .
                .
        }
    }
```

Then we add the remaining buttons as follows:

```
import java.applet.Applet;
import java.awt.*;
import java.awt.event.*;

public class employee extends Applet implements ActionListener {

    Button button1, button2, button3, button4;
    TextArea text1;

    public void init(){


        GridBagLayout gridbag = new GridBagLayout();
        GridBagConstraints constraints = new GridBagConstraints();
        setLayout(gridbag);
        constraints.weighty = 1;
        constraints.fill = GridBagConstraints.BOTH;

        constraints.weightx = 1;
        button1 = new Button("Britta");
        gridbag.setConstraints(button1, constraints);
        add(button1);
        button1.addActionListener(this);

        constraints.weightx = 1;
        button2 = new Button("Mark");
        gridbag.setConstraints(button2, constraints);
        add(button2);
        button2.addActionListener(this);

        constraints.weightx = 1;
        button3 = new Button("Nancy");
        gridbag.setConstraints(button3, constraints);
        add(button3);
        button3.addActionListener(this);

        constraints.weightx = 1;
        button4 = new Button("Ted");
        constraints.gridwidth = GridBagConstraints.REMAINDER;
```

Skill 7

```
→        gridbag.setConstraints(button4, constraints);
→        add(button4);
→        button4.addActionListener(this);
                    .
                    .
                    .

    }
}
```

Note in particular the following line, which we use when adding the final button to the row of buttons:

```
constraints.gridwidth = GridBagConstraints.REMAINDER;
```

This line tells the GridBagLayout that we are done with the current row of controls and that it should take the remainder of the space left for the current (and last) button in this row.

Now that the top row (all buttons) is complete, we add the next row, which is made up of the text area control. Again, we set `constraints.gridwidth` to `GridBagConstraints.REMAINDER`, this time to indicate that there is only one item in this row: the text area:

```
import java.applet.Applet;
import java.awt.*;
import java.awt.event.*;

public class employee extends Applet implements ActionListener {

    Button button1, button2, button3, button4;
    TextArea text1;

    public void init(){

        GridBagLayout gridbag = new GridBagLayout();
        GridBagConstraints constraints = new GridBagConstraints();
        setLayout(gridbag);
        constraints.weighty = 1;
        constraints.fill = GridBagConstraints.BOTH;

        constraints.weightx = 1;
        button1 = new Button("Britta");
        gridbag.setConstraints(button1, constraints);
        add(button1);
        button1.addActionListener(this);
                    .
                    .
                    .
```

```
→          text1 = new TextArea();
→          constraints.gridwidth = GridBagConstraints.REMAINDER;
→          gridbag.setConstraints(text1, constraints);
→          add(text1);
        }
    }
```

Now our GridBag layout is set up. All that remains is to display the correct employee number when the user clicks a button in our applet. As we might expect, we use an actionPerformed() method as follows:

```
public class employee extends Applet implements ActionListener {

     Button button1, button2, button3, button4;
     TextArea text1;

     public void init(){

          GridBagLayout gridbag = new GridBagLayout();
          GridBagConstraints constraints = new GridBagConstraints();
          setLayout(gridbag);
          constraints.weighty = 1;
          constraints.fill = GridBagConstraints.BOTH;

          constraints.weightx = 1;
          button1 = new Button("Britta");
          gridbag.setConstraints(button1, constraints);
          add(button1);
          button1.addActionListener(this);
                    .
                    .
                    .
          text1 = new TextArea();
          constraints.gridwidth = GridBagConstraints.REMAINDER;
          gridbag.setConstraints(text1, constraints);
          add(text1);

     }

→    public void actionPerformed(ActionEvent e){
→         if(e.getSource() == button1){
→              text1.setText("ID: 838939");
→         }
→         if(e.getSource() == button2){
→              text1.setText("ID 8533834");
→         }
→         if(e.getSource() == button3){
```

```
→                    text1.setText("ID 3583893");
→               }
→               if(e.getSource() == button4){
→                    text1.setText("ID 4893439");
→               }
         }
    }
```

Our applet is complete. As you can see below, our controls appear as we want them and in the places we want them. We've set up a GridBagLayout successfully. When you click a button, the corresponding employee number appears. Our employee directory is a success. The code for this applet appears in `employee.java`.

employee.java

```java
import java.applet.Applet;
import java.awt.*;
import java.awt.event.*;

public class employee extends Applet implements ActionListener {

    Button button1, button2, button3, button4;
    TextArea text1;

    public void init(){

        GridBagLayout gridbag = new GridBagLayout();
        GridBagConstraints constraints = new GridBagConstraints();
        setLayout(gridbag);
        constraints.weighty = 1;
```

```
                     constraints.fill = GridBagConstraints.BOTH;

                     constraints.weightx = 1;
                     button1 = new Button("Britta");
                     gridbag.setConstraints(button1, constraints);
                     add(button1);
                     button1.addActionListener(this);

                     constraints.weightx = 1;
                     button2 = new Button("Mark");
                     gridbag.setConstraints(button2, constraints);
                     add(button2);
                     button2.addActionListener(this);

                     constraints.weightx = 1;
                     button3 = new Button("Nancy");
                     gridbag.setConstraints(button3, constraints);
                     add(button3);
                     button3.addActionListener(this);

                     constraints.weightx = 1;
                     button4 = new Button("Ted");
                     constraints.gridwidth = GridBagConstraints.REMAINDER;
                     gridbag.setConstraints(button4, constraints);
                     add(button4);
                     button4.addActionListener(this);

                     text1 = new TextArea();
                     constraints.gridwidth = GridBagConstraints.REMAINDER;
                     gridbag.setConstraints(text1, constraints);
                     add(text1);

             }

        public void actionPerformed(ActionEvent e){
             if(e.getSource() == button1){
                 text1.setText("ID: 838939");
             }
             if(e.getSource() == button2){
                 text1.setText("ID 8533834");
             }
             if(e.getSource() == button3){
                 text1.setText("ID 3583893");
             }
             if(e.getSource() == button4){
                 text1.setText("ID 4893439");
             }
        }
    }
```

We've come far in this chapter, seeing how to use scrolling lists, choice controls, the GridBagLayout, applet parameters, and more. Let's turn now to the next chapter, in which we start to explore some new Java techniques—using popup windows and menus.

Are You Experienced?

Now you can...

- ☑ use choice controls in Java programs to present a drop-down list of options to the user

- ☑ use scrolling lists to present a scrollable list of options to the user

- ☑ customize applet performance by passing parameters to applets—this is very useful when you want to use one .class file to handle different inputs in different Web pages

J. Jones 356-555-3398.

PROGRAMMERS
C, C, VB, Cobol, exp. Call 534-555-6543 or fax 534-555-6544.

PROGRAMMING
MRFS Inc. is looking for a Sr. Windows NT developer. Reqs. 3-5 yrs. Exp. In C under Windows, Win95 & NT, using Visual C. Excl. OO design & implementation skills a must. OLE2 & ODBC are a plus. Salary & bnfts. Resume & salary history to HR. 8779 HighTech Way, Computer City, AR

PROGRAMMERS
Contractors Wanted for short & long term assignments; Visual C, MFC Unix C/C, SQL Oracle Dev elop ers PC Help Desk Support Windows NT & NetWare Telecommunications Visual Basic, Access, HTMT, CGI, Perl MMI & Co., 885-555-9933

PROGRAMMER World Wide Web Links wants your HTML & Photoshop skills. Develop great WWW sites. Local & global customers. Send samples & resume to WWWL, 2000 Apple Road, Santa Rosa, CA.

TECHNICAL WRITER Software firm seeks writer/editor for manuals, research notes, project mgmt. Min 2 years tech. writing, DTP & programming experience. Send resume & writing samples to: Software Systems. Dallas, TX.

TECHNICAL Software development firm looking for Tech Trainers. Ideal candidates have programming experience in Visual C, HTML & JAVA. Need quick self starter. Call (443) 555-6868 for interview.

TECHNICAL WRITER/ Premier Computer Corp is seeking a combination of technical skills, knowledge and experience in the following areas: UNIX, Windows 95/NT, Visual Basic, on-line help & documentation and the Internet. Candidates must possess excellent writing skills, and be comfortable working in a quality vs. deadline driven environment. Competitive salary. Fax resume & samples to Karen Fields, Premier Computer Corp. 444 Industrial Blvd. Concord, CA. Or send to our website at www.premier.com.

WEB DESIGNER
BA/BS or equivalent programming/multimedia production. 3 years of experience in use and design of WWW services streaming audio and video HTML, PERL, CGI, GIF, JPEG. Demonstrated interpersonal, organization, communication, multi-tasking skills. Send resume to The Learning People at www.learning.com.

WEBMASTER-TECHNICAL
BSCS or equivalent, 2 years of experience in CGI, Windows 95/NT, UNIX, C, Java, Perl. Demonstrated ability to design, code, debug and test on-line services. Send resume to The Learning People at www.learning.com.

PROGRAMMER World Wide Web Links wants your HTML & Photoshop skills. Develop great WWW sites.

ing tools. Experienced in documentation preparation & programming languages (Access, C, FoxPro) are a plus. Financial or banking customer service support is required along with excellent verbal & written communication skills with multi levels of end-users. Send resume to KKUP Enterprises. 45 Orange Blvd. Orange, CA.

COMPUTERS Small Web Design firm seeks indiv. w/NT. Webserver & Database management exp. Fax resume to 556-555-4221.

COMPUTER/ Visual C/C. Visual Basic Exp'd Systems Analysts/Programmers for growing software dev. team in Roseburg. Computer Science or related degree preferred. Develop adv. Engineering applications for engineering firm. Fax resume to 707-555-8744.

COMPUTER Web Master for dynamic SF Internet co. Site, Dev, test, coord, train. 2 yrs prog. Exp. C C. Web C, FTP, fax resume to Best Staffing 845-555-7722.

COMPUTERS Programmer/Analyst Design and maintain C based SQL database applications. Required skills: Visual Basic, C, SQL, ODBC. Document existing and new applications. Novell or NT exp. a plus. Fax resume & salary history to 235-555-9935.

GRAPHIC DESIGNER
Webmaster's Weekly is seeking a creative Graphic Designer to design high impact marketing collateral, including direct mail promos. CD-ROM packages, ads and WWW pages. Must be able to juggle multiple projects and learn new skills on the job very rapidly. Web design experience a big plus. technical troubleshooting also a plus. Call 435-555-1235.

GRAPHICS - ART DIRECTOR - WEB-MULTIMEDIA
Leading internet development company has an outstanding opportunity for a talented, high-end Web Experienced Art Director. In addition to a great portfolio and fresh ideas, the ideal candidate has excellent communication and presentation skills. Working as a team with innovative producers and programmers, you will create dynamic, interactive web sites and application interfaces. Some programming experience required. Send samples and resume to: SuperSites, 333 Main, Seattle, WA.

MARKETING
Fast paced software and services provider looking for MARKETING COMMUNICATIONS SPECIALIST to be responsible for its webpage.

PROGRAMMERS Multiple short term assignments available. Visual C, 3 positions SQL ServerNT Server. 2 positions JAVA & HTML long term NetWare Various locations. Call for more info. 356-555-3398.

PROGRAMMERS
C, C, VB, Cobol, exp.
Call 534-555-6543
or fax 534-555-6544.

PROGRAMMING
MRFS Inc. is looking for a Sr. Windows NT developer. Reqs. 3-5 yrs. Exp. In C under Windows, Win95 & NT, using Visual C. Excl. OO design & implementation skills a must. OLE2 & ODBC are a plus. Resume & salary history to HR. 8779 HighTech Way, Computer City, AR

PROGRAMMERS/ Contractors Wanted for short & long term assignments Visual C MFC Unix C/C, SQL Oracle Developers PC Help Desk Support Windows NT & NetWare Telecommunications Visual Basic, Access, HTMT, CGI, Perl MMI & Co., 885-555-9933

PROGRAMMER World Wide Web Links wants your HTML & Photoshop skills. Develop great WWW sites. Local & global customers. Send samples & resume to WWWL, 2000 Apple Road, Santa Rosa, CA.

TECHNICAL WRITER Software firm seeks writer/editor for manuals, research notes, project mgmt. Min 2 years tech. writing, DTP & programming experience. Send resume & writing samples to: Software Systems, Dallas, TX.

COMPUTER PROGRAMMER
Ad agency seeks programmer w/exp. in UNIX/NT Platforms, Web Server, CGI/Perl. Programmer Position avail. on a project basis with the possibility to move into F/T, Fax resume & salary req. to R. Jones 334-555-8332.

TECHNICAL WRITER Premier Computer Corp is seeking a combination of technical skills, knowledge and experience in the following areas: UNIX, Windows 95/NT, Visual Basic, on-line help & documentation, and the internet. Candidates must possess excellent writing skills, and be comfortable working in a quality vs. deadline driven environment. Competitive salary. Fax resume & samples to Karen Fields, Premier Computer Corp., 444 Industrial Blvd. Concord, CA. Or send to our website at www.premier.com.

WEB DESIGNER
BA/BS or equivalent programming/multimedia production 3 years of experience in use and design of WWW services streaming audio and video HTML, PERL, CGI, GIF, JPEG. Demonstrated interpersonal, organization, communication, multi-tasking skills. Send resume to The Learning People at www.learning.com.

WEBMASTER-TECHNICAL
BSCS or equivalent, 2 years of experience in CGI, Windows 95/NT,

COMPUTERS Small Web Design firm seeks indiv. w/NT. Webserver & Database management exp. Fax resume to 556-555-4221.

COMPUTER Visual C/C. Visual Basic Exp'd Systems Analysts/Programmers for growing software dev. team in Roseburg. Computer Science or related degree preferred. Develop adv. Engineering applications for engineering firm. Fax resume to 707-555-8744.

COMPUTER Web Master for dynamic SF Internet co. Site. Dev, test, coord, train. 2 yrs prog. Exp. C C, Web C, FTP, fax resume to Best Staffing 845-555-7722.

COMPUTERS/ QA SOFTWARE TESTERS Qualified candidates should have 2 yrs exp. performing integration & system testing using automated testing tools. Experienced in documentation preparation & programming languages (Access, C, FoxPro) are a plus. Financial or banking customer service support is required along with excellent verbal & written communication skills with multi levels of end-users. Send resume to KKUP Enterprises. 45 Orange Blvd. Orange, CA.

COMPUTERS Programmer/Analyst Design and maintain C based SQL database applications. Required skills: Visual Basic, C, SQL, ODBC. Document existing and new applications. Novell or NT exp. a plus. Fax resume & salary history to 235-555-9935.

GRAPHIC DESIGNER
Webmaster's Weekly is seeking a creative Graphic Designer to design high impact marketing collater al, including direct mail promo's. CD-ROM packages, ads and WWW pages. Must be able to juggle multiple projects and learn new skills on the job very rapidly. Web design experience a big plus, technical troubleshooting also a plus. Call 435-555-1235.

GRAPHICS - ART DIRECTOR - WEB-MULTIMEDIA
Leading internet development company has an outstanding opportunity for a talented, high-end Web Experienced Art Director. In addition to a great portfolio and fresh ideas, the ideal candidate has excellent communication and presentation skills. Working as a team with innovative producers and programmers, you will create dynamic, interactive web sites and application interfaces. Some programming experience required. Send samples and resume to: SuperSites, 333 Main, Seattle, WA.

COMPUTER PROGRAMMER
Ad agency seeks programmer w/exp. in UNIX/NT Platforms, Web Server, CGI/Perl. Programmer Position avail. on a project basis with the possibility to move into F/T, Fax resume & salary req. to R. Jones 334-555-8332.

PROGRAMMERS / Established software company seeks program-

ment. Must be a self-starter, energetic, organized. Must have 2 web experience. Programming plus. Call 985-555-9854

PROGRAMMERS Multiple term assignments available: C, 3 positions SQL ServerNT S 2 positions JAVA & HTML long NetWare Various locations. G more info. 356-555-3398.

PROGRAMMERS
C, C, VB, Cobol, exp. Call 534 6543 or fax 534-555-6544.

PROGRAMMING
MRFS Inc. is looking for a Windows NT developer. Req yrs. Exp. In C under Wind Win95 & NT, using Visual C OO design & implementation a must. OLE2 & ODBC are a Excl. Salary & bnfts. Resum salary history to HR. 8779 Hig Way, Computer City, AR

PROGRAMMERS Contr. Wanted for short & long term a ments: Visual C, MFCUnix C/C Oracle Developers PC Help Support Windows NT & Net Telecommunications Visual Access, HTMT, CGI, Perl MMI 885-555-9933

PROGRAMMER World Wide Links wants your HTML & Phot skills. Develop great WWW Local & global customers. Send ples & resume to WWWL, Apple Road, Santa Rosa, CA.

TECHNICAL WRITER Software seeks writer/editor for mai research notes, project mgmt. years tech. writing, DTP & pro ming experience. Send resu writing samples to: Sof Systems, Dallas, TX.

TECHNICAL Software develo firm looking for Tech Trainers, candidates have programming rience in Visual C, HTML & Need quick self starter. Call 555-6868 for interview.

TECHNICAL WRITER Pr Computer Corp is seeking a c nation of technical skills, know and experience in the foll areas: UNIX, Windows 95/NT, Basic, on-line help & documen and the internet. Candidates possess excellent writing skill be comfortable working in a c vs. deadline driven environ Competitive salary. Fax resu samples to Karen Fields. P Computer Corp., 444 Industria Concord, CA. Or send to our w at www.premier.com.

WEB DESIGNER
BA/BS or equivalent pro ming/multimedia productio years of experience in use design of WWW services stre audio and video HTML, PERL GIF, JPEG. Demonstrated int sonal, organization, commun multi-tasking skills. Send resu The Learning People at www ing.com.

WEBMASTER-TECHNI

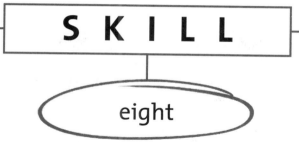

SKILL

eight

8

Creating Windows
and Menus

- ❑ Working with popup windows
- ❑ Using Java menus
- ❑ Creating and using popup menus
- ❑ Adding menu items to menus
- ❑ Showing and hiding windows
- ❑ Determining which menu items the user selected

In Skill 7, we took a look at Choice controls and Scrolling Lists. Here, we'll continue our exploration by taking a look at the process of creating windows and menus in Java. These are all very powerful techniques—they enable us to add new windows entirely separate from our applet and to add menus to such windows. In this Skill, we'll also explore Java 1.1 popup menus.

Handling Java Windows

Let's start by learning how to show a new window on the screen. For example, we can create an applet like the one shown in Figure 8.1, with two buttons, Show Window and Hide Window. When the user clicks the Show Window button, we can display a new (free-floating) window with a message in it, as shown in Figure 8.2.

When the user clicks the "Hide window" button, we can hide the window again. Let's put this applet together now. Create a new file named windows.java and add the applet's main class now:

```
import java.applet.Applet;
import java.awt.*;
import java.awt.event.*;

public class windows extends Applet {

}
```

FIGURE 8.1   An applet with two buttons

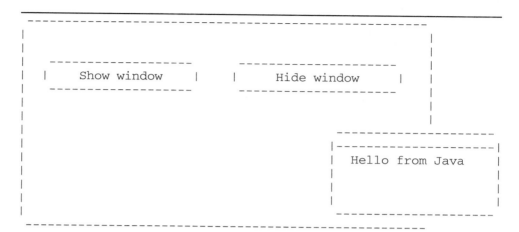

FIGURE 8.2   Clicking the Show Window button displays a window with a message in it.

The next step is to declare a window object so we can work with it, showing it to the user and hiding it again when required. We'll call this new window object window1. This object will be based on the Java Frame class, which creates a frame window on the screen.

 NOTE   Frame windows are surrounded by a frame, which often may be resized.

Next we'll derive our own class, named demoframe, from the Frame class. In this case, the declaration of our window object looks like this:

```java
import java.applet.Applet;
import java.awt.*;
import java.awt.event.*;

public class windows extends Applet {

        demoframe window1;
              .
              .
              .
    }
```

Now that we've declared our `window1` object as an object of the new `demoframe` class, let's write the Java code for this class. We add the following code to the end of the `windows.java` file now, where we declare the new `demoframe` class:

```
import java.applet.Applet;
import java.awt.*;
import java.awt.event.*;

public class windows extends Applet {

     demoframe window1;

}

class demoframe extends Frame {

}
```

The Java `Frame` class's methods appear in Table 8.1.

T A B L E 8 . 1 : The Java `Frame` class's methods

Method	Does This
Frame()	Constructs a Frame (starts as invisible).
Frame(String)	Constructs Frame with given title.
addNotify()	Creates Frame's peer.
dispose()	Disposes of the object.
getCursorType()	Gets cursor type. Deprecated.
getIconImage()	Gets icon for Frame.
getMenuBar()	Gets menu bar for Frame.
getTitle()	Gets title of Frame.
isResizable()	Gets true if user can resize Frame.
paramString()	Gets parameter string of object.
processEvent(AWTEvent)	Processes events on this frame.
processWindowEvent(WindowEvent)	Processes window events by dispatching them to WindowListener objects.
remove(MenuComponent)	Removes given menu bar from object
removeWindowListener(WindowListener)	Removes given window listener.
setCursor(int)	Sets cursor to a given cursor. Deprecated.

```
        MenuBar Menubar1;
→       MenuItem menuitem1, menuitem2, menuitem3;

        TextField text1;

        MenuFrame(String title){
              super(title);
              text1 = new TextField("");
              setLayout(new GridLayout(1, 1));
              add(text1);
              Menubar1 = new MenuBar();

              Menu1 = new Menu("File");
                         .
                         .
                         .
        }
  }
```

The Java `MenuItem` class's methods appear in Table 8.3.

TABLE 8.3: The Java `MenuItem` class's methods

Method	Does This
MenuItem()	Constructs a new MenuItem with an empty label and no keyboard shortcut.
MenuItem(String)	Constructs a new MenuItem with the given label and no keyboard shortcut.
MenuItem(String, MenuShortcut)	Creates a MenuItem with an associated keyboard shortcut.
addActionListener(ActionListener)	Adds the given action listener to receive action events from this menu item.
addNotify()	Creates the menu item's peer.
deleteShortcut()	Deletes any MenuShortcut associated with this MenuItem.
disable()	Deprecated. Replaced by setEnabled(boolean).
disableEvents(long)	Disables the events defined by the given event mask parameter from being delivered to this menu item.
enable()	Deprecated. Replaced by setEnabled(boolean).
enable(boolean)	Deprecated. Replaced by setEnabled(boolean).
enableEvents(long)	Enables the events defined by the given event mask parameter to be delivered to this menu item.

Skill 8

TABLE 8.3 CONTINUED: The Java `MenuItem` class's methods

Method	Does This
getActionCommand()	Returns the command name of the action event fired by this menu item.
getLabel()	Gets the label for this menu item.
getShortcut()	Returns the MenuShortcut associated with this MenuItem, or null if none has been given.
isEnabled()	Checks whether the menu item is enabled.
paramString()	Returns the String parameter of the menu item.
processActionEvent(ActionEvent)	Processes action events occurring on this menu item by dispatching them to any registered ActionListener objects.
processEvent(AWTEvent)	Processes events on this menu item.
removeActionListener(ActionListener)	Removes the given action listener so it no longer receives action events from this menu item.
setActionCommand(String)	Sets the command name of the action event fired by this menu item.
setEnabled(boolean)	Sets whether or not this menu item can be chosen.
setLabel(String)	Sets the label to be the given label.
setShortcut(MenuShortcut)	Sets this MenuItem's MenuShortcut.

We'll begin with our first menu item: "Hello." We create that item and add it to the menu object this way:

```
class MenuFrame extends Frame {

     Menu Menu1;
     MenuBar Menubar1;
➜    MenuItem menuitem1;

     TextField text1;

     MenuFrame(String title){
         super(title);
         text1 = new TextField("");
         setLayout(new GridLayout(1, 1));
         add(text1);
         Menubar1 = new MenuBar();

         Menu1 = new Menu("File");
```

```
→      menuitem1 = new MenuItem("Hello");
→      Menu1.add(menuitem1);
                        .
                        .
                        .
```

We want to be notified when the user clicks Hello, so we install an ActionListener now:

```
→  class MenuFrame extends Frame implements ActionListener {

        Menu Menu1;
        MenuBar Menubar1;
        MenuItem menuitem1, menuitem2, menuitem3;

        TextField text1;

        MenuFrame(String title){
            super(title);
            text1 = new TextField("");
            setLayout(new GridLayout(1, 1));
            add(text1);
            Menubar1 = new MenuBar();

            Menu1 = new Menu("File");

            menuitem1 = new MenuItem("Hello");
            Menu1.add(menuitem1);
→           menuitem1.addActionListener(this);
                        .
                        .
                        .
```

Now we've installed our first menu item. In the same way, we install the two remaining items:

```
    class MenuFrame extends Frame implements ActionListener {

        Menu Menu1;
        MenuBar Menubar1;
→       MenuItem menuitem1, menuitem2, menuitem3;

        TextField text1;

        MenuFrame(String title){
            super(title);
            text1 = new TextField("");
            setLayout(new GridLayout(1, 1));
```

Skill 8

```
        add(text1);
        Menubar1 = new MenuBar();

        Menu1 = new Menu("File");

        menuitem1 = new MenuItem("Hello");
        Menu1.add(menuitem1);
        menuitem1.addActionListener(this);

➜       menuitem2 = new MenuItem("from");
➜       Menu1.add(menuitem2);
➜       menuitem2.addActionListener(this);

➜       menuitem3 = new MenuItem("Java");
➜       Menu1.add(menuitem3);
➜       menuitem3.addActionListener(this);
                    .
                    .
                    .
    }
}
```

Now we've created our File menu. The next step is to add this menu to our menubar, which we do with the add() method this way:

```
class MenuFrame extends Frame implements ActionListener {

    Menu Menu1;
    MenuBar Menubar1;
    MenuItem menuitem1, menuitem2, menuitem3;

    TextField text1;

    MenuFrame(String title){
        super(title);
        text1 = new TextField("");
        setLayout(new GridLayout(1, 1));
        add(text1);
        Menubar1 = new MenuBar();

        Menu1 = new Menu("File");

        menuitem1 = new MenuItem("Hello");
        Menu1.add(menuitem1);
        menuitem1.addActionListener(this);

        menuitem2 = new MenuItem("from");
        Menu1.add(menuitem2);
```

```
            menuitem2.addActionListener(this);

            menuitem3 = new MenuItem("Java");
            Menu1.add(menuitem3);
            menuitem3.addActionListener(this);

➔           Menubar1.add(Menu1);
                    .
                    .
                    .
        }

    }
```

Now we add the menubar to our frame window using the **setMenubar()**
method:

```
class MenuFrame extends Frame implements ActionListener {

    Menu Menu1;
    MenuBar Menubar1;
    MenuItem menuitem1, menuitem2, menuitem3;

    TextField text1;

    MenuFrame(String title){
        super(title);
        text1 = new TextField("");
        setLayout(new GridLayout(1, 1));
        add(text1);
        Menubar1 = new MenuBar();

        Menu1 = new Menu("File");

        menuitem1 = new MenuItem("Hello");
        Menu1.add(menuitem1);
        menuitem1.addActionListener(this);

        menuitem2 = new MenuItem("from");
        Menu1.add(menuitem2);
        menuitem2.addActionListener(this);

        menuitem3 = new MenuItem("Java");
        Menu1.add(menuitem3);
        menuitem3.addActionListener(this);

        Menubar1.add(Menu1);
```

```
➜                    setMenuBar(Menubar1);
              }

      }
```

Now our menu system is set up, except for one thing—it doesn't do anything when clicked. To fix that, we add an `actionPerformed()` method now to handle menu item clicks:

```
class MenuFrame extends Frame implements ActionListener {

      Menu Menu1;
      MenuBar Menubar1;
      MenuItem menuitem1, menuitem2, menuitem3;

      TextField text1;

      MenuFrame(String title){
          super(title);
          text1 = new TextField("");
          setLayout(new GridLayout(1, 1));
          add(text1);
          Menubar1 = new MenuBar();

          Menu1 = new Menu("File");

          menuitem1 = new MenuItem("Hello");
          Menu1.add(menuitem1);
          menuitem1.addActionListener(this);

          menuitem2 = new MenuItem("from");
          Menu1.add(menuitem2);
          menuitem2.addActionListener(this);

          menuitem3 = new MenuItem("Java");
          Menu1.add(menuitem3);
          menuitem3.addActionListener(this);

          Menubar1.add(Menu1);

          setMenuBar(Menubar1);
      }

➜     public void actionPerformed(ActionEvent event){
                        .
                        .
                        .
➜         }
      }
```

We can determine which menu item caused the Java event—`menuitem1`, `menuitem2`, or `menuitem3`—using `getSource()` in the `actionPerformed()` method this way:

```java
class MenuFrame extends Frame implements ActionListener {

    Menu Menu1;
    MenuBar Menubar1;
    MenuItem menuitem1, menuitem2, menuitem3;

    TextField text1;

    MenuFrame(String title){
        super(title);
        text1 = new TextField("");
        setLayout(new GridLayout(1, 1));
        add(text1);
        Menubar1 = new MenuBar();

        Menu1 = new Menu("File");

        menuitem1 = new MenuItem("Hello");
        Menu1.add(menuitem1);
        menuitem1.addActionListener(this);

        menuitem2 = new MenuItem("from");
        Menu1.add(menuitem2);
        menuitem2.addActionListener(this);

        menuitem3 = new MenuItem("Java");
        Menu1.add(menuitem3);
        menuitem3.addActionListener(this);

        Menubar1.add(Menu1);

        setMenuBar(Menubar1);
    }

    public void actionPerformed(ActionEvent event){
        if(event.getSource() == menuitem1){
            .
            .
            .
        }
        if(event.getSource() == menuitem2){
            .
            .
```

Skill 8

```
      →                }
      →                if(event.getSource() == menuitem3){
                              .
                              .
                              .
      →                }
                }
        }
```

If the first menu item caused the click event, we want to place "Hello" in the window's text field, "from" for the second menu item, and "Java" for the third menu item. We install those items in our code now:

```
class MenuFrame extends Frame implements ActionListener {

    Menu Menu1;
    MenuBar Menubar1;
    MenuItem menuitem1, menuitem2, menuitem3;

    TextField text1;

    MenuFrame(String title){
        super(title);
        text1 = new TextField("");
        setLayout(new GridLayout(1, 1));
        add(text1);
        Menubar1 = new MenuBar();

        Menu1 = new Menu("File");

        menuitem1 = new MenuItem("Hello");
        Menu1.add(menuitem1);
        menuitem1.addActionListener(this);
                  .
                  .
                  .
        Menubar1.add(Menu1);

        setMenuBar(Menubar1);
    }

    public void actionPerformed(ActionEvent event){
        if(event.getSource() == menuitem1){
            text1.setText("Hello");
        }
        if(event.getSource() == menuitem2){
            text1.setText("from");
```

```
            }
            if(event.getSource() == menuitem3){
                text1.setText("Java");
            }
        }
    }
```

And now MenuFrame class is complete. Now we have a frame window with our menu set up in it; all that remains is to display that frame window when the user clicks the Show Window button. We start that process by adding the Show Window and Hide Window buttons in our main applet's class:

```
import java.applet.Applet;
import java.awt.*;
import java.awt.event.*;

public class menudemo extends Applet {

    Button button1, button2;
    MenuFrame menuWindow;

    public void init(){

        button1 = new Button("Show window");
        add(button1);

        button2 = new Button("Hide window");
        add(button2);

    }
}
```

Next, we set up the ActionListener to handle clicks from those buttons:

```
import java.applet.Applet;
import java.awt.*;
import java.awt.event.*;

public class menudemo extends Applet implements ActionListener{

    Button button1, button2;
    MenuFrame menuWindow;

    public void init(){

        button1 = new Button("Show window");
        add(button1);
        button1.addActionListener(this);
```

Skill 8

```
                     button2 = new Button("Hide window");
                     add(button2);
→                    button1.addActionListener(this);

         }
```

Then we create and resize the frame window that holds our menu like this:

```
import java.applet.Applet;
import java.awt.*;
import java.awt.event.*;

public class menudemo extends Applet implements ActionListener {

      Button button1, button2;
      MenuFrame menuWindow;

      public void init(){

            button1 = new Button("Show window");
            add(button1);
            button1.addActionListener(this);
            button2 = new Button("Hide window");
            add(button2);
            button1.addActionListener(this);

→           menuWindow = new MenuFrame("Menu Demo");
→           menuWindow.resize(100, 100);
      }
}
```

Next, we add our actionPerformed() method and check to see which button caused the click event:

```
import java.applet.Applet;
import java.awt.*;
import java.awt.event.*;

public class menudemo extends Applet implements ActionListener {

      Button button1, button2;
      MenuFrame menuWindow;

      public void init(){

            button1 = new Button("Show window");
            add(button1);
            button1.addActionListener(this);
```

```
            button2 = new Button("Hide window");
            add(button2);
            button1.addActionListener(this);

            menuWindow = new MenuFrame("Menu Demo");
            menuWindow.resize(100, 100);
        }

→     public void actionPerformed(ActionEvent event){
→         if(event.getSource() == button1){
                  .
                  .
                  .
→         }
→         if(event.getSource() == button2){
                  .
                  .
                  .
→         }
        }
    }
```

Finally, we place the menu window on the screen when required and hide it when the user wants to dismiss it:

```
import java.applet.Applet;
import java.awt.*;
import java.awt.event.*;

public class menudemo extends Applet implements ActionListener {

    Button button1, button2;
    MenuFrame menuWindow;

    public void init(){

        button1 = new Button("Show window");
        add(button1);
        button1.addActionListener(this);
        button2 = new Button("Hide window");
        add(button2);
        button1.addActionListener(this);

        menuWindow = new MenuFrame("Menu Demo");
        menuWindow.resize(100, 100);
    }

    public void actionPerformed(ActionEvent event){
```

Skill 8

```
            if(event.getSource() == button1){
→               menuWindow.show();
            }
            if(event.getSource() == button2){
→               menuWindow.hide();
            }
        }
    }
```

And that's it—run the menudemo applet now. Click the Show window button, displaying our menu frame, and open the File menu, as shown below.

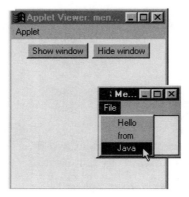

Now click a menu item, such as Java, and you'll see that item appear in the frame window, as shown below. The listing for this applet appears in menudemo.java.

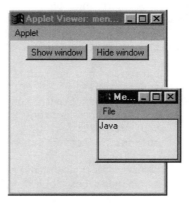

menudemo.java

```java
import java.applet.Applet;
import java.awt.*;
import java.awt.event.*;

public class menudemo extends Applet implements ActionListener {

    Button button1, button2;
    MenuFrame menuWindow;

    public void init(){

        button1 = new Button("Show window");
        add(button1);
        button1.addActionListener(this);
        button2 = new Button("Hide window");
        add(button2);
        button1.addActionListener(this);

        menuWindow = new MenuFrame("Menu Demo");
        menuWindow.resize(100, 100);
    }

    public void actionPerformed(ActionEvent event){
        if(event.getSource() == button1){
            menuWindow.show();
        }
        if(event.getSource() == button2){
            menuWindow.hide();
        }
    }
}

class MenuFrame extends Frame implements ActionListener {

    Menu Menu1;
    MenuBar Menubar1;
    MenuItem menuitem1, menuitem2, menuitem3;

    TextField text1;

    MenuFrame(String title){
        super(title);
        text1 = new TextField("");
        setLayout(new GridLayout(1, 1));
        add(text1);
```

```
            Menubar1 = new MenuBar();

            Menu1 = new Menu("File");

            menuitem1 = new MenuItem("Hello");
            Menu1.add(menuitem1);
            menuitem1.addActionListener(this);

            menuitem2 = new MenuItem("from");
            Menu1.add(menuitem2);
            menuitem2.addActionListener(this);

            menuitem3 = new MenuItem("Java");
            Menu1.add(menuitem3);
            menuitem3.addActionListener(this);

            Menubar1.add(Menu1);

            setMenuBar(Menubar1);
        }

    public void actionPerformed(ActionEvent event){
        if(event.getSource() == menuitem1){
            text1.setText("Hello");
        }
        if(event.getSource() == menuitem2){
            text1.setText("from");
        }
        if(event.getSource() == menuitem3){
            text1.setText("Java");
        }
    }
}
```

And we've completed work on our menudemo applet—now we've got menus working in Java, and we can determine which menu selection the user made. Let's continue on now by exploring more of the power menus can give us.

Building Full Menus

We'll take a look at what more the Java menu system has to offer us. For example, we might add more menu items to an applet, this way—notice that we also use menu separators to separate menu items into groups, as shown in Figure 8.5.

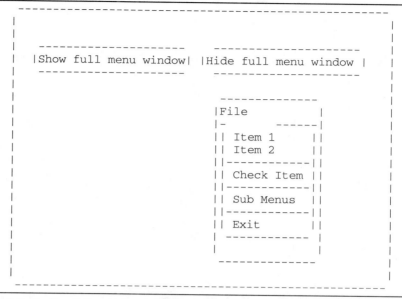

FIGURE 8.5   Using menu separators to separate menu items into groups

Here Item 1 is a normal menu item —when we click it, it will display "Item 1" in the frame window. Item 2 will also display its name—"Item 2"—but then will disable itself so that it can't be selected again. In addition, if the user selects the Sub Menus item, a submenu appears, as shown in Figure 8.6. If the user selects the item labeled Check Item, a check mark will appear in front of that item, as shown in Figure 8.7.

Let's start this applet now. To do so, create a file named `fullmenu.java` and add our usual starting code:

```
import java.applet.Applet;
import java.awt.*;
import java.awt.event.*;

public class fullmenu extends Applet {

}
```

Skill 8

```
----------------------------------------------------
|                                                  |
|   --------------------   --------------------     |
|   |Show full menu window| |Hide full menu window |  |
|   --------------------   --------------------     |
|                          --------------            |
|                          |File        |            |
|                          |-    ------ |            |
|                          || Item 1  ||            |
|                          || Item 2  ||            |
|                          ||----------||            |
|                          || Check Item ||          |
|                          ||----------||            |
|                          || Sub Menus |------      |
|                          ||----------|Hello |      |
|                          || Exit     |from  |      |
|                          | ----------|Java  |      |
|                          |            ------       |
|                          --------------            |
|                                                  |
----------------------------------------------------
```

FIGURE 8.6   When the user selects Sub Menus, a submenu appears.

```
----------------------------------------------------
|                                                  |
|   --------------------   --------------------     |
|   |Show full menu window| |Hide full menu window |  |
|   --------------------   --------------------     |
|                                                  |
|                          --------------            |
|                          |File        |            |
|                          |-    ------ |            |
|                          || Item 1  ||            |
|                          || Item 2  ||            |
|                          ||----------||            |
|                          ||v Check Item||          |
|                          ||----------||            |
|                          || Sub Menus ||           |
|                          ||----------||            |
|                          || Exit     ||            |
|                          | ---------- |            |
|                          |            |            |
|                          --------------            |
|                                                  |
----------------------------------------------------
```

FIGURE 8.7   When the user selects Check Item, a check mark appears.

As before, we create a frame window to support our menu. Here, we can create a new Frame class named menuFrame, and we add two buttons so we can display and hide this frame window as required:

```
import java.applet.Applet;
import java.awt.*;
import java.awt.event.*;
```

→ ```public class fullmenu extends Applet implements ActionListener{```
→ ```   Button button1, button2;```
→ ```   MenuFrame fullmenuWindow;```
```
                  .
                  .
                  .
}
```

As before, we create the code to implement these two buttons, popping the new frame window with the new menu system on the screen as required:

```
import java.applet.Applet;
import java.awt.*;
import java.awt.event.*;

public class fullmenu extends Applet implements ActionListener
{
    Button button1, button2;
    MenuFrame fullmenuWindow;
```

→ ```   public void init(){```
→ ```   button1 = new Button("Show full menu window");```
→ ```   add(button1);```
→ ```   button1.addActionListener(this);```
→
→ ```   button2 = new Button("Hide full menu window");```
→ ```   add(button2);```
→ ```   button2.addActionListener(this);```
→
→ ```   fullmenuWindow = new menuFrame("Full menus");```
→ ```   fullmenuWindow.resize(100, 100);```
→ ```   }```
→
→ ```   public void actionPerformed(ActionEvent event){```
→ ```   if(event.getSource() == button1){```
→ ```   fullmenuWindow.show();```
→ ```   }```
→ ```   if(event.getSource() == button2){```
→ ```   fullmenuWindow.hide();```
→ ```   }```
→ ```   }```
```
}
```

Now we can create our new menu frame window, menuframe. We will also implement the ActionListener interface so that we can handle menu selections:

```
class menuFrame extends Frame implements ActionListener {

}
```

This is the new frame window we'll attach our full menu system to. We now create a constructor for the window, passing the title of the window back to the Java Frame class:

```
class menuFrame extends Frame implements ActionListener {

➤       menuFrame(String title){
➤           super(title);
                .
                .
                .
```

Now we've created the new window class that we will attach our menu to; we'll add a text field to this window class so we can report what menu item was selected. This text field will be called text1. We'll also set up a GridLayout manager for the frame:

```
class menuFrame extends Frame implements ActionListener {

➤       TextField text1;

        menuFrame(String title){
            super(title);
➤           text1 = new TextField("Full menu");
➤           setLayout(new GridLayout(1, 1));
➤           add(text1);
                .
                .
                .
```

After adding a text field to the window and setting up a GridLayout manager, we create our new MenuBar object, giving it one menu, a File menu:

```
class menuFrame extends Frame implements ActionListener {

➤       Menu Menu1;
➤       MenuBar Menubar1;
        TextField text1;

        menuFrame(String title){
```

```
          super(title);
          text1 = new TextField("Full menu");
          setLayout(new GridLayout(1, 1));
          add(text1);
→         Menubar1 = new MenuBar();
→         Menu1 = new Menu("File");
                    .
                    .
                    .
```

The next step is to add our first two menu items, Item 1 and Item 2, as we've done before:

```
class menuFrame extends Frame implements ActionListener {

     Menu Menu1;
     MenuBar Menubar1;
     TextField text1;
→    MenuItem menuitem1, menuitem2;

     menuFrame(String title){
          super(title);
          text1 = new TextField("Full menu");
          setLayout(new GridLayout(1, 1));
          add(text1);
          Menubar1 = new MenuBar();
          Menu1 = new Menu("File");

→         menuitem1 = new MenuItem("Item 1");
→         menuitem1.addActionListener(this);
→         Menu1.add(menuitem1);

→         menuitem2 = new MenuItem("Item 2");
→         menuitem2.addActionListener(this);
→         Menu1.add(menuitem2);
                    .
                    .
                    .
```

We've created our menu now and added two of the items we want in it. At this point, we can add a menu separator, the horizontal line that divides menu items into groups.

Adding a Menu Separator

You use menu separators to separate menu items into functional groups. For example, you might place Cut, Paste, and Copy together in a menu by surrounding them with menu separators. To add a menu separator, we simply use the Menu class's addSeparator() method:

```
class menuFrame extends Frame implements ActionListener {

    Menu Menu1, SubMenu1;
    MenuBar Menubar1;
    TextField text1;
    MenuItem menuitem1, menuitem2;
    CheckboxMenuItem menuitem3;

    menuFrame(String title){
        super(title);
        text1 = new TextField("Full menu");
        setLayout(new GridLayout(1, 1));
        add(text1);
        Menubar1 = new MenuBar();
        Menu1 = new Menu("File");

        menuitem1 = new MenuItem("Item 1");
        menuitem1.addActionListener(this);
        Menu1.add(menuitem1);

        menuitem2 = new MenuItem("Item 2");
        menuitem2.addActionListener(this);
        Menu1.add(menuitem2);

        Menu1.addSeparator();
            .
            .
            .
```

And that's all there is to it—now we've placed a menu separator in our File menu.

TIP   You can also put separators in menus by adding a menu item with a dash (-) for a caption.

Check Box Menu Items

The next step is to add a check box menu item. We can make this item appear checked or unchecked in the File menu. To create such an item, we use the Java class CheckboxMenuItem, giving this item the caption "Check Item," as follows:

```
class menuFrame extends Frame implements ActionListener {
```

```
        Menu Menu1;
        MenuBar Menubar1;
        TextField text1;
        MenuItem menuitem1, menuitem2;
→       CheckboxMenuItem menuitem3;

        menuFrame(String title){
            super(title);
            text1 = new TextField("Full menu");
            setLayout(new GridLayout(1, 1));
            add(text1);
            Menubar1 = new MenuBar();
            Menu1 = new Menu("File");

            menuitem1 = new MenuItem("Item 1");
            menuitem1.addActionListener(this);
            Menu1.add(menuitem1);

            menuitem2 = new MenuItem("Item 2");
            menuitem2.addActionListener(this);
            Menu1.add(menuitem2);

            Menu1.addSeparator();

→           menuitem3 = new CheckboxMenuItem("Check Item");
→           menuitem3.addActionListener(this);
→           Menu1.add(menuitem3);
                    .
                    .
                    .
```

Now, because we have a CheckBoxMenuItem, we'll be able to place a check mark in front of this item when the user selects it.

Incorporating Submenus

Our next step will be to add a *submenu*, or nested menu, which pops up when the user clicks it. What this really means is creating a new Menu object—which we'll call SubMenu1—and installing it in the File menu just as we would any menu item. We'll give the new submenu three items, "Hello," "from," and "Java," as follows:

```
class menuFrame extends Frame implements ActionListener {

→       Menu Menu1, SubMenu1;
        MenuBar Menubar1;
```

```
TextField text1;
MenuItem menuitem1, menuitem2;
CheckboxMenuItem menuitem3;

menuFrame(String title){
    super(title);
    text1 = new TextField("Full menu");
    setLayout(new GridLayout(1, 1));
    add(text1);
    Menubar1 = new MenuBar();
    Menu1 = new Menu("File");
        .
        .
        .
    menuitem3 = new CheckboxMenuItem("Check Item");
    menuitem3.addActionListener(this);
    Menu1.add(menuitem3);

    Menu1.addSeparator();

    SubMenu1 = new Menu("Sub menus");
    SubMenu1.add(new MenuItem("Hello"));
    SubMenu1.add(new MenuItem("from"));
    SubMenu1.add(new MenuItem("Java"));

    Menu1.add(SubMenu1);
        .
        .
        .
```

That's how to create a submenu: as a menu complete in itself, added to its parent menu as a menu item.

Adding an Exit Item to a Menu

Our last menu item will be an Exit item, which any File menu should have. After creating this new menu item, we add it to the File menu, and then add that menu to the menubar. Finally, we install the menubar in our frame window with the setMenuBar() method:

```
class menuFrame extends Frame implements ActionListener {

    Menu Menu1, SubMenu1;
    MenuBar Menubar1;
```

```
TextField text1;
MenuItem menuitem1, menuitem2, menuitem4;
CheckboxMenuItem menuitem3;

menuFrame(String title){
     super(title);
     text1 = new TextField("Full menu");
     setLayout(new GridLayout(1, 1));
     add(text1);
     Menubar1 = new MenuBar();
     Menu1 = new Menu("File");

     menuitem1 = new MenuItem("Item 1");
     menuitem1.addActionListener(this);
     Menu1.add(menuitem1);

     menuitem2 = new MenuItem("Item 2");
     menuitem2.addActionListener(this);
     Menu1.add(menuitem2);

     Menu1.addSeparator();

     menuitem3 = new CheckboxMenuItem("Check Item");
     menuitem3.addActionListener(this);
     Menu1.add(menuitem3);

     Menu1.addSeparator();

     SubMenu1 = new Menu("Sub menus");
     SubMenu1.add(new MenuItem("Hello"));
     SubMenu1.add(new MenuItem("from"));
     SubMenu1.add(new MenuItem("Java"));
     Menu1.add(SubMenu1);

     Menu1.addSeparator();

     menuitem4 = new MenuItem("Exit");
     menuitem4.addActionListener(this);

     Menu1.add(menuitem4);
     Menubar1.add(Menu1);
     setMenuBar(Menubar1);

}
```

Skill 8

Activating Our New Menu Items

Now we're ready to make these new menu items active, and we do that in the `actionPerformed()` method:

```
public void actionPerformed(ActionEvent event){
}
```

First, we activate our standard menu item, Item 1. All this item does is to place the text "Item 1" in the text field `text1`:

```
        public void actionPerformed(ActionEvent event){
➜           if(event.getSource() == menuitem1){
➜               text1.setText("Item 1");
    }                       .
                            .
                            .
    }
```

When the user selects the next menu item, Item 2, we want to display "Item 2" in the text field and then disable the item so the user can't select it again. We disable and enable menu items with the `setEnabled()` method, passing a value of true to enable the item and false to disable it:

```
        public void actionPerformed(ActionEvent event){
            if(event.getSource() == menuitem1){
                text1.setText("Item 1");
            }
➜           if(event.getSource() == menuitem2){
➜               menuitem2.setEnabled(false);
➜               text1.setText("Item 2");
➜           }                   .
                                .
                                .
```

Now that we're using the `setEnabled()` method, we're able to enable and disable menu items.

The next menu item is the check box menu item. When the user clicks that item, we can place a check mark in front of that item with the `setState()` method, passing a value of true to make the check mark visible:

```
        public void actionPerformed(ActionEvent event){
            if(event.getSource() == menuitem1){
                text1.setText("Item 1");
            }
            if(event.getSource() == menuitem2){
```

```
                       menuitem2.setEnabled(false);
                       text1.setText("Item 2");
                   }
→              if(event.getSource() == menuitem3){
→                  ((CheckboxMenuItem)event.getSource()).setState(true);
→              }           .
                           .
                           .

           }
```

TIP   **To get the state of a check box menu item (checked or unchecked) use the** `getState()` **method.**

Finally, we enable the last menu item, menuitem4, the Exit item. To make this item active, we just use the frame window's hide() method:

```
public void actionPerformed(ActionEvent event){
    if(event.getSource() == menuitem1){
        text1.setText("Item 1");
    }
    if(event.getSource() == menuitem2){
        menuitem2.setEnabled(false);
        text1.setText("Item 2");
    }
    if(event.getSource() == menuitem3){
    ((CheckboxMenuItem)event.getSource()).setState(true);
    }
→   if(event.getSource() == menuitem4){
→       hide();
    }
}
```

And now our full menu system is active. Run it now and click the File menu. As you can see in the graphic below, our menu items are installed, complete with menu separators.

Skill 8

Next, select the check item—when you open the menu again, you'll see a check mark in front of this item, as shown below:

In addition, you can open the Sub Menus item to see the submenu, as shown below. Finally, the Exit item is active as well—use it now to leave the fullmenu applet. The code for this applet appears in fullmenu.java.

fullmenu.java

```
import java.applet.Applet;
import java.awt.*;
import java.awt.event.*;

public class fullmenu extends Applet implements ActionListener
{
    Button button1, button2;
    MenuFrame fullmenuWindow;

    public void init(){
        button1 = new Button("Show full menu window");
        add(button1);
        button1.addActionListener(this);
```

```java
        button2 = new Button("Hide full menu window");
        add(button2);
        button2.addActionListener(this);

        fullmenuWindow = new menuFrame("Full menus");
        fullmenuWindow.resize(100, 100);
    }

    public void actionPerformed(ActionEvent event){
        if(event.getSource() == button1){
            fullmenuWindow.show();
        }
        if(event.getSource() == button2){
            fullmenuWindow.hide();
        }
    }
}

class menuFrame extends Frame implements ActionListener {

    Menu Menu1, SubMenu1;
    MenuBar Menubar1;
    TextField text1;
    MenuItem menuitem1, menuitem2, menuitem4;
    CheckboxMenuItem menuitem3;

    menuFrame(String title){
        super(title);
        text1 = new TextField("Full menu");
        setLayout(new GridLayout(1, 1));
        add(text1);
        Menubar1 = new MenuBar();
        Menu1 = new Menu("File");

        menuitem1 = new MenuItem("Item 1");
        menuitem1.addActionListener(this);
        Menu1.add(menuitem1);

        menuitem2 = new MenuItem("Item 2");
        menuitem2.addActionListener(this);
        Menu1.add(menuitem2);

        Menu1.addSeparator();

        menuitem3 = new CheckboxMenuItem("Check Item");
        menuitem3.addActionListener(this);
```

Skill 8

```
        Menu1.add(menuitem3);

        Menu1.addSeparator();

        SubMenu1 = new Menu("Sub menus");
        SubMenu1.add(new MenuItem("Hello"));
        SubMenu1.add(new MenuItem("from"));
        SubMenu1.add(new MenuItem("Java"));

        Menu1.add(SubMenu1);
        Menubar1.add(Menu1);
        setMenuBar(Menubar1);

        Menu1.addSeparator();

        menuitem4 = new MenuItem("Exit");
        menuitem4.addActionListener(this);
        Menu1.add(menuitem4);
    }

    public void actionPerformed(ActionEvent event){
        if(event.getSource() == menuitem1){
            text1.setText("Item 1");
        }
        if(event.getSource() == menuitem2){
            menuitem2.setEnabled(false);
            text1.setText("Item 2");
        }
        if(event.getSource() == menuitem3){
        ((CheckboxMenuItem)event.getSource()).setState(true);
        }
        if(event.getSource() == menuitem4){
            hide();
        }
    }
}
```

You can also add code to create menu items with keyboard shortcuts in Java 1.1. For example, here we add a shortcut of Shift+O to an Open menu item (the boolean parameter in the MenuShortcut constructor indicates whether or not this shortcut uses the Shift key):

```
    menu.add(new MenuItem("Open", new MenuShortcut('o', true));
```

And, in fact, there is another type of menu that Java 1.1 supports: popup menus.

Popup Menus

You've probably seen popup menus—they are usually triggered by the right mouse button, and can pop up anywhere in a window. A popup menu is shown in Figure 8.8.

```
|                                                               |
|                                                               |
|                                                               |
|                          -------------                        |
|                         |Cut          |                       |
|                         |Copy         |                       |
|                         |-------------|                       |
|                         |Paste        |                       |
|                          -------------                        |
|                                                               |
```

FIGURE 8.8   A popup menu

Let's put a popup menu to work now. Create a new file named **popup.java** and add our usual starting code:

```java
import java.applet.Applet;
import java.awt.*;

public class popup extends Applet {
    .
    .
    .
```

We'll add popup menus to this applet now. We add a text field, **text1**, so we can report what menu item was selected. In addition, we create a new object of class **PopupMenu** named, say, **popup**, naming this menu "Edit," as follows:

```java
import java.applet.Applet;
import java.awt.*;

public class popup extends Applet {

    TextField text1;
    PopupMenu popup;

    public void init(){
```

➜
```
          popup = new PopupMenu("Edit");
                            .
                            .
                            .
```

The PopupMenu class's methods appear in Table 8.4

TABLE 8.4: The Java PopupMenu **Class's Methods**

Method	Does This
PopupMenu()	Creates a new popup menu.
PopupMenu(String)	Creates a new popup menu with the given name.
addNotify()	Creates the popup menu's peer.
show(Component, int, int)	Shows the popup menu at the x, y position from an origin component

Now we add three items to this menu: Cut, Copy, and Paste. We also add an ActionListener to make these items active:

```
import java.applet.Applet;
import java.awt.*;
import java.awt.event.*;
```

➜
```
public class popup extends Applet implements ActionListener{

        TextField text1;
        PopupMenu popup;
```
➜
```
        MenuItem menuitem1, menuitem2, menuitem3;

        public void init(){

                popup = new PopupMenu("Edit");
```
➜
```
                menuitem1 = new MenuItem("Cut");
```
➜
```
                menuitem1.addActionListener(this);
```
➜
```
                menuitem2 = new MenuItem("Copy");
```
➜
```
                menuitem2.addActionListener(this);
```
➜
```
                menuitem3 = new MenuItem("Paste");
```
➜
```
                menuitem3.addActionListener(this);
                            .
                            .
                            .
```

Then we can add those new menu items to the popup menu, using its add() method:

```
import java.awt.*;
import java.awt.event.*;
```

```
public class popup extends Applet implements ActionListener {

    TextField text1;
    PopupMenu popup;
    MenuItem menuitem1, menuitem2, menuitem3;

    public void init(){

        popup = new PopupMenu("Edit");
        menuitem1 = new MenuItem("Cut");
        menuitem1.addActionListener(this);
        menuitem2 = new MenuItem("Copy");
        menuitem2.addActionListener(this);
        menuitem3 = new MenuItem("Paste");
        menuitem3.addActionListener(this);
        popup.add(menuitem1);
        popup.add(menuitem2);
        popup.addSeparator();
        popup.add(menuitem3);
            .
            .
            .
```

Next, we add the popup menu to our applet with the applet's add() method, and we create the text field text1. In addition, we'll implement the MouseListener interface to handle mouse events—we'll see how this works in Skill 10 (although you can probably figure it out now, given the Listener interfaces we've already worked with); for now, we just add the following code:

```
import java.awt.*;
import java.awt.event.*;

public class popup extends Applet implements ActionListener,
MouseListener {

    TextField text1;
    PopupMenu popup;
    MenuItem menuitem1, menuitem2, menuitem3;

    public void init(){

        popup = new PopupMenu("Edit");
        menuitem1 = new MenuItem("Cut");
        menuitem1.addActionListener(this);
        menuitem2 = new MenuItem("Copy");
        menuitem2.addActionListener(this);
        menuitem3 = new MenuItem("Paste");
        menuitem3.addActionListener(this);
```

```
                  popup.add(menuitem1);
                  popup.add(menuitem2);
                  popup.addSeparator();
                  popup.add(menuitem3);
→                 add(popup);
→                 text1 = new TextField(20);
→                 add(text1);
→                 addMouseListener(this);
              }
```

To implement mouse handling, we add five methods: mousePressed(), mouseClicked(), mouseReleased(), mouseEntered(), and mouseExited():

```
      public void mousePressed(MouseEvent e){
      }

      public void mouseClicked(MouseEvent e){
      }

      public void mouseReleased(MouseEvent e){
      }

      public void mouseEntered(MouseEvent e){
      }

      public void mouseExited(MouseEvent e){
      }
```

We'll learn more about these methods in Skill 10—for now, we add the following code to the mousePressed() method to check if the right mouse button, the button that brings up the popup menu, was clicked. Here, we check the modifiers member of the MouseEvent object we are passed in mousePressed() to check on the right mouse button:

```
      public void mousePressed(MouseEvent e){
→         if(e.getModifiers() != 0){
                  .
                  .
                  .
→         }
      }
```

If the right mouse button was indeed pressed, we show the popup menu with its show() method at the present mouse location, which we get with the getX() and getY() MouseEvent methods, as follows

```
      public void mousePressed(MouseEvent e){
```

```
         if(e.getModifiers() != 0){
→            popup.show(this, e.getX(), e.getY());
     }
     }
```

At this point, then, the popup menu appears on the screen. We add an `actionPerformed()` method now to handle menu selections:

```
public void actionPerformed(ActionEvent event){

}
```

We add standard menu-handling code here to handle `menuitem1`, `menuitem2`, and `menuitem3` this way, displaying a different text string for each menu item:

```
public void actionPerformed(ActionEvent event){
    if(event.getSource() == menuitem1){
        text1.setText("Hello");
    }
    if(event.getSource() == menuitem2){
        text1.setText("from");
    }
    if(event.getSource() == menuitem3){
        text1.setText("Java");
    }
}
```

And we're finished—run the applet now. You can pop up the popup menu now by clicking the right mouse button, as shown in Figure 8.7. When you click an item in that menu, the corresponding string appears in the text field—our popup menu applet is a success. The code for this applet appears in `popup.java`.

C popup.java

```java
import java.applet.Applet;
import java.awt.*;
import java.awt.event.*;

public class popup extends Applet implements ActionListener,
MouseListener {

    TextField text1;
    PopupMenu popup;
    MenuItem menuitem1, menuitem2, menuitem3;

    public void init(){

        popup = new PopupMenu("Edit");
        menuitem1 = new MenuItem("Cut");
        menuitem1.addActionListener(this);
        menuitem2 = new MenuItem("Copy");
        menuitem2.addActionListener(this);
        menuitem3 = new MenuItem("Paste");
        menuitem3.addActionListener(this);
        popup.add(menuitem1);
        popup.add(menuitem2);
        popup.addSeparator();
        popup.add(menuitem3);
        add(popup);
        text1 = new TextField(20);
        add(text1);
        addMouseListener(this);
    }

    public void mousePressed(MouseEvent e){
        if(e.getModifiers() != 0){
        popup.show(this, e.getX(), e.getY());
    }
    }

    public void mouseClicked(MouseEvent e){
    }

    public void mouseReleased(MouseEvent e){
    }

    public void mouseEntered(MouseEvent e){
    }
```

```
public void mouseExited(MouseEvent e){
}

public void actionPerformed(ActionEvent event){
    if(event.getSource() == menuitem1){
        text1.setText("Hello");
    }
    if(event.getSource() == menuitem2){
        text1.setText("from");
    }
    if(event.getSource() == menuitem3){
        text1.setText("Java");
    }
}
}
```

That's it for the moment for menu handling and popup menus. As you can see, the menu system in Java is a powerful tool, with a great deal of programming strength. In Skill 9, we will continue our exploration of Java by looking at dialog boxes.

Are You Experienced?

Now you can...

- ☑ use Java windows to display information outside an application's window or an applet's Web browser
- ☑ show or hide windows as required
- ☑ give the user a selection of choices with Java menus
- ☑ use submenus, check box menu items, and menu separators
- ☑ use popup menus to give the user additional help
- ☑ determine which menu items the user selected and take the appropriate action

. Jones 356-555-3398.

PROGRAMMING
C. C. VB, Cobol, exp. Call 534-555-6543 or fax 534-555-6544.

PROGRAMMING
MRFS Inc. is looking for a Sr. Windows NT developer. Reqs. 3-5 yrs. Exp. In C. under Windows, Win95 & NT, using Visual C. Excl. OO design & implementation skills. a must. OLE2 & ODBC are a plus. Excl. Salary & bnfts. Resume & salary history to HR, 8779 HighTech Way, Computer City, AR

PROGRAMMERS
Contractors Wanted for short & long term assignments; Visual C. MFC Unix C/C. SQL Oracle Dev elop ers PC Help Desk Support Windows NT & NetWare Telecommunications Visual Basic, Access, HTMT, CGI, Perl MMI & Co., 885-555-9933

PROGRAMMER World Wide Web Links wants your HTML & Photoshop skills. Develop great WWW sites. Local & global customers. Send samples & resume to WWWL, 2000 Apple Road, Santa Rosa, CA.

TECHNICAL WRITER Software firm seeks writer/editor for manuals, research notes, project mgmt. Min 2 years tech. writing, DTP & programming experience. Send resume & writing samples to: Software Systems, Dallas, TX.

TECHNICAL Software development firm looking for Tech Trainers. Ideal candidates have programming experience in Visual C, HTML & JAVA. Need quick self starter Call (443) 555-6868 for interview.

TECHNICAL WRITER/ Premier Computer Corp is seeking a combination of technical skills, knowledge and experience in the following areas: UNIX, Windows 95/NT, Visual Basic, on-line help & documentation and the internet. Candidates must possess excellent writing skills, and be comfortable working in a quality vs. deadline driven environment. Competitive salary. Fax resume & samples to Karen Fields, Premier Computer Corp. 444 Industrial Blvd. Concord, CA. Or send to our website at www.premier.com.

WEB DESIGNER
BA/BS or equivalent programming/multimedia production. 3 years of experience in use and design of WWW services streaming audio and video HTML, PERL, CGI, GIF, JPEG. Demonstrated interpersonal, organization, communication, multi-tasking skills. Send resume to The Learning People at www.learning.com.

WEBMASTER-TECHNICAL
BSCS or equivalent 2 years of experience in CGI, Windows 95/NT, UNIX, C, Java, Perl. Demonstrated ability to design, code, debug and test on-line services. Send resume to The Learning People at www.learning.com.

PROGRAMMER World Wide Web Links wants your HTML & Photoshop skills. Develop great WWW sites. Local & global customers. Send sam-

ing tool, experienced in documentation preparation & programming languages (Access, C, FoxPro) are a plus. Financial or banking customer service support is required along with excellent verbal & written communication skills with multi levels of end-users. Send resume to KKUP Enterprises, 45 Orange Blvd., Orange, CA.

COMPUTERS Small Web Design firm seeks indiv. w/NT. Webserver & Database management exp. Fax resume to 556-555-4221.

COMPUTER/ Visual C/C, Visual Basic Exp'd Systems Analysts/ Programmers for growing software dev. team in Roseburg. Computer Science or related degree preferred. Develop adv. Engineering applications for engineering firm. Fax resume to 707-555-8744.

COMPUTER Web Master for dynamic SF Internet co. Site, Dev. test, coord. train. 2 yrs prog. Exp. C C, Web C, FTP. Fax resume to Best Staffing 845-555-7722.

COMPUTER PROGRAMMER
Ad agency seeks programmer w/exp, in UNIX/NT Platforms, Web Server, CGI/Perl. Programmer Position avail, on a project basis with the possibility to move into F/T. Fax resume & salary req. to R. Jones 334-555-8332.

COMPUTERS Programmer/Analyst Design and maintain C based SQl database applications. Required skills: Visual Basic, C, SQL, ODBC. Document existing and new applications. Novell or NT exp. a plus. Fax resume & salary history to 235-555-9935.

GRAPHIC DESIGNER
Webmaster's Weekly is seeking a creative Graphic Designer to design high impact marketing collater ad, including direct mail promo's. CD-ROM packages, ads and WWW pages. Must be able to juggle multiple projects and learn new skills on the job very rapidly. Web design experience a big plus, technical troubleshooting also a plus. Call 435-555-1235.

GRAPHICS - ART DIRECTOR - WEB-MULTIMEDIA
Leading internet development company has an outstanding opportunity for a talented, high-end Web Experienced Art Director. In addition to a great portfolio and fresh ideas, the ideal candidate has excellent communication and presentation skills. Working as a team with innovative producers and programmers, you will create dynamic, interactive web sites and application interfaces. Some programming experience required. Send samples and resume to: SuperSites, 333 Main, Seattle, WA.

MARKETING
Fast paced software and services provider looking for MARKETING COMMUNICATIONS SPECIALIST to be responsible for its webpage.

PROGRAMMERS Multiple short term assignments available: Visual C, 3 positions SQL ServerNT Server. 2 positions JAVA & HTML, long term NetWare Various locations. Call for more info. 356-555-3398.

PROGRAMMERS
C. C, VB, Cobol, exp.
Call 534-555-6543
or fax 534-555-6544.

PROGRAMMING
MRFS Inc. is looking for a Sr. Windows NT developer. Reqs. 3-5 yrs. Exp. In C. under Windows, Win95 & NT, using Visual C. Excl. OO design & implementation skills a must. OLE2 & ODBC are a plus. Resume & salary history to HR, 8779 HighTech Way, Computer City, AR

PROGRAMMERS/ Contractors Wanted for short & long term assignments; Visual C, MFC Unix C/C, SQL Oracle Developers PC Help Desk Support Windows NT & NetWare Telecommunications Visual Basic, Access, HTMT, CGI, Perl MMI & Co., 885-555-9933

PROGRAMMER World Wide Web Links wants your HTML & Photoshop skills. Develop great WWW sites. Local & global customers. Send samples & resume to WWWL, 2000 Apple Road, Santa Rosa, CA.

TECHNICAL WRITER Software firm seeks writer/editor for manuals, research notes, project mgmt. Min 2 years tech. writing, DTP & programming experience. Send resume & writing samples to: Software Systems, Dallas, TX.

COMPUTER PROGRAMMER
Ad agency seeks programmer w/exp, in UNIX/NT Platforms, Web Server, CGI/Perl. Programmer Position avail on a project basis with the possibility to move into F/T. Fax resume & salary req. to R. Jones 334-555-8332.

TECHNICAL WRITER Premier Computer Corp is seeking a combination of technical skills, knowledge and experience in the following areas: UNIX, Windows 95/NT, Visual Basic, on-line help & documentation, and the internet. Candidates must possess excellent writing skills, and be comfortable working in a quality vs. deadline driven environment. Competitive salary. Fax resume & samples to Karen Fields, Premier Computer Corp., 444 Industrial Blvd, Concord, CA. Or send to our website at www.premier.com

WEB DESIGNER
BA/BS or equivalent programming/multimedia production. 3 years of experience in use and design of WWW services streaming audio and video HTML, PERL, CGI, GIF, JPEG. Demonstrated interpersonal, organization, communication, multi-tasking skills. Send resume to The Learning People at www.learning.com.

WEBMASTER-TECHNICAL
BSCS or equivalent, 2 years of experience in CGI, Windows 95/NT,

COMPUTERS Small Web Design firm seeks indiv. w/NT. Webserver & Database management exp. fax resume to 556-555-4221.

COMPUTER Visual C/C. Visual Basic Exp'd Systems Analysts/ Programmers for growing software dev. team in Roseburg. Computer Science or related degree preferred. Develop adv. Engineering applications for engineering firm. Fax resume to 707-555-8744.

COMPUTER Web Master for dynamic SF Internet co. Site. Dev. test, coord. train. 2 yrs prog. Exp. C C, Web C, FTP. Fax resume to Best Staffing 845-555-7722.

COMPUTERS/ QA SOFTWARE TESTERS Qualified candidates should have 2 yrs exp. performing integration & system testing using automated testing tools. Experienced in documentation preparation & programming languages (Access, C, FoxPro) are a plus. Financial or banking customer service support is required along with excellent verbal & written communication skills with multi levels of end-users. Send resume to KKUP Enterprises, 45 Orange Blvd. Orange, CA.

COMPUTERS Programmer/Analyst Design and maintain C based SQl database applications. Required skills: Visual Basic, C, SQL, ODBC. Document existing and new applications. Novell or NT exp. a plus, Fax resume & salary history to 235-555-9935.

GRAPHIC DESIGNER
Webmaster's Weekly is seeking a creative Graphic Designer to design high impact marketing collater ad, including direct mail promo's. CD-ROM packages, ads and WWW pages. Must be able to juggle multiple projects and learn new skills on the job very rapidly. Web design experience a big plus, technical troubleshooting also a plus. Call 435-555-1235.

GRAPHICS - ART DIRECTOR - WEB-MULTIMEDIA
Leading internet development company has an outstanding opportunity for a talented, high-end Web Experienced Art Director. In addition to a great portfolio and fresh ideas, the ideal candidate has excellent communication and presentation skills. Working as a team with innovative producers and programmers, you will create dynamic, interactive web sites and application interfaces. Some programming experience required. Send samples and resume to: SuperSites, 333 Main, Seattle, WA.

COMPUTER PROGRAMMER
Ad agency seeks programmer w/exp. in UNIX/NT Platforms, Web Server, CGI/Perl. Programmer Position avail on a project basis with the possibility to move into F/T. Fax resume & salary req. to R. Jones 334-555-8332.

PROGRAMMERS / Established software company seeks program-

ment. Must be a self-starter, energetic, organized. Must have 2 yrs web experience. Programming a plus. Call 985-555-9854.

PROGRAMMERS Multiple term assignments available: Visual C, 3 positions SQL ServerNT Server 2 positions JAVA & HTML, long NetWare Various locations. Call more info. 356-555-3398.

PROGRAMMERS
C. C, VB, Cobol, exp. Call 534-6543 or fax 534-555-6544.

PROGRAMMING
MRFS Inc. is looking for a Windows NT developer. Reqs. yrs. Exp. In C. under Wind Win95 & NT, using Visual C. OO design & implementation a must. OLE2 & ODBC are a Excl. Salary & bnfts. Resume salary history to HR, 8779 High Way, Computer City, AR

PROGRAMMERS/ Contract Wanted for short & long term ass ments: Visual C. MFCUnix C/C, Oracle Developers PC Help Support Windows NT & NetW Telecommunications Visual B Access, HTMT, CGI, Perl MMI a 885-555-9933

PROGRAMMER World Wide Links wants your HTML & Photo skills. Develop great WWW Local & global customers. Send ples & resume to WWWL; Apple Road, Santa Rosa, CA.

TECHNICAL WRITER Software seeks writer/editor for man research notes, project mgmt. Mi years tech. writing, DTP & prog ming experience. Send resum writing samples to: Soft Systems, Dallas, TX.

TECHNICAL Software develop firm looking for Tech Trainers, I candidates have programming rience in Visual C, HTML & JA Need quick self starter. Call (555-6868 for interview.

TECHNICAL WRITER Pre Computer Corp is seeking a com nation of technical skills, knowle and experience in the follow areas: UNIX, Windows 95/NT, V Basic, on-line help & documenta and the internet. Candidates possess excellent writing skills. be comfortable working in a qu vs. deadline driven environm Competitive salary. Fax resum samples to Karen Fields, Pre Computer Corp. 444 Industrial Concord, CA. Or send to our we at www.premier.com.

WEB DESIGNER
BA/BS or equivalent prog ming/multimedia production years of experience in use design of WWW services strea audio and video HTML, PERL, GIF, JPEG. Demonstrated inte sonal, organization, communic multi-tasking skills. Send resum The Learning People at www ing.com.

WEBMASTER-TECHNIC

S K I L L

nine

9

Constructing Java Dialog Boxes

- ❑ Creating dialog boxes
- ❑ Showing and hiding dialog boxes
- ❑ Using controls in a dialog box
- ❑ Laying out controls in a dialog box
- ❑ Retrieving values from a dialog box

In this Skill we'll see how to create and use our own dialog boxes. Any Windows user is familiar with dialog boxes—they're those specialized windows that pop up and give you various controls to choose from, controls such as buttons and text fields. You'll see how to add controls to your Java programs, how to lay out the controls in a dialog box, as well as how to transfer values from controls in a dialog box to controls in an applet.

Using Dialog Boxes

Like menus, dialog classes need to be attached to frame windows. For that reason, we can start our dialog box example as we have started our menu example—with an applet that pops a frame window on the screen. When the user clicks a Show Dialog Window button, we can pop a frame window on the screen. We want to let the user pop up a dialog box from this frame window, so we'll put a File menu in this frame window with a menu item "Dialog Box…" in it, as shown in Figure 9.1. When the user selects Dialog Box…, we'll pop up a dialog box with two buttons: OK and Cancel (see Figure 9.2). To remove the dialog box from the screen, the user can just click the OK or Cancel button.

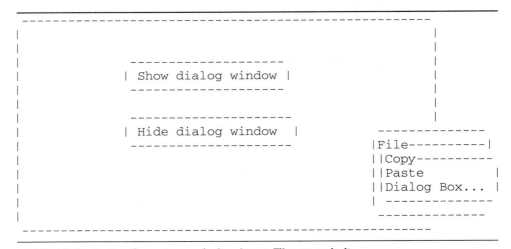

FIGURE 9.1   Our popup window has a File menu in it.

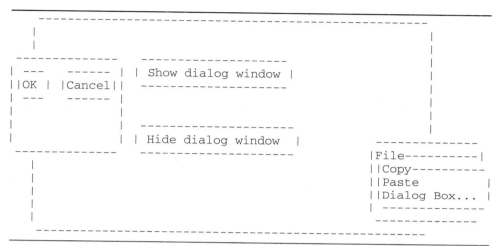

FIGURE 9.2   When the user selects File ➤ Dialog Box..., a dialog box pops up on the screen.

Let's create this applet now. Create a file named `dialogs.java` and add our standard code:

```
import java.applet.Applet;
import java.awt.*;

public class dialogs extends Applet {

}
```

First we add the two buttons we'll use to show and hide the frame window we'll need—here, these two buttons will have the captions "Show Dialog Window" and "Hide Dialog Window." We can name our frame window class `dialogframe` and add an object of that class named `frameWindow`, as follows:

```
import java.applet.Applet;
import java.awt.*;
import java.awt.event.*;

public class dialogs extends Applet
{

    Button button1, button2;
    dialogframe frameWindow;
        .
        .
        .
```

As before, we just connect up those buttons and add code to pop the frame window on the screen this way:

```
import java.applet.Applet;
import java.awt.*;
import java.awt.event.*;
```

→
```
public class dialogs extends Applet implements ActionListener
{

        Button button1, button2;
        dialogframe frameWindow;
```
→
→
→
→
→
→
→
→
→
→
→
→
→
→
→
→
→
→
→
→
→
```
        public void init(){
            button1 = new Button("Show dialog window");
            add(button1);
            button1.addActionListener(this);
            button2 = new Button("Hide dialog window");
            add(button2);
            button2.addActionListener(this);

            frameWindow = new dialogframe("Dialogs");
            frameWindow.resize(100, 100);
        }

        public void actionPerformed(ActionEvent event){
            if(event.getSource() == button1){
                frameWindow.show();
            }
            if(event.getSource() == button2){
                frameWindow.hide();
            }
        }
}
```

Now we can pop the frame window we'll need for our menu onto the screen. The next step is to create the frame window we'll need, dialogframe, and implement the ActionListener interface so we can enable the items in our menubar. Add this text to the end of dialogs.java:

```
class dialogframe extends Frame implements ActionListener {
            .
            .
            .
}
```

We start the dialogframe class with a constructor:

```
class dialogframe extends Frame implements ActionListener {

        dialogframe(String title){
            super(title);
                .
                .
                .

        }
}
```

Next, we add a text field to our dialogframe class to report the menu selections the user has made:

```
class dialogframe extends Frame implements ActionListener {

        TextField text1;

        dialogframe(String title){
            super(title);
            text1 = new TextField("");
            setLayout(new GridLayout(1, 1));
            add(text1);
                .
                .
                .
```

Having added the text field, we add our File menu with three items: Copy, Paste, and Dialog Box..., as follows:

```
class dialogframe extends Frame implements ActionListener {

        Menu Menu1;
        MenuBar Menubar1;
        MenuItem menuitem1, menuitem2, menuitem3;

        TextField text1;

        dialogframe(String title){
            super(title);
            text1 = new TextField("");
            setLayout(new GridLayout(1, 1));
            add(text1);

            Menubar1 = new MenuBar();
            Menu1 = new Menu("File");
```

```
→           menuitem1 = new MenuItem("Copy");
→           Menu1.add(menuitem1);
→           menuitem1.addActionListener(this);

→           menuitem2 = new MenuItem("Paste");
→           Menu1.add(menuitem2);
→           menuitem2.addActionListener(this);

→           menuitem3 = new MenuItem("Dialog box...");
→           Menu1.add(menuitem3);
→           menuitem3.addActionListener(this);

→           Menubar1.add(Menu1);
→           setMenuBar(Menubar1);
                .
                .
                .

    }
```

To actually display the dialog box when the user selects Dialog Box… in our menu, we will create a new class, extending the Java `Dialog` class. We can call our new class `buttondialog` and call the new object of that class `dialogBox`, as follows:

```
class dialogframe extends Frame implements ActionListener {

    Menu Menu1;
    MenuBar Menubar1;
    MenuItem menuitem1, menuitem2, menuitem3;

    TextField text1;
→   buttondialog dialogBox;

    dialogframe(String title){
        super(title);
        text1 = new TextField("");
        setLayout(new GridLayout(1, 1));
        add(text1);
        Menubar1 = new MenuBar();

        Menu1 = new Menu("File");

        menuitem1 = new MenuItem("Copy");
        Menu1.add(menuitem1);
        menuitem1.addActionListener(this);

        menuitem2 = new MenuItem("Paste");
        Menu1.add(menuitem2);
        menuitem2.addActionListener(this);
```

```
            menuitem3 = new MenuItem("Dialog box...");
            Menu1.add(menuitem3);
            menuitem3.addActionListener(this);

            Menubar1.add(Menu1);

            setMenuBar(Menubar1);
            dialogBox = new buttondialog(this, "Dialog", true);
        }
```

→

The Dialog class's methods appear in Table 9.1.

T A B L E   9 . 1 : The Java Dialog class's methods

Method	Does This
Dialog(Frame)	Constructs an initially invisible Dialog with an empty title.
Dialog(Frame, boolean)	Deprecated. Replaced by Dialog(Frame, String, boolean).
Dialog(Frame, String)	Constructs an initially invisible Dialog with a title.
Dialog(Frame, String, boolean)	Constructs an initially invisible Dialog with a title.
addNotify()	Creates the frame's peer.
addWindowListener(WindowListener)	Adds the given window listener to receive window events from this dialog.
getTitle()	Gets the title of the Dialog.
isModal()	Returns true if the Dialog is modal.
isResizable()	Returns true if the user can resize the dialog.
paramString()	Returns the parameter String of this Dialog.
processEvent(AWTEvent)	Processes events on this dialog.
processWindowEvent(WindowEvent)	Processes window events occurring on this dialog by dispatching them to any registered WindowListener objects.
removeWindowListener(WindowListener)	Removes the given window listener so that it no longer receives window events from this dialog.
setModal(boolean)	Specifies whether this Dialog is modal.
setResizable(boolean)	Sets the resizable flag.
SetTitle(String)	Sets the title of the Dialog.
show()	Shows the dialog.

Skill 9

We've allowed the user to pop up a new window with a menu in it on the screen. Now we can make the frame window menu items active. Add an `actionPerformed()` method to `dialogframe` now:

```java
public void actionPerformed(ActionEvent event){

}
```

We make the first two menu items active by simply having them display text in the applet's text field `text1`:

```java
public void actionPerformed(ActionEvent event){
    if(event.getSource() == menuitem1){
        text1.setText("Copy");
    }
    if(event.getSource() == menuitem2){
        text1.setText("Paste");
    }          .
                 .
                 .
}
```

When the user selects Dialog Box..., however, they want to display the dialog box object we have named `dialogBox`. We make that happen by using the `dialogBox` object's `show()` method:

```java
public void actionPerformed(ActionEvent event){
    if(event.getSource() == menuitem1){
        text1.setText("Copy");
    }
    if(event.getSource() == menuitem2){
        text1.setText("Paste");
    }
    if(event.getSource() == menuitem3){
        dialogBox.show();
    }
}
```

Creating a Dialog Box

The next step is to create the dialog box class itself, `buttondialog`. This class supports a dialog box with two buttons, OK and Cancel as shown below.

```
-------------
|  ---     ------  |
| |OK |   |Cancel| |
|  ---     ------  |
|                  |
|                  |
-------------
```

We create the `buttondialog` class now, extending the Java `Dialog` class, and implementing the ActionListener interface so we can enable our OK and Cancel buttons (note that we can implement the ActionListener interface with the `Dialog` class):

```
class buttondialog extends Dialog implements ActionListener {

}
```

And we add those buttons now:

```
class buttondialog extends Dialog implements ActionListener {

        Button OKButton, CancelButton;
                .
                .
                .
```

Next, we add a constructor for our class. In this case, the constructor is passed these values: the host frame window, a title for the dialog box, and a boolean value indicating whether or not the dialog box is *modal*. (If it's modal, the user can't do anything else in your program until they dismiss the dialog box.) We pass these values back to the `Dialog` class's constructor:

```
class buttondialog extends Dialog implements ActionListener {

        Button OKButton, CancelButton;

        buttondialog(Frame hostFrame, String title, boolean dModal){
            super(hostFrame, title, dModal);
                .
                .
                .
```

Next, we resize our dialog box to (100, 100) and install a layout manager. You always need to install a layout manager in dialog boxes; here, we'll use the FlowLayout manager:

```
class buttondialog extends Dialog implements ActionListener {
```

Skill 9

```
Button OKButton, CancelButton;

buttondialog(Frame hostFrame, String title, boolean dModal){
    super(hostFrame, title, dModal);
    resize(100, 100);
    setLayout(new FlowLayout());
        .
        .
        .
```

 WARNING   **If you don't set the size of a dialog box, many Web browsers won't display it.**

We've created the basic dialog box. Now we just create and add our OK and Cancel buttons:

```
class buttondialog extends Dialog implements ActionListener {

    Button OKButton, CancelButton;

    buttondialog(Frame hostFrame, String title, boolean dModal){
        super(hostFrame, title, dModal);
        resize(100, 100);
        setLayout(new FlowLayout());

        OKButton = new Button("OK");
        add(OKButton);
        OKButton.addActionListener((ActionListener)this);

        CancelButton = new Button("Cancel");
        add(CancelButton);
        CancelButton.addActionListener(this);
    }       .
            .
            .
```

We've added our buttons. Now we connect them to our code in an actionPerformed() method:

```
class buttondialog extends Dialog implements ActionListener {

    Button OKButton, CancelButton;

    buttondialog(Frame hostFrame, String title, boolean dModal){
        super(hostFrame, title, dModal);
        resize(100, 100);
```

```
            setLayout(new FlowLayout());

            OKButton = new Button("OK");
            add(OKButton);
            OKButton.addActionListener((ActionListener)this);

            CancelButton = new Button("Cancel");
            add(CancelButton);
            CancelButton.addActionListener(this);
        }

→       public void actionPerformed(ActionEvent event){
                        .
                        .
                        .

→       }
    }
```

These are the two buttons that appear in our dialog box. When the user clicks either button in the dialog box, they are indicating that they want us to take an action (such as closing the dialog box). To respond correctly, we need to know which button was pushed. We determine which button caused an event in actionPerformed, OKButton or CancelButton:

```
class buttondialog extends Dialog implements ActionListener {

    Button OKButton, CancelButton;

    buttondialog(Frame hostFrame, String title, boolean dModal){
        super(hostFrame, title, dModal);
        resize(100, 100);
        setLayout(new FlowLayout());

        OKButton = new Button("OK");
        add(OKButton);
        OKButton.addActionListener((ActionListener)this);

        CancelButton = new Button("Cancel");
        add(CancelButton);
        CancelButton.addActionListener(this);
    }

    public void actionPerformed(ActionEvent event){
→       if(event.getSource() == OKButton){
                    .
                    .
                    .
```

```
→          }
→          if(event.getSource() == CancelButton){
                    .
                    .
                    .
→          }
        }
    }
```

All we do if either button is clicked is hide the dialog box (we'll do more in our next example), using the Dialog class's hide() method. We accomplish this as follows:

```
class buttondialog extends Dialog implements ActionListener {

    Button OKButton, CancelButton;

    buttondialog(Frame hostFrame, String title, boolean dModal){
        super(hostFrame, title, dModal);
        resize(100, 100);
        setLayout(new FlowLayout());

        OKButton = new Button("OK");
        add(OKButton);
        OKButton.addActionListener((ActionListener)this);

        CancelButton = new Button("Cancel");
        add(CancelButton);
        CancelButton.addActionListener(this);
    }

    public void actionPerformed(ActionEvent event){
        if(event.getSource() == OKButton){
→           hide();
        }
→       if(event.getSource() == CancelButton){
            hide();
        }
    }
}
```

And we're finished—you can run the applet now. When you open the frame window and select File ➤ Dialog Box..., the dialog box appears on the screen, as shown in Figure 9.3. When you click the OK or Cancel button, the dialog box disappears from the screen. The listing for this applet appears in dialogs.java.

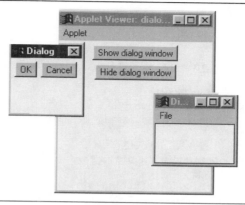

FIGURE 9.3   Our applet supports a dialog box.

dialogs.java

```java
import java.applet.Applet;
import java.awt.*;
import java.awt.event.*;

public class dialogs extends Applet implements ActionListener
{

    Button button1, button2;
    dialogframe frameWindow;

    public void init(){
        button1 = new Button("Show dialog window");
        add(button1);
        button1.addActionListener(this);
        button2 = new Button("Hide dialog window");
        add(button2);
        button2.addActionListener(this);

        frameWindow = new dialogframe("Dialogs");
        frameWindow.resize(100, 100);
    }

    public void actionPerformed(ActionEvent event){
        if(event.getSource() == button1){
            frameWindow.show();
        }
        if(event.getSource() == button2){
```

```
                                frameWindow.hide();
                    }
            }
    }

    class dialogframe extends Frame implements ActionListener {

            Menu Menu1;
            MenuBar Menubar1;
            MenuItem menuitem1, menuitem2, menuitem3;

            TextField text1;
            buttondialog dialogBox;

            dialogframe(String title){
                    super(title);
                    text1 = new TextField("");
                    setLayout(new GridLayout(1, 1));
                    add(text1);
                    Menubar1 = new MenuBar();

                    Menu1 = new Menu("File");

                    menuitem1 = new MenuItem("Copy");
                    Menu1.add(menuitem1);
                    menuitem1.addActionListener(this);

                    menuitem2 = new MenuItem("Paste");
                    Menu1.add(menuitem2);
                    menuitem2.addActionListener(this);

                    menuitem3 = new MenuItem("Dialog box...");
                    Menu1.add(menuitem3);
                    menuitem3.addActionListener(this);

                    Menubar1.add(Menu1);

                    setMenuBar(Menubar1);
                    dialogBox = new buttondialog(this, "Dialog", true);
            }

            public void actionPerformed(ActionEvent event){
                    if(event.getSource() == menuitem1){
                        text1.setText("Copy");
                    }
                    if(event.getSource() == menuitem2){
                        text1.setText("Paste");
                    }
                    if(event.getSource() == menuitem3){
                        dialogBox.show();
```

```
            }
        }
    }

class buttondialog extends Dialog implements ActionListener {

    Button OKButton, CancelButton;

    buttondialog(Frame hostFrame, String title, boolean dModal){
        super(hostFrame, title, dModal);
        resize(100, 100);
        setLayout(new FlowLayout());
        OKButton = new Button("OK");
        add(OKButton);

OKButton.addActionListener((ActionListener)this);
        CancelButton = new Button("Cancel");
        add(CancelButton);
        CancelButton.addActionListener(this);
    }

    public void actionPerformed(ActionEvent event){
        if(event.getSource() == OKButton){
            hide();
        }
        if(event.getSource() == CancelButton){
            hide();
        }
    }
}
```

So far, then, we've seen how to build and display a rudimentary dialog box. However, we haven't retrieved any values that the user entered into the dialog box or set up the layout of our dialog box controls in any significant way.

Building a Popup Calculator

Let's put together a more complete dialog box example now. This time, we'll pop up a window with a File menu that contains one item, Calculator…, as shown in Figure 9.4. When the user clicks that item, we can pop up the layout calculator we developed earlier as a dialog box—with an added Exit button to close the dialog box when not needed (see Figure 9.5). When the calculator is closed, we can read the answer and display it in a text field in the main applet, as shown in Figure 9.6.

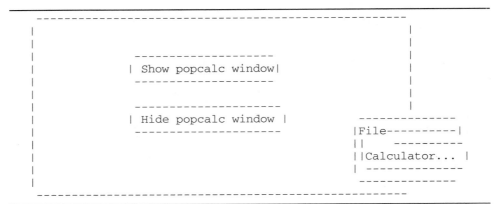

FIGURE 9.4   We pop up a window with a File menu onto the screen.

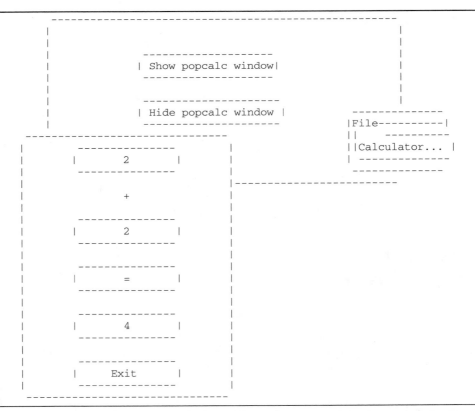

FIGURE 9.5   Our popup calculator allows the user to enter numeric values.

```
--------------------------------------------------------
|                                                      |
|                                                      |
|              --------------------                    |
|             | Show popcalc window|                   |
|              --------------------                    |
|                                                      |
|                                                      |
|              --------------------                    |
|             | Hide popcalc window |         ---------------
|              --------------------          |File----------|
|                                            |The answer is 4|
|                                            |              |
|                                             ---------------
|                                                      |
--------------------------------------------------------
```

FIGURE 9.6   When the calculator is closed, a text field displays the answer.

Let's develop this example now. Create a new file named popcalc.java. We'll need a frame window to display the File menu with the Calculator item in it, so we'll create a class named MenuFrame. The applet class itself will only be responsible for placing that window on the screen, so we write that class as we have above:

```java
import java.applet.Applet;
import java.awt.*;
import java.awt.event.*;

public class popcalc extends Applet implements ActionListener
{

    Button button1, button2;
    MenuFrame frameWindow;

    public void init(){
        button1 = new Button("Show popcalc window");
        add(button1);
        button1.addActionListener(this);
        button2 = new Button("Hide popcalc window");
        add(button2);
        button2.addActionListener(this);

        frameWindow = new MenuFrame("Popup Calculator");
        frameWindow.resize(100, 100);
    }

    public void actionPerformed(ActionEvent event){
```

```
→            if(event.getSource() == button1){
→                frameWindow.show();
→            }
→            if(event.getSource() == button2){
→                frameWindow.hide();
→            }
→        }
    }
```

At this point, the applet is set up to place an object of class MenuFrame on the screen—let's create that class now:

```
class MenuFrame extends Frame implements ActionListener {

    }
```

Here, we add the text field in which we'll display the results from the calculator; we can name that text field text1. Next, we add the menu system itself, with one item, Calculator...:

```
class MenuFrame extends Frame implements ActionListener {

→        Menu Menu1;
→        MenuBar Menubar1;
→        MenuItem menuitem1;

→        TextField text1;

→        MenuFrame(String title){
→            super(title);
→            text1 = new TextField("");
→            setLayout(new GridLayout(1, 1));
→            add(text1);
→            Menubar1 = new MenuBar();
→
→            Menu1 = new Menu("File");

→            menuitem1 = new MenuItem("Calculator...");
→            Menu1.add(menuitem1);
→            menuitem1.addActionListener(this);
→
→            Menubar1.add(Menu1);
→            setMenuBar(Menubar1);
                    .
                    .
        }
```

The popup calculator itself will be a dialog box of the class `calculatordialog`. We'll create an object of that class named `dialogBox` now:

```
class MenuFrame extends Frame implements ActionListener {

    Menu Menu1;
    MenuBar Menubar1;
    MenuItem menuitem1, menuitem2, menuitem3;

    TextField text1;
→   calculatordialog dialogBox;

    MenuFrame(String title){
        super(title);
        text1 = new TextField("");
        setLayout(new GridLayout(1, 1));
        add(text1);
        Menubar1 = new MenuBar();

        Menu1 = new Menu("File");

        menuitem1 = new MenuItem("Calculator...");
        Menu1.add(menuitem1);
        menuitem1.addActionListener(this);

        Menubar1.add(Menu1);

        setMenuBar(Menubar1);
→       dialogBox = new Calculatordialog(this, "Calculator", true);
    }
}
```

When the user clicks the Calculator... menu item, we want to pop up the calculator object on the screen. We do that in an `actionPerformed()` method:

```
class MenuFrame extends Frame implements ActionListener {

    Menu Menu1;
    MenuBar Menubar1;
    MenuItem menuitem1, menuitem2, menuitem3;

    TextField text1;
    calculatordialog dialogBox;
```

Skill 9

```
MenuFrame(String title){
    super(title);
    text1 = new TextField("");
    setLayout(new GridLayout(1, 1));
    add(text1);
    Menubar1 = new MenuBar();

    Menu1 = new Menu("File");

    menuitem1 = new MenuItem("Calculator...");
    Menu1.add(menuitem1);
    menuitem1.addActionListener(this);

    Menubar1.add(Menu1);

    setMenuBar(Menubar1);
    dialogBox = new calculatordialog(this, "Calculator", true);
}

public void actionPerformed(ActionEvent event){
    if(event.getSource() == menuitem1){
        dialogBox.show();
    }
}
}
```

All that's left is to create our calculator class, `calculatordialog`. As with our previous dialog box, we place a constructor in our calculator dialog and pass back to us the parameters passed to the `Dialog` class's constructor:

```
class calculatordialog extends Dialog {

    calculatordialog(Frame hostFrame, String title, boolean dModal){
        super(hostFrame, title, dModal);
        resize(300, 300);
            .
            .
            .
```

Next, we add the controls we'll need for this popup calculator, including the new Exit button at the bottom of the dialog box. The controls we'll use in our calculator are shown in Figure 9.7.

```
---------------------------------------------------------------
|                   |  ------------   |                         |
|      fill1        | |      2      | |       fill2             |
|                   |  ------------   |                         |
|-------------------|-----------------|-------------------------|
|                   |  ------------   |                         |
|      fill3        | |      +      | |       fill4             |
|                   |  ------------   |                         |
|-------------------|-----------------|-------------------------|
|                   |  ------------   |                         |
|      fill5        | |      2      | |       fill6             |
|                   |  ------------   |                         |
|-------------------|-----------------|-------------------------|
|                   |                 |                         |
|     spacer1       |     spacer2     |      spacer3            |
|                   |                 |                         |
|-------------------|-----------------|-------------------------|
|                   |  ------------   |                         |
|      fill7        | |      =      | |       fill8             |
|                   |  ------------   |                         |
|-------------------|-----------------|-------------------------|
|                   |                 |                         |
|     spacer4       |     spacer5     |      spacer6            |
|                   |                 |                         |
|-------------------|-----------------|-------------------------|
|                   |  ------------   |                         |
|      fill9        | |      4      | |       fill10            |
|                   |  ------------   |                         |
|-------------------|-----------------|-------------------------|
|                   |                 |                         |
|     spacer7       |     spacer8     |      spacer9            |
|                   |                 |                         |
|-------------------|-----------------|-------------------------|
|                   |  ------------   |                         |
|      fill11       | |    Exit     | |       fill12            |
|                   |  ------------   |                         |
---------------------------------------------------------------
```

FIGURE 9.7 The controls used in our calculator

Skill 9

We add those new controls in a grid layout, as follows:

```
class calculatordialog extends Dialog implements ActionListener {
        TextField text1, text2, answertext;
        Label pluslabel, fill1, fill2, fill3, fill4, fill5, fill6, fill7,
            fill8, fill9, fill10, fill11, fill12;
        Label spacer1, spacer2, spacer3, spacer4, spacer5, spacer6,
            spacer7, spacer8, spacer9;
        Button button1, button2;

        calculatordialog(Frame hostFrame, String title, boolean dModal){
                super(hostFrame, title, dModal);
                resize(300, 300);
                setLayout(new GridLayout(10, 3));

                fill1 = new Label();
                add(fill1);
                text1 = new TextField(10);
                add(text1);
                fill2 = new Label();
                add(fill2);

                fill3 = new Label();
                add(fill3);
                pluslabel = new Label("+", Label.CENTER);
                add(pluslabel);
                fill4 = new Label();
                add(fill4);

                fill5 = new Label();
                add(fill5);
                text2 = new TextField(10);
                add(text2);
                fill6 = new Label();
                add(fill6);

                spacer1 = new Label();
                add(spacer1);
                spacer2 = new Label();
                add(spacer2);
                spacer3 = new Label();
                add(spacer3);

                fill7 = new Label();
                add(fill7);
```

```
→          button1 = new Button("=");
→          add(button1);
→          button1.addActionListener(this);
→          fill8 = new Label();
→          add(fill8);
→
→          spacer4 = new Label();
→          add(spacer4);
→          spacer5 = new Label();
→          add(spacer5);
→          spacer6 = new Label();
→          add(spacer6);
→
→          fill9 = new Label();
→          add(fill9);
→          answertext = new TextField(10);
→          add(answertext);
→          fill10 = new Label();
→          add(fill10);
→
→          spacer7 = new Label();
→          add(spacer7);
→          spacer8 = new Label();
→          add(spacer8);
→          spacer9 = new Label();
→          add(spacer9);
→
→          fill11 = new Label();
→          add(fill11);
→          button2 = new Button("Exit");
→          add(button2);
→          button2.addActionListener(this);
→          fill12 = new Label();
→          add(fill12);
       }
```

Now we've added to the calculator dialog box all the controls that we'll need, including the = button (button1) and the Exit button (button2). When the user places an integer in the text1 text field, places another integer in the text2 text field, and clicks the = button, we want to add those two values and display their sum in the text field named answertext. We do that by adding an actionPerformed() method and placing this code in it:

```
       public void actionPerformed(ActionEvent e){
→          if(e.getSource() == button1){
```

Skill 9

```
→                       int sum = Integer.parseInt(text1.getText()) +
                        ➥ Integer.parseInt(text2.getText());
→                       answertext.setText(String.valueOf(sum));
→               }               .
                                .
                                .
        }
}
```

After the user completes the calculation and clicks Exit (`button2`), we can take the result from the `answertext` text field and place it in the frame window's text field, which we have named `text1`. We do so as follows:

```
        public void actionPerformed(ActionEvent event){
            if(event.getSource() == menuitem1){
                dialogBox.show();
→               text1.setText("The answer is: " +
                ➥ dialogBox.answertext.getText());
            }
        }
```

And our applet is finished. Start the applet now and select the Calculator item in the frame window's File menu, as shown in Figure 9.8. When the calculator dialog opens, add two numbers, as shown in Figure 9.9. After you click the Exit button, the sum appears in the frame window, as shown in Figure 9.10.

FIGURE 9.8 Our applet supports a popup calculator.

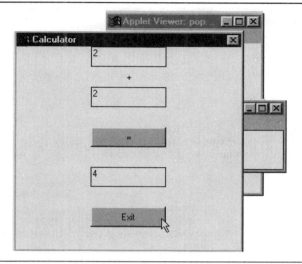

FIGURE 9.9   We add numbers in our popup calculator.

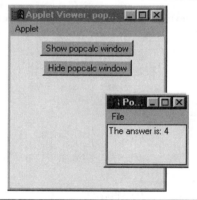

FIGURE 9.10   The calculator dialog places its answer in the frame window.

Now our popup calculator is finished. We're able to lay out our controls in dialog boxes as we want them, and we're able to retrieve values that the user enters in dialog boxes. The listing for this applet appears in popcalc.java.

Skill 9

popcalc.java

```java
import java.applet.Applet;
import java.awt.*;
import java.awt.event.*;

public class popcalc extends Applet implements ActionListener
{

    Button button1, button2;
    MenuFrame frameWindow;

    public void init(){
        button1 = new Button("Show popcalc window");
        add(button1);
        button1.addActionListener(this);
        button2 = new Button("Hide popcalc window");
        add(button2);
        button2.addActionListener(this);

        frameWindow = new MenuFrame("Popup Calculator");
        frameWindow.resize(100, 100);
    }

    public void actionPerformed(ActionEvent event){
        if(event.getSource() == button1){
            frameWindow.show();
        }
        if(event.getSource() == button2){
            frameWindow.hide();
        }
    }
}

class MenuFrame extends Frame implements ActionListener {

    Menu Menu1;
    MenuBar Menubar1;
    MenuItem menuitem1, menuitem2, menuitem3;

    TextField text1;
    Calculatordialog dialogBox;

    MenuFrame(String title){
        super(title);
        text1 = new TextField("");
        setLayout(new GridLayout(1, 1));
```

```
                    add(text1);
                    Menubar1 = new MenuBar();

                    Menu1 = new Menu("File");

                    menuitem1 = new MenuItem("Calculator...");
                    Menu1.add(menuitem1);
                    menuitem1.addActionListener(this);

                    Menubar1.add(Menu1);

                    setMenuBar(Menubar1);
                    dialogBox = new Calculatordialog(this, "Calculator", true);
            }

        public void actionPerformed(ActionEvent event){
                if(event.getSource() == menuitem1){
                    dialogBox.show();
                    text1.setText("The answer is: " +
                ➥ dialogBox.answertext.getText());
                }
            }
        }
}

class Calculatordialog extends Dialog implements ActionListener {

        TextField text1, text2, answertext;
        Label pluslabel, fill1, fill2, fill3, fill4, fill5, fill6, fill7,
      ➥ fill8, fill9, fill10, fill11, fill12;
        Label spacer1, spacer2, spacer3, spacer4, spacer5, spacer6,
      ➥ spacer7, spacer8, spacer9;
        Button button1, button2;

        Calculatordialog(Frame hostFrame, String title, boolean dModal){
                super(hostFrame, title, dModal);
                resize(300, 300);
                setLayout(new GridLayout(10, 3));

                fill1 = new Label();
                add(fill1);
                text1 = new TextField(10);
                add(text1);
                fill2 = new Label();
                add(fill2);

                fill3 = new Label();
                add(fill3);
                pluslabel = new Label("+", Label.CENTER);
```

```
add(pluslabel);
fill4 = new Label();
add(fill4);

fill5 = new Label();
add(fill5);
text2 = new TextField(10);
add(text2);
fill6 = new Label();
add(fill6);

spacer1 = new Label();
add(spacer1);
spacer2 = new Label();
add(spacer2);
spacer3 = new Label();
add(spacer3);

fill7 = new Label();
add(fill7);
button1 = new Button("=");
add(button1);
button1.addActionListener(this);
fill8 = new Label();
add(fill8);

spacer4 = new Label();
add(spacer4);
spacer5 = new Label();
add(spacer5);
spacer6 = new Label();
add(spacer6);

fill9 = new Label();
add(fill9);
answertext = new TextField(10);
add(answertext);
fill10 = new Label();
add(fill10);

spacer7 = new Label();
add(spacer7);
spacer8 = new Label();
add(spacer8);
spacer9 = new Label();
add(spacer9);

fill11 = new Label();
```

```
                add(fill11);
                button2 = new Button("Exit");
                add(button2);
                button2.addActionListener(this);
                fill12 = new Label();
                add(fill12);
        }

        public void actionPerformed(ActionEvent e){
            if(e.getSource() == button1){
                int sum = Integer.parseInt(text1.getText()) +
                ➥ Integer.parseInt(text2.getText());
                answertext.setText(String.valueOf(sum));
            }
            if(e.getSource() == button2){
                hide();
            }
        }
    }
```

We've come far in this Skill, from basic dialog boxes to dialog boxes with layout, from dialog boxes with only the most basic of actions to dialog boxes that report results. In Skill 10, we're going to turn to another favorite with Java and Internet programmers everywhere—graphics programming.

Are You Experienced?

Now you can...

- ☑ create and use dialog boxes

- ☑ show and hide dialog boxes from code as required

- ☑ lay out controls in a dialog box for more control

- ☑ use controls in a dialog box to activate your controls and respond to the user's actions

- ☑ retrieve and use values from dialog box controls in the rest of the program

Skill 9

R. Jones 556-555-3398.

PROGRAMMERS
C, C, VB, Cobol, exp. Call 534-555-6543 or fax 534-555-6544.

PROGRAMMING
MRFS Inc. is looking for a Sr. Windows NT developer. Reqs. 3-5 yrs. Exp. in C under Windows, Win95 & NT, using Visual C. Excl. OO design & implementation skills a must. OLE2 & ODBC are a plus. Excl. Salary & bnfts. Resume & salary history to HR, 8779 HighTech Way, Computer City, AR

PROGRAMMERS
Contractors Wanted for short & long term assignments: Visual C, MFC Unix C/C, SQL Oracle Dev clop ers PC Help Desk Support Windows, NT & NetWare Telecommunications Visual Basic Access, HTMT, CGI, Perl MMI & Co., 885-555-9933

PROGRAMMER World Wide Web Links wants your HTML & Photoshop skills. Develop great WWW sites. Local & global customers. Send samples & resume to WWWL, 2000 Apple Road, Santa Rosa, CA.

TECHNICAL WRITER Software firm seeks writer/editor for manuals, research notes, project mgmt. Min 2 years tech. writing, DTP & programming experience. Send resume & writing samples to: Software Systems, Dallas, TX.

TECHNICAL Software development firm looking for Tech Trainers. Ideal candidates have programming experience in Visual C, HTML & JAVA. Need quick self starter. Call (443) 555-6868 for interview.

TECHNICAL WRITER/ Premier Computer Corp is seeking a combination of technical skills, knowledge and experience in the following areas: UNIX, Windows 95/NT, Visual Basic, on-line help & documentation, and the internet. Candidates must possess excellent writing skills and be comfortable working in a quality vs. deadline driven environment. Competitive salary. Fax resume & samples to Karen Fields, Premier Computer Corp. 444 Industrial Blvd. Concord, CA. Or send to our website at www.premier.com.

WEB DESIGNER
BA/BS or equivalent programming/multimedia production. 3 years of experience in use and design of WWW services streaming audio and video HTML, PERL, CGI, GIF, JPEG. Demonstrated interpersonal, organization communication, multi-tasking skills. Send resume to The Learning People at www.learning.com.

WEBMASTER-TECHNICAL
BSCS or equivalent. 2 years of experience in CGI, Windows 95/NT, UNIX, C, Java, Perl. Demonstrated ability to design code, debug and test on-line services. Send resume to The Learning People at www.learning.com.

PROGRAMMER World Wide Web Links wants your HTML & Photoshop skills. Develop great WWW sites.

ing aool. Experienced in documentation preparation & programming languages (Access, C, FoxPro) are a plus. Financial or banking customer service support is required along with excellent verbal & written communication skills with muti levels of end-users. Send resume to KKUP Enterprises, 45 Orange Blvd. Orange, CA.

COMPUTERS Small Web Design firm seeks indiv. w/NT, Webserver & Database management exp. fax resume to 556-555-4221.

COMPUTER/ Visual C/C, Visual Basic Exp'd Systems Analysts/ Programmers for growing software dev. team in Roseburg. Computer Science or related degree preferred. Develop adv. Engineering applications for engineering firm. Fax resume to 707-555-8744.

COMPUTER Web Master for dynamic SF internet co. Site. Dev. test, coord. train. 2 yrs prog. Exp. C C. Web C FTP. fax resume to Best Staffing 845-555-7722.

COMPUTER
PROGRAMMER
Ad agency seeks programmer w/exp. in UNIX/NT Platforms, Web Server, CGI/Perl. Programmer Position avail. on a project basis with the possibility to move into F/T. Fax resume & salary req to R. Jones 334-555-8332.

COMPUTERS Programmer/Analyst Design and maintain C based SQL database applications, Required skills: Visual Basic, C, SQL, ODBC. Document existing and new applications. Novell or NT exp. a plus. Fax resume & salary history to 235-555-9935.

GRAPHIC DESIGNER
Webmaster's Weekly is seeking a creative Graphic Designer to design high impact marketing collater ad, including direct mail promos. CD-ROM packages, ads and WWW pages. Must be able to juggle multiple projects and learn new skills on the job very rapidly. Web design experience a big plus. technical troubleshooting also a plus. Call 435-555-1235.

GRAPHICS - ART DIRECTOR - WEB-MULTIMEDIA
Leading internet development company has an outstanding opportunity for a talented, high-end Web Experienced Art Director. In addition to a great portfolio and fresh ideas, the ideal candidate has excellent communication and presentation skills. Working as a team with innovative producers and programmers, you will create dynamic, interactive web sites and application interfaces. Some programming experience required. Send samples and resume to: SuperSites, 333 Main, Seattle, WA.

MARKETING
Fast paced software and services provider looking for MARKETING COMMUNICATIONS SPECIALIST to be responsible for its webpage,

PROGRAMMERS Multiple short term assignments available: Visual C 3 positions SQL ServerNT Server. 2 positions JAVA & HTML, long term NetWare Various locations. Call for more info. 356-555-3398.

PROGRAMMERS
C, C, VB, Cobol, exp.
Call 534-555-6543
or fax 534-555-6544.

PROGRAMMING
MRFS Inc. is looking for a Sr. Windows NT developer. Reqs. 3-5 yrs. Exp. in C under Windows, Win95 & NT, using Visual C. Excl. OO design & implementation skills a must. OLE2 & ODBC are a plus. Excl. Salary & bnfts. Resume & salary history to HR, 8779 HighTech Way, Computer City, AR

PROGRAMMERS/ Contractors Wanted for short & long term assignments: Visual C, MFC Unix C/C, SQL Oracle Developers PC Help Desk Support Windows NT & NetWare Telecommunications Visual Basic, Access, HTMT, CGI, Perl MMI & Co., 885-555-9933

PROGRAMMER World Wide Web Links wants your HTML & Photoshop skills. Develop great WWW sites. Local a global customers. Send samples & resume to WWWL, 2000 Apple Road, Santa Rosa, CA.

TECHNICAL WRITER Software firm seeks writer/editor for manuals, research notes, project mgmt. Min 2 years tech. writing, DTP & programming experience. Send resume a writing samples to Software Systems, Dallas, TX.

COMPUTER PROGRAMMER
Ad agency seeks programmer w/exp. in UNIX/NT Platforms, Web Server, CGI/Perl. Programmer Position avail. on a project basis with the possibility to move into F/T. Fax resume & salary req. to R. Jones 334-555-8332.

TECHNICAL WRITER Premier Computer Corp is seeking a combination of technical skills, knowledge and experience in the following areas: UNIX, Windows 95/NT, Visual Basic, on-line help & documentation, and the internet. Candidates must possess excellent writing skills, and be comfortable working in a quality vs. deadline driven environment. Competitive salary. Fax resume & samples to Karen Fields, Premier Computer Corp., 444 Industrial Blvd. Concord, CA. Or send to our website at www.premier.com.

GRAPHICS - ART DIRECTOR - WEB-MULTIMEDIA
Leading internet development company has an outstanding opportunity for a talented, high-end Web Experienced Art Director. In addition to a great portfolio and fresh ideas, the ideal candidate has excellent communication and presentation skills. Working as a team with innovative producers and programmers, you will create dynamic, interactive web sites and application interfaces. Some programming experience required. Send samples and resume to: SuperSites, 333 Main, Seattle, WA.

WEB DESIGNER
BA/BS or equivalent programming/multimedia production. 3 years of experience in use and design of WWW services streaming audio and video HTML, PERL, CGI, GIF, JPEG. Demonstrated interpersonal, organization communication, multi-tasking skills. Send resume to The Learning People at www.learning.com.

WEBMASTER-TECHNICAL
BSCS or equivalent, 2 years of experience in CGI, Windows 95/NT,

COMPUTERS Small Web Design firm seeks indiv. w/NT, Webserver & Database management exp. Fax resume to 556-555-4221.

COMPUTER Visual C/C, Visual Basic Exp'd Systems Analysts/ Programmers for growing software dev. team in Roseburg. Computer Science or related degree preferred. Develop adv. Engineering applications for engineering firm. Fax resume to 707-555-8744.

COMPUTER Web Master for dynamic SF Internet co. Site. Dev. test, coord. train. 2 yrs prog. Exp. C C. Web C FTP. fax resume to Best Staffing 845-555-7722.

COMPUTERS/ QA SOFTWARE TESTERS Qualified candidates should have 2 yrs exp. performing integration & system testing using automated testing tools. Experienced in documentation preparation & programming languages (Access, C, FoxPro) are a plus. Financial or banking customer service support is required along with excellent verbal & written communication skills with muti levels of end-users. Send resume to KKUP Enterprises, 45 Orange Blvd. Orange, CA.

COMPUTERS Programmer/Analyst Design and maintain C based SQL database applications. Required skills: Visual Basic, C, SQL, ODBC. Document existing and new applications. Novell or NT exp. a plus. Fax resume & salary history to 235-555-9935.

GRAPHIC DESIGNER
Webmaster's Weekly is seeking a creative Graphic Designer to design high impact marketing collater ad, including direct mail promo's. CD-ROM packages, ads and WWW pages. Must be able to juggle multiple projects and learn new skills on the job very rapidly. Web design experience a big plus. technical troubleshooting also a plus. Call 435-555-1235.

GRAPHICS - ART DIRECTOR - WEB-MULTIMEDIA
Leading internet development company has an outstanding opportunity for a talented, high-end Web Experienced Art Director. In addition to a great portfolio and fresh ideas, the ideal candidate has excellent communication and presentation skills. Working as a team with innovative producers and programmers, you will create dynamic, interactive web sites and application interfaces. Some programming experience required. Send samples and resume to: SuperSites, 333 Main, Seattle, WA.

COMPUTER PROGRAMMER
Ad agency seeks programmer w/exp. in UNIX/NT Platforms, Web Server, CGI/Perl. Programmer Position avail. on a project basis with the possibility to move into F/T. Fax resume & salary req. to R. Jones 334-555-8332.

PROGRAMMERS / Established software company seeks program-

ment. Must be a self-starter, getic, organized. Must have 2 web experience. Programming plus. Call 985-555-9854

PROGRAMMERS Multiple term assignments available: C 3 positions SQL ServerNT S 2 positions JAVA & HTML, long NetWare Various locations. Ca more info. 356-555-3398.

PROGRAMMERS
C, C, VB, Cobol, exp. Call 534-6543 or fax 534-555-6544.

PROGRAMMING
MRFS Inc. is looking for a Windows NT developer. Req yrs. Exp. in C under Win Win95 & NT using Visual C OO design & implementation a must. OLE2 & ODBC are a Excl. Salary & bnfts. Resum salary history to HR, 8779 Hig Way, Computer City, AR

PROGRAMMERS/ Contr Wanted for short & long term a ments: Visual C, MFCUnix C/C Oracle Developers PC Help Support Windows NT & Net Telecommunications Visual Access, HTMT, CGI, Perl MMI 885-555-9933

PROGRAMMER World Wide Links wants your HTML & Phot skills. Develop great WWW Local & global customers. Send ples & resume to WWWL, Apple Road, Santa Rosa, CA.

TECHNICAL WRITER Software seeks writer/editor for ma research notes, project mgmt. years tech. writing, DTP & pro ming experience. Send resu writing samples to: Sof Systems, Dallas, TX.

TECHNICAL Software develo firm looking for Tech Trainers. candidates have programming rience in Visual C HTML & Need quick self starter. Call 555-6868 for interview.

TECHNICAL WRITER Pr Computer Corp is seeking a c nation of technical skills, know and experience in the foll areas: UNIX, Windows 95/NT, Basic, on-line help & docume and the internet. Candidates possess excellent writing skills be comfortable working in a q vs. deadline driven environ Competitive salary. Fax resu samples to Karen Fields. Pr Computer Corp. 444 Industrial Concord, CA. Or send to our w at www.premier.com.

WEB DESIGNER
BA/BS or equivalent pro ming/multimedia production years of experience in use design of WWW services stre audio and video HTML, PERL GIF, JPEG. Demonstrated intr sonal, organization communic multi-tasking skills. Send resume The Learning People at www. ing.com.

WEBMASTER-TECHNI

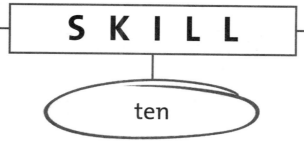

SKILL

ten

10

Java Graphics!

- ❏ Using the mouse
- ❏ Handling mouse events
- ❏ Drawing rectangles and rounded rectangles
- ❏ Drawing ovals and circles
- ❏ Drawing lines
- ❏ Drawing freehand with the mouse
- ❏ Printing in Java

In this chapter, we're going to start exploring a topic very popular among Java programmers—graphics. We'll see how to work with the elementary graphics methods in Java: drawing lines, rectangles, circles and ovals. We'll even design and run a graphics applet named dauber which will allow the user to draw their own graphics with the mouse. At the end of the chapter, we'll take a look at the Java 1.1 support for printing. Let's begin now by seeing how to use the mouse so we can add mouse support to our dauber applet.

Using the Mouse

To learn how to use the mouse, set up a new file named mousedemo.java. We can add a text field to our mousedemo applet, as shown in Figure 10.1.

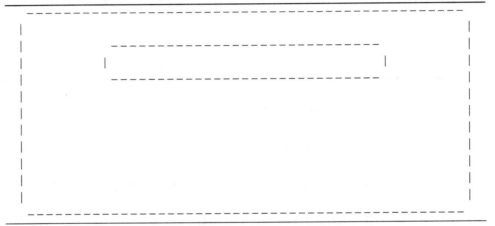

FIGURE   10.1   Adding a text field to the applet

Then, when a mouse event—such as a mouse button going down or up—occurs, we can report the event in the text field. For example, if the mouseEntered() method is called in our applet, we can report that the mouse has entered our applet's boundaries, as shown in Figure 10.2. When the user presses a mouse button, we can report its position in our applet in pixels, as shown in Figure 10.3.

We'll also report when the user clicks the mouse (see Figure 10.4) and when the mouse leaves the boundaries of the applet (see Figure 10.5).

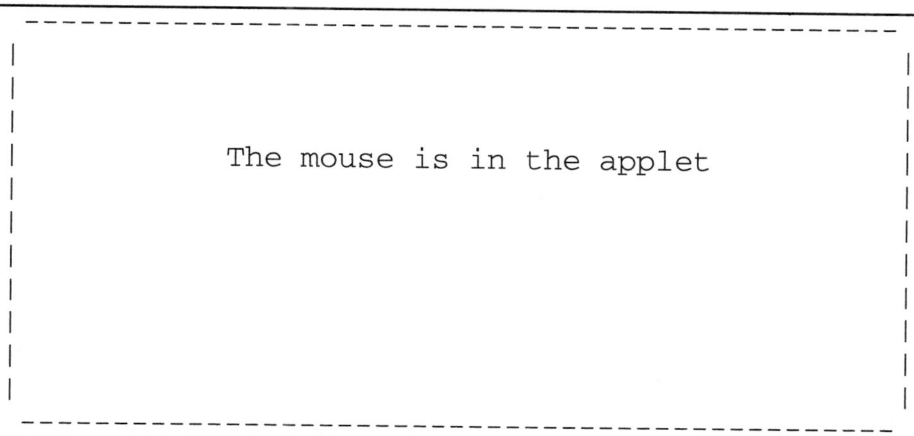

The mouse is in the applet

FIGURE 10.2 Our message reports that the mouse has entered the applet.

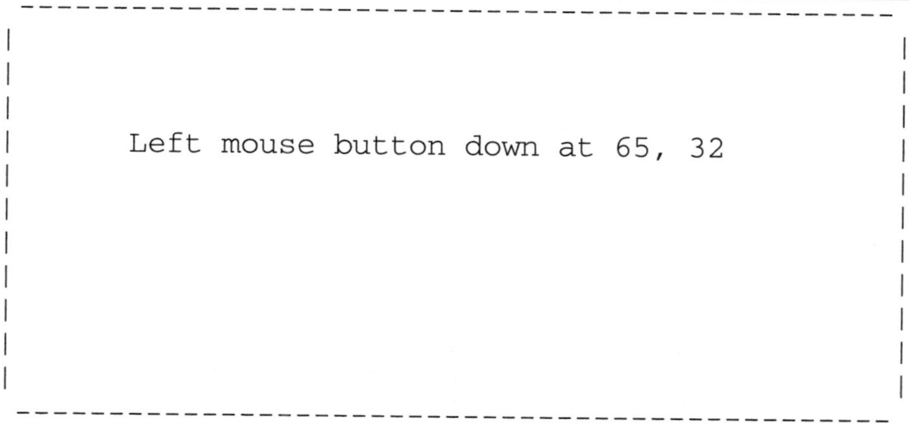

Left mouse button down at 65, 32

FIGURE 10.3 Reporting the position where the user pressed a mouse button

Skill 10

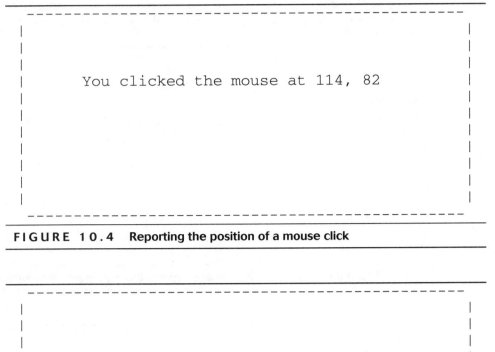

FIGURE 10.4   Reporting the position of a mouse click

The mouse is out of the applet

FIGURE 10.5   When the mouse leaves the applet this message appears.

Let's start writing our Java code now. We can give our text field the name mousetext. We add the declaration of this text field to our applet as follows:

```
import java.applet.Applet;
import java.awt.*;

public class mousedemo extends Applet {
```

➡   ```
       TextField mousetext;
       ```

    }

Next, we create this text field in the init() method:

```
import java.applet.Applet;
import java.awt.*;

public class mousedemo extends Applet {

    TextField mousetext;

    public void init(){
        mousetext = new TextField(25);
        add(mousetext);
             .
             .
             .
    }
```

Using MouseListener

Now we connect the *MouseListener* interface to our applet so we'll be able to handle mouse events:

```
import java.applet.Applet;
import java.awt.*;
import java.awt.event.*;

public class mousedemo extends Applet implements MouseListener{

    TextField mousetext;

    public void init(){
        mousetext = new TextField(25);
        add(mousetext);
        addMouseListener(this);
    }          .
               .
               .
```

Now our text field and our applet are ready to go. It's time to examine the mouse support that Java includes for us.

Mouse events like clicking or moving the mouse are handled in mouse event methods. The first mouse event we'll take a look at is the mousePressed event. (this is different from the mousePressed event used in Java 1.0. All of the mouse
```

handling methods have changed in Java 1.1.) If we define a `mousePressed()` method in our applet, the method will be called when a mouse button is pressed while the mouse is in the boundaries of our applet. Let's add a `mousePressed()` method to our applet now.

Using `mousePressed()`

The `mousePressed()`method looks like this:

```java
import java.applet.Applet;
import java.awt.*;
import java.awt.event.*;

public class mousedemo extends Applet implements MouseListener {

    TextField mousetext;

    public void init(){
        mousetext = new TextField(25);
        add(mousetext);
        addMouseListener(this);
    }

    public void mousePressed(MouseEvent e){

    }
}
```

This method will be called if the mouse button is pressed while the mouse is in our applet. The `MouseEvent` object holds the position of the mouse when the mouse button was pressed, and we can get that location with the `MouseEvent` `getX()` and `getY()` methods. In addition, the `MouseEvent` class member named `modifiers` (which we get with the `getModifiers()` method) will be 0 if the left mouse button went down, and non-zero otherwise. We can use that information to display which button was clicked now.

 NOTE   Java currently handles only two mouse buttons, even though some mice have three buttons.

We first check to see if the `modifiers` member is 0, which means the left mouse button was clicked:

```java
import java.applet.Applet;
import java.awt.*;
```

```
import java.awt.event.*;

public class mousedemo extends Applet implements MouseListener {

    TextField mousetext;

    public void init(){
        mousetext = new TextField(25);
        add(mousetext);
        addMouseListener(this);
    }

    public void mousePressed(MouseEvent e){
        if(e.getModifiers() == 0){
                .
                .
                .
        }
    }
}
```

If the modifiers member is 0, we report that the left mouse button was pressed. We place the text "Left mouse button down at" and the location of the mouse in our text field named mousetext:

```
import java.applet.Applet;
import java.awt.*;
import java.awt.event.*;

public class mousedemo extends Applet implements MouseListener {

    TextField mousetext;

    public void init(){
        mousetext = new TextField(25);
        add(mousetext);
        addMouseListener(this);
    }

    public void mousePressed(MouseEvent e){
        if(e.getModifiers() == 0){
            mousetext.setText("Left mouse button down at " +
            ➥ e.getX() + "," + e.getY());
        }   .
            .
            .
    }
}
```

Otherwise, there's only one other possibility, and we indicate that the right mouse button went down in an `else` clause:

```java
import java.applet.Applet;
import java.awt.*;
import java.awt.event.*;

public class mousedemo extends Applet implements MouseListener {

    TextField mousetext;

    public void init(){
        mousetext = new TextField(25);
        add(mousetext);
        addMouseListener(this);
    }

    public void mousePressed(MouseEvent e){
        if(e.getModifiers() == 0){
            mousetext.setText("Left mouse button down at " +
            ➥ e.getX() + "," + e.getY());
        }
        else{
            mousetext.setText("Right mouse button down at " +
            ➥ e.getX() + "," + e.getY());
        }
    }
}
```

NOTE   **The general form of the Java `if` statement is:**

```java
if(conditional){
[code block 1]
}
else{
[code block 2]
}
```

where the code in code block 1 is executed if the conditional expression evaluates to true, and the code in code block 2 is executed otherwise.

And that's it—we've handled the `mousePressed` event. Now let's take a look at the `mouseClicked` event.

Using mouseClicked()

The mouseClicked() method is called when the mouse is clicked, and we add that method to the applet now:

```java
import java.applet.Applet;
import java.awt.*;
import java.awt.event.*;

public class mousedemo extends Applet implements MouseListener {

    TextField mousetext;

    public void init(){
        mousetext = new TextField(25);
        add(mousetext);
        addMouseListener(this);
    }

    public void mousePressed(MouseEvent e){
        if(e.getModifiers() == 0){
            mousetext.setText("Left mouse button down at " +
            ➥ e.getX() + "," + e.getY());
        }
        else{
            mousetext.setText("Right mouse button down at " +
            ➥ e.getX() + "," + e.getY());
        }
    }

    public void mouseClicked(MouseEvent e){
                .
                .
                .
    }
}
```

Here, we'll just report the location of the mouse click, as follows:

```java
import java.applet.Applet;
import java.awt.*;
import java.awt.event.*;

public class mousedemo extends Applet implements MouseListener {

    TextField mousetext;

    public void init(){
        mousetext = new TextField(25);
```

```
                add(mousetext);
                addMouseListener(this);
        }

        public void mousePressed(MouseEvent e){
            if(e.getModifiers() == 0){
                mousetext.setText("Left mouse button down at " +
                ➡ e.getX() + "," + e.getY());
            }
            else{
                mousetext.setText("Right mouse button down at " +
                ➡ e.getX() + "," + e.getY());
            }
    }

        public void mouseClicked(MouseEvent e){
➡           mousetext.setText("You clicked the mouse at " + e.getX() +
            ➡ "," + e.getY());
        }
    }
```

That's it—now we've handled the `mousePressed()` and `mouseClicked()` methods. The next mouse method is `mouseReleased()`.

Using `mouseReleased()`

To identify when a mouse button is released, use the `mouseReleased()` event. The `mouseReleased` event is handled in the `mouseReleased()` method:

```
import java.applet.Applet;
import java.awt.*;
import java.awt.event.*;

public class mousedemo extends Applet implements MouseListener {

    TextField mousetext;

    public void init(){
        mousetext = new TextField(25);
        add(mousetext);
        addMouseListener(this);
    }

    public void mousePressed(MouseEvent e){
        if(e.getModifiers() == 0){
            mousetext.setText("Left mouse button down at " +
            ➡ e.getX() + "," + e.getY());
        }
```

```
                    else{
                        mousetext.setText("Right mouse button down at " +
                        ➥ e.getX() + "," + e.getY());
                    }
            }

➜       public void mouseReleased(MouseEvent e){
                            .
                            .
                            .
➜           }
        }
```

That's one way to identify that a mouse button is released. We can also indicate that the mouse button went up using the following method:

```
import java.applet.Applet;
import java.awt.*;
import java.awt.event.*;

public class mousedemo extends Applet implements MouseListener {

        TextField mousetext;

        public void init(){
            mousetext = new TextField(25);
            add(mousetext);
            addMouseListener(this);
        }

        public void mousePressed(MouseEvent e){
            if(e.getModifiers() == 0){
                mousetext.setText("Left mouse button down at " +
                ➥ e.getX() + "," + e.getY());
            }
            else{
                mousetext.setText("Right mouse button down at " +
                ➥ e.getX() + "," + e.getY());
            }
        }

➜       public void mouseReleased(MouseEvent e){
➜           mousetext.setText("The mouse button is up");
➜       }
        }
```

And that's it—we've reported what happened by placing text, "The mouse button is up," in our text field named mousetext. That takes care of mousePressed(), mouseClicked, and mouseReleased(). Next, we'll take a look at mouseEntered().

Using mouseEntered()

The mouseEntered event occurs when the mouse enters the boundaries of our applet on the screen. Place the following code in our applet to handle this event:

```
import java.applet.Applet;
import java.awt.*;
import java.awt.event.*;

public class mousedemo extends Applet implements MouseListener {

    TextField mousetext;

    public void init(){
        mousetext = new TextField(25);
        add(mousetext);
        addMouseListener(this);
    }

    public void mousePressed(MouseEvent e){
        if(e.getModifiers() == 0){
            mousetext.setText("Left mouse button down at " +
            ➥ e.getX() + "," + e.getY());
        }
        else{
            mousetext.setText("Right mouse button down at " +
            ➥ e.getX() + "," + e.getY());
        }
    }

    public void mouseClicked(MouseEvent e){
        mousetext.setText("You clicked the mouse at " + e.getX() +
        ➥ "," + e.getY());
    }

    public void mouseReleased(MouseEvent e){
        mousetext.setText("The mouse button is up");
    }

➜   public void mouseEntered(MouseEvent e){
                        .
                        .
                        .
➜       }

    }
```

Using the mouseEntered() method, we can report that the mouse has entered our applet by placing the message, "The mouse is in the applet," into the mousetext:

```
import java.applet.Applet;
import java.awt.*;
import java.awt.event.*;

public class mousedemo extends Applet implements MouseListener {

    TextField mousetext;

    public void init(){
        mousetext = new TextField(25);
        add(mousetext);
        addMouseListener(this);
    }

    public void mousePressed(MouseEvent e){
        if(e.getModifiers() == 0){
            mousetext.setText("Left mouse button down at " +
            ➥ e.getX() + "," + e.getY());
        }
        else{
            mousetext.setText("Right mouse button down at " +
            ➥ e.getX() + "," + e.getY());
        }
    }

    public void mouseClicked(MouseEvent e){
        mousetext.setText("You clicked the mouse at " + e.getX() +
        ➥ "," + e.getY());
    }

    public void mouseReleased(MouseEvent e){
        mousetext.setText("The mouse button is up");
    }

    public void mouseEntered(MouseEvent e){
        mousetext.setText("The mouse is in the applet");
    }
}
```

TIP   If you take advantage of the mouseEntered event in a Java frame window, you can change the mouse cursor to whatever you want with the Frame class setCursor() method when the mouse is in your window.

Skill 10

The last of the mouse events is the mouseExited event; we will take a look at that now.

Using mouseExited()

As you might expect—having seen the mouseEntered event—the mouseExited event occurs when the mouse leaves our applet. Place the following code in our applet to handle the mouseExited event:

```java
import java.applet.Applet;
import java.awt.*;
import java.awt.event.*;

public class mousedemo extends Applet implements MouseListener {

    TextField mousetext;

    public void init(){
        mousetext = new TextField(25);
        add(mousetext);
        addMouseListener(this);
    }

    public void mousePressed(MouseEvent e){
        if(e.getModifiers() == 0){
            mousetext.setText("Left mouse button down at " +
            ➡ e.getX() + "," + e.getY());
        }
        else{
            mousetext.setText("Right mouse button down at " +
            ➡ e.getX() + "," + e.getY());
        }
    }

    public void mouseClicked(MouseEvent e){
        mousetext.setText("You clicked the mouse at " + e.getX() +
        ➡ "," + e.getY());
    }

    public void mouseReleased(MouseEvent e){
        mousetext.setText("The mouse button is up");
    }

    public void mouseEntered(MouseEvent e){
        mousetext.setText("The mouse is in the applet");
    }
```

```
→        public void mouseExited(MouseEvent e){
                        .
                        .
                        .

→        }
    }
```

In our case, we'll just report that the mouse left the applet with a message, as follows:

```
import java.applet.Applet;
import java.awt.*;
import java.awt.event.*;

public class mousedemo extends Applet implements MouseListener {

    TextField mousetext;

    public void init(){
        mousetext = new TextField(25);
        add(mousetext);
        addMouseListener(this);
    }

    public void mousePressed(MouseEvent e){
        if(e.getModifiers() == 0){
            mousetext.setText("Left mouse button down at " +
            ➡ e.getX() + "," + e.getY());
        }
        else{
            mousetext.setText("Right mouse button down at " +
            ➡ e.getX() + "," + e.getY());
        }
    }

    public void mouseClicked(MouseEvent e){
        mousetext.setText("You clicked the mouse at " + e.getX() +
        ➡ "," + e.getY());
    }

    public void mouseReleased(MouseEvent e){
        mousetext.setText("The mouse button is up");
    }

    public void mouseEntered(MouseEvent e){
        mousetext.setText("The mouse is in the applet");
    }
```

```
       public void mouseExited(MouseEvent e){
→          mousetext.setText("The mouse is out of the applet");
       }
   }
```

And now our mousedemo applet is ready to use. In the graphic below, our mousedemo applet is indicating that the mouse has entered the applet:

If the user presses the left mouse button, the applet displays the message shown below.

As you can tell by playing around with this applet for a while, all the other mouse events are active as well. The code for this applet appears in mousedemo.java.

mousedemo.java

```java
import java.applet.Applet;
import java.awt.*;
import java.awt.event.*;

public class mousedemo extends Applet implements MouseListener {

    TextField mousetext;

    public void init(){
        mousetext = new TextField(25);
        add(mousetext);
        addMouseListener(this);
    }

    public void mousePressed(MouseEvent e){
        if(e.getModifiers() == 0){
            mousetext.setText("Left mouse button down at " +
            ➡ e.getX() + "," + e.getY());
        }
        else{
            mousetext.setText("Right mouse button down at " +
            ➡ e.getX() + "," + e.getY());
        }
    }

    public void mouseClicked(MouseEvent e){
        mousetext.setText("You clicked the mouse at " + e.getX() +
        ➡ "," + e.getY());
    }

    public void mouseReleased(MouseEvent e){
        mousetext.setText("The mouse button is up");
    }

    public void mouseEntered(MouseEvent e){
        mousetext.setText("The mouse is in the applet");
    }

    public void mouseExited(MouseEvent e){
        mousetext.setText("The mouse is out of the applet");
    }
}
```

Skill 10

Now that we've seen how to use the mouse in a Java applet, we're ready to create our dauber applet, which will let the user to create graphics like lines, rectangles, and circles with the mouse.

The Dauber Applet

To explore how graphics works in Java, we'll create the dauber applet now. We can present the user with a collection of drawing "tools"—as shown in Figure 10.6, these tools will be buttons the user can select from. After the user selects a drawing tool (i.e., by clicking a drawing tool button), they can draw the figure they chose with the mouse.

```
---------------------------------------------------------------------
|                                                                     |
|    -------------     ----    ----    ----    -------    -------     |
|    |Draw freehand|   |Line|  |Oval|  |Rect|  |3D Rect|  |Rounded|   |
|    -------------     ----    ----    ----    -------    -------     |
|                                                                     |
|                                                                     |
|                                                                     |
|                                                                     |
|                                                                     |
|                                                                     |
|                                                                     |
|                                                                     |
|                                                                     |
|                                                                     |
|                                                                     |
---------------------------------------------------------------------
```

FIGURE 10.6   We wil present the user with a collection of drawing tools.

To draw a rectangle, the user clicks the Rect button, moves the mouse to the place where they'd like their new graphics figure to begin, presses and holds the mouse button, drags the mouse to the other end of the graphics figure, and releases the mouse button. When the mouse button goes up, we draw the figure the user has described.

Let's see drawing in action. Create a new file named dauber.java now. Open the file and add the new dauber class now:

```
public class dauber extends Applet
{                 .
                  .
                  .
```

Creating Dauber's Drawing Tools

We can add our drawing tools now as buttons—we will examine six types of graphics here: lines, ovals (including circles), rectangles, 3D rectangles, rounded rectangles, and freehand drawing. We'll need six buttons, which we'll set up as follows:

```
public class dauber extends Applet
{
        Button buttonDraw, buttonLine, buttonOval, buttonRect,
        ➥ button3DRect, buttonRounded;
            .
            .
            .
```

Next, we add the six buttons and create them in the init() method:

```
public class dauber extends Applet {

        Button buttonDraw, buttonLine, buttonOval, buttonRect,
        ➥ button3DRect, buttonRounded;

        public void init() {

                buttonDraw = new Button("Draw Freehand");
                buttonLine = new Button("Line");
                buttonOval = new Button("Oval");
                buttonRect = new Button("Rect");
                button3DRect = new Button("3D Rect");
                buttonRounded = new Button("Round");
                    .
                    .
                    .

        }
```

To arrange those buttons, we'll use the default FlowLayout manager here. We just add the buttons to that layout now, as well as adding an ActionListener for each button as follows:

```
    public class dauber extends Applet implements ActionListener{
```

```
Button buttonDraw, buttonLine, buttonOval, buttonRect,
➥ button3DRect;
Button buttonRounded;

public void init() {

        buttonDraw = new Button("Draw Freehand");
        buttonLine = new Button("Line");
        buttonOval = new Button("Oval");
        buttonRect = new Button("Rect");
        button3DRect = new Button("3D Rect");
        buttonRounded = new Button("Round");

        add(buttonDraw);
        buttonDraw.addActionListener(this);
        add(buttonLine);
        buttonLine.addActionListener(this);
        add(buttonOval);
        buttonOval.addActionListener(this);
        add(buttonRect);
        buttonRect.addActionListener(this);
        add(button3DRect);
        button3DRect.addActionListener(this);
        add(buttonRounded);
        buttonRounded.addActionListener(this);
                    .
                    .
                    .
}
```

Now that our buttons have been installed, we can make them active. But note that the drawing does not take place when the user clicks a drawing tool—it takes place when the user releases the mouse button. That is, we'll draw the required figure in the `mouseReleased()` method.

How will we know what figure to draw? We'll have to know which button the user clicked, so we'll set some *boolean* flags, one for each drawing tool, when the user clicks one of the drawing tools.

 NOTE   A boolean flag is just a boolean variable (which can take the values true or false) used to indicate the state (true or false) of some option in a program. For example, `windowvisibleboolean` may be a boolean flag, which, if true, indicates that a particular window is visible.

Creating Dauber's Boolean Flags

We will create and initialize our boolean flags now. If the user clicks the line drawing tool, we will set the flag named bLineFlag to true; if they click the rectangle drawing tool, we will set the flag named bRectFlag to true, and so on. Our flags will be: bDrawFlag, bLineFlag, bOvalFlag, bRectFlag, b3DRectFlag, and bRoundedFlag, and we'll start out with all of them set to false:

```
public class dauber extends Applet implements ActionListener {

        Button buttonDraw, buttonLine, buttonOval, buttonRect,
    ➥ button3DRect, buttonRounded;

➔       boolean bMouseDownFlag = false;
➔       boolean bMouseUpFlag = false;
➔       boolean bDrawFlag = false;
➔       boolean bLineFlag = false;
➔       boolean bOvalFlag = false;
➔       boolean bRectFlag = false;
➔       boolean b3DRectFlag = false;
➔       boolean bRoundedFlag = false;
                  .
                  .
                  .
```

We will keep track of the mouse in our dauber applet because we draw our graphics figures after the mouse button goes up, so we add two new flags, bMouseDownFlag and bMouseUpFlag as follows:

```
public class dauber extends Applet implements ActionListener {

        Button buttonDraw, buttonLine, buttonOval, buttonRect,
    ➥ button3DRect, buttonRounded;

➔       boolean bMouseDownFlag = false;
➔       boolean bMouseUpFlag = false;
➔       boolean bDrawFlag = false;
➔       boolean bLineFlag = false;
➔       boolean bOvalFlag = false;
➔       boolean bRectFlag = false;
➔       boolean b3DRectFlag = false;
➔       boolean bRoundedFlag = false;
                  .
                  .
                  .
```

After we make these flags active, we'll know in any method of the applet which drawing tool the user has selected and what the mouse state is. That's what's important to us—what we're being asked to draw and when we can draw it. We will connect the buttons we've installed to these flags, and then we won't need to think about the buttons any more.

 TIP We are dividing our program into a user interface part (using buttons) and a separate drawing part (using flags). Dividing the parts of a program into self-contained (and therefore easily debugged) parts is usually a good programming practice. Long, monolithic programs get to be very unwieldy very quickly.

We make the drawing tool buttons active in an `actionPerformed()` method that we can add to our applet now:

```
public void actionPerformed(ActionEvent e){
                   .
                   .
                   .
}
```

First, we can check whether the user clicked the Draw Freehand button to start freehand drawing. The name of this button is `buttonDraw`, and we check whether it was clicked this way:

```
public void actionPerformed(ActionEvent e){
    if(e.getSource() == buttonDraw){
                   .
                   .
                   .
    }
}
```

If so, we can toggle the setting of the freehand drawing flag, `bDrawFlag`, and we do that with the Java exclamation point (!) operator, which reverses boolean values (a value of true becomes false, and a value of false becomes true):

```
public void actionPerformed(ActionEvent e){
    if(e.getSource() == buttonDraw){
→       bDrawFlag = !bDrawFlag;
                   .
                   .
                   .
    }
```

In addition, now that the user has clicked the Draw Freehand button, we set the other button's flags to false:

```
public void actionPerformed(ActionEvent e){
    if(e.getSource() == buttonDraw){
        bDrawFlag = !bDrawFlag;
        bLineFlag = false;
        bOvalFlag = false;
        bRectFlag = false;
        b3DRectFlag = false;
        bRoundedFlag = false;
    }
                .
                .
                .
}
```

We can connect the other buttons up to their boolean flags as follows:

```
public void actionPerformed(ActionEvent e){
    if(e.getSource() == buttonDraw){
        bDrawFlag = !bDrawFlag;
        bLineFlag = false;
        bOvalFlag = false;
        bRectFlag = false;
        b3DRectFlag = false;
        bRoundedFlag = false;
    }
    if(e.getSource() == buttonLine){
        bLineFlag = !bLineFlag;
        bDrawFlag = false;
        bOvalFlag = false;
        bRectFlag = false;
        b3DRectFlag = false;
        bRoundedFlag = false;
    }
    if(e.getSource() == buttonOval){
        bOvalFlag = !bOvalFlag;
        bLineFlag = false;
        bDrawFlag = false;
        bRectFlag = false;
        b3DRectFlag = false;
        bRoundedFlag = false;
    }
    if(e.getSource() == buttonRect){
        bRectFlag = !bRectFlag;
        bLineFlag = false;
        bOvalFlag = false;
```

Skill 10

```
→                        bDrawFlag = false;
→                        b3DRectFlag = false;
→                        bRoundedFlag = false;
→               }
→               if(e.getSource() == button3DRect){
→                        b3DRectFlag = !b3DRectFlag;
→                        bLineFlag = false;
→                        bOvalFlag = false;
→                        bRectFlag = false;
→                        bDrawFlag = false;
→                        bRoundedFlag = false;
→               }
→               if(e.getSource() == buttonRounded){
→                        bRoundedFlag = !bRoundedFlag;
→                        bLineFlag = false;
→                        bOvalFlag = false;
→                        bRectFlag = false;
→                        b3DRectFlag = false;
→                        bDrawFlag = false;
→               }
→       }
```

And so, we've connected our buttons to the settings of associated boolean flags. We don't have to worry about the buttons anymore since from now on, we can just check the boolean flags we set up.

Drawing in the Dauber Applet

Now the user turns from the drawing tool buttons to using the mouse to outline the graphics figure they want to draw. They will press the mouse button at some location in our applet that we can call the anchor point, and then they will move the mouse to a new location, which we call the drawto point. When they release the mouse button, our applet will draw the graphics figure, as bounded by the anchor and drawto points:

That's how we'll proceed, then—we'll record the location at which the mouse went down in the mousePressed() method and start the drawing process in the mouseReleased() method. Let's look at the mousePressed() method now.

Using mousePressed() in Dauber

In the mousePressed event, we want to record the beginning point of the graphics figure, the point we have called the anchor point. We can store points in Java using the Java Point class, which has two data members: x and y. We'll declare two Point objects, ptAnchor and ptDrawTo in our applet as follows:

```
public class dauber extends Applet implements ActionListener {

        Button buttonDraw, buttonLine, buttonOval, buttonRect,
        ➥ button3DRect, buttonRounded;

        Point ptAnchor, ptDrawTo;

        boolean bMouseDownFlag = false;
        boolean bMouseUpFlag = false;
        boolean bDrawFlag = false;
        boolean bLineFlag = false;
        boolean bOvalFlag = false;
        boolean bRectFlag = false;
        boolean b3DRectFlag = false;
        boolean bRoundedFlag = false;
                .
                .
                .
```

The x coordinate of a point like ptAnchor can be reached as ptAnchor.x and the y coordinate as prAnchor.y.

Adding MouseListener Support to Dauber

Now we'll add the mouse support we need. We'll implement the MouseListener interface for mousePressed()and mouseReleased(). In addition, we'll use the mouseDragged() method when we draw freehand with the mouse. To use mouseDragged(), we need a new listener—MouseMotionListener—and we add that like as follows:

```
public class dauber extends Applet implements ActionListener,
MouseListener, MouseMotionListener {
```

Next, we install our new listeners:

```
public class dauber extends Applet implements ActionListener,
MouseListener, MouseMotionListener {
```

```
Button buttonDraw, buttonLine, buttonOval, buttonRect,
➥ button3DRect, buttonRounded;

Point ptAnchor, ptDrawTo;

boolean bMouseDownFlag = false;
boolean bMouseUpFlag = false;
boolean bDrawFlag = false;
boolean bLineFlag = false;
boolean bOvalFlag = false;
boolean bRectFlag = false;
boolean b3DRectFlag = false;
boolean bRoundedFlag = false;

public void init() {

    buttonDraw = new Button("Draw Freehand");
    buttonLine = new Button("Line");
    buttonOval = new Button("Oval");
    buttonRect = new Button("Rect");
    button3DRect = new Button("3D Rect");
    buttonRounded = new Button("Round");
                .
                .
                .

    button3DRect.addActionListener(this);
    add(buttonRounded);
    buttonRounded.addActionListener(this);
➜   addMouseListener(this);
➜   addMouseMotionListener(this);
}               .
                .
                .
```

Having added the MouseMotionListener, we next add the mouse methods we'll use: `mousePressed()`, `mouseReleased()`, and `mouseDragged()`:

```
public void mousePressed(MouseEvent e){
                .
                .
                .
}

public void mouseReleased(MouseEvent e){
                .
                .
                .
}
```

```
public void mouseDragged(MouseEvent e){
        .
        .
        .
}

public void mouseClicked(MouseEvent e){}

public void mouseEntered(MouseEvent e){}

public void mouseExited(MouseEvent e){}

public void mouseMoved(MouseEvent e){}
```

The location at which the mouse went down is passed to us with the e.getX() and e.getY() methods, and we want to store that location in the anchor point object, ptAnchor. We do so by creating a new object of the Point class, passing the x and y coordinates as arguments to the Point class's constructor:

```
      public void mousePressed(MouseEvent e){
➡         ptAnchor = new Point(e.getX(), e.getY());
              .
              .
              .
      }
```

DO EXTRA ANCHOR POINTS WASTE MEMORY?

Memory-frugal C++ programmers may worry about lines of code like

```
      ptAnchor = new Point(x, y);
```

because the user may click the mouse button several times while using our applet and so execute this line each time. What happens to the old anchor points—do those objects just remain in memory, taking up space? Should we delete them?

It turns out there is not a delete operator in Java like the one in C++. But that's not a big problem because when no object variables refer to a particular object, Java deallocates that object's memory automatically (a process called automatic garbage collection). If you want to save memory space by getting rid of objects that are no longer needed, simply set their variables to null for example:

```
      framewindow = null;
```

Skill 10

Now that the mouse button is down, we set the mouse boolean flags, bMouseDownFlag and bMouseUpFlag to indicate the following:

```
      public void mousePressed(MouseEvent e){
➜         bMouseDownFlag = true;
➜         bMouseUpFlag = false;
          ptAnchor = new Point(e.getX(), e.getY());
      }
```

We'll set the same flags when the mouse button goes back up in the mouseReleased() method.

Using mouseReleased() in Dauber

We set the mouse boolean flags like this in the mouseReleased() method:

```
      public void mouseReleased(MouseEvent e){
➜         bMouseDownFlag = false;
➜         bMouseUpFlag = true;
               .
               .
               .
      }
```

Note that when the mouse button goes up the user is indicating the end point of the graphics figure—the drawto point. We can record the drawto point as follows, using the x and y location of the mouse.

```
      public void mouseReleased(MouseEvent e){
          bMouseDownFlag = false;
          bMouseUpFlag = true;

➜         ptDrawTo = new Point(e.getX(), e.getY());
               .
               .
               .
      }
```

Now we have the two points we'll need to draw our figure, ptAnchor and ptDrawTo. The actual drawing should be done in the paint() method— that is where we are passed an object of the Graphics class to use in painting our applet. To force the paint event to occur, we call `repaint()` in the `mouseReleased()` method as follows:

```
public void mouseReleased(MouseEvent e){
    bMouseDownFlag = false;
    bMouseUpFlag = true;

    ptDrawTo = new Point(e.getX(), e.getY());
    repaint();
}
```

Now we're ready to draw. We will start with one of the most common graphics figures—the line.

Drawing Lines in Dauber

When the user clicks the Line button, they can draw lines in our applet, stretching from the point we have called `ptAnchor` to the point we have called `ptDrawTo`, as shown in Figure 10.7.

```
-------------------------------------------------------------
|                                                           |
|   -------------     ----     ----    ----    -------     -------    |
|  |Draw freehand|   |Line|   |Oval|  |Rect|  |3D Rect|   |Rounded|   |
|   -------------     ----     ----    ----    -------     -------    |
|                                                           |
|                                                           |
|                                                           |
|                                                           |
|                                                           |
|    anchor point  -------------------- drawto point        |
|                                                           |
|                                                           |
|                                                           |
|                                                           |
|                                                           |
-------------------------------------------------------------
```

FIGURE 10.7 The line extends from the anchor point to the drawto point.

Now that the mouse button has been released, the `paint()` method is called, and we can draw the line. Add the `paint()` method now:

```
public void paint (Graphics g) {
        .
        .
        .
}
```

Because there can be many causes for the paint event, we first check to make sure that the mouse button went up—by checking the variables **bMouseUpFlag** and **bLineFlag** to make sure we are supposed to be drawing a line. If so, we should draw our figure as follows:

```
public void paint (Graphics g) {

        if(bLineFlag && bMouseUpFlag){
                .
                .
                .
        }
}
```

If we are expected to draw a line, the line is to stretch from the anchor point to the drawto point. We use the `Graphics` class's `drawLine()` method to draw this line, and we pass it the start and end coordinates of the line as follows:

```
public void paint (Graphics g) {

        if(bLineFlag && bMouseUpFlag){
                g.drawLine(ptAnchor.x, ptAnchor.y, ptDrawTo.x, ptDrawTo.y);
        }
}
```

And now our line appears in the applet, as shown in Figure 10.8. The `drawLine()` method is just one of the methods of the `Graphics` class—that class's methods appear in Table 10.1.

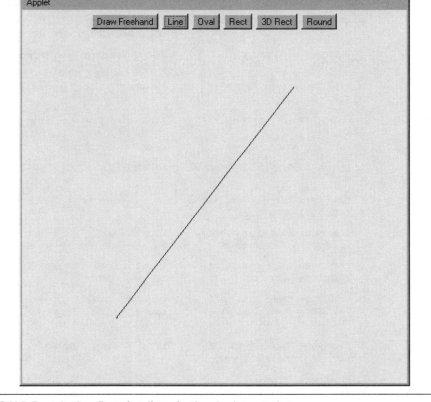

FIGURE 10.8   Drawing lines in the dauber applet

T A B L E 1 0 . 1 : The methods of the Graphics class

Method	Does This
Graphics()	Constructs a new Graphics object.
clearRect(int, int, int, int)	Clears the given rectangle by filling it with the current background color.
clipRect(int, int, int, int)	Intersects the current clip with the given rectangle.
copyArea(int, int, int, int, int, int)	Copies an area of the Component.
create()	Creates a new Graphics object that is a copy of this Graphics object.

TABLE 10.1 CONTINUED: The methods of the Graphics class

Method	Does This
create(int, int, int, int)	Creates a new Graphics object based on this Graphics object but with a new translation and clip area.
dispose()	Disposes of the system resources used by this graphics context.
draw3DRect(int, int, int, int, boolean)	Draws a 3-D highlighted outline of the given rectangle.
drawArc(int, int, int, int, int, int)	Draws the outline of an arc covering the given rectangle, starting at startAngle and extending for arcAngle degrees, using the current color.
drawBytes(byte[], int, int, int, int)	Draws the given bytes using the current font and color.
drawChars(char[], int, int, int, int)	Draws the given characters using the current font and color.
drawImage(Image, int, int, Color, ImageObserver)	Draws as much of the given image as is currently available at the given coordinate with the given solid background.
drawImage(Image, int, int, ImageObserver)	Draws as much of the given image as is currently available at the given coordinate (x, y).
drawImage(Image, int, int, int, int, Color, ImageObserver)	Draws as much of the given image as has already been scaled to fit inside the given rectangle with the given solid background color.
drawImage(Image, int, int, int, int, ImageObserver)	Draws as much of the given image as has already been scaled to fit inside the given rectangle.
drawImage(Image, int, int, int, int, int, int, int, int, Color, ImageObserver)	Draws as much of the given area of the given image as is currently available, scaling it to fit inside the given area of destination drawable surface with the given solid the background color.
drawImage(Image, int, int, int, int, int, int, int, int, ImageObserver)	Draws as much of the given area of the given image as is available, scaling it to fit inside the given area of the destination drawable surface.
drawLine(int, int, int, int)	Draws a line between the coordinates (x1,y1) and (x2,y2) using the current color.
drawOval(int, int, int, int)	Draws the outline of an oval covering the given rectangle using the current color.
drawPolygon(int[], int[], int)	Draws the outline of a polygon defined by arrays of x coordinates and y coordinates using the current color.
drawPolygon(Polygon)	Draws the outline of a polygon defined by the given Polygon object using the current color.
drawPolyline(int[], int[], int)	Draws a sequence of connected lines defined by arrays of x coordinates and y coordinates using the current color.

TABLE 10.1 CONTINUED: The methods of the Graphics class

Method	Does This
drawRect(int, int, int, int)	Draws the outline of the given rectangle using the current color.
drawRoundRect(int, int, int, int, int, int)	Draws the outline of the given rounded corner rectangle using the current color.
drawString(String, int, int)	Draws the given String using the current font and color.
fill3DRect(int, int, int, int, boolean)	Paints a 3-D highlighted rectangle filled with the current color.
fillArc(int, int, int, int, int, int)	Fills an arc bounded by the given rectangle, starting at startAngle and extending for arcAngle degrees, with the current color.
fillOval(int, int, int, int)	Fills an oval bounded by the given rectangle with the current color.
fillPolygon(int[], int[], int)	Fills a polygon defined by arrays of coordinates and y coordinates with the current color using an even-odd fill rule.
fillPolygon(Polygon)	Fills the polygon defined by the given Polygon object with the current color using an even-odd fill rule.
fillRect(int, int, int, int)	Fills the given rectangle with the current color.
fillRoundRect(int, int, int, int, int, int)	Fills the given rounded corner rectangle with the current color.
finalize()	Disposes of this graphics context once it is no longer referenced.
getClip()	Returns a Shape object representing the current clipping area.
getClipBounds()	Returns the bounding rectangle of the current clipping area.
getClipRect()	Deprecated. Replaced by getClipBounds().
getColor()	Gets the current color.
getFont()	Gets the current font.
getFontMetrics()	Gets the font metrics of the current font.
getFontMetrics(Font)	Gets the font metrics for the given font.
setClip(int, int, int, int)	Sets the current clip to the rectangle given by the given coordinates.
setClip(Shape)	Set the current clipping area to an arbitrary clip shape.
setColor(Color)	Sets the current color to the given color.
setFont(Font)	Sets the font for all subsequent text rendering operations.
setPaintMode()	Sets the logical pixel operation function to the Paint, or overwrite mode.

Skill 10

TABLE 10.1 CONTINUED: The methods of the Graphics class

Method	Does This
setXORMode(Color)	Sets the logical pixel operation function to the XOR mode, which alternates pixels between the current color and a new given XOR color.
toString()	Returns a String object representing this Graphics object's value.
translate(int, int)	Translates the origin of the graphics context to a point in the current coordinate system.

Now that you've learned how to create lines, we'll move on to creating circles and ovals.

Creating Circles and Ovals in Dauber

When the user clicks the Oval tool button, they can draw circles and ovals, as shown in Figure 10.9.

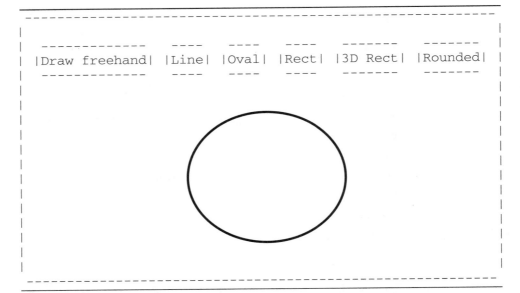

FIGURE 10.9   Drawing a circle

Let's work on creating circles now. We can do that with the Graphics class's drawOval() method (with which you can draw both ovals and circles). This method—like the other graphics methods we'll see in this chapter—works slightly differently from the drawLine() method we just used. In drawLine(), we only needed to pass the (x, y) coordinates of the beginning and end of the line. With other graphics methods like drawOval() and drawRect(), we need to pass the upper left corner of the figure's bounding rectangle and its width and height:

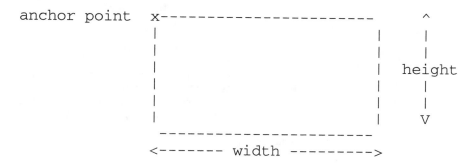

```
anchor point   x----------------------          ^
               |                        |        |
               |                        |        |
               |                        |   height
               |                        |        |
               |                        |        |
               |                        |        V
               ----------------------
               <------- width --------->
```

It looks as if we can pass the anchor point as the upper left corner of the figure's bounding rectangle. However, there is no special reason that the user would have placed the anchor point at the upper left—in fact, the anchor point may even be at the lower right. Therefore, we will reorder the anchor point and the drawto point to make sure that the anchor point is at the upper left, and the drawto point is at the lower right. (The Java graphics methods require that we pass them the point we know to be the upper left of the image we want to draw.)

We can reorder these points in the mouseReleased() method, just before we paint the graphics figure the user has requested in our applet. As mentioned, we won't need to rearrange the two bounding points for the drawLine() method, but we will for the other graphics methods. For that reason, we first make sure we are not drawing a line by checking the bLineFlag variable in an if statement, as follows:

```
        public void mouseReleased(MouseEvent e){
            bMouseDownFlag = false;
            bMouseUpFlag = true;
            ptDrawTo = new Point(e.getX(), e.getY());
→           if(!bLineFlag){
                        .
                        .
                        .

            }
            repaint();
        }
```

If we are not drawing a line, we can continue on, rearranging the point named ptAnchor to be the top left of our figure's bounding rectangle and the ptDrawTo point to be the bottom left of the bounding rectangle. We do that simply by numerically comparing values in each of these points.

We can use the Java Math class's min() and max() methods to compare values. The min() method takes two values and returns the lesser; the max() method takes two values and returns the greater. That means that we can sort the anchor and drawto points as follows:

```
public void mouseReleased(MouseEvent e){
    bMouseDownFlag = false;
    bMouseUpFlag = true;
    ptDrawTo = new Point(e.getX(), e.getY());
    If(!bLineFlag){
    ptDrawTo = new Point(Math.max(e.getX(), ptAnchor.x),
    ➥ Math.max(e.getY(), ptAnchor.y));
        ptAnchor = new Point(Math.min(e.getX(), ptAnchor.x),
        ➥ Math.min(e.getY(), ptAnchor.y));
    }
    repaint();
}
```

Here we are using the Java Math class, and that class is part of the java.lang package. We need to import that class in the beginning of our applet as follows so Java can find the min() and max() methods:

```
import java.awt.Graphics;
import java.awt.*;
import java.awt.event.*;
import java.lang.Math;
import java.applet.Applet;

public class dauber extends Applet implements ActionListener,
MouseListener, MouseMotionListener {

    Button buttonDraw, buttonLine, buttonOval, buttonRect,
    ➥ button3DRect, buttonRounded;
        .
        .
        .
```

Now we're ready to draw ovals and circles with the drawOval() method. We place the code to draw these figures in the paint() method, which currently looks like this:

```
public void paint (Graphics g) {
    int loop_index;
    int drawWidth, drawHeight;

    if(bLineFlag && bMouseUpFlag){
        g.drawLine(ptAnchor.x, ptAnchor.y, ptDrawTo.x, ptDrawTo.y);
    }
    if(bOvalFlag && bMouseUpFlag){
        drawWidth = ptDrawTo.x - ptAnchor.x;
        drawHeight = ptDrawTo.y - ptAnchor.y;
```

```
        g.drawOval(ptAnchor.x, ptAnchor.y, drawWidth, drawHeight);
                 .
                 .
                 .
    }
```

Here, by examining the boolean flag bMouseUpFlag, we check to make sure that the user has released the mouse button and that we should draw the oval or circle. If the flag is set, we are supposed to draw a figure. Next, we check the bOvalFlag boolean flag to see if we are supposed to be drawing an oval:

```
public void paint (Graphics g) {
    int loop_index;
    int drawWidth, drawHeight;

    if(bLineFlag && bMouseUpFlag){
        g.drawLine(ptAnchor.x, ptAnchor.y, ptDrawTo.x, ptDrawTo.y);
    }
    if(bOvalFlag && bMouseUpFlag){
             .
             .
             .
    }
```

To draw the oval or circle, we'll need the width and height of the figure. Now that we've ordered our drawto and anchor points, we can find those dimensions by simple subtraction, as follows:

```
public void paint (Graphics g) {
    int loop_index;
    int drawWidth, drawHeight;

    if(bLineFlag && bMouseUpFlag){
        g.drawLine(ptAnchor.x, ptAnchor.y, ptDrawTo.x, ptDrawTo.y);
    }
    if(bOvalFlag && bMouseUpFlag){
        drawWidth = ptDrawTo.x - ptAnchor.x;
        drawHeight = ptDrawTo.y - ptAnchor.y;
             .
             .
             .
}
```

We use the Graphics class drawOval() method to draw the oval or circle. We pass it the coordinates of the upper left point of the figure's bounding rectangle—that is, our anchor point—and the figure's width and height:

```
public void paint (Graphics g) {
    int loop_index;
    int drawWidth, drawHeight;
```

```
        if(bLineFlag && bMouseUpFlag){
            g.drawLine(ptAnchor.x, ptAnchor.y, ptDrawTo.x, ptDrawTo.y);
        }
        if(bOvalFlag && bMouseUpFlag){
            drawWidth = ptDrawTo.x - ptAnchor.x;
            drawHeight = ptDrawTo.y - ptAnchor.y;
            g.drawOval(ptAnchor.x, ptAnchor.y, drawWidth, drawHeight);
                    .
                    .
                    .

}
```

Now we have drawn ovals and circles. Our circles and ovals appear on the screen, as shown in Figure 10.10.

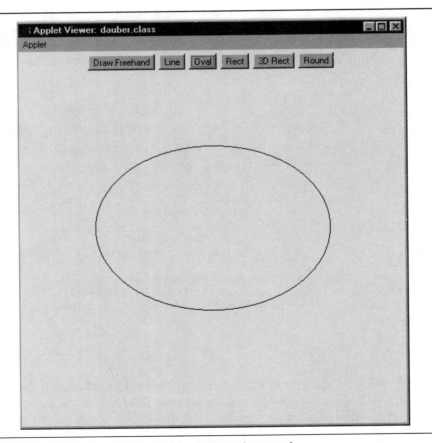

FIGURE 10.10   Our dauber applet can draw ovals.

Using Dauber to Draw Rectangles

Our next step is to draw rectangles. The user can draw rectangles by clicking the Rect button and using the mouse, as shown in Figure 10.11.

```
 ---------------------------------------------------------------
|                                                               |
|   -------------    ----    ----    ----    --------    ------- |
|  |Draw freehand|  |Line|  |Oval|  |Rect|  |3D Rect|  |Rounded||
|   -------------    ----    ----    ----    --------    ------- |
|                                                               |
|                                                               |
|                         -----------------                     |
|                        |                 |                    |
|                        |                 |                    |
|                        |                 |                    |
|                         -----------------                     |
|                                                               |
|                                                               |
|                                                               |
|                                                               |
 ---------------------------------------------------------------
```

FIGURE 10.11   Drawing a rectangle in dauber

We've already included all the mouse support that we'll need to draw rectangles. The Graphics method we'll use to draw rectangles is drawRect(), and we'll use that method in our applet's paint() method. We'll need to pass the upper left point of our rectangle and its width and height. First, we make sure that we are supposed to be drawing rectangles by checking the bRectFlag boolean flag (set when the user clicks the Rect button):

```
public void paint (Graphics g) {
    int loop_index;
    int drawWidth, drawHeight;

    if(bLineFlag && bMouseUpFlag){
        g.drawLine(ptAnchor.x, ptAnchor.y, ptDrawTo.x, ptDrawTo.y);
    }
    if(bOvalFlag && bMouseUpFlag){
        drawWidth = ptDrawTo.x - ptAnchor.x;
        drawHeight = ptDrawTo.y - ptAnchor.y;
```

```
                              g.drawOval(ptAnchor.x, ptAnchor.y, drawWidth, drawHeight);
                      }
➜              if(bRectFlag && bMouseUpFlag){
                              .
                              .
                              .
➜              }
```

If we are indeed drawing rectangles, we use the drawRect() method, passing it the four parameters it needs: the upper left point of the rectangle's x and y coordinates, as well as the rectangle's width and height:

```
public void paint (Graphics g) {
      int loop_index;
      int drawWidth, drawHeight;

      if(bLineFlag && bMouseUpFlag){
            g.drawLine(ptAnchor.x, ptAnchor.y, ptDrawTo.x, ptDrawTo.y);
      }
      if(bOvalFlag && bMouseUpFlag){
            drawWidth = ptDrawTo.x - ptAnchor.x;
            drawHeight = ptDrawTo.y - ptAnchor.y;
            g.drawOval(ptAnchor.x, ptAnchor.y, drawWidth, drawHeight);
      }
      if(bRectFlag && bMouseUpFlag){
➜            drawWidth = ptDrawTo.x - ptAnchor.x;
➜            drawHeight = ptDrawTo.y - ptAnchor.y;
➜            g.drawRect(ptAnchor.x, ptAnchor.y, drawWidth, drawHeight);
      }
}
```

Now the user can draw rectangles in our dauber applet, as shown in Figure 10.12.

Drawing 3D Rectangles in Dauber

It's also possible to draw "3D" rectangles in dauber, and that works just as it did for drawing rectangles, except that we use the draw3DRect() method (adding a final parameter set to true is supposed to make the 3D rectangle appear raised):

```
public void paint (Graphics g) {
      int loop_index;
      int drawWidth, drawHeight;

      if(bLineFlag && bMouseUpFlag){
            g.drawLine(ptAnchor.x, ptAnchor.y, ptDrawTo.x, ptDrawTo.y);
      }
      if(bOvalFlag && bMouseUpFlag){
            drawWidth = ptDrawTo.x - ptAnchor.x;
            drawHeight = ptDrawTo.y - ptAnchor.y;
```

```
        g.drawOval(ptAnchor.x, ptAnchor.y, drawWidth, drawHeight);
    }
    if(bRectFlag && bMouseUpFlag){
        drawWidth = ptDrawTo.x - ptAnchor.x;
        drawHeight = ptDrawTo.y - ptAnchor.y;
        g.drawRect(ptAnchor.x, ptAnchor.y, drawWidth, drawHeight);
    }
➜   if(b3DRectFlag && bMouseUpFlag){
➜       drawWidth = ptDrawTo.x - ptAnchor.x;
➜       drawHeight = ptDrawTo.y - ptAnchor.y;
➜       g.draw3DRect(ptAnchor.x, ptAnchor.y, drawWidth,drawHeight, true);
            .
            .
            .
```

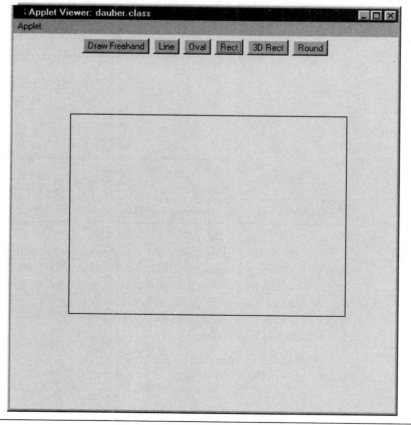

FIGURE 10.12   Our dauber applet can draw rectangles.

Drawing a 3D rectangle, however, results in simply a rectangle—at least in the current version of Java.

Drawing Rounded Rectangles in Dauber

Now that we are able to draw rectangles, it turns out that we can draw rectangles with rounded corners easily. When the user clicks the button we've labeled Rounded, they can use the mouse to draw rounded rectangles, as shown in Figure 10.13.

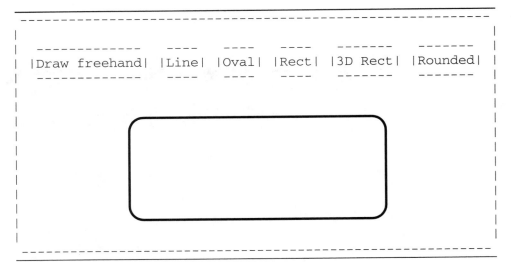

FIGURE 10.13   Drawing a rectangle with rounded corners

Because we've stored the anchor and drawto points already, all the mouse handling has already been done when it comes time to draw our new rounded rectangle—we can determine the rectangle's width and height, and we already know the location of its upper left corner. All we have to do in the paint() method is check if we are supposed to draw a rounded rectangle by examining the bRoundedFlag boolean flag:

```
public void paint (Graphics g) {
int loop_index;
int drawWidth, drawHeight;

if(bLineFlag && bMouseUpFlag){
```

```
              g.drawLine(ptAnchor.x, ptAnchor.y, ptDrawTo.x, ptDrawTo.y);
         }
         if(bOvalFlag && bMouseUpFlag){
              drawWidth = ptDrawTo.x - ptAnchor.x;
              drawHeight = ptDrawTo.y - ptAnchor.y;
              g.drawOval(ptAnchor.x, ptAnchor.y, drawWidth, drawHeight);
                    .
                    .
                    .
         if(bRoundedFlag && bMouseUpFlag){
                    .
                    .
                    .
         }
```

If we are supposed to draw rounded rectangles, we can call the Graphics method drawRoundRect(). This method takes the usual parameters—the coordinates of the upper left of the rectangle, as well as its height and width—and two new parameters as well. These new parameters control the rounding of the corners. The first parameter is the width of the rounding arc (in pixels) and the second parameter is the height of the rounding arc. In our case, we will give both of these parameters the value of 10:

```
public void paint (Graphics g) {
     int loop_index;
     int drawWidth, drawHeight;

     if(bLineFlag && bMouseUpFlag){
          g.drawLine(ptAnchor.x, ptAnchor.y, ptDrawTo.x, ptDrawTo.y);
     }
     if(bOvalFlag && bMouseUpFlag){
          drawWidth = ptDrawTo.x - ptAnchor.x;
          drawHeight = ptDrawTo.y - ptAnchor.y;
          g.drawOval(ptAnchor.x, ptAnchor.y, drawWidth, drawHeight);
                .
                .
                .
     if(bRoundedFlag && bMouseUpFlag){
          drawWidth = ptDrawTo.x - ptAnchor.x;
          drawHeight = ptDrawTo.y - ptAnchor.y;
          g.drawRoundRect(ptAnchor.x, ptAnchor.y, drawWidth,
          ➥ drawHeight, 10, 10);
     }
```

And now the user can draw rounded rectangles, as shown in Figure 10.14.

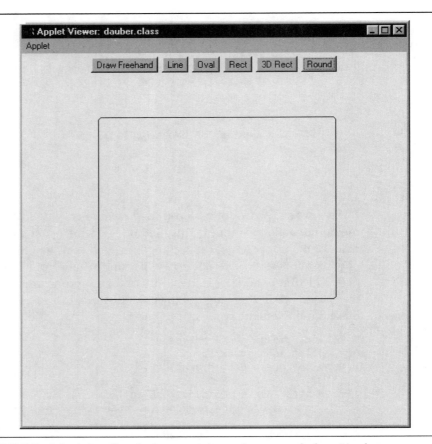

FIGURE 10.14   Our dauber applet can draw rounded rectangles.

That's it for the standard graphics figures: lines, circles, ovals, rectangles, and rounded rectangles. However, we can go one better—we can support freehand drawing in our dauber applet, letting the user draw with the mouse. We'll take a look at that next.

Dauber and Freehand Drawing

After the user clicks the freehand drawing tool—the button labeled Draw Freehand—they can draw with the mouse, as shown in Figure 10.15.

```
--------------------------------------------------------------
|                                                              |
|                                                              |
|  ------------    ----    ----    ----    -------    -------   |
|  |Draw freehand|  |Line|  |Oval|  |Rect|  |3D Rect|  |Rounded|  |
|  ------------    ----    ----    ----    -------    -------   |
|                                                              |
|                                                              |
|                                                              |
|                                                              |
|                                                              |
|                                                              |
|                                                              |
|                                                              |
|                                                              |
--------------------------------------------------------------
```

FIGURE 10.15   A freehand drawing

The user can do this by pressing the mouse button at some starting location in our applet and dragging the mouse. To handle this new capability, we can use the mouseDrag() method:

```
public void mouseDragged(MouseEvent e){
        .
        .
        .

}
```

This method is called when the user drags the mouse. We can check if they have selected the Draw tool by looking at the bDrawFlag boolean flag:

```
public void mouseDragged(MouseEvent e){
    if(bDrawFlag){
        .
        .
        .
    }
}
```

One way of drawing freehand with the mouse is to record the mouse locations as the mouse is dragged around in our applet and then "connect the dots." That is, we store each point we get in the `mouseDrag` event and then draw from point to point in the `paint()` method.

We start that process by storing the points we get in the `mouseDrag` event in an array of `Point` objects named, say, `pts[]`. We can declare an array of, say, 1000 `Point` objects. The syntax of declaring an array in Java is like this: `Type name[] = new Type[number]`. This means we can declare our array of points as follows:

```
import java.awt.Graphics;
import java.awt.*;
import java.awt.event.*;
import java.lang.Math;
import java.applet.Applet;

public class dauber extends Applet implements ActionListener,
➥ MouseListener, MouseMotionListener {

    Button buttonDraw, buttonLine, buttonOval, buttonRect,
    ➥ button3DRect, buttonRounded;

➔    Point pts[] = new Point[1000];
    Point ptAnchor, ptDrawTo;
                  .
                  .
                  .
```

> **NOTE**
>
> Technically, Java only supports one-dimensional arrays. Two dimensional arrays are really arrays of one-dimensional arrays. For example, here is how we declare and initialize a 3 x 3 two-dimensional array of String objects:
>
> ```
> String stringarray[][] =
> {
>     {"Hello", "there", "USA"},
>     {"Hello", "there", "Asia"},
>     {"Hello", "there", "World!"},
> };
> ```

Now we've set up the array of points to store the mouse locations as the user moves the mouse. In addition, we will need an index value in that array so that we will be able to tell where to add the next point and how many points there are to draw. We can call that array index `ptindex`:

```
import java.awt.Graphics;
import java.awt.*;
import java.awt.event.*;
```

```
import java.lang.Math;
import java.applet.Applet;

public class dauber extends Applet implements ActionListener,
➥ MouseListener, MouseMotionListener {

        Button buttonDraw, buttonLine, buttonOval, buttonRect,
        ➥ button3DRect, buttonRounded;

        Point pts[] = new Point[1000];
        Point ptAnchor, ptDrawTo;
➔      int ptindex = 0;
                          .
                          .
                          .
```

Now our point array is set up, and we can add points to it in the `mouseDrag()` method. The point passed to us is the current location of the mouse, so we add that to our `points[]` array this way, incrementing `ptindex` after we have done so:

```
        public void mouseDragged(MouseEvent e){
            if(bDrawFlag){
➔              pts[ptindex] = new Point(e.getX(), e.getY());
➔              ptindex++;
                          .
                          .
                          .
            }
        }
```

> **NOTE**
>
> The C++ operator ++ simply increments a variable. Used this way, as a postfix operator: `pts[ptindex++] = new Point(x, y);`, it adds 1 to the variable ptindex after the whole statement is executed. Used as a prefix operator: `pts[++ptindex] = new Point(x, y);`, it adds 1 to ptindex before the rest of the statement is executed, and so we use that new, incremented value as the array index. The operator ++ is an operator that may be overloaded, so you should not assume that it always adds 1 when used—it may have been redefined for a certain class to add, say, 1000, or even the characters "abc."

We add a new point made from the x and y parameters passed to us, store it in the `pts[]` array, and then increment the array index named `ptindex`. After we have stored the point, we call `repaint()` to draw the points in the array on the screen:

```
        public void mouseDragged(MouseEvent e){
            if(bDrawFlag){
```

```
                                 pts[ptindex] = new Point(e.getX(), e.getY());
                                 ptindex++;
   ➜                            repaint();
                         }
                }
```

All that remains is to add code to the paint() method to draw the points in the pts[] array. First in the paint() method, we check to make sure we are supposed to be drawing freehand by examining the bDrawFlag boolean flag:

```
public void paint (Graphics g) {
    int loop_index;
    int drawWidth, drawHeight;

    if(bLineFlag && bMouseUpFlag){
        g.drawLine(ptAnchor.x, ptAnchor.y, ptDrawTo.x, ptDrawTo.y);
    }
    if(bOvalFlag && bMouseUpFlag){
        drawWidth = ptDrawTo.x - ptAnchor.x;
        drawHeight = ptDrawTo.y - ptAnchor.y;
        g.drawOval(ptAnchor.x, ptAnchor.y, drawWidth, drawHeight);
                        .
                        .
                        .
   ➜    if(bDrawFlag){
                        .
                        .
                        .
   ➜            }
    }
```

If we are to draw freehand, that means we will draw the points in the pts[] array. We can loop over all those points, from 0 to the value in ptindex with a for loop. In general, this loop looks just like it would in C or C++:

```
for(initial statement; conditional test; increment statement){
        loop body
}
```

You use the initial statement to set up a loop index, the conditional test to see if you have looped enough, and the increment statement to increment (or decrement) your loop index. In our case, we can loop over all the points in the points[] array as follows:

```
public void paint (Graphics g) {
```

```
            int loop_index;
            int drawWidth, drawHeight;

            if(bLineFlag && bMouseUpFlag){
                g.drawLine(ptAnchor.x, ptAnchor.y, ptDrawTo.x, ptDrawTo.y);
            }
            if(bOvalFlag && bMouseUpFlag){
                drawWidth = ptDrawTo.x - ptAnchor.x;
                drawHeight = ptDrawTo.y - ptAnchor.y;
                g.drawOval(ptAnchor.x, ptAnchor.y, drawWidth, drawHeight);
                        .
                        .
                        .
            if(bRoundedFlag && bMouseUpFlag){
                drawWidth = ptDrawTo.x - ptAnchor.x;
                drawHeight = ptDrawTo.y - ptAnchor.y;
                g.drawRoundRect(ptAnchor.x, ptAnchor.y, drawWidth,
              ➡ drawHeight, 10, 10);
            }
            if(bDrawFlag){
➡   for(loop_index = 0; loop_index < ptindex - 1; loop_index++){
                        .
                        .
                        .
➡               }
            }
        }
```

NOTE   There are three types of loops in Java—for, while, and do loops. Their syntax looks like this:

```
for(initial statement; conditional test; increment statement){
        loop body
}

while(conditional test){
        loop body
}

do{
        loop body
}while(conditional test(/)[/]
```

Skill 10

We will then connect the dots, drawing a line from one point to the next, which will display a continuous freehand drawing on the screen. We will draw all these line segments with the `Graphics drawLine()` method:

```
public void paint (Graphics g) {
    int loop_index;
    int drawWidth, drawHeight;

    if(bLineFlag && bMouseUpFlag){
        g.drawLine(ptAnchor.x, ptAnchor.y, ptDrawTo.x, ptDrawTo.y);
    }
    if(bOvalFlag && bMouseUpFlag){
        drawWidth = ptDrawTo.x - ptAnchor.x;
        drawHeight = ptDrawTo.y - ptAnchor.y;
        g.drawOval(ptAnchor.x, ptAnchor.y, drawWidth, drawHeight);
             .
             .
             .
    if(bDrawFlag){
        for(loop_index = 0; loop_index < ptindex - 1; loop_index++){
            g.drawLine(pts[loop_index].x, pts[loop_index].y,
            ➥ pts[loop_index + 1].x, pts[loop_index + 1].y);
        }
    }
}
```

➡

NOTE   You may wonder why we used lines to connect the points we stored when the mouse moved across our applet, instead of just drawing the points themselves. The reason is that the `mouseDrag()` method is not called for each pixel the mouse moves over—there are only a limited number of mouse events generated each second, and if we just drew the individual points we got, we'd end up with a series of unconnected points trailing over the screen.

That's all there is to it—now run the dauber applet and click the Draw button. When you do, you can draw freehand with the mouse, as shown in Figure 10.16. That's it for freehand drawing—and that's it for our dauber applet. We've come far in this applet—from handling the mouse to drawing graphics like lines, circles, ovals, rectangles and more. We've gotten a good start in graphics handling. You can find the code for this applet in dauber.java.

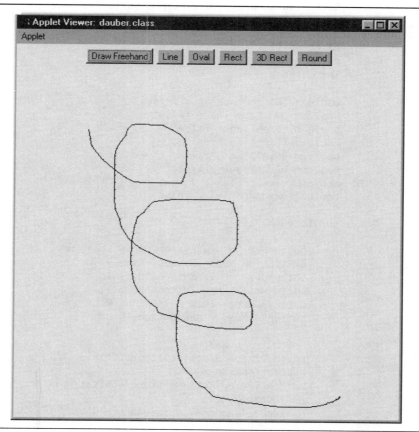

FIGURE 10.16 Our dauber applet supports freehand drawing.

C dauber.java

```java
import java.awt.Graphics;
import java.awt.*;
import java.awt.event.*;
import java.lang.Math;
import java.applet.Applet;

public class dauber extends Applet implements ActionListener, MouseListener,
➥ MouseMotionListener {
```

```java
Button buttonDraw, buttonLine, buttonOval, buttonRect, button3DRect,
➥ buttonRounded;

Point pts[] = new Point[1000];
Point ptAnchor, ptDrawTo;
int ptindex = 0;

boolean bMouseDownFlag = false;
boolean bMouseUpFlag = false;
boolean bDrawFlag = false;
boolean bLineFlag = false;
boolean bOvalFlag = false;
boolean bRectFlag = false;
boolean b3DRectFlag = false;
boolean bRoundedFlag = false;

public void init() {

    buttonDraw = new Button("Draw Freehand");
    buttonLine = new Button("Line");
    buttonOval = new Button("Oval");
    buttonRect = new Button("Rect");
    button3DRect = new Button("3D Rect");
    buttonRounded = new Button("Round");

    add(buttonDraw);
    buttonDraw.addActionListener(this);
    add(buttonLine);
    buttonLine.addActionListener(this);
    add(buttonOval);
    buttonOval.addActionListener(this);
    add(buttonRect);
    buttonRect.addActionListener(this);
    add(button3DRect);
    button3DRect.addActionListener(this);
    add(buttonRounded);
    buttonRounded.addActionListener(this);
    addMouseListener(this);
    addMouseMotionListener(this);
}

public void mousePressed(MouseEvent e){
    bMouseDownFlag = true;
    bMouseUpFlag = false;
    ptAnchor = new Point(e.getX(), e.getY());
}
```

```java
public void mouseReleased(MouseEvent e){
    bMouseDownFlag = false;
    bMouseUpFlag = true;
    ptDrawTo = new Point(e.getX(), e.getY());
        if(!bLineFlag){
        ptDrawTo = new Point(Math.max(e.getX(), ptAnchor.x),
        ➥ Math.max(e.getY(), ptAnchor.y));
        ptAnchor = new Point(Math.min(e.getX(), ptAnchor.x),
        ➥ Math.min(e.getY(), ptAnchor.y));
    }
    repaint();
}

public void mouseDragged(MouseEvent e){
    if(bDrawFlag){
        pts[ptindex] = new Point(e.getX(), e.getY());
        ptindex++;
        repaint();
    }
}

public void mouseClicked(MouseEvent e){}

public void mouseEntered(MouseEvent e){}

public void mouseExited(MouseEvent e){}

public void mouseMoved(MouseEvent e){}

public void paint (Graphics g) {
    int loop_index;
    int drawWidth, drawHeight;

    if(bLineFlag && bMouseUpFlag){
        g.drawLine(ptAnchor.x, ptAnchor.y, ptDrawTo.x, ptDrawTo.y);
    }
    if(bOvalFlag && bMouseUpFlag){
        drawWidth = ptDrawTo.x - ptAnchor.x;
        drawHeight = ptDrawTo.y - ptAnchor.y;
        g.drawOval(ptAnchor.x, ptAnchor.y, drawWidth, drawHeight);
    }
    if(bRectFlag && bMouseUpFlag){
        drawWidth = ptDrawTo.x - ptAnchor.x;
        drawHeight = ptDrawTo.y - ptAnchor.y;
        g.drawRect(ptAnchor.x, ptAnchor.y, drawWidth, drawHeight);
    }
```

```
            if(b3DRectFlag && bMouseUpFlag){
                drawWidth = ptDrawTo.x - ptAnchor.x;
                drawHeight = ptDrawTo.y - ptAnchor.y;
                g.draw3DRect(ptAnchor.x, ptAnchor.y, drawWidth,
                ➥ drawHeight, true);
            }
            if(bRoundedFlag && bMouseUpFlag){
                drawWidth = ptDrawTo.x - ptAnchor.x;
                drawHeight = ptDrawTo.y - ptAnchor.y;
                g.drawRoundRect(ptAnchor.x, ptAnchor.y, drawWidth,
                ➥ drawHeight, 10, 10);
            }
            if(bDrawFlag){
                for(loop_index = 0; loop_index < ptindex - 1; loop_index++){
                    g.drawLine(pts[loop_index].x, pts[loop_index].y,
                    ➥ pts[loop_index + 1].x, pts[loop_index + 1].y);
                }
            }
        }
    }

    public void actionPerformed(ActionEvent e){
        if(e.getSource() == buttonDraw){
            bDrawFlag = !bDrawFlag;
            bLineFlag = false;
            bOvalFlag = false;
            bRectFlag = false;
            b3DRectFlag = false;
            bRoundedFlag = false;
        }
        if(e.getSource() == buttonLine){
            bLineFlag = !bLineFlag;
            bDrawFlag = false;
            bOvalFlag = false;
            bRectFlag = false;
            b3DRectFlag = false;
            bRoundedFlag = false;
        }
        if(e.getSource() == buttonOval){
            bOvalFlag = !bOvalFlag;
            bLineFlag = false;
            bDrawFlag = false;
            bRectFlag = false;
            b3DRectFlag = false;
            bRoundedFlag = false;
        }
        if(e.getSource() == buttonRect){
            bRectFlag = !bRectFlag;
```

```
                   bLineFlag = false;
                   bOvalFlag = false;
                   bDrawFlag = false;
                   b3DRectFlag = false;
                   bRoundedFlag = false;
              }
              if(e.getSource() == button3DRect){
                   b3DRectFlag = !b3DRectFlag;
                   bLineFlag = false;
                   bOvalFlag = false;
                   bRectFlag = false;
                   bDrawFlag = false;
                   bRoundedFlag = false;
              }
              if(e.getSource() == buttonRounded){
                   bRoundedFlag = !bRoundedFlag;
                   bLineFlag = false;
                   bOvalFlag = false;
                   bRectFlag = false;
                   b3DRectFlag = false;
                   bDrawFlag = false;
              }
         }
    }
```

We've gotten our dauber applet working. We're able to use the mouse to receive input and draw lines, rectangles, 3D rectangles, ovals, circles, and rounded rectangles. We've added quite a few new skills to our Java arsenal in this chapter. There's one more skill we're going to add in this chapter—printing.

Printing from Java

It is possible to print graphics from Java 1.1 programs, and we'll take a look at that here. In this case, our goal might be to print a simple graphics figure—just a box with a diagonal line.

We'll need the getToolkit() method here, so we start by deriving a class named printgraphics, from the Frame class because that class includes the getToolkit() method:

```
class printgraphics extends Frame {
         .
         .
         .
}
```

Java Security

You may ask why we don't derive our class from the `Applet` class (the `Applet` class also contains the `getToolKit()` method). The answer is that in Java 1.1, security is currently set up so that Applets can't print on the printer. However, Java *applications* can, and we'll install this new `printgraphics` class in a Java application in a minute. Next, we add a constructor to the new `printgraphics` class like this:

```
     class printgraphics extends Frame {
➤        printgraphics() {
                 .
                 .
                 .
➤         }
     }
```

Here in the `printgraphics` constructor, we create an object of class `PrintJob`, indicating what object we want the print job for, the name we want to give our print job, and a reference to a `Properties` object, which we will set to null:

```
     class printgraphics extends Frame {
         printgraphics() {
➤   PrintJob p = getToolkit().getPrintJob(this, "Print graphics", null);
                 .
                 .
                 .

         }
     }
```

Now we have a print job, and the next step is to get a `Graphics` object for this print job so we can actually create the graphics we want to print. We do that with the `getGraphics()` method:

```
     class printgraphics extends Frame {
         printgraphics() {
             PrintJob p = getToolkit().getPrintJob(this, "Print graphics",
             ➥ null);
➤            Graphics g = p.getGraphics();
                 .
                 .
                 .

         }
     }
```

Now we draw the graphics we want in the new `Graphics` object, just as we did in the dauber applet:

```java
class printgraphics extends Frame {
    printgraphics() {
        PrintJob p = getToolkit().getPrintJob(this, "Print graphics", null);
        Graphics g = p.getGraphics();
→       g.drawRect(1, 1, 40, 40);
→       g.drawLine(1, 1, 40, 40);
              .
              .
              .
    }
}
```

To start the printing, we have to dispose of the `Graphics` object, which we do with its `dispose()` method:

```java
class printgraphics extends Frame {
    printgraphics() {
        PrintJob p = getToolkit().getPrintJob(this, "Print graphics", null);
        Graphics g = p.getGraphics();
        g.drawRect(1, 1, 40, 40);
        g.drawLine(1, 1, 40, 40);
→       g.dispose();
              .
              .
              .
    }
}
```

And finally, we end the print job with the `end()` method this way:

```java
class printgraphics extends Frame {
    printgraphics() {
        PrintJob p = getToolkit().getPrintJob(this, "Print graphics", null);
        Graphics g = p.getGraphics();
        g.drawRect(1, 1, 40, 40);
        g.drawLine(1, 1, 40, 40);
        g.dispose();
→       p.end();
    }
}
```

At this point, then, the graphics image we have drawn is printed. However, this class only does the printing—we still need to set up our application itself, and we'll do that now.

Java Applications

We've only used applets in this book so far, because they are still the most popular type of Java programs, but Java can also create applications, which are not intended to be embedded in a Web page (although you can run applications as applets). To create an application, you just set up a public class, as you would for an applet. We can name this class app, and put it in a file named app.java:

```
public class app {
    .
    .
    .
}
```

What distinguishes applications from applets is that applications have a main() method, where code is executed first (note that having a main() method does not stop a program from being executed as an applet):

```
    public class app {
→       public static void main(String[] argv) {
            .
            .
            .
→       }
    }
```

The String array passed to the application holds the command-line arguments pass to the application. In this first, small application, we might just display "Hello from Java" on the screen, and we do that with the System.out.println() method:

```
public class app {
    public static void main(String[] argv) {
        System.out.println("Hello from Java");
    }
}
```

When we run this application, we'll see "Hello from Java" appear. To do that, compile the application by typing **javac app**. To run the application, use the java.exe interpreter which comes with the JDK 1.1 like this at the command line (i.e., in DOS):

```
c:\java1-1\app>java app
```

When you do, you'll see our "Hello from Java" message:

```
c:\java1-1\app>java app
Hello from Java
```

Let's run the code in our `printgraphics` class now. To do that, we just create a new application class named `printer`, that creates an object of the `printgraphics` class—when we do that, the `printgraphics` constructor will start the printing job, printing the graphics we want printed:

```
   import java.awt.*;
   import java.awt.event.*;

   public class printer {
→      public static void main(String[] argv) {
→          printgraphics w = new printgraphics();
→      }
   }
```

And that's it—create `printer.class` now and run it with the Java interpreter to see the graphics printed out. A standard Print dialog box will appear (as with any Windows program that prints) where you can select how many copies you want to print, and so on. After clicking the OK button, our graphics image is printed. Our printer application is a success, and the code for this application appears in `printer.java`.

TIP   You can also show the Frame window in our application, if you like—just resize the window (with `resize()`) to give it a size, and use the window's `show()` method.

printer.java

```
import java.awt.*;
import java.awt.event.*;

public class printer {
    public static void main(String[] argv) {
        printgraphics w = new printgraphics();
    }
}

class printgraphics extends Frame {
    printgraphics() {
        PrintJob p = getToolkit().getPrintJob(this, "Print graphics", null);
```

Skill 10

```
Graphics g = p.getGraphics();
g.drawRect(1, 1, 40, 40);
g.drawLine(1, 1, 40, 40);
g.dispose();
p.end();
    }
}
```

We've gotten a good introduction to the mouse, graphics handling, and printing in Java 1.1. Let's turn now to another powerful graphics topic—handling images. In the Skill 11, you'll learn how to read images in and how to work with them.

Are You Experienced?

Now you can...

- ☑ **use the mouse and handle mouse events**
- ☑ **draw lines, rectangles, ovals, circles, and 3D rectangles in Java**
- ☑ **let the user draw freehand with the mouse**
- ☑ **print from Java applications usingthe** `getPrintJob()` **method**

R. Jones 356-555-3398.

PROGRAMMERS
C, C, Cobol, exp. Call 534-555-6543 or fax 534-555-6544.

PROGRAMMING
MRFS Inc. is looking for a Sr. Windows NT developer. Reqs. 3-5 yrs. Exp. In C under Windows, Win95 & NT, using Visual C. Excl. OO design & implementation skills a must. OLE2 & ODBC are a plus. Exd. Salary & bnfts. Resume & salary history to HR, 8779 HighTech Way, Computer City, AR

PROGRAMMERS
Contractors Wanted for short & long term assignments: Visual C, MFC Unix C/C, SQL Oracle Dev elop ers PC Help Desk Support Windows NT & NetWare Telecommunications Visual Basic, Access, HTMT, CGI, Perl MMI & Co.. 885-555-9933

PROGRAMMER World Wide Web Links wants your HTML & Photoshop skills. Develop great WWW sites. Local & global customers. Send samples & resume to WWWL, 2000 Apple Road, Santa Rosa, CA.

TECHNICAL WRITER Software firm seeks writer/editor for manuals, research notes, project mgmt. Min 2 years tech. writing, DTP & programming experience. Send resume & writing samples to: Software Systems, Dallas, TX.

TECHNICAL Software development firm looking for Tech Trainers. Ideal candidates have programming experience in Visual C, HTML & JAVA. Need quick self starter. Call (443) 555-6868 for interview.

TECHNICAL WRITER/ Premier Computer Corp is seeking a combination of technical skills, knowledge and experience in the following areas: UNIX, Windows 95/NT, Visual Basic, on-line help & documentation, and the internet. Candidates must possess excellent writing skills, and be comfortable working in a quality vs. deadline driven environment. Competitive salary. Fax resume & samples to Karen Fields, Premier Computer Corp, 444 Industrial Blvd. Concord, CA. Or send to our website at www.premier.com.

WEB DESIGNER
BA/BS or equivalent programming/multimedia- production. 3 years of experience in use and design of WWW services streaming audio and video HTML, PERL, CGI, GIF, JPEG. Demonstrated interpersonal, organization, communication, multi-tasking skills. Send resume to The Learning People at www.learning.com.

WEBMASTER-TECHNICAL
BSCS or equivalent. 2 years of experience in CGI, Windows 95/NT, UNIX, C, Java, Perl. Demonstrated ability to design, code, debug and test on-line services. Send resume to The Learning People at www.learning.com.

PROGRAMMER World Wide Web Links wants your HTML & Photoshop skills. Develop great WWW sites.

ing tools. Experienced in documentation preparation & programming languages (Access, C, FoxPro) are a plus. Financial or banking customer service support is required along with excellent verbal & written communication skills with multi levels of end-users. Send resume to KKUP Enterprises. 45 Orange Blvd. Orange, CA.

COMPUTERS Small Web Design firm seeks indiv. w/NT, Webserver & Database management exp. Fax resume to 556-555-4221.

COMPUTER/ Visual C/C, Visual Basic Exp'd Systems Analysts/Programmers for growing software dev. team in Roseburg. Computer Science or related degree preferred. Develop adv. Engineering applications for engineering firm. Fax resume to 707-555-8744.

COMPUTER Web Master for dynamic SF Internet co. Site. Dev., test, coord. train. 2 yrs prog. Exp. C C Web C FTP. Fax resume to Best Staffing 845-555-7722.

COMPUTER PROGRAMMER
Ad agency seeks programmer w/exp. in UNIX/NT Platforms, Web Server, CGI/Perl. Programmer Position avail. on a project basis with the possibility to move into F/T. Fax resume & salary req. to R. Jones 334-555-8332.

COMPUTERS Programmer/Analyst Design and maintain C based SQL database applications. Required skills: Visual Basic, C, SQL, ODBC. Document existing and new applications. Novell or NT exp. a plus. Fax resume & salary history to 235-555-9935.

GRAPHIC DESIGNER
Webmaster's Weekly is seeking a creative Graphic Designer to design high impact marketing collater al, including direct mail promos. CD-ROM packages, ads and WWW pages. Must be able to juggle multiple projects and learn new skills on the job very rapidly. Web design experience a big plus, technical troubleshooting also a plus. Call 435-555-1235.

GRAPHICS - ART DIRECTOR - WEB-MULTIMEDIA
Leading internet development company has an outstanding opportunity for a talented, high-end Web Experienced Art Director. In addition to a great portfolio and fresh ideas, the ideal candidate has excellent communication and presentation skills. Working as a team with innovative producers and programmers, you will create dynamic, interactive web sites and application interfaces. Some programming experience required. Send samples and resume to: SuperSites, 333 Main, Seattle, WA.

MARKETING
Fast paced software and services provider looking for MARKETING COMMUNICATIONS SPECIALIST to be responsible for its webpage,

PROGRAMMERS Multiple short term assignments available: Visual C, 3 positions SQL ServerNT Server, 2 positions JAVA & HTML, long term NetWare Various locations. Call for more info. 356-555-3398.

PROGRAMMERS
C, C, VB, Cobol, exp.
Call 534-555-6543
or fax 534-555-6544.

PROGRAMMING
MRFS Inc. is looking for a Sr. Windows NT developer. Reqs. 3-5 yrs. Exp. In C under Windows, Win95 & NT, using Visual C. Excl. OO design & implementation skills a must. OLE2 & ODBC are a plus. Excl. Resume & salary history to HR, 8779 HighTech Way, Computer City, AR

PROGRAMMERS/ Contractors Wanted for short & long term assignments: Visual C, MFC Unix C/C, SQL Oracle Developers PC Help Desk Support Windows NT & NetWare Telecommunications Visual Basic, Access, HTMT, CGI, Perl MMI & Co.. 885-555-9933

PROGRAMMER World Wide Web Links wants your HTML & Photoshop skills. Develop great WWW sites. Local & global customers. Send samples & resume to WWWL, 2000 Apple Road, Santa Rosa, CA.

TECHNICAL WRITER Software firm seeks writer/editor for manuals, research notes, project mgmt. Min 2 years tech. writing, DTP & programming experience. Send resume & writing samples to: Software Systems, Dallas, TX.

COMPUTER PROGRAMMER
Ad agency seeks programmer w/exp. in UNIX/NT Platforms, Web Server, CGI/Perl. Programmer Position avail. on a project basis with the possibility to move into F/T. Fax resume & salary req. to R. Jones 334-555-8332.

TECHNICAL WRITER Premier Computer Corp is seeking a combination of technical skills, knowledge and experience in the following areas: UNIX, Windows 95/NT, Visual Basic, on-line help & documentation, and the internet. Candidates must possess excellent writing skills, and be comfortable working in a quality vs. deadline driven environment. Competitive salary. Fax resume & samples to Karen Fields, Premier Computer Corp, 444 Industrial Blvd Concord, CA. Or send to our website at www.premier.com.

WEB DESIGNER
BA/BS or equivalent programming/multimedia production. 3 years of experience in use and design of WWW services streaming audio and video HTML, PERL, CGI, GIF, JPEG. Demonstrated interpersonal, organization, communication, multi-tasking skills. Send resume to The Learning People at www.learning.com.

WEBMASTER-TECHNICAL
BSCS or equivalent, 2 years of experience in CGI, Windows 95/NT,

COMPUTERS Small Web Design firm seeks indiv. w/NT, Webserver & Database management exp. fax resume to 556-555-4221.

COMPUTER Visual C/C, Visual Basic Exp'd Systems Analysts/Programmers for growing software dev. team in Roseburg. Computer Science or related degree preferred. Develop adv. Engineering applications for engineering firm. Fax resume to 707-555-8744.

COMPUTER Web Master for dynamic SF Internet co. Site. Dev., test, coord. train. 2 yrs prog. Exp. C C Web C FTP. Fax resume to Best Staffing 845-555-7722.

COMPUTERS/ QA SOFTWARE TESTERS Qualified candidates should have 2 yrs exp. performing integration & system testing using automated testing tools. Experienced in documentation preparation & programming languages (Access, C, FoxPro) are a plus. Financial or banking customer service support is required along with excellent verbal & written communication skills with multi levels of end-users. Send resume to KKUP Enterprises, 45 Orange Blvd. Orange, CA.

COMPUTERS Programmer/Analyst Design and maintain C based SQL database applications. Required skills: Visual Basic, C, SQL, ODBC. Document existing and new applications. Novell or NT exp. a plus. Fax resume & salary history to 235-555-9935.

GRAPHIC DESIGNER
Webmaster's Weekly is seeking a creative Graphic Designer to design high impact marketing collater al, including direct mail promo's. CD-ROM packages, ads and WWW pages. Must be able to juggle multiple projects and learn new skills on the job very rapidly. Web design experience a big plus, technical troubleshooting also a plus. Call 435-555-1235.

GRAPHICS - ART DIRECTOR - WEB-MULTIMEDIA
Leading internet development company has an outstanding opportunity for a talented, high-end Web Experienced Art Director. In addition to a great portfolio and fresh ideas, the ideal candidate has excellent communication and presentation skills. Working as a team with innovative producers and programmers you will create dynamic, interactive web sites and application interfaces. Some programming experience required. Send samples and resume to: SuperSites, 333 Main, Seattle, WA.

COMPUTER PROGRAMMER
Ad agency seeks programmer w/exp. in UNIX/NT Platforms, Web Server, CGI/Perl. Programmer Position avail. on a project basis with the possibility to move into F/T. Fax resume & salary req. to R. Jones 334-555-8332.

PROGRAMMERS / Established software company seeks program-

ment. Must be a self-starter, energetic, organized. Must have 2 years web experience. Programming a plus. Call 985-555-9654.

PROGRAMMERS Multiple term assignments available: C, 3 positions SQL ServerNT S. 2 positions JAVA & HTML, long NetWare Various locations. Call more info. 356-555-3398.

PROGRAMMERS
C, C, VB, Cobol, exp. Call 534-6543 or fax 534-555-6544.

PROGRAMMING
MRFS Inc. is looking for a Windows NT developer. Reqs yrs. Exp. In C under Windows, Win95 & NT, using Visual C. OO design & implementation a must. OLE2 & ODBC are a Excl. Salary & bnfts. Resume salary history to HR, 8779 High Way, Computer City, AR

PROGRAMMERS/ Contra Wanted for short & long term as ments: Visual C, MFCUnix C/C, Oracle Developers PC Help Support Windows NT & Net Telecommunications Visual E Access, HTMT, CGI, Perl MMI 885-555-9933

PROGRAMMER World Wide Links wants your HTML & Photo skills. Develop great WWW Local & global customers. Send ples & resume to WWWL, Apple Road, Santa Rosa, CA.

TECHNICAL WRITER Software seeks writer/editor for man research notes, project mgmt. years tech. writing, DTP & pro ming experience. Send resu writing samples to: Sof Systems, Dallas, TX.

TECHNICAL Software develop firm looking for Tech Trainers. candidates have programming rience in Visual C, HTML & Need quick self starter. Call 555-6868 for interview.

TECHNICAL WRITER Pr Computer Corp is seeking a c nation of technical skills, know and experience in the foll areas: UNIX, Windows 95/NT, Basic, on-line help & document and the internet. Candidates possess excellent writing skills be comfortable working in a q vs. deadline driven environ Competitive salary. Fax resu samples to Karen Fields, Pr Computer Corp, 444 Industrial Concord, CA. Or send to our w at www.premier.com.

WEB DESIGNER
BA/BS or equivalent pro ming/multimedia productio years of experience in use design of WWW services stre audio and video HTML, PERL GIF, JPEG. Demonstrated int sonal, organization, communi multi-tasking skills. Send resu The Learning People at www. ing.com.

WEBMASTER-TECHNI

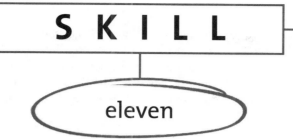

SKILL

eleven

Displaying and Stretching Images

❑ How to load images into an applet

❑ Manipulating images

❑ Displaying images

❑ Creating a clickable image map

❑ Navigating a Web browser to a new URL

In Skill 11, we're going to examine the ins and outs of Java image handling. As you can imagine, image handling is a very popular topic. In this Skill, we'll see how to read images into our applet, display them and stretch them to new shapes. We'll also see how to support *image maps*—those clickable images you see on the Web. Let's start at once with our first example, which will read an image and stretch it as we direct.

The Imagesizer Applet

We'll start off our image-handling discussion with a simple applet that reads an image. Then, the user can press the mouse in one location and drag it to another. When they release the mouse button, we can draw the image in the coordinates they've given, as shown in Figure 11.1. If the user selects a different size, we can draw the image again, using the new coordinates, as shown in Figure 11.2. This process can continue as many times as the user likes:

FIGURE 1 1 . 1   We can let the user specify coordinates for an image.

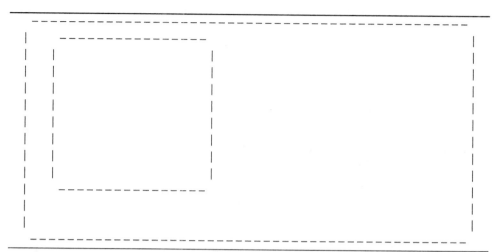

FIGURE 11.2   The user can change the size of the image.

Let's see how this works now. Create a new file named, say, imagesizer.java. In this applet, we'll read in a graphics figure and allow the user to resize it. We might use an image like the one shown below. We can name that image figure.jpg.

TIP   We are able to read in both .jpg, and .gif files into our applets.

Create the imagesizer class now:

```
import java.awt.*;
import java.awt.event.*;
import java.applet.Applet;
```

```
public class imagesizer extends Applet {
                  .
                  .
                  .
}
```

We'll need to store the image after we read it in, and we can do that in a Java Image object which we can name image:

```
import java.awt.*;
import java.awt.event.*;
import java.applet.Applet;

public class imagesizer extends Applet {
```

➜
```
        Image image;
                  .
                  .
                  .
```

The Image class is the class that we'll be using throughout this Skill because it provides Java's support for image handling. The Image class's methods appear in Table 11.1.

T A B L E   1 1 . 1 : The Image **class's methods**

Method	Does This
Image()	Constructs a new Image object.
createScaledImage(int, int, int)	Creates a scaled version of this image.
flush()	Flushes resources of this Image object.
GetGraphics()	Gets a graphics object for this image.
getHeight(ImageObserver)	Gets the height of image in pixels.
GetProperty(String, ImageObserver)	Gets a property of image.
getSource()	Gets object that actually produces image's pixels.
getWidth(ImageObserver)	Get the width of image in pixels.

Now we have the file we want to read, figure.jpg, and we've declared the Image object we'll store that image in, image. The next step is to read in that image, and we do that with the Java Applet class method getImage(). One way to use getImage() is to pass an object of the Java URL class to getImage(), which specifies the URL of the image to read.

The URL class just holds URLs; its methods appear in Table 11.2. If we know the absolute URL of an image, we can create an URL object like this: `url = new URL("http://www.javasoft.com");`.

TABLE 11.2: The URL class's methods

Method	Does This
URL(String)	Creates a URL from the unparsed absolute URL.
URL(String, String, int, String)	Creates an absolute URL from the given protocol, host, port, and file.
URL(String, String, String)	Creates an absolute URL from the given protocol, host, and file.
URL(URL, String)	Creates a URL from the unparsed URL in the given context. If spec is an absolute URL it is used as is.
equals(Object)	Compares two URLs.
GetContent()	Gets the contents from this opened connection.
getFile()	Gets the file name.
getHost()	Gets the host name, if applicable.
getPort()	Gets the port number.
GetProtocol()	Gets the protocol name.
getRef()	Gets the ref.
hashCode()	Creates an integer suitable for hash table indexing.
OpenConnection()	Creates (if not already in existance) a URLConnection object that contains a connection to the remote object referred to by the URL.
OpenStream()	Opens an input stream.
sameFile(URL)	Compares two URLs.
set(String, String, int, String, String)	Sets the fields of the URL.
SetURLStreamHandlerFactory (URLStreamHandlerFactory)	Sets the URLStreamHandler factory.
toExternalForm()	Reverses the parsing of the URL.
toString()	Converts to a human-readable form.

Another way to use the `getImage()` method is to pass the URL of the directory containing the image and the name of the image file like this: `getImage(url, "figure.jpg");`. In our case, we'll assume the figure is in the same directory as

the file figure.jpg, and we'll use the handy Applet method getCodeBase().
This method returns the URL of the .class file we are executing, and that means
we can read our image in the applet's init() method as follows:

```
import java.awt.*;
import java.awt.event.*;
import java.applet.Applet;

public class imagesizer extends Applet {

    Image image;

    public void init() {
        image = getImage(getCodeBase(), "figure.jpg");
                        .
                        .
                        .
    }
```

The line of code marked above reads the image into our applet and stores it in the
Image object, image. In addition, we add a MouseListener to our applet in init():

```
import java.awt.*;
import java.awt.event.*;
import java.applet.Applet;

public class imagesizer extends Applet implements MouseListener{

    Image image;
    boolean bMouseDownFlag = false;
    boolean bMouseUpFlag = false;
    Point ptAnchor, ptDrawTo;

    public void init() {
        image = getImage(getCodeBase(), "figure.jpg");
        addMouseListener(this);
    }
```

We'll set up our applet much like we set up our dauber applet: when the user
presses the mouse button, we can set the anchor point, and when they release it,
we can draw our image in the given rectangle:

```
anchor point  x---------------
              |               |
              |               |
              |               |
              ---------------x drawto point
```

We add those points to our applet now:

```
import java.awt.*;
import java.awt.event.*;
import java.applet.Applet;

public class imagesizer extends Applet implements MouseListener {

        Image image;
→       Point ptAnchor, ptDrawTo;
                .
                .
                .
```

In addition, we keep track of the mouse state with two flags, bMouseUpFlag and bMouseDownFlag, as we did in the dauber applet. We add those flags to our applet now:

```
import java.awt.*;
import java.awt.event.*;
import java.applet.Applet;

public class imagesizer extends Applet implements MouseListener {

        Image image;
→       boolean bMouseDownFlag = false;
→       boolean bMouseUpFlag = false;
        Point ptAnchor, ptDrawTo;
                .
                .
                .
```

When the user presses the mouse button, we can store the location at which they did so (the anchor point) and set the mouse flags in the mousePressed() method:

```
→       public void mousePressed(MouseEvent e){
→           bMouseDownFlag = true;
→           bMouseUpFlag = false;
→           ptAnchor = new Point(e.getX(), e.getY());
→       }
```

Next, we add the mouseReleased() method:

```
        public void mouseReleased(MouseEvent e){
                .
                .
                .
        }
```

Here we first set the mouse flags:

```
       public void mouseReleased(MouseEvent e){
→          bMouseDownFlag = false;
→          bMouseUpFlag = true;
                   .
                   .
                   .
       }
```

When the user releases the mouse button, we can set the DrawTo point. In fact, we should order the Anchor and DrawTo points as we did in our dauber applet so the Anchor point is at upper left and the DrawTo point is at lower right:

```
       public void mouseReleased(MouseEvent e){
           bMouseDownFlag = false;
           bMouseUpFlag = true;

           ptDrawTo = new Point(Math.max(e.getX(), ptAnchor.x),
           ➥ Math.max(e.getY(), ptAnchor.y));
           ptAnchor = new Point(Math.min(e.getX(), ptAnchor.x),
           ➥ Math.min(e.getY(), ptAnchor.y));
                   .
                   .
                   .
       }
```

Now we're ready to draw the image. We do that in the paint() method, so we call repaint() here to make sure paint() is called:

```
       public void mouseReleased(MouseEvent e){
           bMouseDownFlag = false;
           bMouseUpFlag = true;

           ptDrawTo = new Point(Math.max(e.getX(), ptAnchor.x),
           ➥ Math.max(e.getY(), ptAnchor.y));
           ptAnchor = new Point(Math.min(e.getX(), ptAnchor.x),
           ➥ Math.min(e.getY(), ptAnchor.y));
→          repaint();
       }
```

Displaying Images in Java

Because we have the image in the image object, and the coordinates in which to draw it, we can now draw our image. Add the paint() method below.

```
public void paint (Graphics g) {
        .
        .
        .
}
```

First, we check to make sure we should be drawing our image by making sure the mouse is up:

```
public void paint (Graphics g) {

    if(bMouseUpFlag){
        .
        .
        .
    }
}
```

If the mouse is up, we will use the `drawImage()` method to draw our image in the given coordinates. To do that, we'll need the width and height of our image, and we get those measurements as follows:

```
public void paint (Graphics g) {
    int drawWidth, drawHeight;

    if(bMouseUpFlag){
→       drawWidth = ptDrawTo.x - ptAnchor.x;
→       drawHeight = ptDrawTo.y - ptAnchor.y;
                .
                .
                .

    }
}
```

Next, we will draw a rectangle to surround our image with:

```
public void paint (Graphics g) {
    int drawWidth, drawHeight;

    if(bMouseUpFlag){
        drawWidth = ptDrawTo.x - ptAnchor.x;
        drawHeight = ptDrawTo.y - ptAnchor.y;
→       g.drawRect(ptAnchor.x, ptAnchor.y, drawWidth, drawHeight);
            .
            .
            .

    }
}
```

Now we draw the image with `drawImage()`. All we have to do is to pass the image and the coordinates we want it drawn in—`drawImage()` will stretch the image as required—and a reference to an *ImageObserver* object. This object watches the process of drawing images, and in this case, we'll just pass a reference to our applet object with a `this` keyword:

```
public void paint (Graphics g) {
    int drawWidth, drawHeight;

    if(bMouseUpFlag){
        drawWidth = ptDrawTo.x - ptAnchor.x;
        drawHeight = ptDrawTo.y - ptAnchor.y;
        g.drawRect(ptAnchor.x, ptAnchor.y, drawWidth,
        ➥ drawHeight);
        g.drawImage(image, ptAnchor.x, ptAnchor.y, drawWidth,
        ➥ drawHeight, this);
    }
}
```

And that's all there is to drawing images—now the user can draw our image using the mouse, as shown below. The code for this applet appears in `imagesizer.java`.

imagesizer.java

```
import java.awt.*;
import java.awt.event.*;
import java.lang.Math;
import java.applet.Applet;

public class imagesizer extends Applet implements MouseListener {

    Image image;
    boolean bMouseDownFlag = false;
    boolean bMouseUpFlag = false;
    Point ptAnchor, ptDrawTo;

    public void init() {
        image = getImage(getCodeBase(), "figure.jpg");
        addMouseListener(this);
    }

    public void mousePressed(MouseEvent e){
        bMouseDownFlag = true;
        bMouseUpFlag = false;
        ptAnchor = new Point(e.getX(), e.getY());
    }

    public void mouseReleased(MouseEvent e){
        bMouseDownFlag = false;
        bMouseUpFlag = true;

        ptDrawTo = new Point(Math.max(e.getX(), ptAnchor.x),
        ➥ Math.max(e.getY(), ptAnchor.y));
        ptAnchor = new Point(Math.min(e.getX(), ptAnchor.x),
        ➥ Math.min(e.getY(), ptAnchor.y));
        repaint();
    }

    public void mouseClicked(MouseEvent e){}

    public void mouseEntered(MouseEvent e){}

    public void mouseExited(MouseEvent e){}

    public void paint (Graphics g) {
        int drawWidth, drawHeight;
```

Skill 11

```
                if(bMouseUpFlag){
                     drawWidth = ptDrawTo.x - ptAnchor.x;
                     drawHeight = ptDrawTo.y - ptAnchor.y;
                     g.drawRect(ptAnchor.x, ptAnchor.y, drawWidth, drawHeight);
                     g.drawImage(image, ptAnchor.x, ptAnchor.y, drawWidth,
                     ➥ drawHeight, this);
                }
           }
      }
```

Now that we've seen how to load an image in, let's take a look at how to "interact" with an image. In this case, we'll see how to support image maps, those clickable maps you see on the World Wide Web.

Using Image Maps

An image map is an image you can click in a Web browser to move to a new URL. An image map might have several active areas, as shown in Figure 11.3.

```
 ---------------------------------------------
|                                             |
|                              ----------     |
|        ----------           | Click Me |    |
|       | Click Me |           ----------     |
|        ----------                           |
|                                             |
|                                             |
|                                             |
|                           ----------        |
|                          | Click Me |       |
|                           ----------        |
|                                             |
|                                             |
 ---------------------------------------------
```

FIGURE 11.3 An image map with three active areas

When the user clicks one of these areas, the Web browser takes them to a new URL. The image map we'll use in this example, `imap.gif`, appears below, where we have hyperlinks to Sun and to Sybex. When the user clicks one of those labeled rectangles, the Web browser will open the appropriate URL.

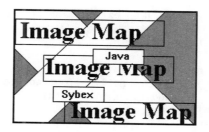

Let's begin this example now. Create a new file called imap.java. We'll need a place to store our image after we load it in and before displaying it, so we create a new Image object named image:

```
public class imap extends Applet
{
     Image image;
          .
          .
          .
```

We load our image map in from the file imap.gif and store it in the object named image in the init() method, as follows:

```
public class imap extends Applet {

     Image image;

     public void init(){
          image = getImage(getCodeBase(), "imap.gif");
     }
```

Next, we display the image in our applet by adding a paint() method:

```
public void paint (Graphics g) {
     g.drawImage(image, 10, 10, 240, 155, this);
}
```

Although the image is displayed, it's still just a part of our applet, so the normal mousePressed and mouseReleased events will occur even when we click the image. That's the key to Java image maps—we just find the location that the user clicked in our applet to see if they have clicked an active area.

We can add mouse support to our applet now by adding a MouseListener and the mouse methods as follows:

```
import java.applet.Applet;
import java.awt.*;
import java.awt.event.*;
```

```
→    public class imap extends Applet implements MouseListener{

         Image Imap;

         public void init(){
             Imap = getImage(getCodeBase(), "imap.gif");
             addMouseListener(this);
         }
→        public void mousePressed(MouseEvent e){
                       .
                       .
                       .
→        }
→        public void mouseClicked(MouseEvent e){}
→        public void mouseReleased(MouseEvent e){}
→        public void mouseEntered(MouseEvent e){}
→        public void mouseExited(MouseEvent e){}
```

Open the mousePressed() method now:

```
         public void mousePressed(MouseEvent e){
                       .
                       .
                       .
         }
```

First, we get the location of the mouse and store it in the variables x and y:

```
         public void mousePressed(MouseEvent e){
→            int x = e.getX();
→            int y = e.getY();
                       .
                       .
                       .
         }
```

Checking an Image Map's Hotspots

Now we need to determine the location in our image of the *hotspots*—the locations that cause the browser to do something when clicked—once we do, we can check if the mouse went down in one of them.

TIP   To determine the location of the hotspots in your image map, you can use the Windows Paint program; as you move the mouse, the Paint program indicates the current mouse location (in pixels). The Paint program only uses .bmp files. However, many Web browsers, such as the free Microsoft Internet Explorer, can convert image files for you.

We can check to see if the mouse was clicked in the first of these areas, the Java hyperlink, in the mousePressed() method, where we compare the mouse location passed to us in the x and y parameters with the Java hyperlink's coordinates, as follows:

```
public void mousePressed(MouseEvent e){
    int x = e.getX();
    int y = e.getY();
    if( x > 104 && x < 171 && y > 53 && y < 75){
          .
          .
          .
    }
}
```

Here, && is the Java logical AND operator, which means that we are requiring x > 104 AND x < 171 AND y > 53 AND y < 75 to be true.

TIP   There are other logical operators like && in Java. The || operator ORs a number of boolean values together, and the result is true if any of the values are true. There are also the binary (i.e., bit-by-bit numeric) operators &, |, and ^ (XOR). The other common boolean operator is the NOT operator, !, which toggles a boolean–if booleanvalue is true, then !booleanvalue is false.

In fact, the lines of code we just added are not quite right because these are the coordinates of the Sybex hyperlink in the image map, but we started the image map at the location (10, 10) in the paint() method:

```
public void paint (Graphics g) {
    g.drawImage(Imap, 10, 10, 240, 155, this);
}
```

That means we have to add 10 to each coordinate measurement as follows:

```
public void mousePressed(MouseEvent e){
    int x = e.getX();
    int y = e.getY();
```

Skill 11

```
➜     if( x > 104 + 10 && x < 171 + 10 && y > 53 + 10 && y < 75 + 10){
                           .
                           .
                           .
           }
      }
```

If the user did, in fact, click inside the Java hyperlink, we navigate the Web browser to the Java Web site, `http://www.javasoft.com`.

The Java URL Class

To do that, we'll need a new URL class object representing this URL. We can declare a new URL object named `url` and set it to `http://www.javasoft.com` as follows (note that to use the URL class, we have to import the `java.net.*` package):

```
       public void mousePressed(MouseEvent e){
➜           URL newURL = null;
            int x = e.getX();
            int y = e.getY();
            if( x > 104 + 10 && x < 171 + 10 && y > 53 + 10 && y < 75 + 10){
➜                 try { newURL = new URL("http://www.javasoft.com"); }
➜                 catch (MalformedURLException e1) {}
                         .
                         .
                         .
           }
      }
```

Note the `try` and `catch` keywords here. These keywords are used to catch Java *exceptions*, which represent error conditions (we'll see more about Java exceptions later). Because loading in a new URL is an operation that is subject to many errors, Java requires that you enclose this operation in a `try...catch` block like we just did.

Now that we have our new URL object, we can navigate the Web browser to that URL. We do so by working with the Web browser itself, which is called the applet's *context*. Here, we'll use the `Applet` class's `getAppletContext()` method to reach the Web browser and the context's `showDocument()` method to open the new URL:

```
       public void mousePressed(MouseEvent e){
            URL newURL = null;
            int x = e.getX();
            int y = e.getY();
            if( x > 104 + 10 && x < 171 + 10 && y > 53 + 10 && y < 75 + 10){
                  try { newURL = new URL("http://www.javasoft.com"); }
                  catch (MalformedURLException e1) {}
```

→
```
        getAppletContext().showDocument(newURL);
    }                       .
                            .
                            .

}
```

And we've opened the new URL. We can check for the other active spots in our image map, adding them to our applet as follows:

```
public void mousePressed(MouseEvent e){
    URL newURL = null;
    int x = e.getX();
    int y = e.getY();
    if( x > 104 + 10 && x < 171 + 10 && y > 53 + 10 && y < 75 + 10){
        try { newURL = new URL("http://www.javasoft.com"); }
        catch (MalformedURLException e1) {}
        getAppletContext().showDocument(newURL);
    }
    if( x > 54 + 10 && x < 118 + 10 && y > 105 + 10 && y < 125 + 10){
        try {newURL = new URL("http://www.sybex.com");}
        catch (MalformedURLException e2) {}
        getAppletContext().showDocument(newURL);
    }
}
```

And now the imap applet is ready to go, as shown below. When you open the applet in a Web browser that supports Java 1.1, the Web browser will navigate to the corresponding URL. The imap applet is a success. The code for this applet appears in imap.java.

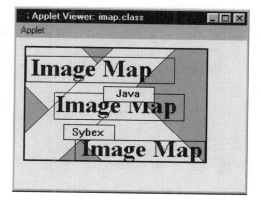

TIP   If you want to show the user what hyperlink the mouse cursor is over in your image map, you can use the `mouseMoved()` method to track the mouse movements, reporting back to the user in a `Label` control.

imap.java

```java
import java.applet.Applet;
import java.awt.*;
import java.awt.event.*;
import java.net.*;

public class imap extends Applet implements MouseListener {

    Image Imap;

    public void init(){
        Imap = getImage(getCodeBase(), "imap.gif");
        addMouseListener(this);
    }

    public void mousePressed(MouseEvent e){
        URL newURL = null;
        int x = e.getX();
        int y = e.getY();
        if( x > 104 + 10 && x < 171 + 10 && y > 53 + 10 && y < 75 + 10){
            try {newURL = new URL("http://www.javasoft.com");}
            catch (MalformedURLException e1) {}
            getAppletContext().showDocument(newURL);
        }
        if( x > 54 + 10 && x < 118 + 10 && y > 105 + 10 && y < 125 + 10){
            try {newURL = new URL("http://www.sybex.com");}
            catch (MalformedURLException e2) {}
            getAppletContext().showDocument(newURL);
        }
    }

    public void mouseClicked(MouseEvent e){}

    public void mouseReleased(MouseEvent e){}

    public void mouseEntered(MouseEvent e){}

    public void mouseExited(MouseEvent e){}
```

```
public void paint (Graphics g) {
    g.drawImage(Imap, 10, 10, 240, 155, this);
}
```
}

You've learned a lot about image maps, from loading images to displaying them, from stretching images to creating a clickable image map. In Skill 12, we'll turn to a another popular Java topic: font handling.

Are You Experienced?

Now you can...

☑ **load images into an applet using** `getImage()`

☑ **stretch images to the size you want, zooming in or out as you like**

☑ **create one of the most popular aspects of the Java-enabled Web page, the clickable image map**

☑ **use the Java** URL **class to navigate a Web browser to a new URL**

2. Jones 356-555-3398.

PROGRAMMERS
C, C, VB, Cobol, exp. Call 534-555-6543 or fax 534-555-6544.

PROGRAMMING
MRFS Inc. is looking for a Sr. Windows NT developer. Reqs. 3-5 yrs. Exp. In C under Windows, Win95 & NT, using Visual C. Excl. OO design & implementation skills a must. OLE2 & ODBC are a plus. Salary & bnfts. Resume & salary history to HR, 8779 HighTech Way, Computer City, AR

PROGRAMMERS
Contractors Wanted for short & long term assignments: Visual C, MFC Unix C/C, SQL Oracle Dev elopers PC Help Desk Support Windows NT & NetWare Telecommunications Visual Basic, Access, HTMT, CGI, Perl MMI & Co., 885-555-9933

PROGRAMMER World Wide Web Links wants your HTML & Photoshop skills. Develop great WWW sites. Local & global customers. Send samples & resume to WWWL, 2000 Apple Road, Santa Rosa, CA.

TECHNICAL WRITER Software firm seeks writer/editor for manuals, research notes, project mgmt. Min 2 years tech. writing, DTP & programming experience. Send resume & writing samples to: Software Systems, Dallas, TX.

TECHNICAL Software development firm looking for Tech Trainers. Ideal candidates have programming experience in Visual C, HTML & JAVA. Need quick self starter. Call (443) 555-6868 for interview.

TECHNICAL WRITER/ Premier Computer Corp is seeking a combination of technical skills, knowledge and experience in the following areas: UNIX, Windows 95/NT, Visual Basic, on-line help & documentation and the Internet. Candidates must possess excellent writing skills, and be comfortable working in a quality vs. deadline driven environment. Competitive salary. Fax resume & Samples to Karen Fields, Premier Computer Corp. 444 Industrial Blvd. Concord, CA. Or send to our website at www.premier.com.

WEB DESIGNER
BA/BS or equivalent programming/multimedia production. 3 years of experience in use and design of WWW services streaming audio and video HTML, PERL, CGI, GIF, JPEG. Demonstrated interpersonal, organization, communication, multi-tasking skills. Send resume to The Learning People at www.learning.com.

WEBMASTER-TECHNICAL
BSCS or equivalent, 2 years of experience in CGI, Windows 95/NT, UNIX, C, Java, Perl. Demonstrated ability to design, code, debug and test on-line services. Send resume to The Learning People at www.learning.com.

PROGRAMMER World Wide Web Links wants your HTML & Photoshop skills. Develop great WWW sites.

...ing tools. Experienced in documentation preparation & programming languages (Access, C FoxPro) are a plus. Financial or banking customer service support is required along with excellent verbal & written communication skills with multi levels of end-users. Send resume to KKUP Enterprises, 45 Orange Blvd, Orange, CA.

COMPUTERS Small Web Design firm seeks indiv. w/NT, Webserver & Database management exp. fax resume to 556-555-4221.

COMPUTER/ Visual C/C, Visual Basic Exp'd Systems Analysts/ Programmers for growing software dev. team in Roseburg. Computer Science or related degree preferred. Develop adv. Engineering applications for engineering firm. fax resume to 707-555-8744.

COMPUTER Web Master for dynamic SF Internet co. Site. Dev, test, coord, train. 2 yrs prog. Exp. C C Web C FTP. fax resume to Best Staffing 845-555-7722.

COMPUTER PROGRAMMER
Ad agency seeks programmer w/exp. in UNIX/NT Platforms, Web Server, CGI/Perl. Programmer Position avail. on a project basis with the possibility to move into F/T. fax resume & salary req. to R. Jones 334-555-8332.

COMPUTERS Programmer/Analyst Design and maintain C based SQL database applications. Required skills: Visual Basic, C, SQL, ODBC. Document existing and new applications. Novell or NT exp. a plus. Fax resume & salary history to 235-555-9935.

GRAPHIC DESIGNER
Webmaster's Weekly is seeking a creative Graphic Designer to design high impact marketing collater ad, including direct mail promois. CD-ROM packages, ads and WWW pages. Must be able to juggle multiple projects and learn new skills on the job very rapidly. Web design experience a big plus, technical troubleshooting also a plus. Call 435-555-1235.

GRAPHICS - ART DIRECTOR - WEB-MULTIMEDIA
Leading internet development company has an outstanding opportunity for a talented, high-end Web Experienced Art Director. In addition to a great portfolio and fresh ideas, the ideal candidate has excellent communication and presentation skills. Working as a team with innovative producers and programmers, you will create dynamic, interactive web sites and application interfaces. Some programming experience required. Send samples and resume to: SuperSites, 333 Main, Seattle. WA.

MARKETING
Fast paced software and services provider looking for MARKETING COMMUNICATIONS SPECIALIST to be responsible for its webpage,

---

PROGRAMMERS Multiple short term assignments available: Visual C. 3 positions SQL ServerNT Server, 2 positions JAVA & HTML, long term NetWare Various locations. Call for more info. 356-555-3398.

PROGRAMMERS
C, C, VB, Cobol, exp.
Call 534-555-6543
or fax 534-555-6544

PROGRAMMING
MRFS Inc. is looking for a Sr. Windows NT developer. Reqs. 3-5 yrs. Exp. In C under Windows, Win95 & NT, using Visual C. Excl. OO design & implementation skills a must. OLE2 & ODBC are a plus. Excl. Salary & bnfts. Resume & salary history to HR, 8779 HighTech Way, Computer City, AR

PROGRAMMERS/ Contractors Wanted for short & long term assignments: Visual C, MFC Unix C/C, SQL Oracle Developers PC Help Desk Support Windows NT & NetWare Telecommunications Visual Basic, Access, HTMT, CGI, Perl MMI & Co., 885-555-9933

PROGRAMMER World Wide Web Links wants your HTML & Photoshop skills. Develop great WWW sites. Local & global customers. Send samples & resume to WWWL, 2000 Apple Road, Santa Rosa, CA.

TECHNICAL WRITER Software firm seeks writer/editor for manuals, research notes, project mgmt. Min 2 years tech. writing, DTP & programming experience. Send resume & writing samples to: Software Systems, Dallas, TX.

COMPUTER PROGRAMMER
Ad agency seeks programmer w/exp. in UNIX/NT Platforms, Web Server, CGI/Perl. Programmer Position avail. on a project basis with the possibility to move into F/T. Fax resume & salary req. to R. Jones 334-555-8332.

TECHNICAL WRITER Premier Computer Corp is seeking a combination of technical skills, knowledge and experience in the following areas: UNIX, Windows 95/NT, Visual Basic, on-line help & documentation and the internet. Candidates must possess excellent writing skills, and be comfortable working in a quality vs. deadline driven environment. Competitive salary. Fax resume & samples to Karen Fields, Premier Computer Corp., 444 Industrial Blvd. Concord, CA. Or send to our website at www.premier.com.

WEB DESIGNER
BA/BS or equivalent programming/multimedia production. 3 years of experience in use and design of WWW services streaming audio and video HTML, PERL, CGI, GIF, JPEG. Demonstrated interpersonal, organization, communication, multi-tasking skills. Send resume to The Learning People at www.learning.com.

WEBMASTER-TECHNICAL
BSCS or equivalent, 2 years of experience in CGI, Windows 95/NT,

PROGRAMMERS / Established software company seeks program-

COMPUTERS Small Web Design Firm seeks indiv. w/NT. Webserver & Database management exp. fax resume to 556-555-4221.

COMPUTER Visual C/C, Visual Basic Exp'd Systems Analysts/ Programmers for growing software dev. team in Roseburg. Computer Science or related degree preferred. Develop adv. Engineering applications for engineering firm. Fax resume to 707-555-8744.

COMPUTER Web Master for dynamic SF Internet co. Site. Dev, test, coord, train. 2 yrs prog. Exp. C C Web C FTP. Fax resume to Best Staffing 845-555-7722.

COMPUTERS/ QA SOFTWARE TESTERS Qualified candidates should have 2 yrs exp. performing integration & system testing using automated testing tools. Experienced in documentation preparation & programming languages (Access, C, FoxPro) are a plus. Financial or banking customer service support is required along with excellent verbal & written communication skills with multi levels of end-users. Send resume to KKUP Enterprises, 45 Orange Blvd. Orange, CA.

COMPUTERS Programmer/Analyst Design and maintain C based SQL database applications. Required skills: Visual Basic, C, SQL, ODBC. Document existing and new applications. Novell or NT exp. a plus. Fax resume & salary history to 235-555-9935.

GRAPHIC DESIGNER
Webmaster's Weekly is seeking a creative Graphic Designer to design high impact marketing collater ad, including direct mail promo's. CD-ROM packages, ads and WWW pages. Must be able to juggle multiple projects and learn new skills on the job very rapidly. Web design experience a big plus, technical troubleshooting also a plus. Call 435-555-1235.

GRAPHICS - ART DIRECTOR - WEB-MULTIMEDIA
Leading internet development company has an outstanding opportunity for a talented, high-end Web Experienced Art Director. In addition to a great portfolio and fresh ideas, the ideal candidate has excellent communication and presentation skills. Working as a team with innovative producers and programmers, you will create dynamic, interactive web sites and application interfaces. Some programming experience required. Send samples and resume to: SuperSites, 333 Main, Seattle, WA.

COMPUTER PROGRAMMER
Ad agency seeks programmer w/exp. in UNIX/NT Platforms, Web Server, CGI/Perl. Programmer Position avail. on a project basis with the possibility to move into F/T. Fax resume & salary req. to R. Jones 334-555-8332.

PROGRAMMERS / Established software company seeks program-

---

ment. Must be a self-starter, energetic, organized. Must have 2 y web experience. Programming plus. Call 985-555-9854.

PROGRAMMERS Multiple term assignments available: C. 3 positions SQL ServerNT S 2 positions JAVA & HTML, long NetWare Various locations. Ca more info. 356-555-3398.

PROGRAMMERS
C, C, VB, Cobol, exp. Call 534 6543 or fax 534-555-6544.

PROGRAMMING
MRFS Inc. Is looking for a Windows NT developer. Reqs yrs. Exp. In C under Wind Win95 & NT, using Visual C OO design & implementation a must. OLE2 & ODBC are a Excl. Salary & bnfts. Resum salary history to HR. 8779 Hig Way, Computer City, AR

PROGRAMMERS/ Contra Wanted for short & long term a ments: Visual C. MFCUnix C/C, Oracle Developers PC Help Support Windows NT & NetW Telecommunications Visual I Access, HTMT, CGI, Perl MMI 885-555-9933

PROGRAMMER World Wide Links wants your HTML & Photo skills. Develop great WWW Local & global customers. Send ples & resume to WWWL, Apple Road, Santa Rosa, CA.

TECHNICAL WRITER Software seeks writer/editor for man research notes, project mgmt. M years tech. writing, DTP & pro ming experience. Send resum writing samples to: Soft Systems, Dallas, TX.

TECHNICAL Software develop firm looking for Tech Trainers, candidates have programming rience in Visual C, HTML & Need quick self starter. Call 555-6868 for interview.

TECHNICAL WRITER Pr Computer Corp is seeking a co nation of technical skills, know and experience in the follo areas: UNIX, Windows 95/NT, Basic, on-line help & document and the internet. Candidates possess excellent writing skills be comfortable working in a q vs. deadline driven environ Competitive salary. Fax resu samples to -Karen Fields. Pr Computer Corp. 444 Industrial Concord, CA. Or send to our w at www.premier.com.

WEB DESIGNER
BA/BS or equivalent prov ming/multimedia productio years of experience in us design of WWW services strea audio and video HTML, PERL GIF, JPEG. Demonstrated int sonal, organization, communic multi-tasking skills. Send resu The Learning People at www ing.com.

WEBMASTER-TECHNI

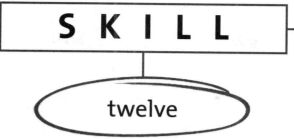

S K I L L

twelve

12

Setting and Modifying Text and Fonts

- ❑ **Setting a program's font**
- ❑ **Using the system clipboard**
- ❑ **Making text bold and italic**
- ❑ **Reading keyboard input**
- ❑ **Determining a text string's length on the screen**
- ❑ **Centering text**
- ❑ **Using the** FontMetric **class**

In Skill 11, we worked with images. In this Skill, we'll work on the presentation of text in Java. So far, we've used text in text fields and labels, but now we'll take over the process directly as we display text in our programs without those controls. Text is just another type of graphic; we'll see how to determine a text string's length and height as it appears on the screen so we can place it as we want it. We'll also see how to switch to various fonts, such as Times New Roman or Courier, and how to make text italic or bold. Finally, we'll see the Java 1.1 techniques of using the system clipboard.

Creating the Scribbler Applet

We'll write an applet called scribbler, which will present the user with a series of buttons representing various font options, such as italics, bold, Roman, and Courier, as shown in Figure 12.1. After the user selects the font options they want, they can type text, which we'll read directly from the keyboard (in the keyPressed() method) and display in our applet. The text will appear as a centered string in the font, with the font options the user wants.

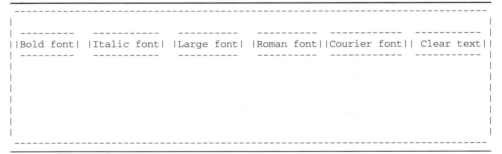

FIGURE 12.1   Buttons representing font options

Let's start this applet now. Create the new file named scribbler.java now, and create the new scribbler class now. We'll start by setting up the buttons in our applet. There are six buttons, and we name the buttons after their functions: boldbutton (makes text bold), italicbutton (makes text italic), largebutton (sets the font to a large typesize), romanbutton (switches to the Roman font), courierbutton (switches to the Courier font), and clearbutton (clears the text string). We add these buttons now:

```
    public class scribbler extends Applet{
→       Button boldbutton, italicbutton, largebutton;
→       Button romanbutton, courierbutton, clearbutton;
                    .
                    .
                    .
```

Next, we create these buttons in the init() method and add them to our applet's layout:

```
    public class scribbler extends Applet {

        Button boldbutton, italicbutton, largebutton;
        Button romanbutton, courierbutton, clearbutton;

        public void init()
        {
→           boldbutton = new Button("Bold font");

→           italicbutton = new Button("Italic font");

→           largebutton = new Button("Large font");

→           romanbutton = new Button("Roman font");

→           courierbutton = new Button("Courier font");

            clearbutton = new Button("Clear text");

→           add(boldbutton);
→           add(italicbutton);
→           add(largebutton);
→           add(romanbutton);
→           add(courierbutton);
→           add(clearbutton);
        }        .
                 .
                 .
```

In addition, we add an ActionListener to each button and make that ActionListener our applet as follows:

```
→   public class scribbler extends Applet implements ActionListener{

        Button boldbutton, italicbutton, largebutton;
        Button romanbutton, courierbutton, clearbutton;
```

```
         public void init()
         {
             boldbutton = new Button("Bold font");
→            boldbutton.addActionListener(this);

             italicbutton = new Button("Italic font");
→            italicbutton.addActionListener(this);

             largebutton = new Button("Large font");
→            largebutton.addActionListener(this);

             romanbutton = new Button("Roman font");
→            romanbutton.addActionListener(this);

             courierbutton = new Button("Courier font");
→            courierbutton.addActionListener(this);

             clearbutton = new Button("Clear text");
→            clearbutton.addActionListener(this);

             add(boldbutton);
             add(italicbutton);
             add(largebutton);
             add(romanbutton);
             add(courierbutton);
             add(clearbutton);
                    .
                    .
                    .
         }
```

As in our artist applet, we set up a boolean flag for each of the buttons except for the clear button (the clear button can clear the text string as soon as it is clicked—we do not have to wait for the paint() method to be executed):

```
    public class scribbler extends Applet implements ActionListener {

         Button boldbutton, italicbutton, largebutton;
         Button romanbutton, courierbutton, clearbutton;
→        boolean bBoldFlag = false;
→        boolean bItalicFlag = false;
→        boolean bLargeFlag = false;
→        boolean bRomanFlag = true;
→        boolean bCourierFlag = false;

         public void init()
         {
             boldbutton = new Button("Bold font");
```

```
boldbutton.addActionListener(this);

italicbutton = new Button("Italic font");
italicbutton.addActionListener(this);

largebutton = new Button("Large font");
largebutton.addActionListener(this);

romanbutton = new Button("Roman font");
romanbutton.addActionListener(this);

courierbutton = new Button("Courier font");
courierbutton.addActionListener(this);

clearbutton = new Button("Clear text");
clearbutton.addActionListener(this);

add(boldbutton);
add(italicbutton);
add(largebutton);
add(romanbutton);
add(courierbutton);
add(clearbutton);
        .
        .
        .
}
```

All of our boolean flags are set to false initially, except the flag bRomanFlag, since we will use Roman as our default font. To make these boolean flags active, we set up an actionPerformed() method in the scribbler class:

```
public void actionPerformed(ActionEvent event){
        .
        .
        .
}
```

We will handle the first of the buttons—the one with the caption "Bold font"—now. When the user clicks this button, they want to make the text they will type boldface, so we could set the boolean flag bBoldFlag to true. But this way, how can the user turn off boldface typing? It's better to *toggle* the bold setting on and off, and we do that with the negation operator (!) as follows, where we just reverse the setting of the bBoldFlag flag:

```
public void actionPerformed(ActionEvent event){
```

```
       if(event.getSource() == boldbutton){
              bBoldFlag = !bBoldFlag;
       }               .
                       .
                       .

}
```

When we click the Bold button, that gives the *input focus*—the target of keyboard strokes in Windows—to the button itself. When the user types again, no further text will appear, as the applet itself lost the focus when the button gained it. (The button has the focus, and buttons don't display keystrokes.) For that reason, we have the applet request the focus back again as follows after we have handled the button click, using the `requestFocus()` method:

```
   public void actionPerformed(ActionEvent event){
       if(event.getSource() == boldbutton){
              bBoldFlag = !bBoldFlag;
➡             requestFocus();
       }               .
                       .
                       .

   }
```

The first three font settings can be toggled on and off: boldface, italics, and large (versus normal) text, and we set them up as follows:

```
       public void actionPerformed(ActionEvent event){
           if(event.getSource() == boldbutton){
➡             bBoldFlag = !bBoldFlag;
➡             requestFocus();
➡         }
➡         if(event.getSource() == italicbutton){
➡             bItalicFlag = !bItalicFlag;
➡             requestFocus();
➡         }
➡         if(event.getSource() == largebutton){
➡             bLargeFlag = !bLargeFlag;
➡             requestFocus();
➡         }               .
                          .
                          .

       }
```

If, however, the user clicks a button with the caption "Roman font" or "Courier font" we can't just toggle a boolean flag. There are two font name flags: **bRomanFlag** and bCourierFlag; because only one can be true at a time, when we set one true, we must set the other one false:

```java
public void actionPerformed(ActionEvent event){
    if(event.getSource() == boldbutton){
        bBoldFlag = !bBoldFlag;
        requestFocus();
    }
    if(event.getSource() == italicbutton){
        bItalicFlag = !bItalicFlag;
        requestFocus();
    }
    if(event.getSource() == largebutton){
        bLargeFlag = !bLargeFlag;
        requestFocus();
    }
    if(event.getSource() == romanbutton){
        bRomanFlag = true;
        bCourierFlag = false;
        requestFocus();
    }
    if(event.getSource() == courierbutton){
        bCourierFlag = true;
        bRomanFlag = false;
        requestFocus();
    }           .
                .
                .
}
```

So far, then, we've made our Bold, Italic, Large, Roman, and Courier buttons active. All that remains is to activate the Clear Text button, which the user clicks when they want to clear the text they've typed. We'll store that text in a String object named text:

```java
import java.applet.Applet;
import java.awt.*;
import java.awt.event.*;

public class scribbler extends Applet implements ActionListener {

    String text = "";

    Button boldbutton, italicbutton, largebutton;
    Button romanbutton, courierbutton, clearbutton;
    boolean bBoldFlag = false;
    boolean bItalicFlag = false;
```

```
boolean bLargeFlag = false;
boolean bRomanFlag = true;
boolean bCourierFlag = false;

        .
        .
        .
```

And we clear the text object by simply setting it to a null or empty string when the user clicks the Clear button:

```
public void actionPerformed(ActionEvent event){
    if(event.getSource() == boldbutton){
        bBoldFlag = !bBoldFlag;
        requestFocus();
    }
    if(event.getSource() == italicbutton){
        bItalicFlag = !bItalicFlag;
        requestFocus();
    }
    if(event.getSource() == largebutton){
        bLargeFlag = !bLargeFlag;
        requestFocus();
    }
    if(event.getSource() == romanbutton){
        bRomanFlag = true;
        bCourierFlag = false;
        requestFocus();
    }
    if(event.getSource() == courierbutton){
        bCourierFlag = true;
        bRomanFlag = false;
        requestFocus();
    }
    if(event.getSource() == clearbutton){
        text = "";
        requestFocus();
    }
    repaint();
}
```

Note that we also include a call to repaint() at the end of the action method. This is so the user can see the result of clicking a button immediately, without having to wait for the new key to be struck. And that brings us to the question, just how do we read direct keyboard input in Java?

Working with the Keyboard

So far, we've used text fields and text areas to handle all of our keyboard input. It is possible, however, to read keys directly in Java using the keyTyped() method. To use this method, we have to implement the KeyListener interface, and we do that as follows:

```
import java.applet.Applet;
import java.awt.*;
import java.awt.event.*;

public class scribbler extends Applet implements ActionListener, KeyListener {
    String text = "";

    Button boldbutton, italicbutton, largebutton;
    Button romanbutton, courierbutton, clearbutton;
    boolean bBoldFlag = false;
    boolean bItalicFlag = false;
    boolean bLargeFlag = false;
    boolean bRomanFlag = true;
    boolean bCourierFlag = false;

    public void init()
    {
        boldbutton = new Button("Bold font");
        boldbutton.addActionListener(this);

        italicbutton = new Button("Italic font");
        italicbutton.addActionListener(this);

        largebutton = new Button("Large font");
        largebutton.addActionListener(this);

        romanbutton = new Button("Roman font");
        romanbutton.addActionListener(this);

        courierbutton = new Button("Courier font");
        courierbutton.addActionListener(this);

        clearbutton = new Button("Clear text");
        clearbutton.addActionListener(this);

        add(boldbutton);
        add(italicbutton);
```

```
        add(largebutton);
        add(romanbutton);
        add(courierbutton);
        add(clearbutton);

→       addKeyListener(this);
        requestFocus();
    }
```

Now we're ready to add the three key-handling methods of the KeyListener interface, keyTyped(), keyPressed(), and keyReleased(), each of which is passed a KeyEvent object:

```
    public void keyTyped(KeyEvent e) {}

    public void keyPressed(KeyEvent e) {}

    public void keyReleased(KeyEvent e) {}
```

We'll use the keyTyped() method here:

```
    public void keyTyped(KeyEvent e) {
                    .
                    .
                    .
    }
```

Here, we want to add the just-typed key to the string of text we already have in memory: the String object named text. We get that key by using the KeyEvent getKeyChar() method, and we add it to the text string the user has already typed as follows:

```
    public void keyTyped(KeyEvent e) {
→       text = text + e.getKeyChar();
                    .
                    .
                    .
    }
```

The real work of the applet is done in the paint() method, and we force a paint event now with the repaint() method:

```
    public void keyTyped(KeyEvent e) {
        text = text + e.getKeyChar();
→       repaint();
    }
```

NOTE   **Unless you are familiar with C++, you may be surprised to see a line like**

```
text = text + e.getKeyChar();
```

because text **is an object of the Java** String **class. However, in Java and in C++, operators like the** + **operator can be overloaded to work with object of various classes. The** + **operator is overloaded to work with** String **objects.**

Let's write our paint() method now; that's where the guts of this applet are.

Working with Fonts

When we enter the paint() method, we already have a string of text—that is, the String object named text—to display. Our goal is to display that text using the font settings the user has indicated (which are now mirrored in the settings of our boolean flags) so that the text appears centered in our applet, as shown in Figure 12.2.

```
 ----------------------------------------------------------------------------
|                                                                            |
| ---------   -----------   ---------   -----------  -------------  ----------|
||Bold font| |Italic font| |Large font| |Roman font||Courier font|| Clear text||
| ---------   -----------   ---------   -----------  -------------  ----------|
|                                                                            |
|                                                                            |
|                          This is centered text.                            |
|                                                                            |
|                                                                            |
|                                                                            |
 ----------------------------------------------------------------------------
```

FIGURE 12.2   The applet centers the text.

In the paint() method, we'll set up the type, the size, and the actual typeface of the font we will use to display the characters in the text object, and we'll set up an object of class Font with this information. Then we'll simply install that Font object in the Graphics object passed to us in paint() and draw our string.

We start our paint() method by setting up the variables we'll need and setting the font type to default values. For example, the name of the font we'll use is stored as a string, like "Roman" or "Courier," and our default will be Roman:

```
public void paint(Graphics g)
{
```

Skill 12

→
```
        String fontname = "Roman";
                    .
                    .
                    .
```

TIP   If you don't know what fonts are installed on your system, you can check in the Windows 95 registry with the Windows REGEDIT tool, `regedit.exe`, which Windows 95 places in the `c:\windows` directory. You can also see what fonts are available by using a word processing program like Microsoft Word. Another option is to look in the Control Panel and click the Fonts icon.

The type of font—plain, bold, or italic—is set up in an integer variable that can take one of these pre-defined Font class constants: Font.PLAIN, Font.BOLD, or Font.ITALIC. Our default will be plain text, Font.PLAIN:

```
public void paint(Graphics g)
{
        String fontname = "Roman";
→       int type = Font.PLAIN;
                    .
                    .
                    .
```

The point size of the font is also stored as an integer. Our default font size will be 24 point:

```
public void paint(Graphics g)
{
        String fontname = "Roman";
        int type = Font.PLAIN;
→       int size = 24;
                    .
                    .
                    .
```

We've set up the default values for our font. Next, we create the Font object itself—which we name font—that we will load into the Graphics object passed to us in the paint() method:

```
public void paint(Graphics g)
{
        String fontname = "Roman";
        int type = Font.PLAIN;
        int size = 24;
```

→   Font font;
             .
             .
             .

The methods of the Java Font class appear in Table 12.1.

TABLE 12.1: The Font class's methods

Method	Does This
Font(String, int, int)	Creates font object with given name, style (Font.BOLD, Font.PLAIN, or Font.ITALIC), and point size.
decode(String)	Gets the specified font using the name passed in.
equals(Object)	Compares font to specified font.
getFamily()	Gets family name of font.
getFont(String)	Gets a font from system properties list.
getFont(String, Font)	Gets given font from system properties list.
getName()	Gets logical name of font.
getPeer()	Gets the peer of the font.
getSize()	Gets point size of font.
getStyle()	Gets font style.
hashCode()	Gets the font hashcode.
isBold()	Returns true if font is bold.
isItalic()	Returns true if font is italic.
isPlain()	Returns true if font is plain.
toString()	Converts font to a string.

The next step is to set up the variables fontname, type, and size according to how the user wants them so that we can use them to set up the Font object. To do so, we just check the various boolean flags we have set up and set these three variables accordingly:

```
public void paint(Graphics g)
{
    String fontname = "Roman";
    int type = Font.PLAIN;
    int size = 24;
    Font font;
```

Skill 12

```
➜        if(bBoldFlag){
➜              type = type | Font.BOLD;
➜        }
➜        if(bItalicFlag){
➜              type = type | Font.ITALIC;
➜        }
➜        if(bLargeFlag){
➜              size = 48;
➜        }
➜        if(bRomanFlag){
➜              fontname = "Roman";
➜        }
➜        if(bCourierFlag){
➜              fontname = "Courier";
➜        }              .
                       .
                       .
```

T TIP   **Because text can be italic and bold at the same time, you can use the bitwise OR operator (|) to combine font types. For example, valid font types include:** `Font.PLAIN | Font.ITALIC` **or** `Font.BOLD | Font.ITALIC`.

At this point, then, we have the font's name, its size, and its type (i.e., plain or bold, italic or not). We create the Font object now and install it in our Graphics object using the setFont() method as follows:

```
public void paint(Graphics g)
{
     String fontname = "Roman";
     int type = Font.PLAIN;
     int size = 24;
     Font font;

     if(bBoldFlag){
           type = type | Font.BOLD;
     }              .
                    .
                    .
➜    font = new Font(fontname, type, size);
➜    g.setFont(font);
}
```

And now the font the user selected, in the font style they want, is installed. When we draw text in the Graphics object with drawString(), the text will appear in this new font.

However, we want to do more—we want to make sure the text appears centered in the applet. We do that with a FontMetrics object.

Working with the
FontMetrics **Class**

To make sure our text string is centered in the applet, we have to know how much space the string will take up on the screen, both horizontally and vertically, and we do that with a FontMetrics object (in addition, we'll have to find out how wide and how tall our applet is in pixels). First, we add a new FontMetrics object to our applet:

```
import java.applet.Applet;
import java.awt.*;
import java.awt.event.*;

public class scribbler extends Applet implements ActionListener, KeyListener {

    String text = "";
    int x = 0;
    int y = 0;

    Button boldbutton, italicbutton, largebutton;
    Button romanbutton, courierbutton, clearbutton;
    boolean bBoldFlag = false;
    boolean bItalicFlag = false;
    boolean bLargeFlag = false;
    boolean bRomanFlag = true;
    boolean bCourierFlag = false;
    FontMetrics fontmetrics;
            .
            .
            .
```

Then we create this FontMetrics object, passing it the font object we have set up so it will be able to return information about strings displayed in that font:

```
    public void paint(Graphics g)
    {
        String fontname = "Roman";
        int type = Font.PLAIN;
        int size = 24;
        Font font;
```

Skill 12

```
                      if(bBoldFlag){
                            type = type | Font.BOLD;
                      }
                      if(bItalicFlag){
                            type = type | Font.ITALIC;
                      }
                      if(bLargeFlag){
                            size = 48;
                      }
                      if(bRomanFlag){
                            fontname = "Roman";
                      }
                      if(bCourierFlag){
                            fontname = "Courier";
                      }

                      font = new Font(fontname, type, size);
                      g.setFont(font);

➜                     fontmetrics = getFontMetrics(font);
                            .
                            .
                            .
```

The FontMetrics class's methods appear in Table 12.2.

T A B L E   1 2 . 2 : The FontMetric class's methods

Method	Does This
FontMetrics(Font)	Creates a FontMetrics object using given font.
bytesWidth(byte[], int, int)	Returns the width of a byte array.
charWidth(int)	Gets width of given character.
charWidth(char)	Gets width of given character.
charsWidth(char[], int, int)	Gets width of character array.
getAscent()	Gets font ascent.
getDescent()	Gets font descent.
getFont()	Gets the font.
getHeight()	Gets total height of this font.
getLeading()	Gets standard line spacing for font.
getMaxAdvance()	Gets maximum advance width of any character.
getMaxAscent()	Gets maximum ascent of characters.

TABLE 12.2 CONTINUED: The `FontMetric` class's methods

Method	Does This
getMaxDescent()	Gets maximum descent of characters.
getWidths()	Gets widths of first 256 characters.
stringWidth(String)	Gets width of given String.
toString()	Gets String representation for object.

Getting the Width of a Text String

Now we will be able to retrieve the width of the text this way:

```
width = fontmetrics.stringWidth(text);
```

and the height this way:

```
height = fontmetrics.getHeight();
```

NOTE   The height of the line of text is a constant—not dependent on string length—so we don't have to pass the line of text itself to the `getHeight()` method.

We'll also need the height and width of our applet, and we'll find those values with the `Applet` method `size()`, which returns an object of the Java `Dimension` class. The `width` and `height` members of this `Dimension` object will give us the width and height of our applet.

The last thing to keep in mind is that when we pass the location of a string to `drawString()` so that it can appear on the screen, the location we pass is actually the bottom left of the string on the screen—*not* the top left as many Windows programmers expect.

Centering Displayed Text

Putting together all we've learned in this Skill means that we find the x and y location at which to print our string as follows, making sure it is centered in the applet's display:

```
public void paint(Graphics g)
{
    String fontname = "Roman";
```

Skill 12

```
int type = Font.PLAIN;
int size = 24;
Font font;

if(bBoldFlag){
    type = type | Font.BOLD;
}
if(bItalicFlag){
    type = type | Font.ITALIC;
}
if(bLargeFlag){
    size = 48;
}
if(bRomanFlag){
    fontname = "Roman";
}
if(bCourierFlag){
    fontname = "Courier";
}

font = new Font(fontname, type, size);
g.setFont(font);

fontmetrics = getFontMetrics(font);
x =(size().width - fontmetrics.stringWidth(text)) / 2;
y = (size().height + fontmetrics.getHeight()) / 2;
            .
            .
            .

}
```

We also need to declare the new integer variables x and y, which hold the location of the text string in the applet:

```
import java.applet.Applet;
import java.awt.*;
import java.awt.event.*;

public class scribbler extends Applet implements ActionListener, KeyListener {

    String text = "";
    int x = 0;
    int y = 0;

    Button boldbutton, italicbutton, largebutton;
    Button romanbutton, courierbutton, clearbutton;
    boolean bBoldFlag = false;
    boolean bItalicFlag = false;
```

```
boolean bLargeFlag = false;
boolean bRomanFlag = true;
boolean bCourierFlag = false;
FontMetrics fontmetrics;
      .
      .
      .
```

All that remains now is to display the text string itself, and we do that with drawString():

```
public void paint(Graphics g)
{
      String fontname = "Roman";
      int type = Font.PLAIN;
      int size = 24;
      Font font;

      if(bBoldFlag){
            type = type | Font.BOLD;
      }
      if(bItalicFlag){
            type = type | Font.ITALIC;
      }
      if(bLargeFlag){
            size = 48;
      }
      if(bRomanFlag){
            fontname = "Roman";
      }
      if(bCourierFlag){
            fontname = "Courier";
      }

      font = new Font(fontname, type, size);
      g.setFont(font);

      fontmetrics = getFontMetrics(font);
      x =(size().width - fontmetrics.stringWidth(text)) / 2;
      y = (size().height + fontmetrics.getHeight()) / 2;

      g.drawString(text, x, y);
}
```

Select a few font options–in Figure 12.3, we've selected bold italic font and typed a few characters. As you can see, our scribbler applet is a success. The code for this applet appears in scribbler.java.

FIGURE 12.3   The scribbler applet lets the user specify various font options.

scribbler.java

```java
import java.applet.Applet;
import java.awt.*;
import java.awt.event.*;

public class scribbler extends Applet implements ActionListener, KeyListener {

    String text = "";
    int x = 0;
    int y = 0;

    Button boldbutton, italicbutton, largebutton;
    Button romanbutton, courierbutton, clearbutton;
    boolean bBoldFlag = false;
    boolean bItalicFlag = false;
    boolean bLargeFlag = false;
    boolean bRomanFlag = true;
    boolean bCourierFlag = false;
    FontMetrics fontmetrics;

    public void init()
    {
```

```
            boldbutton = new Button("Bold font");
            boldbutton.addActionListener(this);

            italicbutton = new Button("Italic font");
            italicbutton.addActionListener(this);

            largebutton = new Button("Large font");
            largebutton.addActionListener(this);

            romanbutton = new Button("Roman font");
            romanbutton.addActionListener(this);

            courierbutton = new Button("Courier font");
            courierbutton.addActionListener(this);

            clearbutton = new Button("Clear text");
            clearbutton.addActionListener(this);

            add(boldbutton);
            add(italicbutton);
            add(largebutton);
            add(romanbutton);
            add(courierbutton);
            add(clearbutton);

            addKeyListener(this);
            requestFocus();
        }

        public void actionPerformed(ActionEvent event){
            if(event.getSource() == boldbutton){
                bBoldFlag = !bBoldFlag;
                requestFocus();
            }
            if(event.getSource() == italicbutton){
                bItalicFlag = !bItalicFlag;
                requestFocus();
            }
            if(event.getSource() == largebutton){
                bLargeFlag = !bLargeFlag;
                requestFocus();
            }
            if(event.getSource() == romanbutton){
                bRomanFlag = true;
                bCourierFlag = false;
                requestFocus();
            }
            if(event.getSource() == courierbutton){
```

Skill 12

```
            bCourierFlag = true;
            bRomanFlag = false;
            requestFocus();
        }
        if(event.getSource() == clearbutton){
            text = "";
            requestFocus();
        }
        repaint();
    }

    public void paint(Graphics g)
    {
        String fontname = "Roman";
        int type = Font.PLAIN;
        int size = 24;
        Font font;

        if(bBoldFlag){
            type = type | Font.BOLD;
        }
        if(bItalicFlag){
            type = type | Font.ITALIC;
        }
        if(bLargeFlag){
            size = 48;
        }
        if(bRomanFlag){
            fontname = "Roman";
        }
        if(bCourierFlag){
            fontname = "Courier";
        }

        font = new Font(fontname, type, size);
        g.setFont(font);

        fontmetrics = getFontMetrics(font);
        x =(size().width - fontmetrics.stringWidth(text)) / 2;
        y = (size().height + fontmetrics.getHeight()) / 2;

        g.drawString(text, x, y);
    }

    public void keyTyped(KeyEvent e) {
        text = text + e.getKeyChar();
        repaint();
```

```
          }

          public void keyPressed(KeyEvent e) {}

          public void keyReleased(KeyEvent e) {}

      }
```

And now we're displaying text the user typed in with the font options they've picked. While we're working with text in Java, let's take a look at one more way of handling text—using the clipboard.

Using the Clipboard from Java

To see how to use the clipboard in Java, we'll place a small text string, "Hello from Java," into the clipboard. Then we'll be able to paste that text string into other programs, like Microsoft Word (using Word's Paste menu item). Create a new file named clipboarder.java now. This program will be a Java application because, as is the case with printing, applets cannot access the clipboard for security reasons. Add the application's main class to clipboarder.java now:

```
public class clipboarder {
            .
            .
            .
}
```

Because this is a Java application, we add a main() method:

```
public class clipboarder {
      public static void main(String[] argv) {
                  .
                  .
                  .
      }
}
```

Here we can simply create a new object of the class we'll name writetext, which will write to the clipboard. We create that object this way:

```
public class clipboarder {
      public static void main(String[] argv) {
```

➡
```
                    writetext w = new writetext();
        }
    }
```

Next, we will write the writetext class. We'll need a frame window to implement the ClipboardOwner interface, so we start with the following code:

```
class writetext extends Frame {
        .
        .
        .
}
```

To handle clipboard operations, we add the ClipboardOwner interface this way:

➡
```
class writetext extends Frame implements ClipboardOwner {
        .
        .
        .
}
```

Now we create the writetext class's constructor and the lostOwnership() method which is required to implement this interface:

```
class writetext extends Frame implements ClipboardOwner {
```
➡
```
    writetext() {
    }
```
➡
```
    public void lostOwnership(Clipboard clipboard, Transferable contents){}
}
```

We get an object of the Clipboard class as follows:

```
class writetext extends Frame implements ClipboardOwner {
    writetext() {
```
➡
```
        Clipboard clipboard = getToolkit().getSystemClipboard();
        .
        .
        .
    }

    public void lostOwnership(Clipboard clipboard, Transferable contents){}
}
```

The Java Clipboard class's methods appear in Table 12.3—you place text in the clipboard with setContents(), and you retrieve it with getContents().

TABLE 12.3: The Clipboard class's methods

Method	Does This
Clipboard(String)	Creates a clipboard object.
getContents(Object)	Returns a transferable object representing the current contents of the clipboard.
getName()	Returns the name of this clipboard object.
setContents(Transferable, ClipboardOwner)	Sets the current contents of the clipboard to the specified transferable object and registers the specified clipboard owner as the owner of the new contents.

Next, we create the string of text we want to place in the clipboard with the Java StringSelection class; in this case, that string is simply "Hello from Java."

```
class writetext extends Frame implements ClipboardOwner {
    writetext() {
        Clipboard clipboard = getToolkit().getSystemClipboard();
        StringSelection contents = new StringSelection("Hello from Java");
                    .
                    .
                    .
    }

    public void lostOwnership(Clipboard clipboard, Transferable contents){}
}
```

Finally, we place the string into the clipboard with the Clipboard class's setContents() method:

```
class writetext extends Frame implements ClipboardOwner {
    writetext() {
        Clipboard clipboard = getToolkit().getSystemClipboard();
        StringSelection contents = new StringSelection("Hello from Java");
        clipboard.setContents(contents, this);
    }

    public void lostOwnership(Clipboard clipboard, Transferable contents){}
}
```

Use javac.exe to compile clipboarder.java and java.exe to run it. When the application runs, the string "Hello from Java" is placed in the clipboard, and we can paste it into other applications, like Microsoft Word, as shown in Figure 12.4. The code for this application appears in clipboarder.java.

Skill 12

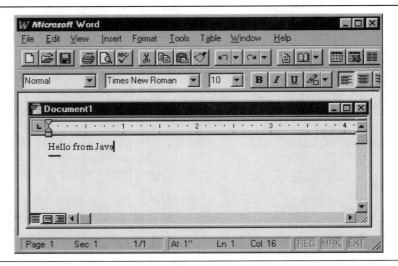

FIGURE 12.4   We can place text into the clipboard and paste it into other applications such as Microsoft Word.

 clipboarder.java

```
public class clipboarder {
    public static void main(String[] argv) {
        writetext w = new writetext();
    }
}

class writetext extends Frame implements ClipboardOwner {
    writetext() {
        Clipboard clipboard = getToolkit().getSystemClipboard();
        StringSelection contents = new StringSelection("Hello from Java");
        clipboard.setContents(contents, this);
    }

    public void lostOwnership(Clipboard clipboard, Transferable contents){}
}
```

As you can see, working with fonts can be an indispensable technique, allowing you display text in Java in a wide variety of formats. In Skill 13, we'll turn to an important and very popular Java topic: graphics animation.

Are You Experienced?

Now you can...

- ☑ set a program's font by using `setFont()`
- ☑ make text bold or italic as you require
- ☑ read keys directly from the keyboard, using the `KeyListener` methods
- ☑ use the `FontMetric` class to determine a text string's length
- ☑ center displayed text
- ☑ copy and paste text to and from other applications with the system clipboard

2. Jones 556-555-3398.

PROGRAMMERS
C. C. VB, Cobol, exp. Call 534-555-
6543 or fax 534-555-6544.

PROGRAMMING
MRFS Inc. is looking for a Sr.
Windows NT developer. Reqs. 3-5
yrs. Exp. In C under Windows,
Win95 & NT, using Visual C. Excl. OO
design & implementation skills a
must. OLE2 & ODBC are a plus. Excl.
Salary & bnfts. Resume & salary his-
tory to HR. 8779 HighTech Way,
Computer City, AR

PROGRAMMERS
Contractors Wanted for short & long
term assignments; Visual C, MFC
Unix C/C, SQL Oracle Dev elop ers
PC Help Desk Support Windows NT
& NetWare Telecommunications
Visual Basic, Access, HTMT, CGI,
Perl MMI & Co., 885-555-9933

PROGRAMMER World Wide Web
Links wants your HTML & Photoshop
skills. Develop great WWW sites.
Local & global customers. Send sam-
ples & resume to WWWL, 2000
Apple Road, Santa Rosa, CA.

TECHNICAL WRITER Software firm
seeks writer/editor for manuals,
research notes, project mgmt. Min 2
years tech. writing. Send resume &
writing samples to: Software
Systems, Dallas, TX.

TECHNICAL Software development
firm looking for Tech Trainers, Ideal
candidates have programming experience in Visual C, HTML & JAVA.
Need quick self starter. Call (443)
555-6868 for interview.

TECHNICAL WRITER/ Premier
Computer Corp is seeking a combination of technical skills, knowledge
and experience in the following
areas: UNIX, Windows 95/NT, Visual
Basic, on-line help & documentation,
and the internet. Candidates must
possess excellent writing skills, and
be comfortable working in a quality
vs. deadline driven environment.
Competitive salary. Fax resume &
samples to Karen Fields, Premier
Computer Corp. 444 Industrial Blvd.
Concord, CA. Or send to our website
at www.premier.com.

WEB DESIGNER
BA/BS or equivalent program-
ming/multimedia production. 3
years of experience in use and
design of WWW services streaming
audio and video HTML, PERL, CGI,
GIF, JPEG. Demonstrated interpersonal, organization, communication,
multi-tasking skills. Send resume to
The Learning People at www.learn-
ing.com.

WEBMASTER-TECHNICAL
BSCS or equivalent. 2 years of
experience in CGI, Windows 95/NT,
UNIX, C, Java, Perl. Demonstrated
ability to design, code, debug and
test on-line services. Send resume to
The Learning People at www.learn-
ing.com.

PROGRAMMER World Wide Web
Links wants your HTML & Photoshop
skills. Develop great WWW sites.

---

ing tools. Experience is docu-
tation preparation & programming
languages (Access, C, FoxPro) are a
plus. Financial or banking customer
service support is required along
with excellent verbal & written communication skills with multi levels of
end-users. Send resume to KKUP
Enterprises. 45 Orange Blvd.
Orange, CA.

COMPUTERS Small Web Design
firm seeks indiv. w/NT, Webserver &
Database management exp. Fax
resume to 556-555-4221.

COMPUTER/ Visual C/C Visual
Basic Exp'd Systems Analysts/
Programmers for growing software
dev. team in Roseburg. Computer
Science or related degree preferred.
Develop adv. Engineering applica-
tions for engineering firm. Fax
resume to 707-555-8744.

COMPUTER Web Master for dynamic SF Internet co. Site. Dev. test,
coord. train. 2 yrs prog. Exp. C C.
Web C FTP. Fax resume to Best
Staffing 845-555-7722.

**COMPUTER
PROGRAMMER**
Ad agency seeks programmer
w/exp. in UNIX/NT Platforms, Web
Server, CGI/Perl. Programmer Position avail. on a project basis with the
possibility to move into F/T. Fax
resume & salary req. to R. Jones
334-555-8332.

COMPUTERS Programmer/Analyst
Design and maintain C based SQL
database applications. Required
skills: Visual Basic, C SQL, ODBC.
Document existing and new applications. Novell or NT exp. a plus. Fax
resume & salary history to
235-555-9935.

GRAPHIC DESIGNER
Webmaster's Weekly is seeking a
creative Graphic Designer to design
high impact marketing collater al,
including direct mail promos.
CD-ROM packages, ads and WWW
pages. Must be able to juggle multiple projects and learn new skills
on the job very rapidly. Web design
experience a big plus, technical
troubleshooting also a plus. Call
435-555-1235.

**GRAPHICS - ART DIRECTOR -
WEB-MULTIMEDIA**
Leading internet development company has an outstanding opportunity for a talented, high-end Web
Experienced Art Director. In addition
to a great portfolio and fresh ideas,
the ideal candidate has excellent
communication and presentation
skills. Working as a team with innovative producers and programmers,
you will create dynamic, interactive
web sites and application interfaces.
Some programming experience
required. Send samples and resume
to: SuperSites, 333 Main, Seattle,
WA.

MARKETING
Fast paced software and services
provider looking for MARKETING
COMMUNICATIONS SPECIALIST to
be responsible for its webpage.

PROGRAMMERS Multiple short
term assignments available: Visual C,
3 positions SQL ServerNT Server. 4
positions JAVA & HTML, long term
NetWare Various locations. Call for
more info. 356-555-3398.

PROGRAMMERS
C. C. VB, Cobol, exp
Call 534-555-6543
or fax 534-555-6544.

PROGRAMMING
MRFS Inc. is looking for a Sr. Windows
NT developer. Reqs. 3-5 yrs. Exp. In
C under Windows, Win95 & NT,
using Visual C. Excl. OO design &
implementation skills a must. OLE2 &
ODBC are a plus. Excl. Salary & bnfts.
Resume & salary history to HR. 8779
HighTech Way, Computer City, AR

PROGRAMMERS/ Contractors
Wanted for short & long term
assignments: Visual C, MFC Unix C/C
SQL Oracle Developers PC Help
Desk Support Windows NT &
NetWare Telecommunications Visual
Basic, Access, HTMT, CGI, Perl MMI
& Co., 885-555-9933

PROGRAMMER World Wide Web
Links wants your HTML & Photoshop
skills. Develop great WWW sites.
Local & global customers. Send sam-
ples & resume to WWWL, 2000
Apple Road, Santa Rosa, CA.

TECHNICAL WRITER Software firm
seeks writer/editor for manuals,
research notes, project mgmt. Min 2
years tech. writing. DTP & programming experience. Send resume &
writing samples to: Software
Systems, Dallas, TX.

COMPUTER PROGRAMMER
Ad agency seeks programmer w/exp.
in UNIX/NT Platforms, Web Server,
CGI/Perl. Programmer Position avail.
on a project basis with the possibility to move into F/T. Fax resume &
salary req. to R. Jones 334-555-
8332.

TECHNICAL WRITER Premier
Computer Corp is seeking a combination of technical skills, knowledge
and experience in the following
areas: UNIX, Windows 95/NT, Visual
Basic, on-line help & documentation,
and the internet. Candidates must
possess excellent writing skills, and
be comfortable working in a quality
vs. deadline driven environment.
Competitive salary. Fax resume &
samples to Karen Fields, Premier
Computer Corp. 444 Industrial Blvd.
Concord, CA. Or send to our website
at www.premier.com.

WEB DESIGNER
BA/BS or equivalent program-
ming/multimedia production. 3
years of experience in use and
design of WWW services streaming
audio and video HTML, PERL, CGI,
GIF, JPEG. Demonstrated interpersonal, organization, communication,
multi-tasking skills. Send resume to
The Learning People at www.learn-
ing.com.

WEBMASTER-TECHNICAL
BSCS or equivalent. 2 years of
experience in CGI, Windows 95/NT,

COMPUTERS Small Web Design
firm seeks indiv. w/NT, Webserver &
Database management exp. Fax
resume to 556-555-4221.

COMPUTER Visual C/C, Visual
Basic Exp'd Systems Analysts/
Programmers for growing software
dev. team in Roseburg. Computer
Science or related degree preferred.
Develop adv. Engineering applica-
tions for engineering firm. Fax
resume to 707-555-8744.

COMPUTER Web Master for dynamic SF Internet co. Site. Dev. test,
coord. train. 2 yrs prog. Exp. C C.
Web C FTP. Fax resume to Best
Staffing 845-555-7722.

COMPUTERS/ QA SOFTWARE
TESTERS Qualified candidates should
have 2 yrs exp. performing integration & system testing using automated testing tools. Experienced in documentation preparation & programming languages (Access, C, FoxPro)
are a plus. Financial or banking customer service support is required
along with excellent verbal & written
communication skills with multi levels
of end-users. Send resume to KKUP
Enterprises, 45 Orange Blvd.
Orange, CA.

COMPUTERS Programmer/Analyst
Design and maintain C based SQL
database applications. Required
skills: Visual Basic C, SQL, ODBC,
Document existing and new applications. Novell or NT exp. a plus.
Fax resume & salary history to
235-555-9935.

GRAPHIC DESIGNER
Webmaster's Weekly is seeking a
creative Graphic Designer to design
high impact marketing collater al,
including direct mail promo's. CD-
ROM packages, ads and WWW
pages. Must be able to juggle multiple projects and learn new skills
on the job very rapidly. Web design
experience a big plus, technical
troubleshooting also a plus. Call
435-555-1235.

**GRAPHICS - ART DIRECTOR -
WEB-MULTIMEDIA**
Leading internet development company has an outstanding opportunity for a talented, high-end Web
Experienced Art Director. In addition
to a great portfolio and fresh ideas,
the ideal candidate has excellent
communication and presentation
skills. Working as a team with innovative producers and programmers,
you will create dynamic, interactive
web sites and application interfaces.
Some programming experience
required. Send samples and resume
to: SuperSites, 333 Main, Seattle,
WA

COMPUTER PROGRAMMER
Ad agency seeks programmer w/exp.
in UNIX/NT Platforms, Web Server,
CGI/Perl. Programmer Position avail.
on a project basis with the possibility to move into F/T. Fax resume &
salary req. to R. Jones 334-555-
8332.

PROGRAMMERS / Established
software company seeks program-

---

ment. Must be a self-starter,
getic, organized. Must have 2
web experience. Programmi
plus. Call 985-555-9854

PROGRAMMERS Multiple
term assignments available:
C, 3 positions SQL ServerNT S
2 positions JAVA & HTML, lon
NetWare Various locations. C
more info. 356-555-3398.

PROGRAMMERS
C. C. VB, Cobol, exp. Call 534
6543 or fax 534-555-6544.

PROGRAMMING
MRFS Inc. is looking for a
Windows NT developer. Req
yrs. Exp. In C under Win
Win95 & NT, using Visual C.
OO design & implementation
a must. OLE2 & ODBC are a
Excl. Salary & bnfts. Resum
salary history to HR. 8779 Hig
Way, Computer City, AR

PROGRAMMERS Contr
Wanted for short & long term a
ments. Visual C, MFCUnix C/C
Oracle Developers PC Help
Support Windows NT & Ne
Telecommunications Visual
Access, HTMT, CGI, Perl MMI
885-555-9933

PROGRAMMER World Wide
Links wants your HTML & Phot
skills. Develop great WWW
local & global customers. Send
ples & resume to WWWL.
Apple Road, Santa Rosa, CA.

TECHNICAL WRITER Softwar
seeks writer/editor for ma
research notes, project mgmt.
years tech. writing. DTP & pro
ming experience. Send resu
writing samples to: So
Systems, Dallas, TX.

TECHNICAL Software develo
firm looking for Tech Trainers,
candidates have programming
rience in Visual C, HTML &
Need quick self starter. Call
555-6868 for interview.

TECHNICAL WRITER P
Computer Corp is seeking a
nation of technical skills, kno
and experience in the foll
areas: UNIX, Windows 95/NT,
Basic, on-line help & documen
and the internet. Candidate
possess excellent writing skil
be comfortable working in a
vs. deadline driven enviro
Competitive salary. Fax resu
samples to Karen Fields. P
Computer Corp. 444 Industria
Concord, CA. Or send to our w
at www.premier.com.

WEB DESIGNER
BA/BS or equivalent pre
ming/multimedia producti
years of experience in us
design of WWW services stre
audio and video HTML, PER
GIF, JPEG. Demonstrated in
sonal, organization, communi
multi-tasking skills. Send rese
The Learning People at www
ing.com.

WEBMASTER-TECHN

SKILL thirteen

Understanding Graphics Animation

- ❏ **Creating animated programs**
- ❏ **Using** Canvas **controls**
- ❏ **Using the Sun** Animator **class**
- ❏ **Examining how animation works**
- ❏ **Reducing screen flicker**
- ❏ **Customizing an animation applet**

In Skill 12, we saw how to work with text and fonts. Here, we'll take a guided tour of a very popular Java topic: graphics animation. For a long time, Web pages were static things of images and text. Java brought animation to Web pages, and that was one of the chief reasons for its popularity. There are other ways to animate Web pages now: embedding video files like .avi files, using looping .gif images (which hold a number of internal images), or using other packages like VB Script. However, Java remains the animation tool of choice for most Web programmers.

The fundamentals of animation are simply placing a series of images on the screen in rapid succession to give the impression of movement. We start with one image, as shown in Figure 13.1, and then rapidly move on to the next, as shown in Figure 13.2.

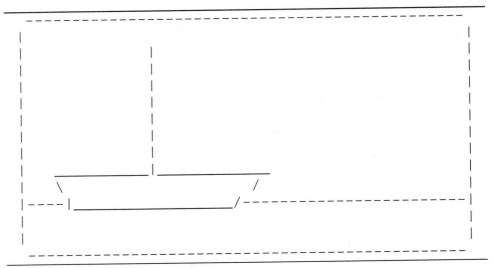

FIGURE 13.1 **Our first image is on the left.**

Flipping quickly though images this way creates the animation. Graphics animation was one of the biggest reasons that Java took the Internet by storm. Let's start now with our first animation applet.

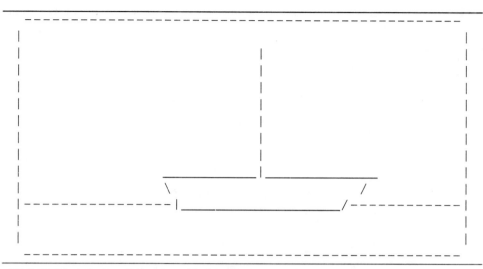

FIGURE 13.2   Our second image is closer to the center.

Creating Basic Animation

In our first animation example, we will draw a graphics image and move it across the screen. For this purpose, we'll use a Canvas control. Canvas controls are very useful Java controls that you can draw in; we'll draw an image in a Canvas control and use that control's setLocation() method to animate the image. Let's put this to work now. Create a new file named canvaser.java and add our standard starting code:

```
import java.applet.Applet;
import java.awt.*;

public class canvaser extendsApplet {
               .
               .
               .
}
```

We'll create a new class derived from the Java Canvas class and place our image in that new control. Here, we can draw a small box in our Canvas control, and we'll call this new Canvas control class BoxCanvas. We create an object of that class in our applet as follows. (We'll create the BoxCanvas class in a minute.)

```
import java.applet.Applet;
import java.awt.*;

public class canvaser extends Applet {
```

➜   BoxCanvas boxcanvas;
            .
            .
            .

The Canvas class's methods appear in Table 13.1.

TABLE 1 3 . 1 : The Java Canvas **class's methods**

Method	Does This
Canvas()	Constructs a new Canvas.
addNotify()	Creates the peer of the canvas.
paint(Graphics)	Paints the canvas in the default background color.

We create and add the boxcanvas control to our applet in the init() method as follows:

```
import java.applet.Applet;
import java.awt.*;

public class canvaser extends Applet {
```

➜   BoxCanvas boxcanvas;

            public void init(){
➜   boxcanvas = new BoxCanvas();
➜   boxcanvas.resize(100, 100);
➜   add(boxcanvas);
                  .
                  .
                  .

Let's add a button with the caption "Move Rectangle" to our applet; when the user clicks the button, we can move the box across the screen. We add that button, button1, this way:

```
import java.applet.Applet;
import java.awt.*;
```

```
→   import java.awt.event.*;

→   public class canvaser extends Applet implements ActionListener {

        BoxCanvas boxcanvas;
→       Button button1;

        public void init(){
            boxcanvas = new BoxCanvas();
            boxcanvas.resize(100, 100);
            add(boxcanvas);
→           button1 = new Button("Move Rectangle");
→           add(button1);
→           button1.addActionListener(this);
        }
                .
                .
                .
```

To make our new button active, we add an `actionPerformed()` method:

```
import java.applet.Applet;
import java.awt.*;
import java.awt.event.*;

public class canvaser extends Applet implements ActionListener {

        BoxCanvas boxcanvas;
        Button button1;

        public void init(){
            boxcanvas = new BoxCanvas();
            boxcanvas.resize(100, 100);
            add(boxcanvas);
            button1 = new Button("Move Rectangle");
            add(button1);
            button1.addActionListener(this);
        }

→       public void actionPerformed(ActionEvent event){
                .
                .
                .
→       }
    }
```

And we check to make sure our button was the control that caused this event:

```
import java.applet.Applet;
import java.awt.*;
```

```
import java.awt.event.*;

public class canvaser extends Applet implements ActionListener {

    BoxCanvas boxcanvas;
    Button button1;

    public void init(){
        boxcanvas = new BoxCanvas();
        boxcanvas.resize(100, 100);
        add(boxcanvas);
        button1 = new Button("Move Rectangle");
        add(button1);
        button1.addActionListener(this);
    }

    public void actionPerformed(ActionEvent event){
➔       if(event.getSource() == button1){
                    .
                    .
                    .
➔               }
        }
    }
```

If the button has indeed been clicked, we set up a for loop, using a loop index named loop_index, which will loop 150 times:

```
import java.applet.Applet;
import java.awt.*;
import java.awt.event.*;

public class canvaser extends Applet implements ActionListener {

    BoxCanvas boxcanvas;
    Button button1;

    public void init(){
        boxcanvas = new BoxCanvas();
        boxcanvas.resize(100, 100);
        add(boxcanvas);
        button1 = new Button("Move Rectangle");
        add(button1);
        button1.addActionListener(this);
    }

    public void actionPerformed(ActionEvent event){
        if(event.getSource() == button1){
```

```
→    for(loop_index = 0; loop_index < 150; loop_index++){
                         .
                         .
                         .
                    }
                }
            }
    }
```

And we use the Canvas control's setLocation() method (all controls have this method built in to move the Canvas control across the screen:

```java
import java.applet.Applet;
import java.awt.*;
import java.awt.event.*;

public class canvaser extends Applet implements ActionListener {

    BoxCanvas boxcanvas;
    Button button1;

    public void init(){
        boxcanvas = new BoxCanvas();
        boxcanvas.resize(100, 100);
        add(boxcanvas);
        button1 = new Button("Move Rectangle");
        add(button1);
        button1.addActionListener(this);
    }

    public void actionPerformed(ActionEvent event){
        if(event.getSource() == button1){
            for(loop_index = 0; loop_index < 150; loop_index++){
                boxcanvas.setLocation(loop_index, 0);
            }
        }
    }
}
```

All that remains now is to create the BoxCanvas class. We create that class now, extending the Java Canvas class. Add the following code to the end of the canvaser.java file:

```java
class BoxCanvas extends java.awt.Canvas {
        .
        .
        .
}
```

Here, we want to draw a box in the control, so we override the `paint()` method and draw that box with the `drawRect()` method:

```
class BoxCanvas extends java.awt.Canvas {

    public void paint (Graphics g) {
        g.drawRect(10, 50, 40, 40);
    }
}
```

You can run the applet now, as shown below. When you click the button, the box moves across the screen, from left to right. Our first animation example—created simply by moving a `Canvas` control—is a success. The code for this applet appears in `canvaser.java`.

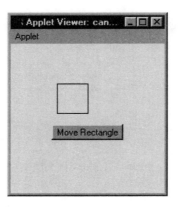

canvaser.java

```
import java.applet.Applet;
import java.awt.*;
import java.awt.event.*;

public class canvaser extends java.applet.Applet implements ActionListener {

    BoxCanvas boxcanvas;
    Button button1;

    public void init(){
        boxcanvas = new BoxCanvas();
        boxcanvas.resize(100, 100);
        add(boxcanvas);
        button1 = new Button("Move Rectangle");
```

```
            add(button1);
            button1.addActionListener(this);
        }

    public void actionPerformed(ActionEvent event){
        if(event.getSource() == button1){
            for(loop_index = 0; loop_index < 150; loop_index++){
                boxcanvas.setLocation(loop_index, 0);
            }
        }
    }
}

class BoxCanvas extends java.awt.Canvas {

    public void paint (Graphics g) {
        g.drawRect(10, 50, 40, 40);
    }
}
```

Our canvaser example showed us a quick and easy method of animation, but of course moving an image around is relatively crude. Java offers a great deal more animation power. Let's explore the other standard Java animation techniques now.

Our First True Animation Example

Java animation is very powerful. One of the reasons it is powerful is *multi-threading*. (We'll see a great deal more about threads in Skill 15.) A thread is an execution stream, and so far, all our programs have only had one thread. Java programs can have a number of such threads, each executing code in the same program, and each running at the same time. In this way, we can run the animation at the same time as the rest of our applet, without interference. Let's take a look at this now.

We can create an example animation applet with a circular image in it, as shown in Figure 13.3. When the applet runs, we can have our graphics image appear to spin. We'll use four images to create the illusion of motion in this applet, flashing these images on the screen, one at a time.

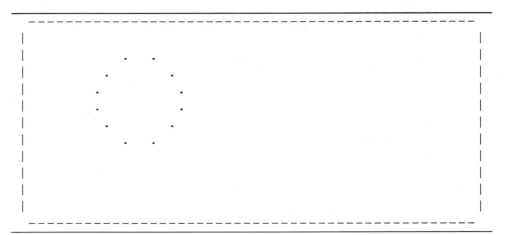

FIGURE 13.3   An applet with a circular image

These four images appear below. We'll use a small colored disk and animate it to give the impression that it is spinning.

Let's put this technique to work now. Create a new file named **spinner.java** and install our usual starting code there:

```
import java.awt.*;
import java.applet.Applet;

public class spinner extends Applet {
            .
            .
            .
}
```

We will start our new applet by reading in the four images, which we might save in the four files `spin1.gif` through `spin4.gif`. First, we set up an Image array to hold those images, named `spinImages[]`:

```java
import java.awt.*;
import java.applet.Applet;

public class spinner extends Applet {

    Image spinImages[] = new Image[4];
             .
             .
             .
```

Next, we load the images themselves in the `init()` method:

```java
import java.awt.*;
import java.applet.Applet;

public class spinner extends Applet implements Runnable{

    Image spinImages[] = new Image[4];

    public void init() {
        spinImages[0] = getImage(getCodeBase(), "spin1.gif");
        spinImages[1] = getImage(getCodeBase(), "spin2.gif");
        spinImages[2] = getImage(getCodeBase(), "spin3.gif");
        spinImages[3] = getImage(getCodeBase(), "spin4.gif");
    }
```

Now our images are ready to go. We're ready to introduce multi-threading to our applet.

Working with Multi-Threading

As we'll see in Skill 15, the basis of multi-threading in Java is the three methods, `start()`, `run()`, and `stop()`:

```java
start()
{
}

run()
{
}
```

```
stop()
{
}
```

Usually, Java programs have one thread, the main thread, running. However, we can start a new thread in the `start()` method. The code that we want this thread to run appears in the `run()` method. This means that the code in that method will be run automatically as the main thread continues on with the rest of the applet. We stop the thread in the `stop()` method, which is called when the applet is unloaded or the application finishes.

 NOTE It's important to stop the thread in the `stop()` method, or your applet will continue to run in a Web browser, even when the user goes on to other pages.

Let's install the code we'll need for our animation applet now. We'll create a new thread, named `spinThread` to handle our animation. We'll start the new thread in the `start()` method, run our animation in the `run()` method, and stop the thread in the `stop()` method.

Handling the `start()` Method

We add the new thread, `spinThread`, to our applet now:

```
import java.awt.*;
import java.applet.Applet;

public class spinner extends Applet {

    Image spinImages[] = new Image[4];
    Thread spinThread;
        .
        .
        .
```

The Java `Thread` class's methods appear in Table 13.2

T A B L E 1 3 . 2 : The Java `Thread` class's methods

Method	Does This
Thread()	Constructs a new Thread.
Thread(Runnable)	Constructs a new Thread which applies the run() method of the given target.

TABLE 13.2 CONTINUED: The Java Thread class's methods

Method	Does This
Thread(Runnable, String)	Constructs a new Thread with the given name and applies the run() method of the given target.
Thread(String)	Constructs a new Thread with the given name.
Thread(ThreadGroup, Runnable)	Constructs a new Thread in the given Thread group that applies the run() method of the given target.
Thread(ThreadGroup, Runnable, String)	Constructs a new Thread in the given Thread group with the given name and applies the run() method of the given target.
Thread(ThreadGroup, String)	Constructs a new Thread in the given Thread group with the given name.
activeCount()	Returns the current number of active Threads in this Thread group.
checkAccess()	Checks whether the current Thread is allowed to modify this Thread.
countStackFrames()	Returns the number of stack frames in this Thread.
currentThread()	Returns a reference to the currently executing Thread object.
destroy()	Destroy a thread, without any cleanup.
dumpStack()	A debugging procedure to print a stack trace for the current Thread.
enumerate(Thread[])	Copies into the given array references to every active Thread in this Thread's group.
getName()	Gets and returns this Thread's name.
getPriority()	Gets and returns the Thread's priority.
getThreadGroup()	Gets and returns this Thread group.
interrupt()	Sends an interrupt to a thread.
interrupted()	Asks if thread is interrupted.
isAlive()	Returns a boolean indicating if the Thread is active.
isDaemon()	Returns the daemon flag of the Thread.
isInterrupted()	Asks if some Thread (not necessarily self) has been interrupted.
join()	Waits forever for this Thread to die.
join(long)	Waits for this Thread to die.

TABLE 13.2 CONTINUED: The Java Thread class's methods

Method	Does This
join(long, int)	Waits for the Thread to die, with more precise time.
resume()	Resumes this Thread execution.
run()	The actual body of this Thread.
setDaemon(boolean)	Marks this Thread as a daemon Thread or a user Thread.
setName(String)	Sets the Thread's name.
setPriority(int)	Sets the Thread's priority.
sleep(long)	Causes the currently executing Thread to sleep for the given number of milliseconds.
sleep(long, int)	Sleep, in milliseconds and additional nanosecond.
start()	Starts this Thread.
stop()	Stops a Thread by tossing an object.
stop(Throwable)	Stops a Thread by tossing an object.
suspend()	Suspends this Thread's execution.
toString()	Returns a String representation of the Thread, including the thread's name, priority, and thread group.
yield()	Causes the currently executing Thread object to yield.

To handle multi-threading, we have to implement the *Runnable* interface, which we do as follows. (We'll see more about this interface later.)

```
import java.awt.*;
import java.applet.Applet;

public class spinner extends Applet implements Runnable{
        Image spinImages[] = new Image[4];
        Thread spinThread;
            .
            .
            .
```

Now we add the start() method:

```
import java.awt.*;
import java.applet.Applet;
```

```
public class spinner extends Applet implements Runnable{

    Image spinImages[] = new Image[4];
    Thread spinThread;

    public void init() {
        spinImages[0] = getImage(getCodeBase(), "spin1.gif");
        spinImages[1] = getImage(getCodeBase(), "spin2.gif");
        spinImages[2] = getImage(getCodeBase(), "spin3.gif");
        spinImages[3] = getImage(getCodeBase(), "spin4.gif");
    }

→   public void start() {

                    .
                    .
                    .

→   }
```

First, we create our new thread object as follows:

```
import java.awt.*;
import java.applet.Applet;

public class spinner extends Applet implements Runnable{

    Image spinImages[] = new Image[4];
    Thread spinThread;

    public void init() {
        spinImages[0] = getImage(getCodeBase(), "spin1.gif");
        spinImages[1] = getImage(getCodeBase(), "spin2.gif");
        spinImages[2] = getImage(getCodeBase(), "spin3.gif");
        spinImages[3] = getImage(getCodeBase(), "spin4.gif");
    }

    public void start() {
→       spinThread = new Thread(this);
                    .
                    .
                    .

    }
```

Next, we start that thread running with its start() method. That is, we start executing the code in the run() method, as follows:

```
import java.awt.*;
import java.applet.Applet;

public class spinner extends Applet implements Runnable{
```

```
        Image spinImages[] = new Image[4];
        Thread spinThread;

        public void init() {
            spinImages[0] = getImage(getCodeBase(), "spin1.gif");
            spinImages[1] = getImage(getCodeBase(), "spin2.gif");
            spinImages[2] = getImage(getCodeBase(), "spin3.gif");
            spinImages[3] = getImage(getCodeBase(), "spin4.gif");
        }

        public void start() {
            spinThread = new Thread(this);
→           spinThread.start();
        }
```

Now the start() method is ready to go, and we'll turn to the stop() method.

Handling the stop() Method

We've started our new thread, but we have to be able to stop it. We do that in the stop() method, as follows:

```
    public void start() {
            spinThread = new Thread(this);
            spinThread.start();
    }

→   public void stop() {
            .
            .
            .
→   }
```

When the stop() method is called, we should stop our thread, and we do that with the Thread class's stop() method:

```
    public void start() {
            spinThread = new Thread(this);
            spinThread.start();
    }

    public void stop() {
→           spinThread.stop();
    }
```

And the stop() method is all set. Now we'll turn to the run() method, where the real work takes place.

Skill 13

Handling the run() Method

Now our thread enters the run() method. Here, we'll do something you don't see every day in programming—we'll set up a loop that keeps looping forever. Actually, this loop only runs until the stop() method is called, terminating the thread: the loop is not really infinite after all. We'll use a Java while loop here, which keeps executing while its conditional statement is true, and since we'll set that statement to true, it will loop until interrupted:

```java
public void start() {
        spinThread = new Thread(this);
        spinThread.start();
    }

    public void stop() {
        spinThread.stop();
    }

    public void run() {
        while(true){
            .
            .
            .
        }
    }
```

Here's where we'll perform our animation. To do so, we'll simply keep flashing a new image on the screen continually. We'll set up an index we can loop over named spinIndex; this will be our index into our array of images, spinImages[]. We'll also load the current image to display now in an Image object named nowImage:

```java
import java.awt.*;
import java.applet.Applet;

public class spinner extends Applet implements Runnable{

    Image spinImages[] = new Image[4];
    Image nowImage;
    int spinIndex = 0;
    Thread spinThread;
```

Now we can keep loading a new image into nowImage each time the loop is executed this way, as follows:

```java
public void run() {
        while(true){
```

```
→       nowImage = spinImages[spinIndex++];
→       if(spinIndex > 3)spinIndex = 0;
                   .
                   .
                   .

            }
        }
```

At this point, then, the image in nowImage is continually updated, and the next step is to display it on the screen. We can do that in the paint() method (where we get a Graphics object to draw with), so we force a paint event now by calling repaint():

```
        public void run() {
            while(true){
                nowImage = spinImages[spinIndex++];
                if(spinIndex > 3)spinIndex = 0;
→               repaint();
                   .
                   .
```

In the paint() method, we simply draw the image nowImage on the screen:

```
        public void run() {
            while(true){
                nowImage = spinImages[spinIndex++];
                if(spinIndex > 3)spinIndex = 0;
                repaint();
                   .
                   .
                   .

            }
        }

        public void paint (Graphics g) {
→           if(nowImage != null) g.drawImage(nowImage, 10, 10, this);
            }
        }
```

NOTE   We make sure nowImage is not null before drawing it. We do so to make sure that the images are loaded in before we try to display them.

Drawing images like this is fine as far as it goes but flashes the images on the screen with great rapidity—as fast as the computer could do it. We want the user to have time to view each image, not just a blur of action, so we slow things down with the Thread class's sleep() method. This method puts the thread to "sleep" for the number of milliseconds (thousandths of a second) that we pass to it. We can make each image appear for .2 seconds by passing a value of 200 milli-seconds to sleep() as follows:

```java
public void run() {
    while(true){
        nowImage = spinImages[spinIndex++];
        if(spinIndex > 3)spinIndex = 0;
        repaint();
        Thread.sleep(200);
    }
}



public void paint (Graphics g) {
    if(nowImage != null) g.drawImage(nowImage, 10, 10, this);
}
}
```

Actually, Java insists that we place that statement in a try{} block, with an accompanying catch{} block in case there is an error, and so instead of the code listed above, we enter the following:

```java
public void run() {
    while(true){
        nowImage = spinImages[spinIndex++];
        if(spinIndex > 3)spinIndex = 0;
        repaint();
        try {Thread.sleep(200);}
        catch(InterruptedException e) { }
    }
}

public void paint (Graphics g) {
    if(nowImage != null) g.drawImage(nowImage, 10, 10, this);
}
}
```

You can run the applet now, as shown below. The image spins around and around, as it should. The code for this applet appears in spinner.java.

spinner.java

```java
import java.awt.*;
import java.applet.Applet;

public class spinner extends Applet implements Runnable{

    Image spinImages[] = new Image[4];
    Image nowImage;
    int spinIndex = 0;
    Thread spinThread;

    public void init() {
        spinImages[0] = getImage(getCodeBase(), "spin1.gif");
        spinImages[1] = getImage(getCodeBase(), "spin2.gif");
        spinImages[2] = getImage(getCodeBase(), "spin3.gif");
        spinImages[3] = getImage(getCodeBase(), "spin4.gif");
    }

    public void start() {
        spinThread = new Thread(this);
        spinThread.start();
    }

    public void stop() {
        spinThread.stop();
    }

    public void run() {
        while(true){
            nowImage = spinImages[spinIndex++];
            if(spinIndex > 3)spinIndex = 0;
```

```
                    repaint();
                    try {Thread.sleep(200);}
                    catch(InterruptedException e) { }
                }
            }

        public void paint (Graphics g) {
            if(nowImage != null) g.drawImage(nowImage, 10, 10, this);
        }
    }
```

If you watch the spinner applet, you'll see that the spinner applet flickers occasionally. If you make the spinner spin faster, there will be even more flicker. There is a way to get rid of screen flicker, for the most part anyway, and we'll take a look at that now.

Eliminating Screen Flicker

One of the main reasons that the applet flickers is that each time the `paint()` method is called, the `update()` method is called first, which clears the entire applet display. That means that between successive images, our applet's display is entirely repainted with the background color. There is no need for this repainting—the spinner images are all the same size, each one exactly covers the previous one, and so there is no need to clear the whole applet between images. Let's stop the flickering now.

Stopping Java from Clearing an Applet's Display

Here, we will stop the `update()` method from clearing the applet each time we place a new image on the screen. We can do that by overriding the `update()` method ourselves:

```
public class spinner extends Applet implements Runnable{

    Image spinImages[] = new Image[4];
    Image nowImage;
    int spinIndex = 0;
    Thread spinThread;

    public void init() {
        spinImages[0] = getImage(getCodeBase(), "spin1.gif");
        spinImages[1] = getImage(getCodeBase(), "spin2.gif");
```

```
                spinImages[2] = getImage(getCodeBase(), "spin3.gif");
                spinImages[3] = getImage(getCodeBase(), "spin4.gif");
        }
                         .
                         .
                         .
        public void run() {
             while(true){
                nowImage = spinImages[spinIndex++];
                if(spinIndex > 3)spinIndex = 0;
                repaint();
                try {Thread.sleep(200);}
                catch(InterruptedException e) { }
             }
        }

        public void paint (Graphics g) {
             if(nowImage != null) g.drawImage(nowImage, 10, 10, this);
        }

➜       public void update(Graphics g) {

                         .
                         .
                         .

➜          }
        }
```

Here, we skip the step of clearing the applet's display entirely and simply call the paint() method as follows:

```
import java.awt.*;
import java.applet.Applet;

public class spinner extends Applet implements Runnable{

        Image spinImages[] = new Image[4];
        Image nowImage;
        int spinIndex = 0;
        Thread spinThread;

        public void init() {
             spinImages[0] = getImage(getCodeBase(), "spin1.gif");
             spinImages[1] = getImage(getCodeBase(), "spin2.gif");
             spinImages[2] = getImage(getCodeBase(), "spin3.gif");
             spinImages[3] = getImage(getCodeBase(), "spin4.gif");
        }
                         .
                         .
                         .
```

```
public void run() {
    while(true){
        nowImage = spinImages[spinIndex++];
        if(spinIndex > 3)spinIndex = 0;
        repaint();
        try {Thread.sleep(200);}
        catch(InterruptedException e) { }
    }
}

public void paint (Graphics g) {
    if(nowImage != null) g.drawImage(nowImage, 10, 10, this);
}

public void update(Graphics g) {
    paint(g);
}
}
```

We've done a lot of good—now the applet isn't cleared between images. However, we can do more. The paint() method still paints the entire applet display each time it is called. It turns out we can restrict the drawing operations to just part of the applet's display, and in this case, that means we can restrict drawing to just the space in which our images appear. This saves time and reduces flicker.

Restricting Drawing to a Section of the Applet

To restrict drawing operations to a specific region of the display, we use the Graphics class's clipRect() method. Using this method means that drawing operations will only take place in the rectangle given; we can make that rectangle correspond to the location of our images this way:

```
public void update(Graphics g) {
    g.clipRect(10, 10, 100, 100);
    paint(g);
}
```

Our new version of the spinner applet works just as the first one did, but without the screen flicker. The new version of spinner is a success. The code for this applet appears in spinner.java, version 2 (The version 2 of the spinner.java file can be found in the spinner2 directory where you installed the example source code.)

C   spinner.java, version 2

```java
import java.awt.*;
import java.applet.Applet;

public class spinner extends Applet implements Runnable{

    Image spinImages[] = new Image[4];
    Image nowImage;
    int spinIndex = 0;
    Thread spinThread;

    public void init() {
        spinImages[0] = getImage(getCodeBase(), "spin1.gif");
        spinImages[1] = getImage(getCodeBase(), "spin2.gif");
        spinImages[2] = getImage(getCodeBase(), "spin3.gif");
        spinImages[3] = getImage(getCodeBase(), "spin4.gif");
    }

    public void start() {
        spinThread = new Thread(this);
        spinThread.start();
    }

    public void stop() {
        spinThread.stop();
    }

    public void run() {
        while(true){
            nowImage = spinImages[spinIndex++];
            if(spinIndex > 3)spinIndex = 0;
            repaint();
            try {Thread.sleep(200);}
            catch(InterruptedException e) { }
        }
    }

    public void paint (Graphics g) {
        if(nowImage != null) g.drawImage(nowImage, 10, 10, this);
    }

    public void update(Graphics g) {
        g.clipRect(10, 10, 100, 100);
        paint(g);
    }
}
```

So far, we've seen several ways of creating graphics animation in Java. It turns out that Sun has created a class that it distributes as an example to support animation.

The Sun Animator Class

You can use Sun's Animator class to create motion in your applets. The Sun Animator class comes with the JDK 1.1 as an example. To use this class, you pass various parameters to the Animator class as parameters in your Web page. Here is Sun's own documentation for the Animator class:

```
<APPLET CODE="Animator.class"
WIDTH = "aNumber"                   the width (in pixels) of
                                    the widest frame
HEIGHT = "aNumber">                 the height (in pixels) of
                                    the tallest frame

<PARAM NAME="IMAGESOURCE"
VALUE="aDirectory">                 the directory that has the
                                    animation frames (a series of
                                    pictures in GIF or JPEG
                                    format, by default named
                                    T1.gif, T2.gif, ...)

<PARAM NAME="STARTUP"
VALUE="aFile">                      an image to display at
                                    load time

<PARAM NAME="BACKGROUND"
VALUE="aFile">                      an image to paint the
                                    frames against

<PARAM NAME="STARTIMAGE"
VALUE="aNumber">                    number of the starting
                                    frame (1..n)

<PARAM NAME="ENDIMAGE"
VALUE="aNumber">                    number of the end frame
                                    (1..n)

<PARAM NAME="NAMEPATTERN"
VALUE="dir/prefix%N.suffix">        a pattern to use for
                                    generating names
                                    based on STARTIMAGE and
                                    ENDIMAGE (See below.)

<PARAM NAME="PAUSE"
VALUE="100">                        milliseconds to pause
                                    between images
                                    default (can be overriden
                                    by PAUSES)

<PARAM NAME="PAUSES"
VALUE="300|200||400|200">           millisecond delay per
```

```
                                              frame. Blank
                                              uses default PAUSE value
<PARAM NAME="REPEAT"
VALUE="true">                                 repeat the sequence?
<PARAM NAME="POSITIONS"
VALUE="100@200||200@100||200@200|100@100|105@105">
                                              positions (X@Y) for each
                                              frame. Blank means use previous
                                              frame's position

<PARAM NAME="IMAGES"
VALUE="3|3|2|1|2|3|17">                        explicit order for frames
                                              (see below)

<PARAM NAME="SOUNDSOURCE"
VALUE="aDirectory">                           the directory that has the
                                              audio files

<PARAM NAME="SOUNDTRACK"
VALUE="aFile">                                an audio file to play
                                              throughout

<PARAM NAME="SOUNDS"
SOUNDS="aFile.au|||||bFile.au">               audio files keyed to
                                              individual frames

</APPLET>
```

To use the Animator class, all you have to do is to name your images T1.gif, T2.gif, T3.gif, and so on, and then set the endimage parameter to the number of images you have. For example, here's how we would set up our spinner images with the Animator class:

```
<HTML>
<BODY>

<CENTER>
<H1>Our animation example</H1>
<APPLET CODE = Animator.class WIDTH = 300 HEIGHT = 200>
<PARAM NAME = endimage VALUE = 4>
<PARAM NAME = pause VALUE = 200>
<PARAM NAME = repeat VALUE = true>
</APPLET>
</CENTER>

</HTML>
</BODY>
```

Copy the classes in the Animator example folder to the folder with this Web page and copy over the spin1.gif to spin4.gif files as T1.gif to T4.gif, placing them in the same folder. Then use the Applet Viewer to take a look at this Web page. This displays our spinner on the screen.

We've gotten our start in graphics animation, and thanks to Java, it's been easy. There are more animation techniques available in Java. One of them is *double buffering,* which lets us handle complex animation images. We'll explore that technique and more in the Skill 14.

Are You Experienced?

Now you can...

- ☑ create animated graphics programs
- ☑ support an easy method of animation in Java by using the Canvas **control**
- ☑ reduce screen flicker by overriding the update() **method**
- ☑ use the Sun Animator **class**

Jones 356-555-3398.

PROGRAMMERS
C, C, VB, Cobol, exp. Call 534-555-6543 or fax 534-555-6544.

PROGRAMMING
MRFS Inc. is looking for a Sr. Windows NT developer. Reqs. 3-5 yrs. Exp. in C under Windows, Win95 & NT, using Visual C, Excl. OO design & implementation skills a must. OLE2 & ODBC are a plus. Excl. Salary & bnfts. Resume & salary history to HR, 8779 HighTech Way, Computer City, AR

PROGRAMMERS
Contractors Wanted for short & long term assignments: Visual C, MFC Unix C/C, SQL Oracle Dev elop ers PC Help Desk Support Windows NT & NetWareTelecommunications Visual Basic, Access, HTMT, CGI, Perl MMI & Co. 885-555-9933

PROGRAMMER World Wide Web Links wants your HTML & Photoshop skills. Develop great WWW sites. Local & global customers. Send samples & resume to WWWL, 2000 Apple Road, Santa Rosa, CA.

TECHNICAL WRITER Software firm seeks writer/editor for manuals, research notes, project mgmt. Min 2 years tech. writing, DTP & programming experience. Send resume to: Software Systems, Dallas, TX.

TECHNICAL Software development firm looking for Tech Trainers. Ideal candidates have programming experience in Visual C, HTML & JAVA. Need quick self starter Call (443) 555-6868 for interview.

TECHNICAL WRITER/ Premier Computer Corp is seeking a combination of technical skills, knowledge and experience in the following areas: UNIX, Windows 95/NT, Visual Basic, on-line help & documentation, and the internet. Candidates must possess excellent writing skills, and be comfortable working in a quality vs. deadline driven environment. Competitive salary. Fax resume & samples to Karen Fields, Premier Computer Corp., 444 Industrial Blvd. Concord, CA. Or send to our website at www.premier.com.

WEB DESIGNER
BA/BS or equivalent programming/multimedia production. 3 years of experience in use and design of WWW services streaming audio and video HTML, PERL, CGI, GIF, JPEG. Demonstrated interpersonal, organization, communication, multi-tasking skills. Send resume to The Learning People at www.learning.com.

WEBMASTER-TECHNICAL
BSCS or equivalent, 2 years of experience in CGI, Windows 95/NT, UNIX, C, Java, Perl. Demonstrated ability to design, code, debug and test on-line services. Send resume to The Learning People at www.learning.com.

PROGRAMMER World Wide Web Links wants your HTML & Photoshop skills. Develop great WWW sites.

---

ing tools. Experienced in documentation preparation & programming languages (Access, C, FoxPro) are a plus. Financial or banking customer service support is required along with excellent verbal & written communication skills with multi levels of end-users. Send resume to KKUP Enterprises, 45 Orange Blvd, Orange, CA.

COMPUTERS Small Web Design firm seeks indiv. w/NT. Webserver & Database management exp. Fax resume to 556-555-4221.

COMPUTER/ Visual C/C, Visual Basic Exp'd Systems Analysts/ Programmers for growing software dev. team in Roseburg. Computer Science or related degree preferred. Develop adv. Engineering applications for engineering firm. Fax resume to 707-555-8744.

COMPUTER Web Master for dynamic SF internet co. Site Dev., test, coord., train. 2 yrs prog. Exp. C C. Web C, FTP. Fax resume to Best Staffing 845-555-7722.

COMPUTER PROGRAMMER
Ad agency seeks programmer w/exp. in UNIX/NT Platforms, Web Server, CGI/Perl. Programmer Position avail. on a project basis with the possibility to move into F/T. Fax resume & salary req. to R. Jones 334-555-8332.

COMPUTERS Programmer/Analyst Design and maintain C based SQL database applications. Required skills: Visual Basic, C, SQL, ODBC, Document, existing and new applications. Novell or NT exp. a plus. Fax resume & salary history to 235-555-9935.

GRAPHIC DESIGNER
Webmaster's Weekly is seeking a creative Graphic Designer to design high impact marketing collater al, including direct mail promo's. CD-ROM packages, ads and WWW pages. Must be able to juggle multiple projects and learn new skills on the job very rapidly. Web design experience a big plus, technical troubleshooting also a plus. Call 435-555-1235.

GRAPHICS - ART DIRECTOR - WEB-MULTIMEDIA
Leading internet development company has an outstanding opportunity for a talented, high-end Web Experienced Art Director. In addition to a great portfolio and fresh ideas, the ideal candidate has excellent communication and presentation skills. Working as a team with innovative producers and programmers, you will create dynamic, interactive web sites and application interfaces. Some programming experience required. Send samples and resume to: SuperSites, 333 Main, Seattle, WA.

MARKETING
Fast paced software and services provider looking for MARKETING COMMUNICATIONS SPECIALIST to

---

PROGRAMMERS Multiple short term assignments available: Visual C 3 positions SQL ServerNT Server. 2 positions JAVA & HTML, long term NetWare Various locations. Call for more info. 356-555-3398.

PROGRAMMERS
C, C, VB, Cobol, exp.
Call 534-555-6543
or fax 534-555-6544.

PROGRAMMING
MRFS inc. is looking for a Sr. Windows NT developer. Reqs. 3-5 yrs. Exp. in C under Windows, Win95 & NT. using Visual C. Excl. OO design & implementation skills a must. OLE2 & ODBC are a plus. Excl. Salary & bnfts. Resume & salary history to HR, 8779 HighTech Way, Computer City, AR

PROGRAMMERS/ Contractors Wanted for short & long term assignments: Visual C, MFC Unix C/C, SQL Oracle Developers PC Help Desk Support Windows NT & NetWareTelecommunications Visual Basic, Access, HTML, CGI, Perl MMI & Co. 685-555-9933

PROGRAMMER World Wide Web Links wants your HTML & Photoshop skills. Develop great WWW sites. Local & global customers. Send samples & resume to WWWL, 2000 Apple Road, Santa Rosa, CA.

TECHNICAL WRITER Software firm seeks writer/editor for manuals, research notes, project mgmt. Min 2 years tech. writing, DTP & programming experience. Send resume & writing samples to: Software Systems, Dallas, TX.

COMPUTER PROGRAMMER
Ad agency seeks programmer w/exp. in UNIX/NT Platforms, Web Server, CGI/Perl. Programmer Position avail. on a project basis with the possibility to move into F/T. Fax resume & salary req. to R. Jones 334-555-8332.

TECHNICAL WRITER Premier Computer Corp is seeking a combination of technical skills, knowledge and experience in the following areas: UNIX, Windows 95/NT, Visual Basic, on-line help & documentation, and the internet. Candidates must possess excellent writing skills, and be comfortable working in a quality vs. deadline driven environment. Competitive salary. Fax resume & samples to Karen Fields, Premier Computer Corp., 444 Industrial Blvd. Concord, CA. Or send to our website at www.premier.com.

WEB DESIGNER
BA/BS or equivalent programming/multimedia production. 3 years of experience in use and design of WWW services streaming audio and video HTML, PERL, CGI, GIF, JPEG. Demonstrated interpersonal, organization, communication, multi-tasking skills. Send resume to The Learning People at www.learning.com.

WEBMASTER-TECHNICAL
BSCS or equivalent, 2 years of

COMPUTERS Small Web Design Firm seeks indiv. w/NT. Webserver & Database management exp. Fax resume to 556-555-4221.

COMPUTER Visual C/C, Visual Basic Exp'd Systems Analysts/ Programmers for growing software dev. team in Roseburg. Computer Science or related degree preferred. Develop adv. Engineering applications for engineering firm. Fax resume to 707-555-8744.

COMPUTER Web Master for dynamic SF Internet co. Site. Dev., test. coord., train. 2 yrs prog. Exp. C C. Web C, FTP. Fax resume to Best Staffing 845-555-7722.

COMPUTERS/ QA SOFTWARE
TESTERS Qualified candidates should have 2 yrs exp. performing integration & system testing using automated testing tools. Experienced in documentation preparation & programming languages (Access, C, FoxPro) are a plus. Financial or banking customer service support is required along with excellent verbal & written communication skills with multi levels of end-users. Send resume to KKUP Enterprises, 45 Orange Blvd. Orange, CA.

COMPUTERS Programmer/Analyst Design and maintain C based SQL database applications. Required skills: Visual Basic, C, SQL, ODBC. Document existing and new applications. Novell or NT exp. a plus. Fax resume & salary history to 235-555-9935.

GRAPHIC DESIGNER
Webmaster's Weekly is seeking a creative Graphic Designer to design high impact marketing collater al, including direct mail promo's. CD-ROM packages, ads and WWW pages. Must be able to juggle multiple projects and learn new skills on the job very rapidly. Web design experience a big plus, technical troubleshooting also a plus. Call 435-555-1235.

GRAPHICS - ART DIRECTOR - WEB-MULTIMEDIA
Leading Internet development company has an outstanding opportunity for a talented, high-end Web Experienced Art Director. In addition to a great portfolio and fresh ideas, the ideal candidate has excellent communication and presentation skills. Working as a team with innovative producers and programmers, you will create dynamic, interactive web sites and application interfaces. Some programming experience required. Send samples and resume to: SuperSites, 333 Main, Seattle, WA.

COMPUTER PROGRAMMER
Ad agency seeks programmer w/exp. in UNIX/NT Platforms, Web Server, CGI/Perl. Programmer Position avail. on a project basis with the possibility to move into F/T. Fax resume & salary req. to R. Jones 334-555-8332.

PROGRAMMERS / Established software

---

ment. Must be a self-starter, energetic, organized. Must have 2 yrs web experience. Programming plus. Call 985-555-9854.

PROGRAMMERS Multiple term assignments available: V C, 3 positions SQL ServerNT S 2 positions JAVA & HTML, long NetWare Various locations. Call more info. 356-555-3398.

PROGRAMMERS
C, C, VB, Cobol, exp. Call 534-6543 or fax 534-555-6544.

PROGRAMMING
MRFS Inc. is looking for a Windows NT developer. Reqs. yrs. Exp. In C under Wind Win95 & NT. using Visual C OO design & implementation a must. OLE2 & ODBC are a Excl. Salary & bnfts. Resu salary history to HR, 8779 High Way. Computer City, AR

PROGRAMMERS/ Contra Wanted for short & long term as ments: Visual C, MFCUnix C/C Oracle Developers PC Help Support Windows NT & Net Telecommunications Visual Access, HTML, CGI, Perl MMI 885-555-9933

PROGRAMMER World Wide Links wants your HTML & Photo skills. Develop great WWW Local & global customers. Send ples & resume to WWWL. Apple Road. Santa Rosa, CA.

TECHNICAL WRITER Software seeks writer/editor for man research notes, project mgmt. years tech. writing, DTP & prog ming experience. Send resu writing samples to: Soft Systems, Dallas, TX.

TECHNICAL Software develop firm looking for Tech Trainers. candidates have programming e rience in Visual C, HTML & Need quick self starter. Call 555-6868 for interview.

TECHNICAL WRITER Pre Computer Corp is seeking a co nation of technical skills, know and experience in the areas: UNIX, Windows 95/NT Basic, on-line help & document. and the internet. Candidates possess excellent writing skills. be comfortable working in a gr vs. deadline driven environ Competitive salary. Fax resu samples to Karen Fields, Pr Computer Corp., 444 Industrial Concord, CA. Or send to our w at www.premier.com.

WEB DESIGNER
BA/BS or equivalent pro ming/multimedia production years of experience in use design of WWW services str audio and video HTML, PERL GIF, JPEG. Demonstrated int sonal, organization, communic multi-tasking skills. Send resu The Learning People at www ing.com.

More Graphics Animation Power

- ❑ **Using double buffering for faster animation updating**

- ❑ **Using the card layout to animate panels of controls**

- ❑ **Updating our dauber applet to include animation**

- ❑ **Creating graphics images in memory**

In Skill 13, you got your start in animation. Here, we're going to continue that work by examining some popular animation techniques. One of those is *double-buffering*, which is a method that allows you to construct complicated graphics images in memory and then flash them on the screen, rather than having to construct them on the screen as the user watches. We'll also see how to update our dauber painting program in this Skill. Finally, we'll look at one more Java layout: the *card* layout, which lets you flash panels of controls or images onto the screen as you like, animating them. We'll start at once with the double-buffering technique now.

Working with Double Buffering

Double buffering allows you to develop complex graphics images off-screen and then flash them on the screen when they are complete. You wouldn't want to create the graphics you want to animate on the screen, in front of the user, frame by frame, as the user watches. It is far better to create each image in memory first and display it only when ready. This technique, double buffering, is a powerful Java technique that you'll learn how to use now.

For this example, our graphics images won't be all that complex. We'll develop just a series of white boxes, as shown in Figure 14.1. In succeeding frames, the innermost rectangle becomes larger, so as we work through all 20 images in an animation example, it looks as though the rectangle is growing from upper left to the lower right, as shown in Figure 14.2. None of these images will exist on disk. We'll create them in memory and then display them on the screen.

Create a new file named `doublebuffer.java`. We will need an image object in memory that we can draw in—this will be our "buffer" image. We create this image object as an object of the Image class, calling it `memoryimage`:

```
import java.awt.*;
import java.applet.Applet;

public class doublebuffer extends Applet {

        Image memoryimage;
              .
              .
              .
```

Skill 14

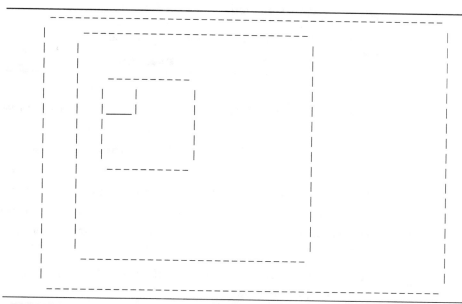

FIGURE 14.1   We'll develop simple graphics images for this example.

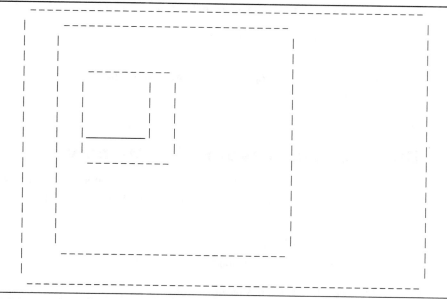

FIGURE 14.2   Over the course of our example, the innermost rectangle will get larger.

The Image class's methods appear in Table 14.1.

TABLE 14.1: The Java Image class's methods

Method	Does This
Image()	Creates a new Image object.
createScaledImage(int, int, int)	Creates a scaled version of this image.
flush()	Flushes all resources being used by this Image object.
getGraphics()	Gets a graphics object to draw into this image.
getHeight(ImageObserver)	Gets the actual height of the image.
getProperty(String, ImageObserver)	Gets a property of the image by name.
getSource()	Gets the object that produces the pixels for the image.
getWidth(ImageObserver)	Gets the actual width of the image.

We create that new object in the init() method as follows, giving our image a size (in pixels) of 100 x 100:

```
import java.awt.*;
import java.applet.Applet;

public class doublebuffer extends Applet {

    Image memoryimage;

    public void init() {
        memoryimage = createImage(100, 100);
    }
        .
        .
        .
```

Drawing in Images Stored in Memory

To actually draw in our image in memory, we need a Graphics object. We can get a Graphics object for our memory image, naming that object memorygraphics:

```
import java.awt.*;
import java.applet.Applet;

public class doublebuffer extends Applet {

    Image memoryimage;
```

```
Graphics memorygraphics;

public void init() {
    memoryimage = createImage(100, 100);
    memorygraphics = memoryimage.getGraphics();
}
        .
        .
        .
}
```

Now let's start our new thread, which will perform the actual animation. In this case, we give the new thread the name doublebufferthread:

```
import java.awt.*;
import java.applet.Applet;

public class doublebuffer extends Applet {

    Image memoryimage;
    Graphics memorygraphics;
    Thread doublebufferthread;

    public void init() {
        memoryimage = createImage(100, 100);
        memorygraphics = memoryimage.getGraphics();
    }
        .
        .
        .
```

We create and start that new thread in the start() method and implement the Runnable interface as well:

```
import java.awt.*;
import java.applet.Applet;

public class doublebuffer extends Applet implements Runnable{

    Image memoryimage;
    Graphics memorygraphics;
    Thread doublebufferthread;

    public void init() {
        memoryimage = createImage(100, 100);
        memorygraphics = memoryimage.getGraphics();
    }

    public void start() {
        doublebufferthread = new Thread(this);
```

```
→          doublebufferthread.start();
→      }            .
                    .
                    .
   }
```

In addition, we add code to stop the new thread in the stop() method, as
follows:

```
import java.awt.*;
import java.applet.Applet;

public class doublebuffer extends Applet implements Runnable{

    Image memoryimage;
    Graphics memorygraphics;
    Thread doublebufferthread;

    public void init() {
        memoryimage = createImage(100, 100);
        memorygraphics = memoryimage.getGraphics();
    }

    public void start() {
        doublebufferthread = new Thread(this);
        doublebufferthread.start();
    }

→   public void stop() {
→       doublebufferthread.stop();
→   }            .
                 .
                 .

   }
```

Implementing the run() Method

Finally, we create the run() method. In this case, we simply cause the paint()
method to be called repeatedly by calling repaint() every .2 seconds:

```
import java.awt.*;
import java.applet.Applet;

public class doublebuffer extends Applet implements Runnable{

    Image memoryimage;
    Graphics memorygraphics;
```

```
Thread doublebufferthread;

public void init() {
    memoryimage = createImage(100, 100);
    memorygraphics = memoryimage.getGraphics();
}

public void start() {
    doublebufferthread = new Thread(this);
    doublebufferthread.start();
}

public void stop() {
    doublebufferthread.stop();
}

public void run() {
    while(true){
        repaint();
        try {Thread.sleep(200);}
        catch(InterruptedException e) { }
    }
}
```

We'll put the real code in the paint() method, so open that method now:

```
public void paint (Graphics g) {
            .
            .
            .
}
```

We will need a loop index to keep track of the current size of our rectangle.
Let's call the index loop_index and add it to our applet as follows:

```
import java.awt.*;
import java.applet.Applet;

public class doublebuffer extends Applet implements Runnable{

    Image memoryimage;
    Graphics memorygraphics;
    Thread doublebufferthread;
    int loop_index = 0;
            .
            .
            .
```

In this example, we'll make each box five pixels larger than the last, so we'll increment the `loop_index` variable by five each time the `paint()` method is called:

```java
public void paint (Graphics g) {

    loop_index += 5;
        .
        .
        .

}
```

And if that loop index exceeds 100 pixels (the size of the image), we can set it back to 5:

```java
public void paint (Graphics g) {

    loop_index += 5;
    if(loop_index >= 100) loop_index = 5;
        .
        .
        .

}
```

Now we can draw the box itself in our `memorygraphics` object. Because we also want to draw over any previous boxes, we'll start by drawing a white rectangle to clear the display. To do that, first set the drawing color in the applet to white (with red, green, and blue color values of 255, 255, and 255) with the Graphics `setColor()` method, which we use with our memory graphics object, `memorygraphics`:

```java
public void paint (Graphics g) {

    loop_index += 5;
    if(loop_index >= 100) loop_index = 5;

    memorygraphics.setColor(new Color(255, 255, 255));
        .
        .
        .

}
```

Next, we draw our filled-in rectangle with the `fillRect()` method to erase any previous rectangles:

```java
public void paint (Graphics g) {

    loop_index += 5;
    if(loop_index >= 100) loop_index = 5;
```

```
        memorygraphics.setColor(new Color(255, 255, 255));
        memorygraphics.fillRect(0, 0, 100, 100);
                                .
                                .
                                .
    }
```

At this point, we are ready to draw our box in the memory image, so we set the drawing color back to black (color values 0, 0, 0):

```
    public void paint (Graphics g) {

        loop_index += 5;
        if(loop_index >= 100) loop_index = 5;

        memorygraphics.setColor(new Color(255, 255, 255));
        memorygraphics.fillRect(0, 0, 100, 100);
        memorygraphics.setColor(new Color(0, 0, 0));
                                .
                                .
                                .
    }
```

Then we draw the box itself using the loop_index (incremented by 5 each time we draw an image) as the extent of the box:

```
    public void paint (Graphics g) {

        loop_index += 5;
        if(loop_index >= 100) loop_index = 5;

        memorygraphics.setColor(new Color(255, 255, 255));
        memorygraphics.fillRect(0, 0, 100, 100);
        memorygraphics.setColor(new Color(0, 0, 0));
        memorygraphics.drawRect(0, 0, loop_index, loop_index);
                                .
                                .
                                .
    }
```

And finally, we draw the new image with the Graphics class's drawImage() method:

```
    public void paint (Graphics g) {

        loop_index += 5;
        if(loop_index >= 100) loop_index = 5;

        memorygraphics.setColor(new Color(255, 255, 255));
```

```
        memorygraphics.fillRect(0, 0, 100, 100);
        memorygraphics.setColor(new Color(0, 0, 0));
        memorygraphics.drawRect(0, 0, loop_index, loop_index);

→       g.drawImage(memoryimage, 10, 10, this);
    }
```

You can run the applet now, as shown below. The boxes appear to grow steadily from the upper left, and then they disappear and start out small again, repeating the process over and over. The code for this applet appears in doublebuffer.java.

doublebuffer.java

```java
import java.awt.*;
import java.applet.Applet;

public class doublebuffer extends Applet implements Runnable{

    Image memoryimage;
    Graphics memorygraphics;
    Thread doublebufferthread;
    int loop_index = 0;

    public void init() {
        memoryimage = createImage(100, 100);
        memorygraphics = memoryimage.getGraphics();
    }

    public void start() {
        doublebufferthread = new Thread(this);
        doublebufferthread.start();
```

```
          }

          public void stop() {
              doublebufferthread.stop();
          }

          public void run() {
              while(true){
                  repaint();
                  try {Thread.sleep(200);}
                  catch(InterruptedException e) { }
              }
          }

          public void paint (Graphics g) {

              loop_index += 5;
              if(loop_index >= 100) loop_index = 5;

              memorygraphics.setColor(new Color(255, 255, 255));
              memorygraphics.fillRect(0, 0, 100, 100);
              memorygraphics.setColor(new Color(0, 0, 0));
              memorygraphics.drawRect(0, 0, loop_index, loop_index);

              g.drawImage(memoryimage, 10, 10, this);
          }
      }
```

Using double-buffering techniques, then, we can prepare graphics "off-screen" and pop them up on the screen as needed. This is very useful if you want to support and draw complex images.

Updating the Dauber Applet

Another method of animation involves dynamically "stretching" images on the screen in reaction to the user's mouse movements. This method doesn't use the start(), stop(), and run() methods, but nonetheless, it gives the impression of movement, this time in response to the user's direction. This technique involves several new drawing methods, and we'll look into that now as we update our dauber painting applet to allow the user to stretch images as they draw them.

When the user draws using our dauber applet, they press the mouse at one location, move the mouse to another location, and release the mouse button.

When they do, the image appears. But in between those two actions, there is nothing to be seen on the screen. However, popular paint programs animate this process by displaying an image that the user can stretch as they like with the mouse. We can incorporate this feature in the dauber applet. This feature is an example of user-driven animation—the process will be the same in essence as the animation techniques we have explored so far: drawing a figure, erasing it, and drawing a new figure, but this time, the user directs the action. This technique involves a new drawing technique, XOR drawing, which we'll learn now. When we're done, the user will be able to draw a line like the one shown in Figure 14.3. As the user draws, the line will stretch to match the mouse movements, as shown in Figure 14.4.

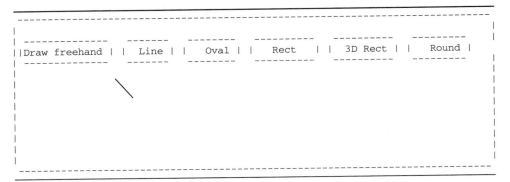

FIGURE 1 4 . 3 **The user can draw a line.**

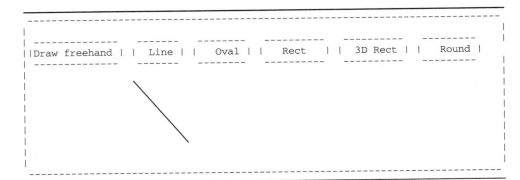

FIGURE 1 4 . 4 **The line stretches as the user draws.**

Let's put this idea to work now. Here's how it works: the user starts by pressing the mouse to establish the anchor point, and then moves the mouse to a new point, the drawto point, as shown below:

```
anchor point x-----------------------
               |                       |
               |                       |
               |                       |
               |                       |
               -----------------------x drawto point
```

Next, the user moves on as they drag the mouse, stretching the figure to a new drawto point, past the old drawto point, as shown below:

```
anchor point x----------------------
               |                     |
               |                     |
               |                     |
               ---------------------x old drawto point

                                     x drawto point
```

To give the impression that the user has stretched the graphics figure, we erase the old graphics figure:

```
anchor point x




                                    x old drawto point

                                    x drawto point
```

Then, we draw the new graphics figure, stretching from the anchor point to the new drawto point:

And the process continues in this manner—drawing to a new drawto point, then a new one and a new one, and so on. Each time, we have to erase the old figure and draw a new one.

Let's start writing code now. First, we have to keep track of the old drawto point, and we do that by adding a new point, ptOldDrawTo, to the dauber applet:

```
import java.awt.Graphics;
import java.awt.*;
import java.awt.event.*;
import java.lang.Math;
import java.applet.Applet;

public class dauber extends Applet implements ActionListener, MouseListener,
➥ MouseMotionListener {

    Button buttonDraw, buttonLine, buttonOval, buttonRect, button3DRect;
    Button buttonRounded;

    Point pts[] = new Point[1000];
    Point ptAnchor, ptDrawTo, ptOldDrawTo;
    int ptindex = 0;

    boolean bMouseDownFlag = false;
    boolean bMouseUpFlag = false;
    boolean bDrawFlag = false;
    boolean bLineFlag = false;
    boolean bOvalFlag = false;
    boolean bRectFlag = false;
    boolean b3DRectFlag = false;
    boolean bRoundedFlag = false;
            .
            .
            .
```

Next, we set the old drawto point when the user presses the mouse in the `mousePressed()` method:

```
public void mousePressed(MouseEvent e){
    bMouseDownFlag = true;
    bMouseUpFlag = false;
    ptOldDrawTo = new Point(e.getX(), e.getY());
    ptDrawTo = new Point(e.getX(), e.getY());
    ptAnchor = new Point(e.getX(), e.getY());
}
```

In addition, when the user drags the mouse, we need to update the drawto point. We will copy the old drawto point to the ptOldDrawTo point, and update the new ptDrawTo point. Then, in the `paint()` method, we can erase the old figure, drawn from the anchor point to the old drawto point, and draw the new figure, from the anchor point to the new drawto point. We start in the `mouseDragged()` method by making the current drawto point the old drawto point (so the current graphics figure can be drawn over):

```
public void mouseDragged(MouseEvent e){
    if(bDrawFlag){
        pts[ptindex] = new Point(e.getX(), e.getY());
        ptindex++;
    }
    else{
        ptOldDrawTo = ptDrawTo;
               .
               .
               .
    }
    repaint();
}
```

Next, we update the drawto point itself to the current location of the mouse, and call `repaint()`:

```
public void mouseDragged(MouseEvent e){
    if(bDrawFlag){
        pts[ptindex] = new Point(e.getX(), e.getY());
        ptindex++;
    }
    else{
        ptOldDrawTo = ptDrawTo;
        ptDrawTo = new Point(e.getX(), e.getY());
    }
    repaint();
}
```

In the `paint()` method, we'll erase the old figure (stretching from `ptAnchor` to `ptOldDrawTo`) and draw the new figure (stretching from `ptAnchor` to `ptDrawTo`).

In addition, when the user releases the mouse button, we do the same thing so the screen is updated one last time and the figure is drawn in its final state:

```
public void mouseReleased(MouseEvent e){
        bMouseDownFlag = false;
        bMouseUpFlag = true;
→       ptOldDrawTo = ptDrawTo;
→       ptDrawTo = new Point(e.getX(), e.getY());
        if(!bLineFlag){
            ptDrawTo = new Point(Math.max(ptAnchor.x, ptDrawTo.x),
              ➥ Math.max(ptAnchor.y, ptDrawTo.y));
            ptAnchor = new Point(Math.min(ptDrawTo.x, ptAnchor.x),
              ➥ Math.min(ptDrawTo.y, ptAnchor.y));
        }
        repaint();
    }
```

Now we will update the `paint()` method to make use of these changes.

Updating the Dauber `paint()` Method

Here, in the `paint()` method, we want to erase the current graphics figure, which stretches from `ptAnchor` to `ptOldDrawTo`, and draw the new graphics figure, which stretches from `ptAnchor` to `ptDrawTo`.

We'll use XOR drawing to do this. The XOR exclusive OR operator is a unique one. It operates much like the OR operator. The OR operator takes binary values like 0 and 1, and it combines them. In all cases but 0 ORed with 0, the result is 1:

```
        OR
        0     1
      -------
0   |   0     1
1   |   1     1
```

The XOR operator is a little different. Here, when we XOR 1 and 1, we do not get 1, but 0. For all other cases, XOR works just like OR.

```
        XOR
        0     1
      -------
  0   |   0     1
→ 1   |   1     0
```

What this means in practice is that when you XOR a number with itself, you get 0. The interesting thing is that when you XOR number A with number B, you get a certain result, number C. However, when you XOR C with B again, you get A back. This property is useful for, among other things, placing mouse cursors on the screen. When you place the mouse cursor on the screen, you can XOR the pixels in the cursor's image with the pixels on the screen, pixel by pixel. The cursor appears. When you want to get rid of it, you just repeat the same process again—XORing the cursor with the screen at the same location again—and the screen is restored. There is no need to store the screen before placing the mouse cursor on the screen.

Let's put XOR to work. Our first task will be to erase the old figure, stretching from ptAnchor to ptOldDrawTo. Our drawing color is black, so we install that now in our Graphics object:

```
public void paint (Graphics g) {
    int loop_index;
    int figureWidth, figureHeight;
    Point topLeft;

    if(bDrawFlag){
        for(loop_index = 0; loop_index < ptindex - 1; loop_index++){
        g.drawLine(pts[loop_index].x, pts[loop_index].y,
        ➥ pts[loop_index + 1].x, pts[loop_index + 1].y);
        }
        return;
    }

    g.setColor(new Color(0, 0, 0));
        .
        .
        .
```

Next, we set the XOR drawing mode with the Graphics setXORMode() method.

Setting the XOR Mode

Here, we'll set the XOR drawing mode with the background color. This means that when we draw over black pixels (black is the current drawing color) on the screen, they will be changed to the background color:

```
public void paint (Graphics g) {
    int loop_index;

    if(bDrawFlag){
```

```
        for(loop_index = 0; loop_index < ptindex - 1; loop_index++){
        g.drawLine(pts[loop_index].x, pts[loop_index].y,
        ➥ pts[loop_index + 1].x, pts[loop_index + 1].y);
        }
        return;
    }

    g.setColor(new Color(0, 0, 0));
➜   g.setXORMode(getBackground());
                .
                .
                .
```

Now the XOR mode is set. We next find the top left point of the graphics figure we want to erase, as well as its width and height:

```
public void paint (Graphics g) {
        int loop_index;
➜       int figureWidth, figureHeight;
➜       Point topLeft;

        if(bDrawFlag){
        for(loop_index = 0; loop_index < ptindex - 1; loop_index++){
        g.drawLine(pts[loop_index].x, pts[loop_index].y,
        ➥ pts[loop_index + 1].x, pts[loop_index + 1].y);
        }
        return;
    }

    g.setColor(new Color(0, 0, 0));
    g.setXORMode(getBackground());

➜   topLeft = new Point(Math.min(ptAnchor.x, ptOldDrawTo.x),
    ➥ Math.min(ptAnchor.y, ptOldDrawTo.y));
➜   figureWidth = Math.abs(ptOldDrawTo.x - ptAnchor.x);
    figureHeight = Math.abs(ptOldDrawTo.y - ptAnchor.y);
                .
                .
                .
```

At this point, we are ready to erase the figure itself, and we do that simply by drawing over it now that we have set the XOR mode correctly:

```
public void paint (Graphics g) {
        int loop_index;
        int figureWidth, figureHeight;
```

```
Point topLeft;

if(bDrawFlag){
    for(loop_index = 0; loop_index < ptindex - 1; loop_index++){
        g.drawLine(pts[loop_index].x, pts[loop_index].y,
    ➥ pts[loop_index + 1].x, pts[loop_index + 1].y);
    }
    return;
}

g.setColor(new Color(0, 0, 0));
g.setXORMode(getBackground());

topLeft = new Point(Math.min(ptAnchor.x, ptOldDrawTo.x),
➥ Math.min(ptAnchor.y, ptOldDrawTo.y));
figureWidth = Math.abs(ptOldDrawTo.x - ptAnchor.x);
figureHeight = Math.abs(ptOldDrawTo.y - ptAnchor.y);

if(bLineFlag){
    g.drawLine(ptAnchor.x, ptAnchor.y, ptOldDrawTo.x,
    ➥ ptOldDrawTo.y);
}
if(bOvalFlag){
    g.drawOval(topLeft.x, topLeft.y, figureWidth, figureHeight);
}
if(bRectFlag){
    g.drawRect(topLeft.x, topLeft.y, figureWidth, figureHeight);
}
if(b3DRectFlag){
    g.draw3DRect(topLeft.x, topLeft.y, figureWidth, figureHeight,
    ➥ true);
}
if(bRoundedFlag){
    g.drawRoundRect(topLeft.x, topLeft.y, figureWidth,
    ➥ figureHeight, 10, 10);
}     .
      .
      .
```

This erases the old graphics figure, which is obsolete now that the user has moved the mouse. We've made considerable progress.

The next step is to draw the new figure, which stretches from ptAnchor to ptDrawTo. To do that, now that the XOR mode is set, we simply set the drawing color to the background color itself. In this way, we'll end up drawing in the current drawing color. Now that we are not drawing to ptOldDrawTo anymore, but to ptDrawTo instead, we have to recalculate the width and height as well, and we do that this way:

```
public void paint (Graphics g) {
        int loop_index;
        int figureWidth, figureHeight;
        Point topLeft;

        if(bDrawFlag){
            for(loop_index = 0; loop_index < ptindex - 1; loop_index++){
            g.drawLine(pts[loop_index].x, pts[loop_index].y,
            ➥ pts[loop_index + 1].x, pts[loop_index + 1].y);
            }
            return;
        }

        g.setColor(new Color(0, 0, 0));
        g.setXORMode(getBackground());
                    .
                    .
                    .
        if(bRoundedFlag){
            g.drawRoundRect(topLeft.x, topLeft.y, figureWidth,
            ➥ figureHeight, 10, 10);
        }
```
➔
➔
```
        g.setColor(getBackground());
        topLeft = new Point(Math.min(ptAnchor.x, ptDrawTo.x),
        ➥ Math.min(ptAnchor.y, ptDrawTo.y));
```
➔
➔
```
        figureWidth = Math.abs(ptDrawTo.x - ptAnchor.x);
        figureHeight = Math.abs(ptDrawTo.y - ptAnchor.y);
                    .
                    .
                    .
```

Finally, we draw the new figure, making it appear on the screen:

```
public void paint (Graphics g) {
        int loop_index;
        int figureWidth, figureHeight;
        Point topLeft;

        if(bDrawFlag){
            for(loop_index = 0; loop_index < ptindex - 1; loop_index++){
            g.drawLine(pts[loop_index].x, pts[loop_index].y,
            ➥ pts[loop_index + 1].x, pts[loop_index + 1].y);
            }
```

Skill 14

```
            return;
        }

        g.setColor(new Color(0, 0, 0));
        g.setXORMode(getBackground());
            .
            .
            .
        if(bRoundedFlag){
            g.drawRoundRect(topLeft.x, topLeft.y, figureWidth,
            ➥ figureHeight, 10, 10);
        }

        g.setColor(getBackground());
        topLeft = new Point(Math.min(ptAnchor.x, ptDrawTo.x),
        ➥ Math.min(ptAnchor.y, ptDrawTo.y));

        figureWidth = Math.abs(ptDrawTo.x - ptAnchor.x);
        figureHeight = Math.abs(ptDrawTo.y - ptAnchor.y);

        if(bLineFlag){
            g.drawLine(ptAnchor.x, ptAnchor.y, ptDrawTo.x, ptDrawTo.y);
        }
        if(bOvalFlag){
            g.drawOval(topLeft.x, topLeft.y, figureWidth, figureHeight);
        }
        if(bRectFlag){
            g.drawRect(topLeft.x, topLeft.y, figureWidth, figureHeight);
        }
        if(b3DRectFlag){
            g.draw3DRect(topLeft.x, topLeft.y, figureWidth, figureHeight,
            ➥ true);
        }
        if(bRoundedFlag){
            g.drawRoundRect(topLeft.x, topLeft.y, figureWidth,
            ➥ figureHeight, 10, 10);
        }
    }
```

And the new version of dauber is ready to run. Run the applet now, as shown in Figure 14.5. When you draw a new figure, that figure stretches until you release the mouse button. The code for this applet appears in dauber.java, version 2.

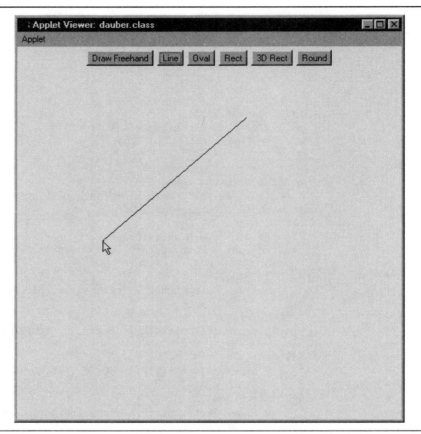

FIGURE 14.5 Now we can stretch figures in dauber, implementing user-driven animation.

dauber.java, version 2

```java
import java.awt.Graphics;
import java.awt.*;
import java.awt.event.*;
import java.lang.Math;
import java.applet.Applet;

public class dauber extends Applet implements ActionListener, MouseListener,
➡ MouseMotionListener {

    Button buttonDraw, buttonLine, buttonOval, buttonRect, button3DRect;
```

```java
Button buttonRounded;

Point pts[] = new Point[1000];
Point ptAnchor, ptDrawTo, ptOldDrawTo;
int ptindex = 0;

boolean bMouseDownFlag = false;
boolean bMouseUpFlag = false;
boolean bDrawFlag = false;
boolean bLineFlag = false;
boolean bOvalFlag = false;
boolean bRectFlag = false;
boolean b3DRectFlag = false;
boolean bRoundedFlag = false;

public void init() {

    buttonDraw = new Button("Draw Freehand");
    buttonLine = new Button("Line");
    buttonOval = new Button("Oval");
    buttonRect = new Button("Rect");
    button3DRect = new Button("3D Rect");
    buttonRounded = new Button("Round");

    add(buttonDraw);
    buttonDraw.addActionListener(this);
    add(buttonLine);
    buttonLine.addActionListener(this);
    add(buttonOval);
    buttonOval.addActionListener(this);
    add(buttonRect);
    buttonRect.addActionListener(this);
    add(button3DRect);
    button3DRect.addActionListener(this);
    add(buttonRounded);
    buttonRounded.addActionListener(this);
    addMouseListener(this);
    addMouseMotionListener(this);
    ptAnchor = new Point(0, 0);
    ptOldDrawTo = new Point(0, 0);
    ptDrawTo = new Point(0, 0);
}

public void mousePressed(MouseEvent e){
    bMouseDownFlag = true;
    bMouseUpFlag = false;
    ptOldDrawTo = new Point(e.getX(), e.getY());
    ptDrawTo = new Point(e.getX(), e.getY());
    ptAnchor = new Point(e.getX(), e.getY());
```

```
        }
        public void mouseReleased(MouseEvent e){
            bMouseDownFlag = false;
            bMouseUpFlag = true;
            ptOldDrawTo = ptDrawTo;
            ptDrawTo = new Point(e.getX(), e.getY());
            if(!bLineFlag){
                ptDrawTo = new Point(Math.max(ptAnchor.x, ptDrawTo.x),
                ➡ Math.max(ptAnchor.y, ptDrawTo.y));
                ptAnchor = new Point(Math.min(ptDrawTo.x, ptAnchor.x),
                ➡ Math.min(ptDrawTo.y, ptAnchor.y));
            }
            repaint();
        }

        public void mouseDragged(MouseEvent e){
            if(bDrawFlag){
                pts[ptindex] = new Point(e.getX(), e.getY());
                ptindex++;
            }
            else{
                ptOldDrawTo = ptDrawTo;
                ptDrawTo = new Point(e.getX(), e.getY());
            }
            repaint();
        }

        public void mouseClicked(MouseEvent e){}

        public void mouseEntered(MouseEvent e){}

        public void mouseExited(MouseEvent e){}

        public void mouseMoved(MouseEvent e){}

        public void paint (Graphics g) {
            int loop_index;
            int figureWidth, figureHeight;
            Point topLeft;

            if(bDrawFlag){
                for(loop_index = 0; loop_index < ptindex - 1; loop_index++){
                g.drawLine(pts[loop_index].x, pts[loop_index].y,
                ➡ pts[loop_index + 1].x, pts[loop_index + 1].y);
                }
                return;
            }
```

```
g.setColor(new Color(0, 0, 0));
g.setXORMode(getBackground());

topLeft = new Point(Math.min(ptAnchor.x, ptOldDrawTo.x),
➡ Math.min(ptAnchor.y, ptOldDrawTo.y));
figureWidth = Math.abs(ptOldDrawTo.x - ptAnchor.x);
figureHeight = Math.abs(ptOldDrawTo.y - ptAnchor.y);

if(bLineFlag){
    g.drawLine(ptAnchor.x, ptAnchor.y, ptOldDrawTo.x,
    ➡ ptOldDrawTo.y);
}
if(bOvalFlag){
    g.drawOval(topLeft.x, topLeft.y, figureWidth, figureHeight);
}
if(bRectFlag){
    g.drawRect(topLeft.x, topLeft.y, figureWidth, figureHeight);
}
if(b3DRectFlag){
    g.draw3DRect(topLeft.x, topLeft.y, figureWidth, figureHeight,
    ➡ true);
}
if(bRoundedFlag){
    g.drawRoundRect(topLeft.x, topLeft.y, figureWidth,
    ➡ figureHeight, 10, 10);
}

g.setColor(getBackground());
topLeft = new Point(Math.min(ptAnchor.x, ptDrawTo.x),
➡ Math.min(ptAnchor.y, ptDrawTo.y));

figureWidth = Math.abs(ptDrawTo.x - ptAnchor.x);
figureHeight = Math.abs(ptDrawTo.y - ptAnchor.y);

if(bLineFlag){
    g.drawLine(ptAnchor.x, ptAnchor.y, ptDrawTo.x, ptDrawTo.y);
}
if(bOvalFlag){
    g.drawOval(topLeft.x, topLeft.y, figureWidth, figureHeight);
}
if(bRectFlag){
    g.drawRect(topLeft.x, topLeft.y, figureWidth, figureHeight);
}
if(b3DRectFlag){
    g.draw3DRect(topLeft.x, topLeft.y, figureWidth, figureHeight,
    ➡ true);
}
if(bRoundedFlag){
    g.drawRoundRect(topLeft.x, topLeft.y, figureWidth,
    ➡ figureHeight, 10, 10);
```

Skill 14

```
            }
      }
      public void actionPerformed(ActionEvent e){
           if(e.getSource() == buttonDraw){
                bDrawFlag = !bDrawFlag;
                bLineFlag = false;
                bOvalFlag = false;
                bRectFlag = false;
                b3DRectFlag = false;
                bRoundedFlag = false;
           }
           if(e.getSource() == buttonLine){
                bLineFlag = !bLineFlag;
                bDrawFlag = false;
                bOvalFlag = false;
                bRectFlag = false;
                b3DRectFlag = false;
                bRoundedFlag = false;
           }
           if(e.getSource() == buttonOval){
                bOvalFlag = !bOvalFlag;
                bLineFlag = false;
                bDrawFlag = false;
                bRectFlag = false;
                b3DRectFlag = false;
                bRoundedFlag = false;
           }
           if(e.getSource() == buttonRect){
                bRectFlag = !bRectFlag;
                bLineFlag = false;
                bOvalFlag = false;
                bDrawFlag = false;
                b3DRectFlag = false;
                bRoundedFlag = false;
           }
           if(e.getSource() == button3DRect){
                b3DRectFlag = !b3DRectFlag;
                bLineFlag = false;
                bOvalFlag = false;
                bRectFlag = false;
                bDrawFlag = false;
                bRoundedFlag = false;
           }
           if(e.getSource() == buttonRounded){
                bRoundedFlag = !bRoundedFlag;
                bLineFlag = false;
                bOvalFlag = false;
                bRectFlag = false;
```

```
            b3DRectFlag = false;
            bDrawFlag = false;
        }
    }
}
```

Our improved dauber applet is complete, and it's pretty powerful, thanks to the Java `Graphics` class.

The last animation topic we'll take up in this Skill is using the card layout manager. With this new layout manager, you can animate not just images, but whole panels complete with controls. Let's look at that now.

Using the Card Layout for Animation

If you want to animate things other than images in Java, there is a Java layout manager that can handle many of the details. For example, if we have a panel filled with label controls (as shown in Figure 14.6), we can use the card layout manager to flash another panel onto the screen (as shown in Figure 14.7).

FIGURE 14.6   A panel with label controls

```
 -------------------
|                   |
|                   |
|   Welcome to Java |
|                   |
|                   |
|                   |
|      This is      |
|                   |
|                   |
|                   |
|      Card Two     |
|                   |
|                   |
|                   |
|                   |
|                   |
 -------------------
```

FIGURE 14.7   A second panel

And we could keep going, cycling panel after panel as long as we liked. In this way, the card layout manager supports animation—not animation of images, but of controls and panels. We'll take a look at this layout manager now, developing the example above.

Create a new file named `carder.java` and place our standard code in it:

```
import java.awt.*;
import java.applet.Applet;

public class carder extends Applet {
          .
          .
          .
```

In addition to the above code, we'll need a thread in this applet to animate our card layout, so implement the Runnable interface now:

```
   import java.awt.*;
   import java.applet.Applet;

➜  public class carder extends Applet implements Runnable{
             .
             .
             .
```

We'll set up three cards in our card layout, of class cardPanel. We'll call those objects panel1, panel2, and panel3. Add those objects to the applet now (we'll create the cardPanel class in a minute):

```
import java.awt.*;
import java.applet.Applet;

public class carder extends Applet implements Runnable{

        cardPanel panel1, panel2, panel3;
                .
                .
                .
```

Now we are ready to add our new card layout to the applet. We do that with a new CardLayout object, and we create that object in the init() method:

```
import java.awt.*;
import java.applet.Applet;

public class carder extends Applet implements Runnable{

        cardPanel panel1, panel2, panel3;

        int cardindex = 0;
        Thread cardThread;
        CardLayout cardlayout;

        public void init() {
                cardlayout = new CardLayout();
                        .
                        .
                        .
```

Next, we install the new layout manager:

```
import java.awt.*;
import java.applet.Applet;

public class carder extends Applet implements Runnable{

        cardPanel panel1, panel2, panel3;

        CardLayout cardlayout;

        public void init() {
```

```
           cardlayout = new CardLayout();
  ➜        setLayout(cardlayout);
                   .
                   .
                   .
```

At this point, we can create the three card panels to install in the card layout. We'll give our cardpanel class a constructor that will take a string so we can label each panel (e.g., "Panel One" or "Panel Two"). We'll create our three new panels as follows, passing an appropriate string to each:

```
import java.awt.*;
import java.applet.Applet;

public class carder extends Applet implements Runnable{

     cardPanel panel1, panel2, panel3;

     CardLayout cardlayout;

     public void init() {
          cardlayout = new CardLayout();
          setLayout(cardlayout);
  ➜       panel1 = new cardPanel("One");
  ➜       panel2 = new cardPanel("Two");
  ➜       panel3 = new cardPanel("Three");
                   .
                   .
                   .
```

We can install these new panels in the Java card layout manager with its add() method. When we use the card layout manager, we need a string for each new panel that we add: "first" for the first card, "second" for the second card, and so forth. In code, the strings look like this:

```
import java.awt.*;
import java.applet.Applet;

public class carder extends Applet implements Runnable{

     cardPanel panel1, panel2, panel3;

     int cardindex = 0;
     Thread cardThread;
     CardLayout cardlayout;

     public void init() {
```

```
        cardlayout = new CardLayout();
        setLayout(cardlayout);
        panel1 = new cardPanel("One");
        panel2 = new cardPanel("Two");
        panel3 = new cardPanel("Three");
→       add("first", panel1);
→       add("second", panel2);
→       add("third", panel3);
            .
            .
            .
```

Now we'll explore the process of using the card layout manager to actually show one of the cards we've installed.

Showing a Card with the Card Layout Manager

To actually show a card—the first card, for example, we use the card layout's show() method, passing the placement strings "first," "second," and so on. To show the first card, we execute the following statement:

```
import java.awt.*;
import java.applet.Applet;

public class carder extends Applet implements Runnable{

    cardPanel panel1, panel2, panel3;

    int cardindex = 0;
    Thread cardThread;
    CardLayout cardlayout;

    public void init() {
        cardlayout = new CardLayout();
        setLayout(cardlayout);
        panel1 = new cardPanel("One");
        panel2 = new cardPanel("Two");
        panel3 = new cardPanel("Three");
        add("first", panel1);
        add("second", panel2);
        add("third", panel3);
→       cardlayout.show(this, "first");
    }
```

That's how we'll show cards in our applet, with the show() method. Now we can implement animation itself.

Animating Control Panels

We'll animate our panels by setting up a new thread, and we'll call that thread cardThread:

```
import java.awt.*;
import java.applet.Applet;

public class carder extends Applet implements Runnable{

    cardPanel panel1, panel2, panel3;

    Thread cardThread;
    CardLayout cardlayout;

    public void init() {
        cardlayout = new CardLayout();
        setLayout(cardlayout);
        panel1 = new cardPanel("One");
        panel2 = new cardPanel("Two");
        panel3 = new cardPanel("Three");
        add("first", panel1);
        add("second", panel2);
        add("third", panel3);
        cardlayout.show(this, "first");
    }
```

We create and start cardThread in the start() method, as follows:

```
    public void start() {
        cardThread = new Thread(this);
        cardThread.start();
    }
```

And we stop it in the stop() method:

```
    public void stop() {
        cardThread.stop();
    }
```

In the run() method, we will cycle between all three cards, showing them one after the other. Add the run() method now, as follows:

```
    public void run() {
        .
        .
        .
    }
```

First, we set up our infinite loop for the animation:

```
public void run() {
    while(true){
            .
            .
            .
    }
}
```

Next, we set up an index—cardindex—to keep track of what panel we are currently showing:

```
import java.awt.*;
import java.applet.Applet;

public class carder extends Applet implements Runnable{

    cardPanel panel1, panel2, panel3;

    int cardindex = 0;
    Thread cardThread;
    CardLayout cardlayout;

    public void init() {
        cardlayout = new CardLayout();
        setLayout(cardlayout);
        panel1 = new cardPanel("One");
        panel2 = new cardPanel("Two");
        panel3 = new cardPanel("Three");
        add("first", panel1);
        add("second", panel2);
        add("third", panel3);
        cardlayout.show(this, "first");
    }
```

We can increment that index and use a *switch* statement to place the correct panel on the screen. We use a switch statement because we can't pass our cardindex directly to the card layout manager. Instead of passing our cardindex directly to the card layout manager, we need to pass String objects like first and second. To do so, we'll use a switch statement that looks like this:

```
switch(++cardindex){
    case 1:
        [code 1]
            .
            .
            .
        break;
```

Skill 14

```
                      case 2:
                          [code 2]
                             .

                             .

                             .
                          break;
                      case 3:
                          [code 3]
                             .

                             .

                             .
                          break;
                      case 4:
                          [code 4]
                             .

                             .

                             .
                          break;
                  }
```

Here, we increment `cardindex` and then execute code in the case that matches the new value in that variable. For example, if `cardindex` holds 3 after being incremented, the code labeled `[code 3]` above will be executed up to the `break` statement. When execution reaches the `break` statement, it leaves the `switch` statement.

 NOTE **If you do not put a `break` statement at the end of a case, execution "falls through" to the following case in a `switch` statement. In addition, instead of a `case` statement, the default statement—usually placed at the end of a list of `case` statements—handles all remaining cases.**

In code, our `switch` statement looks like this:

```
        public void run() {
            while(true){
                switch(++cardindex){
                    case 1:

                    case 2:

                    case 3:

                    case 4:

                       .

                       .

                       .
        }
```

Let's handle case 1 now. Here, we want to show the first card and also pause for 300 milliseconds:

```
public void run() {
        while(true){
                switch(++cardindex){
                        case 1:
→                               cardlayout.show(this, "first");
→                               try {Thread.sleep(300);}
→                               catch(InterruptedException e) { }
→                               break;
                        case 2:

                        case 3:

                        case 4:

                }
```

That shows the first card. Now we can do the same for the other cards, as follows:

```
public void run() {
        while(true){
                switch(++cardindex){
                        case 1:
                                cardlayout.show(this, "first");
                                try {Thread.sleep(300);}
                                catch(InterruptedException e) { }
                                break;
→                       case 2:
→                               cardlayout.show(this, "second");
→                               try {Thread.sleep(300);}
→                               catch(InterruptedException e) { }
→                               break;
→                       case 3:
→                               cardlayout.show(this, "third");
→                               try {Thread.sleep(300);}
→                               catch(InterruptedException e) { }
→                               break;
                        case 4:

                }
                repaint();
        }
    }
}
```

When the cardindex variable reaches a value of 4, we can reset it to 0 again in the fourth case, starting the animation over, as follows:

```
public void run() {
        while(true){
            switch(++cardindex){
                case 1:
                    cardlayout.show(this, "first");
                    try {Thread.sleep(300);}
                    catch(InterruptedException e) { }
                    break;
                case 2:
                    cardlayout.show(this, "second");
                    try {Thread.sleep(300);}
                    catch(InterruptedException e) { }
                    break;
                case 3:
                    cardlayout.show(this, "third");
                    try {Thread.sleep(300);}
                    catch(InterruptedException e) { }
                    break;
                case 4:
                    cardindex = 0;
                    break;
            }

            repaint();
        }
    }
}
```

And we're almost finished; all that remains is to create the cardPanel class, which is based on the Panel class:

```
class cardPanel extends Panel {
        .
        .
        .
}
```

We add a constructor to our cardPanel class, which can take a single parameter, settext, the label of the panel (the label will hold the text "One," "Two," and so on):

```
class cardPanel extends Panel {

    cardPanel(String settext){

    }
}
```

Next, we install three labels in the panel, as follows:

```
class cardPanel extends Panel {
    Label label1, label2, label3;

    cardPanel(String settext){
            .
            .
            .
    }
}
```

And we create those labels, placing the correct text in each of them, including the text we were passed in the settext string:

```
class cardPanel extends Panel {
    Label label1, label2, label3;

    cardPanel(String settext){
        label1 = new Label("Welcome to Java");
        add(label1);
        label2 = new Label("This is");
        add(label2);
        label3 = new Label("Card " + settext);
        add(label3);
    }
}
```

Our carder applet is ready to go. Run it now and you will see the panels appear and disappear in succession, as shown below. The code for this applet appears in carder.java.

carder.java

```java
import java.awt.*;
import java.applet.Applet;

public class carder extends Applet implements Runnable{

    cardPanel panel1, panel2, panel3;

    int cardindex = 0;
    Thread cardThread;
    CardLayout cardlayout;

    public void init() {
        cardlayout = new CardLayout();
        setLayout(cardlayout);
        panel1 = new cardPanel("One");
        panel2 = new cardPanel("Two");
        panel3 = new cardPanel("Three");
        add("first", panel1);
        add("second", panel2);
        add("third", panel3);
        cardlayout.show(this, "first");
    }

    public void start() {
        cardThread = new Thread(this);
        cardThread.start();
    }

    public void stop() {
        cardThread.stop();
    }

    public void run() {
        while(true){
            switch(++cardindex){
                case 1:
                    cardlayout.show(this, "first");
                    try {Thread.sleep(300);}
                    catch(InterruptedException e) { }
                    break;
                case 2:
                    cardlayout.show(this, "second");
                    try {Thread.sleep(300);}
                    catch(InterruptedException e) { }
                    break;
```

```
                            case 3:
                                cardlayout.show(this, "third");
                                try {Thread.sleep(300);}
                                catch(InterruptedException e) { }
                                break;
                            case 4:
                                cardindex = 0;
                                break;
                    }
                    repaint();
                }
            }
        }

        class cardPanel extends Panel {
            Label label1, label2, label3;

            cardPanel(String settext){
                label1 = new Label("Welcome to Java");
                add(label1);
                label2 = new Label("This is");
                add(label2);
                label3 = new Label("Card " + settext);
                add(label3);
            }
        }
```

We've seen a lot in this Skill, including double-buffering, user-directed animation, and using the Card layout manager. We've also been introduced to a very powerful Java technique: multi-threading. We'll explore multi-threading further in Skill 15.

Are You Experienced?

Now you can...

- ☑ develop complex graphics off-screen, rather than in front of the user, and display the graphics when they are ready

- ☑ use the card layout to animate panels of controls, flashing the card panel you want onto the screen as required

- ☑ create user-directed animation

- ☑ use XOR drawing techniques

z Jones
Design
server &
xp. Fax
Visual
nalysts/
oftware
mputer
eferred.
pplica-
m. Fax
dynam-
v., test,
xp. C C.
to Best
Testers
have 2
ation &
ed test-
cumen-
amming
) are a
ustomer
along
en com-
evels of
KKUP
Blvd.
nalyst
ed SQL
equired
ODBC.
pplica-
a plus.
tory to
eking a
design
llateral.
's, CD-
WWW
e multi-
kills on
design
cal trou-
ll 435-
OR -
nt com-
portuni-
nd Web
addition
ideas.
xcellent
ntation
h innov-
ammers.
eractive
terfaces.
erience
resume
Seattle.
oftware
ing for
ATIONS
e for its
ion, and
-starter,
have 2
amming

356-555-3398.

PROGRAMMERS
C. C. VB. Cobol, exp. Call 534-555-6543 or fax 534-555-6544.

PROGRAMMING

MRFS Inc. is looking for a Sr. Windows NT developer. Reqs. 3-5 yrs. Exp. In C under Windows, Win95 & NT, using Visual C. Excl. OO design & implementation skills a must. OLE2 & ODBC are a plus. Excl. Salary & bnfts. Resume & salary history to HR, 8779 HighTech Way, Computer City, AR

PROGRAMMERS

Contractors Wanted for short & long term assignments: Visual C, MFC Unix C/C, SQL Oracle Dev elop ers PC Help Desk Support Windows NT & NetWareTelecommunications Visual Basic, Access, HTMT, CGI, Perl MMI & Co., 885-555-9933

PROGRAMMER World Wide Web Links wants your HTML & Photoshop skills. Develop great WWW sites. Local & global customers. Send samples & resume to WWWL, 2000 Apple Road, Santa Rosa, CA.

TECHNICAL WRITER Software firm seeks writer/editor for manuals, research notes, project mgmt. Min 2 years tech. writing, DTP & programming experience. Send resume & writing samples to: Software Systems, Dallas, TX.

TECHNICAL Software development firm looking for Tech Trainers. Ideal candidates have programming experience in Visual C, HTML & JAVA. Need quick self starter. Call (443) 555-6868 for interview.

TECHNICAL WRITER/ Premier Computer Corp is seeking a combination of technical skills, knowledge and experience in the following areas: UNIX, Windows 95/NT, Visual Basic, on-line help & documentation, and the internet. Candidates must possess excellent writing skills, and be comfortable working in a quality vs. deadline driven environment. Competitive salary. Fax resume & samples to Karen Fields, Premier Computer Corp., 444 Industrial Blvd. Concord, CA. Or send to our website at www.premier.com.

WEB DESIGNER

BA/BS or equivalent programming/multimedia production. 3 years of experience in use and design of WWW services streaming audio and video HTML, PERL, CGI, GIF, JPEG. Demonstrated interpersonal, organization, communication, multi-tasking skills. Send resume to The Learning People at www.learning.com.

WEBMASTER-TECHNICAL

BSCS or equivalent, 2 years of experience in CGI, Windows 95/NT, UNIX, C, Java, Perl. Demonstrated ability to design, code, debug and test on-line services. Send resume to The Learning People at www.learning.com.

PROGRAMMER World Wide Web Links wants your HTML & Photoshop skills. Develop great WWW sites.

ing tools. Experienced in documentation preparation & programming languages (Access, C, FoxPro) are a plus. Financial or banking customer service support is required along with excellent verbal & written communication skills with multi levels of end-users. Send resume to KKUP Enterprises, 45 Orange Blvd., Orange, CA.

COMPUTERS Small Web Design Firm seeks indiv. w/NT, Webserver & Database management exp. Fax resume to 556-555-4221.

COMPUTER/ Visual C/C, Visual Basic Exp'd Systems Analysts/ Programmers for growing software dev. team in Roseburg. Computer Science or related degree preferred. Develop adv. Engineering applications for engineering firm. Fax resume to 707-555-8744.

COMPUTER Web Master for dynamic SF Internet co. Site. Dev., test, coord., train, 2 yrs prog. Exp. C C. Web C. FTP. Fax resume to Best Staffing 845-555-7722.

COMPUTER PROGRAMMER

Ad agency seeks programmer w/exp. in UNIX/NT Platforms, Web Server, CGI/Perl. Programmer Position avail. on a project basis with the possibility to move into F/T. Fax resume & salary req. to R. Jones 334-555-8332.

COMPUTERS Programmer/Analyst Design and maintain C based SQL database applications. Required skills: Visual Basic, C, SQL, ODBC. Document existing and new applications. Novell or NT exp. a plus. Fax resume & salary history to 235-555-9935.

GRAPHIC DESIGNER
Webmaster's Weekly is seeking a creative Graphic Designer to design high impact marketing collater al, including direct mail promo's, CD-ROM packages, ads and WWW pages. Must be able to juggle multiple projects and learn new skills on the job very rapidly. Web design experience a big plus, technical troubleshooting also a plus. Call 435-555-1235.

GRAPHICS - ART DIRECTOR - WEB-MULTIMEDIA
Leading internet development company has an outstanding opportunity for a talented, high-end Web Experienced Art Director. In addition to a great portfolio and fresh ideas, the ideal candidate has excellent communication and presentation skills. Working as a team with innovative producers and programmers, you will create dynamic, interactive web sites and application interfaces. Some programming experience required. Send samples and resume to: SuperSites, 333 Main, Seattle, WA.

MARKETING

Fast paced software and services provider looking for MARKETING COMMUNICATIONS SPECIALIST to be responsible for its webpage.

PROGRAMMERS Multiple short term assignments available: Visual C, 3 positions SQL ServerNT Server, 2 positions JAVA & HTML, long term NetWare Various locations. Call for more info. 356-555-3398.

PROGRAMMERS

C. C. VB, Cobol, exp. Call 534-555-6543 or fax 534-555-6544.

PROGRAMMING
MRFS Inc. is looking for a Sr. Windows NT developer. Reqs. 3-5 yrs. Exp. In C under Windows, Win95 & NT, using Visual C. Excl. OO design & implementation skills a must. OLE2 & ODBC are a plus. Excl. Salary & bnfts. Resume & salary history to HR, 8779 HighTech Way, Computer City, AR

PROGRAMMERS/ Contractors Wanted for short & long term assignments: Visual C, MFC Unix C/C, SQL Oracle Developers PC Help Desk Support Windows NT & NetWareTelecommunications Visual Basic, Access, HTMT, CGI, Perl MMI & Co., 885-555-9933

PROGRAMMER World Wide Web Links wants your HTML & Photoshop skills. Develop great WWW sites. Local & global customers. Send samples & resume to WWWL, 2000 Apple Road, Santa Rosa, CA.

TECHNICAL WRITER Software firm seeks writer/editor for manuals, research notes, project mgmt. Min 2 years tech. writing, DTP & programming experience. Send resume & writing samples to: Software Systems, Dallas, TX.

COMPUTER PROGRAMMER

Ad agency seeks programmer w/exp. in UNIX/NT Platforms, Web Server, CGI/Perl. Programmer Position avail. on a project basis with the possibility to move into F/T. Fax resume & salary req. to R. Jones 334-555-8332.

TECHNICAL WRITER Premier Computer Corp is seeking a combination of technical skills, knowledge and experience in the following areas: UNIX, Windows 95/NT, Visual Basic, on-line help & documentation, and the internet. Candidates must possess excellent writing skills, and be comfortable working in a quality vs. deadline driven environment. Competitive salary. Fax resume & samples to Karen Fields, Premier Computer Corp., 444 Industrial Blvd. Concord, CA. Or send to our website at www.premier.com.

WEB DESIGNER
BA/BS or equivalent programming/multimedia production. 3 years of experience in use and design of WWW services streaming audio and video HTML, PERL, CGI, GIF, JPEG. Demonstrated interpersonal, organization, communication, multi-tasking skills. Send resume to The Learning People at www.learning.com.

WEBMASTER-TECHNICAL
BSCS or equivalent, 2 years of experience in CGI, Windows 95/NT

COMPUTERS Small Web Design Firm seeks indiv. w/NT, Webserver & Database management exp. Fax resume to 556-555-4221.

COMPUTER Visual C/C, Visual Basic Exp'd Systems Analysts/ Programmers for growing software dev. team in Roseburg. Computer Science or related degree preferred. Develop adv. Engineering applications for engineering firm. Fax resume to 707-555-8744.

COMPUTER Web Master for dynamic SF Internet co. Site. Dev., test, coord., train, 2 yrs prog. Exp. C C. Web C. FTP. Fax resume to Best Staffing 845-555-7722.

COMPUTERS/ QA SOFTWARE TESTERS Qualified candidates should have 2 yrs exp. performing integration & system testing using automated testing tools. Experienced in documentation preparation & programming languages (Access, C, FoxPro) are a plus. Financial or banking customer service support is required along with excellent verbal & written communication skills with multi levels of end-users. Send resume to KKUP Enterprises, 45 Orange Blvd., Orange, CA.

COMPUTERS Programmer/Analyst Design and maintain C based SQL database applications. Required skills: Visual Basic, C, SQL, ODBC. Document existing and new applications. Novell or NT exp. a plus. Fax resume & salary history to 235-555-9935.

GRAPHIC DESIGNER

Webmaster's Weekly is seeking a creative Graphic Designer to design high impact marketing collater al, including direct mail promo's, CD-ROM packages, ads and WWW pages. Must be able to juggle multiple projects and learn new skills on the job very rapidly. Web design experience a big plus, technical troubleshooting also a plus. Call 435-555-1235.

GRAPHICS - ART DIRECTOR - WEB-MULTIMEDIA
Leading internet development company has an outstanding opportunity for a talented, high-end Web Experienced Art Director. In addition to a great portfolio and fresh ideas, the ideal candidate has excellent communication and presentation skills. Working as a team with innovative producers and programmers, you will create dynamic, interactive web sites and application interfaces. Some programming experience required. Send samples and resume to: SuperSites, 333 Main, Seattle, WA.

COMPUTER PROGRAMMER

Ad agency seeks programmer w/exp. in UNIX/NT Platforms, Web Server, CGI/Perl. Programmer Position avail. on a project basis with the possibility to move into F/T. Fax resume & salary req. to R. Jones 334-555-8332.

PROGRAMMERS / Established software company seeks program

ment. Must be a self-starter, getic, organized. Must have 2 web experience. Programmi plus. Call 985-555-9854

PROGRAMMERS Multiple term assignments available: C, 3 positions SQL ServerNT S 2 positions JAVA & HTML, long NetWare Various locations. C more info. 356-555-3398.

PROGRAMMERS

C. C. VB, Cobol, exp. Call 534 6543 or fax 534-555-6544.

PROGRAMMING

MRFS Inc. is looking for a Windows NT developer. Req yrs. Exp. In C under Win Win95 & NT, using Visual C OO design & implementation a must. OLE2 & ODBC are a Excl. Salary & bnfts. Resu salary history to HR, 8779 Hi Way, Computer City, AR

PROGRAMMERS/ Contr Wanted for short & long term a ments: Visual C, MFCUnix C/C Oracle Developers PC Help Support Windows NT & Ne Telecommunications Visual Access, HTMT, CGI, Perl MMI 885-555-9933

PROGRAMMER World Wide Links wants your HTML & Phot skills. Develop great WWW Local & global customers. Send ples & resume to WWWL Apple Road, Santa Rosa, CA.

TECHNICAL WRITER Softwar seeks writer/editor for ma research notes, project mgmt. years tech. writing, DTP & pro ming experience. Send resu writing samples to: So Systems, Dallas, TX.

TECHNICAL Software develo firm looking for Tech Trainers candidates have programming rience in Visual C, HTML & Need quick self starter. Call 555-6868 for interview.

TECHNICAL WRITER Pr Computer Corp is seeking a c nation of technical skills, know and experience in the foll areas: UNIX, Windows 95/NT, Basic, on-line help & documen and the internet. Candidates possess excellent writing skill be comfortable working in a vs. deadline driven enviro Competitive salary. Fax res samples to Karen Fields. P Computer Corp., 444 Industri Concord, CA. Or send to our w at www.premier.com.

WEB DESIGNER

BA/BS or equivalent pro ming/multimedia productio years of experience in us design of WWW services stre audio and video HTML, PER GIF, JPEG. Demonstrated in sonal, organization, communi multi-tasking skills. Send res The Learning People at www ing.com.

WEBMASTER-TECHN

S K I L L

fifteen

15

Working with Multi-Threaded Programs and JAR Files

In this Skill, we're going to explore an aspect of Java that we touched on in Skills 13 and 14—multi-threading. Animation gave you a good introduction to this topic; you learned that the way animation works in Java is to have a thread (that is, an independent stream of execution) endlessly place animation frames in an applet while the applet's main thread is able to do other work.

In this Skill, we'll see how to see how to set the priority of the different threads in an applet, how to coordinate threads at work, and how to use multiple threads. Let's start by working through the process of creating a threaded applet.

Creating Thread Objects

To begin our exploration of threads, we'll create an applet with a thread object that repeatedly prints the message "Hello from Java" on the screen. We'll give our applet two buttons, one to start the thread printing its message, and one to stop it, as shown in Figure 15.1.

```
 ------------------------------------------------------
|                                                      |
|                                                      |
|         ---------------      --------------          |
|        | Start thread |     | Stop thread |          |
|         ---------------      --------------          |
|                                                      |
|                                                      |
|                                                      |
|                                                      |
|                                                      |
|                                                      |
|                                                      |
 ------------------------------------------------------
```

FIGURE 15.1   Our applet's two buttons

Create a new file named `threads.java` now. We start with our usual code, and we implement the ActionListener interface for the buttons we'll use:

```java
import java.applet.Applet;
import java.awt.*;
import java.awt.event.*;
```

```
→   public class threads extends Applet implements ActionListener {
                        .
                        .
                        .
    }
```

Next, we add the Start Thread button and the Stop Thread button. We connect them up to our code by installing ActionListeners in each button object:

```
import java.applet.Applet;
import java.awt.*;
import java.awt.event.*;

public class threads extends Applet implements ActionListener {

→       Button button1, button2;

→       public void init(){
→           button1 = new Button("Start thread");
→           add(button1);
→           button1.addActionListener(this);
→           button2 = new Button("Stop thread");
→           add(button2);
→           button2.addActionListener(this);
                        .
                        .
                        .
    }
```

Now we're ready to add our new thread to our applet.

Using the Java Thread Class

Threads in Java are supported by the Thread class; we add a new thread that we'll name printingThread. We will create the printingThread class soon.

 NOTE   **We are intentionally not implementing the Runnable interface in this example; we will make use of the Runnable interface in our next example.**

```
import java.applet.Applet;
import java.awt.*;
import java.awt.event.*;

public class threads extends Applet implements ActionListener {
```

```
→        Button button1, button2;
→        printingThread Thread1;

         public void init(){
             button1 = new Button("Start thread");
             add(button1);
             button1.addActionListener(this);
             button2 = new Button("Stop thread");
             add(button2);
             button2.addActionListener(this);
→            Thread1 = new printingThread();
         }        .
                  .
                  .
```

To start this new thread, we use the Thread class's start() method, and to stop it, we use stop(). This way we connect those methods up to our buttons in the actionPerformed() method:

```
import java.applet.Applet;
import java.awt.*;
import java.awt.event.*;

public class threads extends Applet implements ActionListener {

         Button button1, button2;
         printingThread Thread1;

         public void init(){
             button1 = new Button("Start thread");
             add(button1);
             button1.addActionListener(this);
             button2 = new Button("Stop thread");
             add(button2);
             button2.addActionListener(this);
             Thread1 = new printingThread();
         }

→        public void actionPerformed(ActionEvent e){
→            if(e.getSource() == button1){
→                Thread1.start();
→            }
→            if(e.getSource() == button2){
→                Thread1.stop();
→            }
         }
    }
```

> **NOTE** When the thread is stopped, it is deallocated, so you can use the Start and Stop buttons in our applet only once—if you want to pause a thread, you can use the `suspend()` and `resume()` methods that we'll discuss soon.

Now we create the `printing` Thread class. This class extends the Java Thread class as follows:

```
public class threads extends Applet implements ActionListener {

        Button button1, button2;
        printingThread Thread1;

        public void init(){
            button1 = new Button("Start thread");
            add(button1);
            button1.addActionListener(this);
            button2 = new Button("Stop thread");
            add(button2);
            button2.addActionListener(this);
            Thread1 = new printingThread();
        }                  .
                           .
                           .

    }

→   class printingThread extends Thread {
                    .
                    .
                    .

→   }
```

Because this new class extends the Thread class and not the Applet class, we can't reach the screen (using the Applet class's methods) to work with the new class directly. We also can't extend *both* the Thread and Applet classes at the same time because Java doesn't allow multiple inheritance yet. The Runnable interface was introduced to allow applet classes to be multi-threaded. (Using interfaces is as close to multiple inheritance as Java gets.) In this case, we'll use `System.out.println()` to print our message on the screen in an infinite loop:

```
    class printingThread extends Thread {
→       public void run(){
→           while(true){
```

```
→                    System.out.println("Hello from Java");
→          }
→      }
   }
```

Running the thread applet produces the following display in the DOS window:

```
Hello from Java
Hello from Java
Hello from Java
Hello from Java
Hello from Java
Hello from Java
Hello from Java
Hello from Java
Hello from Java
Hello from Java
Hello from Java
       .
       .
       .
```

Of course, thread objects like the one we've introduced above usually perform more useful tasks in the background. For example, they can perform large-scale mathematical operations, setting flags that the rest of the program can check when the operation is complete. In fact, it's worth noting that we've had to restrict our I/O here to the `println()` method, which is very restricted indeed. Let's explore how to reach the screen more directly.

Working with the Runnable Interface

You've learned how to create `Thread` objects in Java, but you've also learned that if you want to work with graphics on the screen, you'll need something more. That something more is the Runnable interface. For example, in our spinner applet, we implemented the Runnable interface as follows:

```
import java.awt.*;
import java.applet.Applet;

→   public class spinner extends Applet implements Runnable{
               .
               .
               .
```

Then we were able to add a thread object, spinThread, in our applet, as follows:

```
import java.awt.*;
import java.applet.Applet;

public class spinner extends Applet implements Runnable{

        Image spinImages[] = new Image[4];
        Image nowImage;
        int spinIndex = 0;
→       Thread spinThread;

        public void init() {
            spinImages[0] = getImage(getCodeBase(), "spin1.gif");
            spinImages[1] = getImage(getCodeBase(), "spin2.gif");
            spinImages[2] = getImage(getCodeBase(), "spin3.gif");
            spinImages[3] = getImage(getCodeBase(), "spin4.gif");
        }
```

Implementing the Runnable interface means that we can now override the start(), stop() and run() methods, which we do as follows:

```
→       public void start() {
→           spinThread = new Thread(this);
→           spinThread.start();
→       }

→       public void stop() {
→           spinThread.stop();
→       }

→       public void run() {
→           while(true){
→               nowImage = spinImages[spinIndex++];
→               if(spinIndex > 3)spinIndex = 0;
→               repaint();
→               try {Thread.sleep(200);}
→               catch(InterruptedException e) { }
→           }
→       }
```

In this way, we have all the advantages of a thread object without having to create a new thread class. You can see how useful the Runnable interface is and why it was created.

That's an overview of thread use in Java. Let's continue on now to explore some of the power of these thread techniques—we'll rewrite the spinner applet soon.

Skill 15

Controlling Threads and Setting Priority

So far, then, we've set up a new thread and let it run, but we can get far more control over threads than that. For example, we can set the *priority* of a thread with the Thread class's setPriority() method. We can give three priorities to threads, using the pre-defined constants in the Thread class: Thread.MIN_PRIORITY, Thread.NORM_PRIORITY (this is the default), and Thread.MAX_PRIORITY. A minimum-priority thread is used to execute tasks in the background, and maximum-priority threads are used for urgent tasks. For example, if we wanted to give our m_random thread in the last example the maximum priority, we would do so as follows:

```
public void start()
{
    if (m_random == null)
    {
        m_random = new Thread(this);
        m_random.setPriority(Thread.MAX_PRIORITY);
        m_random.start();
    }
}
```

In this way, we have some control over thread execution and can relegate background tasks to the background. For example, we can perform some time-consuming task named, say, bigTask(), as follows in a thread's run() method after that thread has been set to minimum priority:

```
boolean taskCompleted;

public void run() {

    taskCompletedFlag = false;

    bigTask();

    taskCompletedFlag = true;
}
```

 NOTE   Note that we set a global flag, taskCompleted, to false before starting the task and set it true afterwards. In this way, the rest of the program can check on our progress.

This technique gives us some control over the use of threads, but Java gives us more: we can suspend and resume threads at any time. Let's look into that now.

Suspending and Resuming Threads

To see how to suspend and resume threads, we can modify our spinner applet (which spins a colored disk) so that it includes a Suspend button and a Resume button, as shown in Figure 15.2.

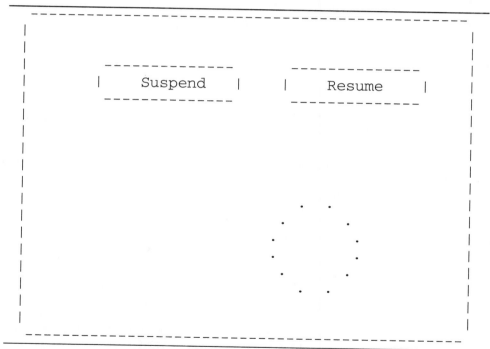

FIGURE 15.2   Adding Suspend and Resume buttons to the spinner applet

When the user clicks the Suspend button, we will suspend the animation thread and the disk will stop rotating. When the user clicks the Resume button, we will resume the thread, and the disk will start rotating again. Let's put this idea to work now. We start by adding the two buttons we'll need, **suspendButton** and **resumeButton**, to the spinner applet and by implementing the ActionListener interface:

```
import java.awt.*;
import java.awt.event.*;
import java.applet.Applet;
```

→   ```
public class spinner extends Applet implements ActionListener, Runnable {

    Image spinImages[] = new Image[4];
    Image nowImage;
    int spinIndex = 0;
    Thread spinThread;
```
→   ```
    Button suspendButton, resumeButton;
            .
            .
            .
```

Next, we add the buttons to our layout:

```
import java.awt.*;
import java.awt.event.*;
import java.applet.Applet;

public class spinner extends Applet implements ActionListener, Runnable {

    Image spinImages[] = new Image[4];
    Image nowImage;
    int spinIndex = 0;
    Thread spinThread;
    Button suspendButton, resumeButton;

    public void init() {
        spinImages[0] = getImage(getCodeBase(), "spin1.gif");
        spinImages[1] = getImage(getCodeBase(), "spin2.gif");
        spinImages[2] = getImage(getCodeBase(), "spin3.gif");
        spinImages[3] = getImage(getCodeBase(), "spin4.gif");
```
→
→
→
→
→
→   ```
        suspendButton = new Button("Suspend");
        add(suspendButton);
        suspendButton.addActionListener(this);
        resumeButton = new Button("Resume");
        add(resumeButton);
        resumeButton.addActionListener(this);
    }
```
```

At this point, we can add the `actionPerformed()` method and check which button was clicked:

```
import java.awt.*;
import java.awt.event.*;
import java.applet.Applet;

public class spinner extends Applet implements ActionListener, Runnable {

    Image spinImages[] = new Image[4];
    Image nowImage;
    int spinIndex = 0;
    Thread spinThread;
    Button suspendButton, resumeButton;

    public void init() {
        spinImages[0] = getImage(getCodeBase(), "spin1.gif");
        spinImages[1] = getImage(getCodeBase(), "spin2.gif");
        spinImages[2] = getImage(getCodeBase(), "spin3.gif");
        spinImages[3] = getImage(getCodeBase(), "spin4.gif");
        suspendButton = new Button("Suspend");
        add(suspendButton);
        suspendButton.addActionListener(this);
        resumeButton = new Button("Resume");
        add(resumeButton);
        resumeButton.addActionListener(this);
    }

    public void actionPerformed(ActionEvent e){
        if(e.getSource() == suspendButton){
            .
            .
            .
        }
        if(e.getSource() == resumeButton){
            .
            .
            .
        }
    }
```

If the user has clicked the Suspend button, we want to suspend the animation thread. That thread is named `spinThread`, so we can suspend it as follows:

```
    public void actionPerformed(ActionEvent e){
        if(e.getSource() == suspendButton){
            spinThread.suspend();
        }
```

```
                    if(e.getSource() == resumeButton){
                              .
                              .
                              .
                    }
          }
```

If the user clicks the Resume button, we want to resume thread execution, which we do with the `resume()` method:

```
          public void actionPerformed(ActionEvent e){
                if(e.getSource() == suspendButton){
                    spinThread.suspend();
                }
                if(e.getSource() == resumeButton){
➜                   spinThread.resume();
                }
          }
```

Start the applet, as shown below. Clicking the Suspend button suspends the animation thread and thus the animation itself; clicking the Resume button resumes thread execution and makes the colored disk spin around again. The code for this new version of the spinner applet appears in `spinner.java`, version 3.

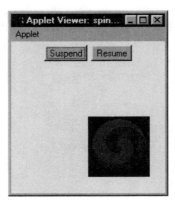

spinner.java, version 3

```
          import java.awt.*;
          import java.awt.event.*;
          import java.applet.Applet;

          public class spinner extends Applet implements ActionListener, Runnable {

                Image spinImages[] = new Image[4];
```

```
Image nowImage;
int spinIndex = 0;
Thread spinThread;
Button suspendButton, resumeButton;

public void init() {
    spinImages[0] = getImage(getCodeBase(), "spin1.gif");
    spinImages[1] = getImage(getCodeBase(), "spin2.gif");
    spinImages[2] = getImage(getCodeBase(), "spin3.gif");
    spinImages[3] = getImage(getCodeBase(), "spin4.gif");
    suspendButton = new Button("Suspend");
    add(suspendButton);
    suspendButton.addActionListener(this);
    resumeButton = new Button("Resume");
    add(resumeButton);
    resumeButton.addActionListener(this);
}

public void actionPerformed(ActionEvent e){
    if(e.getSource() == suspendButton){
        spinThread.suspend();
    }
    if(e.getSource() == resumeButton){
        spinThread.resume();
    }
}

public void start() {
    spinThread = new Thread(this);
    spinThread.start();
}

public void stop() {
    spinThread.stop();
}

public void run() {
    while(true){
        nowImage = spinImages[spinIndex++];
        if(spinIndex > 3)spinIndex = 0;
        repaint();
        try {Thread.sleep(200);}
        catch(InterruptedException e) { }
    }
}

public void paint (Graphics g) {
    if(nowImage != null) g.drawImage(nowImage, 100, 100, this);
}
```

```
public void update(Graphics g) {
    g.clipRect(100, 100, 200, 200);
    paint(g);
}
}
```

We've taken strides toward controlling our threads. Note however, that so far we have worked with only a single thread. What if our applet starts and works with multiple threads? How do we keep them straight? Let's look into this problem now.

Handling Multiple Threads

If we have multiple threads, each of which is supposed to be performing a different task, all these threads execute the same run() method. How do we keep these simultaneously-executing threads separate? We do so by *naming* them.

We'll create a new applet now with two text fields and a button with the caption "Start threads," as shown in Figure 15.3. We can have two threads in this applet, each of which writes incrementing numbers to a text field, as shown in Figure 15.4, after the user clicks the Start Threads button.

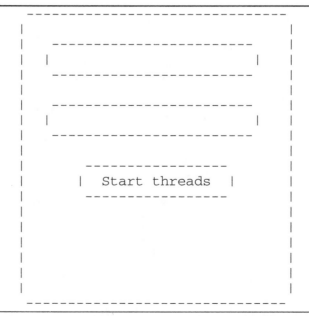

FIGURE 15.3   Our new applet has two text fields and a button.

```
 ---------------------------------
|                                 |
|    ---------------------------   |
|   | 121                      |   |
|    ---------------------------   |
|                                 |
|    ---------------------------   |
|   | 121                      |   |
|    ---------------------------   |
|                                 |
|       -----------------          |
|      |  Start threads  |         |
|       -----------------          |
|                                 |
|                                 |
|                                 |
|                                 |
 ---------------------------------
```

FIGURE 15.4   Each thread writes numbers in a text field.

We'll have only one run() method, but each thread will write to a different text field. We'll have to keep the two threads straight. Create a new file named numbers.java now and place our standard starting code in it:

```
import java.awt.*;
import java.applet.Applet;

public class numbers extends Applet {
        .
        .
        .
}
```

Add the two threads we'll use, naming them Thread1 and Thread2, and implement the Runnable interface:

```
import java.awt.*;
import java.awt.event.*; import java.applet.Applet;

public class numbers extends Applet implements Runnable {
```

```
➜          Thread Thread1, Thread2;
                    .
                    .
                    .
      }
```

We can add our two text fields and the Start Threads button, as well as implementing the ActionListener interface for the button:

```
import java.awt.*;
import java.awt.event.*;
import java.applet.Applet;

public class numbers extends Applet implements Runnable,
➜   ActionListener {

          Thread Thread1, Thread2;
➜         TextField text1, text2;
➜         Button button1;

➜         public void init() {
➜             text1 = new TextField(20);
➜             text2 = new TextField(20);
➜             add(text1);
➜             add(text2);
➜             button1 = new Button("Start threads");
➜             add(button1);
➜             button1.addActionListener(this);
➜         }
      }
```

Next, we arrange for the two threads to start when the user clicks the Start
Threads button:

```
import java.awt.*;
import java.awt.event.*;
import java.applet.Applet;

public class numbers extends Applet implements Runnable,
ActionListener {

          Thread Thread1, Thread2;
          TextField text1, text2;
          Button button1;
```

```
        public void init() {
            text1 = new TextField(20);
            text2 = new TextField(20);
            add(text1);
            add(text2);
            button1 = new Button("Start threads");
            add(button1);
            button1.addActionListener(this);
        }

→       public void actionPerformed(ActionEvent e){
→           if(e.getSource() == button1){
→               Thread1 = new Thread(this);
→               Thread1.start();
→               Thread2 = new Thread(this);
→               Thread2.start();
→           }
→       }
```

We stop the two new threads in the stop() method:

```
public class numbers extends Applet implements Runnable,
ActionListener {

        Thread Thread1, Thread2;
        TextField text1, text2;
        Button button1;

        public void init() {
            text1 = new TextField(20);
            text2 = new TextField(20);
            add(text1);
            add(text2);
            button1 = new Button("Start threads");
            add(button1);
            button1.addActionListener(this);
        }          .
                   .
                   .
→       public void stop() {
→           Thread1.stop();
→           Thread2.stop();
→       }
```

Now let's work on the run() method.

Implementing the run() Method

Both of our threads execute the same run() method. We'll have to distinguish them somehow as they are supposed to write to different text fields. Add the run() method now:

```
public void run() {
        .
        .
        .
}
```

We'll have each thread print out, say, 1000 integers by setting up a for loop:

```
public void run() {
→       int loop_index;
→       for(loop_index = 1; loop_index < 1000; loop_index++){
                .
                .
                .
→       }
}
```

Now we will place the ascending integers into the appropriate text fields: text1 for Thread1 and text2 for Thread2. To do so, we have to know which thread is executing in this copy of the run() method. We keep track by *naming* the threads.

Naming Java Threads

We can give names to threads when we create them. Open the actionPerformed() method now:

```
public void actionPerformed(ActionEvent e){
    if(e.getSource() == button1){
        Thread1 = new Thread(this);
        Thread1.start();
        Thread2 = new Thread(this);
        Thread2.start();
    }
}
```

We give the threads the names "threadname1" and "threadname2" by passing those strings to the thread's constructors:

```
public void actionPerformed(ActionEvent e){
```

```
        if(e.getSource() == button1){
            Thread1 = new Thread(this, "threadname1");
            Thread1.start();
            Thread2 = new Thread(this, "threadname2");
            Thread2.start();
        }
    }
```

Now in the run() method, we can test which thread is executing by using the getName() method. But how do we refer to the current thread so that we can use that method? We do that with the Thread class's currentThread() method. This means that we can test if Thread1 is executing the run() method as follows:

```
public void run() {
    int loop_index;
    for(loop_index = 1; loop_index < 1000; loop_index++){
        if(((Thread.currentThread()). getName()).equals("threadname1")){
            .
            .
            .
        }
    }
}
```

If Thread1 *is* executing the run() method, we can display the thread's output in the text field text1 as follows:

```
public void run() {
    String out_string;
    int loop_index;
    out_string = new String();
    for(loop_index = 1; loop_index < 1000; loop_index++){
        if(((Thread.currentThread()). getName()).equals("threadname1")){
            text1.setText(out_string. valueOf(loop_index));
            .
            .
            .
        }
    }
}
```

Now we can do the same for Thread2, testing for the thread name "threadname2" as follows:

```
public void run() {
    String out_string;
    int loop_index;
```

```
        out_string = new String();
        for(loop_index = 1; loop_index < 1000; loop_index++){
            if(((Thread.currentThread()). getName()).equals("threadname1")){
                text1.setText(out_string. valueOf(loop_index));
            }
            if(((Thread.currentThread()). getName()).equals("threadname2")){
                .
                .
                .
            }
        }
    }
}
```

If the current thread is Thread2, we can display its output in the text field
text2 this way:

```
public void run() {
    String out_string;
    int loop_index;
    out_string = new String();
    for(loop_index = 1; loop_index < 1000; loop_index++){
        if(((Thread.currentThread()). getName()).equals("threadname1")){
            text1.setText(out_string. valueOf(loop_index));
        }
        if(((Thread.currentThread()). getName()).equals("threadname2")){
            text2.setText(out_string. valueOf(loop_index));
        }
    }
}
```

You can now run the numbers applet, as shown below. The code for this applet
appears in numbers.java.

numbers.java

```java
import java.awt.*;
import java.awt.event.*;
import java.applet.Applet;

public class numbers extends Applet implements Runnable,
ActionListener {

    Thread Thread1, Thread2;
    TextField text1, text2;
    Button button1;

    public void init() {
        text1 = new TextField(20);
        text2 = new TextField(20);
        add(text1);
        add(text2);
        button1 = new Button("Start threads");
        add(button1);
        button1.addActionListener(this);
    }

    public void actionPerformed(ActionEvent e){
        if(e.getSource() == button1){
            Thread1 = new Thread(this, "threadname1");
            Thread1.start();
            Thread2 = new Thread(this, "threadname2");
            Thread2.start();
        }
    }

    public void stop() {
        Thread1.stop();
        Thread2.stop();
    }

    public void run() {
        String out_string;
        int loop_index;
        out_string = new String();
        for(loop_index = 1; loop_index < 1000; loop_index++){
            if(((Thread.currentThread()). getName()).equals("threadname1")){
                text1.setText(out_string. valueOf(loop_index));
            }
            if(((Thread.currentThread()). getName()).equals("threadname2")){
```

Skill 15

```
                    text2.setText(out_string. valueOf(loop_index));
                }
            }
        }
    }
```

You've seen how to handle two threads now, but that raises a new issue—what if we want the two threads to work with the same data? For example, if both threads were to work with the same data but execute at different rates (which is determined by the operating system), how would we make sure they didn't interfere with each other?

Setting Up Thread Synchronization

Let's say that we wanted to set up an applet that counts integers steadily from 0 up and displays them. That's fine as long as we only have one thread in the applet. But if we have two threads that do the counting, incrementing and displaying the value in the *same* variable, it could be a problem.

For example, it is possible that thread 1 will be interrupted by thread 2 after incrementing our counter from, say, 1000 to 1001. Thread 2 will then increment our counter from 1001 to 1002 and print, and then control might go back to thread 1, which will print out its value, 1001. This means our series of integers would run: 1000, 1002, 1001..., which is obviously a problem. We will see how to protect the variable that holds the current counter value so that only one thread has access to it at a time until the incrementing and displaying operation is completely finished, thus *synchronizing* the threads.

We start by creating the counting applet now. Create the new file called synchronize.java, adding our standard code and implementing the Runnable interface for our two threads:.

```
import java.awt.*;
import java.applet.Applet;

public class synchronize extends Applet implements Runnable{
            .
            .
            .
    }
```

Now we add our two new threads, Thread1 and Thread2, and start them as follows:

```
import java.awt.*;
import java.applet.Applet;

public class synchronize extends Applet implements Runnable{

    Thread Thread1, Thread2;
        .
        .
        .
    public void start() {
        Thread1 = new Thread(this);
        Thread1.start();
        Thread2 = new Thread(this);
        Thread2.start();
    }

    public void stop() {
        Thread1.stop();
        Thread2.stop();
    }        .
                 .
                 .
```

Let's say that we have a data class named dataClass, with some internal data member named internal_data:

```
class dataClass{
    public int internal_data;
}
```

We can set the internal_data member to 0 in the class's constructor like this:

```
class dataClass{
    public int internal_data;
    public void dataClass(){
        internal_data = 0;
    }
}
```

And we create an object of the dataClass class in our applet, named sensitiveData:

```
import java.awt.*;
import java.applet.Applet;
```

```
 public class synchronize extends Applet implements Runnable{

      Thread Thread1, Thread2;
      dataClass sensitiveData;

      public void init() {
          sensitiveData = new dataClass();
      }
              .
              .
              .
```

Now, in the `run()` method, which both threads will execute, we set up a loop
of 1000 iterations:

```
      public void run() {
          int loop_index;
          for(loop_index = 1; loop_index < 1000; loop_index++){
              .
              .
              .
          }
      }
```

In that loop, each thread will first increment the `sensitiveData` object's
`internal_data` data member:

```
      public void run() {
          String out_string;
          int loop_index;
          out_string = new String();
          for(loop_index = 1; loop_index < 1000; loop_index++){
              sensitiveData.internal_data++;
              .
              .
              .
          }
      }
```

Then we print out the newly-incremented version of the number in
`internal_data`:

```
      public void run() {
          String out_string;
          int loop_index;
          out_string = new String();
          for(loop_index = 1; loop_index < 1000; loop_index++){
              sensitiveData.internal_data++;
```

```
→                      System.out.println("data value = " +
                       ➥ out_string.valueOf(sensitiveData.internal_data));
              }
          }
```

This line is just where the problem is. Between the steps of incrementing and printing out the data, the other thread could have slipped in and completed both tasks, which means that the numbers could appear out of order. In fact, if you run this first version of synchronize.java, you'll see that sometimes this indeed happens—the values do sometimes appear out of order. We'll fix this problem now by creating a new version of synchronize.java. The first version of the applet, with the synchronization problems, appears in synchronize.java, version 1.

C synchronize.java, version 1

```java
import java.awt.*;
import java.applet.Applet;

public class synchronize extends Applet implements Runnable{

    Thread Thread1, Thread2;
    dataClass sensitiveData;

    public void init() {
        sensitiveData = new dataClass();
    }

    public void start() {
        Thread1 = new Thread(this);
        Thread1.start();
        Thread2 = new Thread(this);
        Thread2.start();
    }

    public void stop() {
        Thread1.stop();
        Thread2.stop();
    }

    public void run() {
        String out_string;
        int loop_index;
        out_string = new String();
        for(loop_index = 1; loop_index < 1000; loop_index++){
            sensitiveData.internal_data++;
```

```
                    System.out.println("data value = " +
                 ➥ out_string.valueOf(sensitiveData.internal_data));
            }
        }
    }
```

Let's explore how to fix this problem with synchronized functions.

Synchronizing Functions

Since both `thread1` and `thread2` are working with the same `internal_data` variable, we're in danger of having one thread being interrupted between the time it increments the counter and the time it reads the value back from the counter to display it. In that case, the other thread could have incremented the counter again by that time, and we end up displaying the wrong value. This problem is solved by denying multiple access to the same resource in a program until the currently accessing thread is finished with its work.

One way to deny multiple access to a resource (in our example, the counter variable) is to put all the operations having to do with the counter into a *synchronized* function. To do so, we have to place the sensitive data-handling statements into their own function. Currently, all this code is in the `run()` method:

```
public void run() {
    String out_string;
    int loop_index;
    out_string = new String();
    for(loop_index = 1; loop_index < 1000; loop_index++){
        sensitiveData.internal_data++;
        System.out.println("data value = " +
     ➥ out_string.valueOf(sensitiveData.internal_data));
    }
}
```

W can create a new function, called `printer()` as follows:

```
public void printer(){
        .
        .
        .
}
```

We add the data-handling code here to increment our data and display the new value:

```
    public void printer(){
➜       String out_string;
```

```
→          out_string = new String();
→          sensitiveData.internal_data++;
→          System.out.println("data value = " +
               ➡ out_string.valueOf(sensitiveData.internal_data));
        }
```

Now all the sensitive code is in one function; we can restrict access to that function with the synchronized keyword:

```
→      public synchronized void printer(){
           String out_string;
           out_string = new String();
           sensitiveData.internal_data++;
           System.out.println("data value = " +
              ➡ out_string.valueOf(sensitiveData.internal_data));
       }
   }
```

Now our printer() function is synchronized, which means that only one thread can enter it at a time. In the run() method, all we have to do is to call our new synchronized function, printer():

```
   public void run() {
       int loop_index;
       for(loop_index = 1; loop_index < 500; loop_index++){
→          printer();
       }
   }
```

And we're finished—if you run the new version of this applet, you'll see the same stream of numbers on the screen, but this time they'll be in order. We've been able to coordinate our threads. The code for this improved applet appears in synchronize.java, version 2.

synchronize.java, version 2

```
import java.awt.*;
import java.applet.Applet;

public class synchronize extends Applet implements Runnable{

    Thread Thread1, Thread2;
    dataClass sensitiveData;

    public void init() {
        sensitiveData = new dataClass();
    }
```

Skill 15

```
public void start() {
    Thread1 = new Thread(this);
    Thread1.start();
    Thread2 = new Thread(this);
    Thread2.start();
}

public void stop() {
    Thread1.stop();
    Thread2.stop();
}

public void run() {
    int loop_index;
    for(loop_index = 1; loop_index < 500; loop_index++){
        printer();
    }
}

public synchronized void printer(){
    String out_string;
    out_string = new String();
    sensitiveData.internal_data++;
    System.out.println("data value = " +
    ➡ out_string.valueOf(sensitiveData.internal_data));
}
}

class dataClass{
    public int internal_data;
    public void dataClass(){
        internal_data = 0;
    }
}
```

Creating a separate class like dataClass is a good way to work with multiple threads. However, it's not always convenient to have to place sensitive code into its own function, so Java gives us another way. Let's look into that now.

Synchronizing Code Blocks

The sensitive part of our synchronize.java applet is in the for loop in the run() method:

```
public void run() {
    String out_string;
```

```
        int loop_index;
→       out_string = new String();
→       for(loop_index = 1; loop_index < 500; loop_index++){
→           sensitiveData.internal_data++;
→           System.out.println("data value = " +
                ➥ out_string.valueOf(sensitiveData.internal_data));
→       }
    }
```

As it turns out, Java lets us enclose the sensitive part of our code in a synchronized block. We indicate what data we consider sensitive in parentheses following the synchronized keyword. Here, that's our sensitiveData object, so we set up our synchronized code block this way in the applet:

```
public void run() {
    String out_string;
    int loop_index;
    out_string = new String();
→   synchronized(sensitiveData){
        for(loop_index = 1; loop_index < 500; loop_index++){
            sensitiveData.internal_data++;
            System.out.println("data value = " +
                ➥ out_string.valueOf(sensitiveData.internal_data));
        }
→   }
    }
```

Doing so has the same effect as setting up a synchronized function—we restrict access to the sensitive data such that only one thread has access to it at a time. When you run this applet, you'll see the stream of integers scrolling up the screen, in order. The code for the latest version of this applet appears in synchronize.java, version 3.

synchronize.java, version 3

```
import java.awt.*;
import java.applet.Applet;

public class synchronize extends Applet implements Runnable{

    Thread Thread1, Thread2;
    dataClass sensitiveData;

    public void init() {
        sensitiveData = new dataClass();
    }
```

```
public void start() {
    Thread1 = new Thread(this);
    Thread1.start();
    Thread2 = new Thread(this);
    Thread2.start();
}

public void stop() {
    Thread1.stop();
    Thread2.stop();
}

public void run() {
    String out_string;
    int loop_index;
    out_string = new String();
    synchronized(sensitiveData){
        for(loop_index = 1; loop_index < 500; loop_index++){
            sensitiveData.internal_data++;
            System.out.println("data value = " +
            ➥ out_string.valueOf(sensitiveData:internal_data));
        }
    }
}
}

class dataClass{
    public int internal_data;
    public void dataClass(){
        internal_data = 0;
    }
}
}
```

That's it for synchronizing our threads and for our overview of multi-threaded programming in Java.

Fast Downloading: JAR Files

We've created a lot of applets in this book, and applets are targeted for the World Wide Web. Java 1.1 includes Java Archive (JAR) files, a new way of speeding the downloading process. Before you finish the book, we'll take a look at how to use them.

You can use JAR files to zip and enclose a number of files so they are downloaded all at once in a small package, making the downloading process speedy. To create a JAR file, you use the `jar.exe` tool. For example, our `canvaser.java` applet creates two class files when compiled: `canvaser.class` and `BoxCanvas.class`. We can zip both of those and place them in one JAR file so they are downloaded together. To do that, we use `jar.exe` to create `canvaser.jar` as follows:

```
C:\java1-1\canvaser>jar cvf canvaser.jar *
```

The * at the end means that we will compress all the files in the current directory into this JAR file, and the "cvf" string indicates the options we want to use with the `jar.exe`. These options are listed in Table 15.1.

TABLE 15.1 : Options available with `jar.exe`

Option	Does This
c	Creates a new or empty archive on the standard output.
t	Lists the table of contents from standard output.
x [file]	Extracts all files, or just the named files, from standard input. If file is omitted, all files are extracted; otherwise, only the specified file or files are extracted.
f [jar-file]	The second argument specifies a JAR file to process. In the case of creation, this refers to the name of the JAR file to be created (instead of on stdout). For table or extract, the second argument identifies the JAR file to be listed or extracted.
v	Generates verbose output on stderr.

Now that we've created a JAR file, you upload it to your ISP—this is the file users will download, not the applet's `.class` files. But how do we tell a Java 1.1 enabled Web browser to download and unpack this JAR file? That turns out to be easy: we just add this `<param>` tag to the `<applet>` tag, naming this parameter `archives` and giving as its value our JAR file, `canvaser.jar`:

```
<html>

<!- Web page written for the Sun Applet Viewer>

<head>
<title>canvaser</title>
</head>

<body>
<hr>
```

```
<applet code=canvaser.class
        width=200 height=200>
        <param name=archives value="canvaser.jar">
</applet>

<hr>
</body>
</html>
```

And the Web browser will do the rest. You can run the applet now, as shown below.

In this book, we have seen many aspects of Java at work, including text fields and text areas, radio buttons and check boxes, a popup adding calculator, printing, the Java ScrollPane class, the system clipboard, popup menus, the Delegated event method, scroll bars and scrolling lists, clickable hyperlink-filled images, popup windows, menus, Card layouts, GridBag layouts, dialog boxes, buttons, panels, multi-threading, navigating to URLs, the mouse, a mouse-driven paint program, a mouse-driven image resizer, using the keyboard directly, fonts, animation, the Sun Animator class, JAR files, double buffered graphics animation, and Java applications. All that remains is putting all this power to work for yourself. Happy programming!

Are You Experienced?

Now you can...

- ☑ create Java Thread objects
- ☑ use Applet methods and multi-threading at the same time
- ☑ coordinate multiple threads using synchronization techniques
- ☑ distinguish which thread is executing in the run() method by naming threads
- ☑ prevent threads from accessing sensitive data
- ☑ use JAR files to compress multiple files for easier and faster downloading

356-555-3398.

PROGRAMMERS
C, C, VB, Cobol, exp. Call 534-555-6543 or fax 534-555-6544.

PROGRAMMING
MRFS Inc. Is looking for a Sr. Windows NT developer. Reqs. 3-5 yrs. Exp. In C under Windows, Win95 & NT, using Visual C. Excl. OO design & implementation skills a must. OLE2 & ODBC are a plus. Excl. Salary & bnfts. Resume & salary history to HR. 8779 HighTech Way, Computer City, AR

PROGRAMMERS
Contractors Wanted for short & long term assignments; Visual C, MFC Unix C/C, SQL Oracle Dev elop ers PC Help Desk Support Windows NT & NetWareTelecommunications Visual Basic, Access, HTML, CGI, Perl MMI & Co., 885-555-9933.

PROGRAMMER World Wide Web Links wants your HTML & Photoshop skills. Develop great WWW sites. Local & global customers. Send samples & resume to WWWL, 2000 Apple Road, Santa Rosa, CA.

TECHNICAL WRITER Software firm seeks writer/editor for manuals, research notes, project mgmt. Min 2 years tech. writing, DTP & programming experience. Send resume & writing samples to: Software Systems, Dallas, TX.

TECHNICAL Software development firm looking for Tech Trainers, Ideal candidates have programming experience in Visual C, HTML & JAVA. Need quick self starter. Call (443) 555-6868 for interview.

TECHNICAL WRITER/ Premier Computer Corp is seeking a combination of technical skills, knowledge and experience in the following areas: UNIX, Windows 95/NT, Visual Basic, on-line help & documentation, and the internet. Candidates must possess excellent writing skills and be comfortable working in a quality vs. deadline driven environment. Competitive salary. Fax resume & samples to Karen Fields, Premier Computer Corp. 444 Industrial Blvd. Concord, CA. Or send to our website at www.premier.com.

WEB DESIGNER
BA/BS or equivalent programming/multimedia production. 3 years of experience in use and design of WWW services streaming audio and video HTML, PERL, CGI, GIF, JPEG. Demonstrated interpersonal, organization, communication, multi-tasking skills. Send resume to The Learning People at www.learning.com.

WEBMASTER-TECHNICAL
BSCS or equivalent. 2 years of experience in CGI, Windows 95/NT, UNIX, C, Java, Perl. Demonstrated ability to design, code, debug and test on-line services. Send resume to The Learning People at www.learning.com.

PROGRAMMER World Wide Web Links wants your HTML & Photoshop

---

ing tools. Experienced in documentation preparation & programming languages (Access, C, FoxPro) are a plus. Financial or banking customer service support is required along with excellent verbal & written communication skills with multi levels of end-users. Send resume to KKUP Enterprises, 45 Orange Blvd. Orange, CA.

COMPUTERS Small Web Design Firm seeks indiv. w/NT, Webserver & Database management exp. Fax resume to 556-555-4221.

COMPUTER/ Visual C/C, Visual Basic Exp'd Systems Analysts/ Programmers for growing software dev. team in Roseburg. Computer Science or related degree preferred. Develop adv. Engineering applications for engineering firm. Fax resume to 707-555-8744.

COMPUTER Web Master for dynamic SF Internet co. Site. Dev. test, coord. train. 2 yrs prog. Exp. C C. Web C. FTP. Fax resume to Best Staffing 845-555-7722.

COMPUTER PROGRAMMER
Ad agency seeks programmer w/exp. in UNIX/NT Platforms, Web Server, CGI/Perl. Programmer Position avail on a project basis with the possibility to move into F/T. Fax resume & salary req. to R Jones 334-555-8332.

COMPUTERS Programmer/Analyst Design and maintain C based SQL database applications. Required skills: Visual Basic, C, SQL, ODBC, Document existing and new applications. Novell or NT exp. a plus. Fax resume & salary history to 235-555-9935.

GRAPHIC DESIGNER
Webmaster's Weekly is seeking a creative Graphic Designer to design high impact marketing collater al, including direct mail promos, CD-ROM packages, ads and WWW pages. Must be able to juggle multiple projects and learn new skills on the job very rapidly. Web design experience a big plus. technical troubleshooting also a plus. Call 435-555-1235.

GRAPHICS - ART DIRECTOR - WEB-MULTIMEDIA
Leading internet development company has an outstanding opportunity for a talented, high-end Web Experienced Art Director. In addition to a great portfolio and fresh ideas, the ideal candidate has excellent communication and presentation skills. Working as a team with innovative producers and programmers, you will create dynamic, interactive web sites and application interfaces. Some programming experience required. Send samples and resume to: SuperSites, 333 Main, Seattle, WA.

MARKETING
Fast paced software and services provider looking for MARKETING COMMUNICATIONS SPECIALIST to be responsible for its webpage

---

PROGRAMMERS Multiple short term assignments available: Visual C, 3 positions SQL Server/NT Server, 2 positions JAVA & HTML, long term NetWare. Various locations. Call for more info. 356-555-3398.

PROGRAMMERS
C, C, VB, Cobol, exp.
Call 534-555-6543
or fax 534-555-6544.

PROGRAMMING
MRFS inc. is looking for a Sr. Windows NT developer. Reqs. 3-5 yrs. Exp. In C under Windows, Win95 & NT, using Visual C. Excl. OO design & implementation skills a must. OLE2 & ODBC are a plus. Resume & salary history to HR, 8779 HighTech Way, Computer City, AR

PROGRAMMERS/ Contractors Wanted for short & long term assignments; Visual C, MFC Unix C/C, SQL Oracle Developers PC Help Desk Support Windows NT & NetWareTelecommunications Visual Basic, Access, HTML, CGI, Perl MMI & Co., 885-555-9933

PROGRAMMER World Wide Web Links wants your HTML & Photoshop skills. Develop great WWW sites. Local & global customers. Send samples & resume to WWWL, 2000 Apple Road, Santa Rosa, CA.

TECHNICAL WRITER Software firm seeks writer/editor for manuals, research notes, project mgmt. Min 2 years tech. writing, DTP & programming experience. Send resume & writing samples to: Software Systems, Dallas, TX.

COMPUTER PROGRAMMER
Ad agency seeks programmer w/exp. in UNIX/NT Platforms, Web Server, CGI/Perl. Programmer Position avail on a project basis with the possibility to move into F/T. Fax resume & salary req. to R. Jones 334-555-8332.

TECHNICAL WRITER Premier Computer Corp is seeking a combination of technical skills, knowledge and experience in the following areas: UNIX, Windows 95/NT, Visual Basic, on-line help & documentation, and the internet. Candidates must possess excellent writing skills, and be comfortable working in a quality vs. deadline driven environment. Competitive salary. Fax resume & samples to Karen Fields. Premier Computer Corp. 444 Industrial Blvd. Concord, CA. Or send to our website at www.premier.com.

WEB DESIGNER
BA/BS or equivalent programming/multimedia production. 3 years of experience in use and design of WWW services streaming audio and video HTML, PERL, CGI, GIF, JPEG. Demonstrated interpersonal, organization, communication, multi-tasking skills. Send resume to The Learning People at www.learning.com.

WEBMASTER-TECHNICAL
BSCS or equivalent, 2 years of experience in CGI, Windows 95/NT

COMPUTERS Small Web Design firm seeks indiv. w/NT, Webserver & Database management exp. Fax resume to 556-555-4221.

COMPUTER Visual C/C, Visual Basic Exp'd Systems Analysts/ Programmers for growing software dev. team in Roseburg. Computer Science or related degree preferred. Develop adv. Engineering applications for engineering firm. Fax resume to 707-555-8744.

COMPUTER Web Master for dynamic SF Internet co. Site. Dev. test, coord. train. 2 yrs prog. Exp. C C. Web C. FTP. Fax resume to Best Staffing 845-555-7722.

COMPUTERS/ QA SOFTWARE TESTERS Qualified candidates should have 2 yrs exp. performing integration & system testing using automated testing tools. Experienced in documentation preparation & programming languages (Access, C, FoxPro) are a plus. Financial or banking customer service support is required along with excellent verbal & written communication skills with multi levels of end-users. Send resume to KKUP Enterprises, 45 Orange Blvd. Orange, CA.

COMPUTERS Programmer/Analyst Design and maintain C based SQL database applications. Required skills: Visual Basic, C, SQL, ODBC, Document existing and new applications. Novell or NT exp. a plus. Fax resume & salary history to 235-555-9935.

GRAPHIC DESIGNER
Webmaster's Weekly is seeking a creative Graphic Designer to design high impact marketing collater al, including direct mail promo's, CD-ROM packages, ads and WWW pages. Must be able to juggle multiple projects and learn new skills on the job very rapidly. Web design experience a big plus. technical troubleshooting also a plus. Call 435-555-1235.

GRAPHICS - ART DIRECTOR - WEB-MULTIMEDIA
Leading internet development company has an outstanding opportunity for a talented, high-end Web Experienced Art Director. In addition to a great portfolio and fresh ideas, the ideal candidate has excellent communication and presentation skills. Working as a team with innovative producers and programmers, you will create dynamic, interactive web sites and application interfaces. Some programming experience required. Send samples and resume to: SuperSites, 333 Main, Seattle, WA.

COMPUTER PROGRAMMER
Ad agency seeks programmer w/exp. in UNIX/NT Platforms, Web Server, CGI/Perl. Programmer Position avail on a project basis with the possibility to move into F/T. Fax resume & salary req. to R. Jones 334-555-8332.

PROGRAMMERS / Established software company seeks program-

---

ment. Now be a self-starter, energetic, organized. Must have 2 years web experience. Programming plus. Call 985-555-9854

PROGRAMMERS Multiple term assignments available: Vi C, 3 positions SQL Server/NT Ser 2 positions JAVA & HTML, long t NetWare Various locations. Call more info. 356-555-3398.

PROGRAMMERS
C, C, VB, Cobol, exp. Call 534-5 6543 or fax 534-555-6544.

PROGRAMMING
MRFS Inc. Is looking for a Windows NT developer. Reqs. yrs. Exp. In C under Wind Win95 & NT, using Visual C OO design & implementation a must. OLE2 & ODBC are a Excl. Salary & bnfts. Resum salary history to HR, 8779 High Way, Computer City, AR

PROGRAMMERS/ Contra Wanted for short & long term as ments: Visual C, MFCUnix C/C, Oracle Developers PC Help Support Windows NT & NetW Telecommunications Visual Access, HTML, CGI, Perl MMI & 885-555-9933

PROGRAMMER World Wide Links wants your HTML & Photo skills. Develop great WWW Local & global customers. Send ples & resume to WWWL, Apple Road, Santa Rosa, CA.

TECHNICAL WRITER Software seeks writer/editor for man research notes, project mgmt. years tech. writing, DTP & pro ming experience. Send resu writing samples to: Sof Systems, Dallas, TX.

TECHNICAL Software develo firm looking for Tech Trainers, candidates have programming rience in Visual C, HTML & Need quick self starter. Call 555-6868 for interview.

TECHNICAL WRITER Pr Computer Corp is seeking a C nation of technical skills, know and experience in the foll areas: UNIX, Windows 95/NT, Basic, on-line help & documen and the internet. Candidates possess excellent writing skill be comfortable working in a vs. deadline driven environ Competitive salary. Fax resu samples to Karen Fields. P Computer Corp. 444 Industria Concord, CA. or send to our w at www.premier.com.

WEB DESIGNER
BA/BS or equivalent pro ming/multimedia productio years of experience in use design of WWW services str audio and video HTML, PER GIF, JPEG. Demonstrated in sonal, organization, commun multi-tasking skills. Send re The Learning People at ing.com.

WEBMASTER-TECHN

GLOSSARY

G

Glossary

a

API (Application Programming Interface)

A collection of classes, methods, and data members that you can import into Java.

Applet

A compiled Java program that can be embedded in a Web page and downloaded to run in a Web browser.

AWT (Abstract Windowing Toolkit)

The Java package of user interface methods, which handles graphics and windows.

b

base class

Class from which another class is derived.

boolean

A variable type. Boolean variables may be set to only true or false.

bytecodes

Java executable binary codes which make up applets. Bytecodes are what the compiler produces; they make up .class files.

c

cast

A means of overriding a variable's type, temporarily changing that type to another type.

check box group

A collection of radio buttons. When check boxes are added to a Java CheckBoxGroup object, they become radio buttons.

class

The "template" used to create objects, much like a variable's type (e.g., integer). A class is to an object what a cookie cutter is to a cookie.

class library

Libraries that contain various Java classes. These libraries are called packages in Java.

client

One half of a client/server pair. Clients rely on a server to perform some task for them.

client/server model

Splitting an application into two parts, one part in the client and one part in the server, creates a client/server pair. Applications that work this way use the client/server model.

clipping rectangle

A graphics rectangle bounding a part of the display area to which you want to restrict graphics operations.

compiler

A program that translates Java source code into runnable bytecodes. In other words, a compiler translates .java files into .class files.

constructor

An automatically-run method of a class, used for initialization of an object. A constructor is run whenever an object of the class containing the constructor is created.

container

An object of the Java Container class. A container can contain control objects.

control

Any of the various user interface objects, such as text fields, text areas, scroll bars, and buttons.

critical section

A section of code where threads should be allowed to undertake their tasks without interference. In Java, a critical section is enclosed in a sychronized() block.

d

debugger

An application that lets you execute a Java program while watching the program's state. The execution of a debugger is often line-by-line.

double buffering

A graphics method of preparing images off screen in a memory buffer and then displaying the result on screen.

e

encapsulation

The process of wrapping both data and functions into classes.

event

A user-interface triggered occurrence, such as a mouse click, a button push, or a key strike.

exception

An error message that usually indicates a problem in program flow. For example, when you try to index an array beyond its boundaries, an array-boundary exception occurs.

f

frame

The outline or border of a window or of an individual image in animation.

h

HTML (Hypertext Markup Language)

The programming language used to create Web pages.

i

image map

A "clickable" image with embedded hyperlinks.

inheritance

The process through which derived classes get functionality from their base classes.

ISP (Internet Service Provider)

Usually an external company that provides a machine connected to the Internet, acting as a host machine for individual users.

j

Java Virtual Machine

The system that loads and executes Java byte-code files.

JDK (Java Development Kit)

Sun's set of tools for Java developers.

l

layout

The arrangement of controls in a Java application or applet, usually handled by one or more Java layout managers.

m

member

A short name for a member of a class, meaning a method, embedded data, or a class constant.

method

Member function of a class.

multi-threading

The basis of multi-tasking in a program. In multi-threading, each thread represents an independent execution stream.

n

null

A value usually set to 0 in Java.

o

object

The instance of a class. A class acts as a "template" for an object. A class is to an object as a cookie cutter is to a cookie.

overloading

In object-oriented language, the process of defining multiple methods with the same name but different parameter lists so that the method may be called with different sets of parameters.

overriding

In object-oriented programming, the process of redefining a method originally inherited from a base class.

p

package

In Java lingo, a class library.

panel

A layout construct which holds controls in a specified arrangement for displaying on the screen.

s

server

A general term for a source of data or an application interface that client programs can interact with.

source file

A text file that holds the Java statements to be compiled into an applet or application.

subclass

A class that descends from a given class.

superclass

The class from which a given class is derived.

t

`this` keyword

A Java keyword used to refer to the current object. The `this` keyword is usually passed as a parameter to other methods.

thread

An execution stream in a program. A program may have many threads and therefore be multi-tasking.

throwable object

An object derived from the Java `Exception` class that may be thrown to cause an exception.

thumb

The small box in a scroll bar that the user manipulates, usually with the mouse.

w

Web server

A computer on the Internet that interacts with client programs.

World Wide Web

Large assemblage of documents interconnected through HTTP, FTP, and other protocols over the Internet. Lots of fun and games!

Index

Note to the Reader: Throughout this index **boldface** page numbers indicate primary discussions of a topic. *Italic* page numbers indicate illustrations.

E

F

G

N

R

S

FREE!
SUBSCRIPTION
Don't Miss a Single Issue!

SPECIAL PREMIERE EDITION

JAVA DEVELOPER'S JOURNAL

Subscribe Now!

- Interactive Java
- Applet Development
- CORBACorner
- Java Class Libraries
- Interviews with Java Gurus
- Product Reviews with the JDJ World Class Award
- Tips & Techniques • Infinite Java • Book Reviews
- Java Animation • Games & Graphics... and Much More

www.JavaDevelopersJournal.com

SYS-CON Publications, Inc.
39 East Central Ave Pearl River, NY 10965
Tel: 914-735-1900   Fax: 914-735-3922

JDJ WORLD CLASS AWARD

FREE SUBSCRIPTION CERTIFICATE

☐ 1 Year JDJ $39.95 50% (12 Issues)   *SAVE 50% on a 1 year subscription if you*
☐ 2 Years $129 (24 Issues)   **subscribe NOW! – ONLY $39.95**

☐ **FREE** Trial Subscription (Three Months)   With No Obligation

Name:	☐ M/C ☐ Visa ☐ Amex
Title:	Card#:
Company:	Expiration Date:
Address:	Signature:
City:	St: Zip:
Tel:	Fax:

Java Developer's Journal one year is 11 regular monthly issues plus 1 additional special issue for a total of 12 issues in all. *JDJ* basic annual subscription rate is *$79.00*. NY, NJ, CT residents, please add sales tax. **Canada/Mexico $99**; all **other countries $128**. Subscription begins upon receipt of payment Please allow 4-6 weeks for delivery of first issue. *International subscriptions must be payable in U.S. dollars.*

Java™ Development Kit Version 1.1 Binary Code License

This binary code license ("License") contains rights and restrictions associated with use of the accompanying software and documentation ("Software"). Read the License carefully before installing the Software. By installing the Software you agree to the terms and conditions of this License.

1. Limited License Grant. Sun grants to you ("Licensee") a non-exclusive, non-transferable limited license to use the Software without fee for evaluation of the Software and for development of Java™ compatible applets and applications. Licensee may make one archival copy of the Software. Licensee may not re-distribute the Software in whole or in part, either separately or included with a product. Refer to the Java Runtime Environment Version 1.1 binary code license (http://www.javasoft.com/products/JDK/1.1/index.html) for the availability of runtime code which may be distributed with Java compatible applets and applications.

2. Java Platform Interface. Licensee may not modify the Java Platform Interface ("JPI", identified as classes contained within the "java" package or any subpackages of the "java" package), by creating additional classes within the JPI or otherwise causing the addition to or modification of the classes in the JPI. In the event that Licensee creates any Java-related API and distributes such API to others for applet or application development, Licensee must promptly publish an accurate specification for such API for free use by all developers of Java-based software.

3. Restrictions. Software is confidential copyrighted information of Sun and title to all copies is retained by Sun and/or its licensors. Licensee shall not modify, decompile, disassemble, decrypt, extract, or otherwise reverse engineer Software. Software may not be leased, assigned, or sublicensed, in whole or in part. **Software is not designed or intended for use in on-line control of aircraft, air traffic, aircraft navigation or aircraft communications; or in the design, construction, operation or maintenance of any nuclear facility. Licensee warrants that it will not use or redistribute the Software for such purposes.**

4. Trademarks and Logos. This License does not authorize Licensee to use any Sun name, trademark or logo. Licensee acknowledges that Sun owns the Java trademark and all Java-related trademarks, logos and icons including the Coffee Cup and Duke ("Java Marks") and agrees to: (i) to comply with the Java Trademark Guidelines at http://java.com/trademarks.html; (ii) not do anything harmful to or inconsistent with Sun's rights in the Java Marks; and (iii) assist Sun in protecting those rights, including assigning to Sun any rights acquired by Licensee in any Java Mark.

5. Disclaimer of Warranty. Software is provided "AS IS," without a warranty of any kind. ALL EXPRESS OR IMPLIED REPRESENTATIONS AND WARRANTIES, INCLUDING ANY IMPLIED WARRANTY OF MERCHANTABILITY, FITNESS FOR A PARTICULAR PURPOSE OR NON-INFRINGEMENT, ARE HEREBY EXCLUDED.

6. Limitation of Liability. SUN AND ITS LICENSORS SHALL NOT BE LIABLE FOR ANY DAMAGES SUFFERED BY LICENSEE OR ANY THIRD PARTY AS A RESULT OF USING OR DISTRIBUTING SOFTWARE. IN NO EVENT WILL SUN OR ITS LICENSORS BE LIABLE FOR ANY LOST REVENUE, PROFIT OR DATA, OR FOR DIRECT, INDIRECT, SPECIAL, CONSEQUENTIAL, INCIDENTAL OR PUNITIVE DAMAGES, HOWEVER CAUSED AND REGARDLESS OF THE THEORY OF LIABILITY, ARISING OUT OF THE USE OF OR INABILITY TO USE SOFTWARE, EVEN IF SUN HAS BEEN ADVISED OF THE POSSIBILITY OF SUCH DAMAGES.

7. Termination. Licensee may terminate this License at any time by destroying all copies of Software. This License will terminate immediately without notice from Sun if Licensee fails to comply with any provision of this License. Upon such termination, Licensee must destroy all copies of Software.

8. Export Regulations. Software, including technical data, is subject to U.S. export control laws, including the U.S. Export Administration Act and its associated regulations, and may be subject to export or import regulations in other countries. Licensee agrees to comply strictly with all such regulations and acknowledges that it has the responsibility to obtain licenses to export, re-export, or import Software. Software may not be downloaded, or otherwise exported or re-exported (i) into, or to a national or resident of, Cuba, Iraq, Iran, North Korea, Libya, Sudan, Syria or any country to which the U.S. has embargoed goods; or (ii) to anyone on the U.S. Treasury Department's list of Specially Designated Nations or the U.S. Commerce Department's Table of Denial Orders.

9. Restricted Rights. Use, duplication or disclosure by the United States government is subject to the restrictions as set forth in the Rights in Technical Data and Computer Software Clauses in DFARS 252.227-7013(c) (1) (ii) and FAR 52.227-19(c) (2) as applicable.

10. Governing Law. Any action related to this License will be governed by California law and controlling U.S. federal law. No choice of law rules of any jurisdiction will apply.

11. Severability. If any of the above provisions are held to be in violation of applicable law, void, or unenforceable in any jurisdiction, then such provisions are herewith waived to the extent necessary for the License to be otherwise enforceable in such jurisdiction. However, if in Sun's opinion deletion of any provisions of the License by operation of this paragraph unreasonably compromises the rights or increase the liabilities of Sun or its licensors, Sun reserves the right to terminate the License and refund the fee paid by Licensee, if any, as Licensee's sole and exclusive remedy.

JDK1.1 BCL 2-9-97#

What's on the CD-ROM

The companion CD-ROM contains all the code for the tutorials in this book. You will also find cutting-edge third-party tools to use with Java 1.1.

Products you will find on this CD include:

- **JDK 1.1** is the full Java development package from Sun Microsystems. The JDK is used for creating applets and applications.

- **Jamba 1.1**, an authoring tool from Aimtech, enables Internet developers and Web masters to create interactive, media-rich Java applets and applications without programming or scripting.

- **Mojo 2.0**, from Penumbra Software, is a complete development environment for creating networking applets. Mojo consists of a GUI Designer and a Coder.

- **ED for Windows 3.71**, from Soft As It Gets, is a complete Java development environment that offers powerful editing capabilities and code navigation features.

- **Widgets™**, from Connect! Quick, is a library of sophisticated, prebuilt components for assembling commercial-quality Java applications.

- **JetEffects 2.5**, from Peak Technologies, is a Java animation tool targeted at home and small office Web authors.

- **Vibe DE 1.0**, from Visix Software, is an intuitive integrated development and deployment environment for building Java applications. Vibe is comprised of a Java-specific IDE, which includes a compiler, debugger, and extensive set of class libraries, and ActiveX support.

For installation instructions, see the file `readme.txt` in the CD's root directory.

N **NOTE** CD-ROM can be used with Windows 95 and NT4. UNIX users can access code for the tutorials only. Visit the vendor Web sites for UNIX versions of the third party tools.